VISUAL
INFORMATION

VISUAL INFORMATION

SECOND EDITION

•

RUNE PETTERSSON

•

EDUCATIONAL TECHNOLOGY PUBLICATIONS
ENGLEWOOD CLIFFS, NEW JERSEY 07632

Library of Congress Cataloging-in-Publication Data

Pettersson, Rune, 1943-
   Visual information / Rune Pettersson. — 2nd ed.
      p. cm.
   Rev. ed. of: Visuals for information. © 1989.
   Includes bibliographical references and indexes.
   ISBN 0-87778-262-8
   1. Visual communication. 2. Communication—Audio-visual aids.
I. Pettersson, Rune, 1943-   Visuals for information.   II. Title.
P93.5.P48 1993
302.23—dc20   93-19822
                                                                  CIP

Printed in the United States of America.

Library of Congress Catalog Card Number:
93-19822.

International Standard Book Number:
0-87778-262-8.

First Printing: June, 1993.

ABOUT THE AUTHOR

Rune Pettersson is Manager of Technical Training at ELLEMTEL Telecommunication Systems Laboratories, a Swedish R&D Company. Dr. Pettersson has been teaching "Visuals for Information" at the University of Stockholm and "New Media Development" at the Royal Institute of Technology, Sweden.

He is an affiliate research professor and a member of the faculty of the Institute of Business Graphics at the College of Business Administration at Pennsylvania State University, USA. Dr. Pettersson is vice president of IVLA, the International Visual Literacy Association. He is an International Advisor for the International Division of AECT, the Association for Educational Communications and Technology, in Washington DC. He has been a board member of IEPRC, the International Electronic Publishing Research Centre, and of IPA-EPC, the International Publishers Association-Electronic Publishing Committee. Dr. Pettersson is also a fellow of BOA, Bild och Ord Akademin, The Swedish Academy of Verbovisual Information.

PREFACE

The past few decades have witnessed dramatic developments in technology. A few examples can serve to illustrate the major changes, especially those occurring in the media field.

In 1946, ENIAC, the world's first electronic computer, made its debut. It weighed 30 tons, contained 18,000 tubes, and had a memory capable of storing only 20 numbers. Pocket calculators of today have a much greater capacity, and personal computers can easily store the contents of a book in internal memory.

In 1956, the first regularly scheduled TV transmissions began in Sweden. The American Ampex company introduced the first video tape recorder. It was a large, expensive machine with an insatiable appetite for 2-inch, open-reel tape. In 1988, one-third of all Swedish households (33%) had small, handy video cassette recorders, usually employing 1/2 inch tape. The corresponding figures for the United States and Japan were 46% and 62%, respectively.

In 1962, the first communications satellite, Telstar, was launched into orbit. In 1988, 600,000 Swedish households (8%) could view satellite TV transmissions via local cable TV networks. At some locations in the United States, viewers had a choice of 50–60 programs. Many channels also broadcast around the clock.

In 1973, the Dutch company Philips launched its optical video disc system. This medium permits the storage of truly vast amounts of information. CD-ROM discs of today are only 12 cm in diameter but can store 600 megabytes of information. All the text in several encyclopedias can be made easily accessible in a database stored in a CD-ROM.

Now systems for desktop publishing and desktop video are common. Easy to handle software gives the layman the opportunity to combine verbal and visual messages. Unfortunately, most desktop publishers know little about visual information.

So technical developments have moved at a very rapid pace. Everything suggests that the pace of developments is likely to increase rather than decrease. *Visual messages* in different forms *will become increasingly important*. However, only limited knowledge is available on visual communications, pictures as a means of linguistic communications, and the interplay between verbal and visual messages. Attention must be devoted to issues concerning the production, transmission, and perception of verbo-visual messages.

The author acknowledges his debt to a large number of researchers and practitioners in the field of verbo-visual literacy.

INTRODUCTION

The word "information" is derived from the Latin noun "informatio" which means a "conception" or "idea." "Information" has therefore long been synonymous with "data," "details," or "facts." The word ultimately acquired three additional meanings. Nowadays, it may even refer to the import ascribed to specific data. Then information does not arise until the received data, e.g., a text or a picture, are interpreted by the receiver. The term "information" is also sometimes used for data processed in a computer. "An internal structure which regulates processes" is yet another meaning. The latter meaning is used in computer science and in genetics. The verb "inform" means to supply or convey information or to provide knowledge of and is therefore a unidirectional process, e.g., from one person to another. However, to "communicate" entails an interplay between two or more persons.

Information is a richly varied concept covering many important disciplines and areas of knowledge plus different kinds of information. Most people are involved with communications and communications systems in one way or another. Some of these systems have "soft," human or linguistic dimensions, whereas others possess "hard," technological dimensions. Some subject fields have been well-established for many years. Others are relatively new. These fields can be regarded as independent scientific disciplines. In several instances, there is some overlapping because certain sub-issues are addressed in different disciplines, even if approaches may vary.

Information science

Information science, or *informatics*, is a scientific discipline comprising information in general and storage of information with areas like classification, indexing, cataloging, and bibliographic and other databases. Other important areas are seeking, retrieval, and transmission of information. Information science also comprises various library information service activities like administration, collections, circulation as well as scientific communication, use of information, and information resources management.

The task of an *informatic, i.e., documentalist,* is to collect and tabulate scientific information. This information is often sought in national and international databases.

Information processing

Information processing is a scientific discipline comprising, e.g., mathematical and numerical analysis plus methods and techniques for administrative data processing. The discipline also comprises the study of information searches in databases, information systems, computer aided translation, computer aided education, computer aided problem solving, design, etc.

The term "information processing" is often used as a synonym for data processing, i.e., the execution of a systematic series of operations on data. The term is also sometimes used for studies of the way people process information mentally (see "Psychological information theory" below).

Information theory

Information theory is a scientific discipline which comprises measurement of transmitted information and comparison of various communications systems, especially in telecommunications.

In information theory, the information's contents lack inherent interest. Information theory is based on a mathematical theory presented in the 1940s by the American mathematician Claude E. Shannon. It subsequently came to be known as the Shannon and Weaver mathematical communications model. In this kind of communications system, a sender (e.g., a telex unit) communicates with one or more receivers (other telex units) via a channel. The sender codes the transmitted signal, and the receiver decodes the received signal. Information theory utilizes the *bit* as the smallest unit of information. A bit can either be a one or a zero, representing, e.g., "yes"/ "no" or "on"/ "off."

The Shannon and Weaver communications theory was originally developed for studies of telecommunications and other technical systems. But it has also been used for communications between people.

Psychological information theory

Psychological information theory is the designation for one of the main branches of cognitive psychology. It refers to the study of Man's mental processing of information, i.e., mental information processing. A major principle in cognitive psychology is that Man organizes impressions and knowledge into meaningful units. This process starts at the perception stage.

Psychological information theory describes the brain's work as a process in which the flow of information between different types of memory functions determines whether or not we are able to solve different intellectual problems, such as learning something.

Semantic information theory

In philosophy, semantic information theory refers to the information supplied by a proposition in terms of the proposition's probability, and specifies the principles for measuring information.

Information technology

Information technology (IT) is a science dealing with the technical systems used for making production, distribution, storage, and other information handling more efficient. This includes computer technology and electronics.

The term *information society* is sometimes used in information technology. This is a designation for the society which follows an industrial society and in which Man's thinking power is supported by information processing computer systems and telecommunications techniques. The information society is dominated by the resource "information" instead of energy, raw materials, labor, and capital.

Social information

Social information, i.e., the result of all information measures whose aim is to make it easier for citizens to know what their rights, privileges, and obligations are, is studied in social science subjects. Good social information should be readily accessible, tailored to local requirements, readily grasped, adapted to individual needs, and capable of creating a state of preparedness in the receiver. The information must be closely integrated with the activities of the respective authorities, professionally planned and designed, and disseminated through efficient media.

Information economy

Information economy comprises research on the economic development of information industries. There is a lot of information jobs in all kinds of work-places, and an increasing number of employees are working with information. Other areas of research are the impact of information and communication, the application of information technology in the work-place, the history and geography of information labor and capital, the regulation and provision of information infrastructure, and the use of computers and networks.

Information ergonomics

Information ergonomics comprises research and development of the ergonomic design of Man-machine systems. The design of an information system must be based on studies of the information user's aims, knowledge, experience, and way of working.

Tasks making particularly heavy information demands occur in work at computer terminals, work at complex information panels, and in signal systems (e.g., for the monitoring of industrial processes, etc.). Information ergonomics include lighting, the design of instrument panels, video display units, characters, symbols, signals, etc.

Infology

Infology is the science of verbo-visual presentation of information. On the basis of Man's prerequisites, infology encompasses studies of the way a verbo-visual representation should be designed in order to achieve optimum communications between sender and receiver. Some studies concentrate on the sender, others on the receiver, representation, or communications process as such.

Infology is interdisciplinary and encompasses many aspects from already "established fields" such as aesthetics, art, audio-visual media, cinema, computer science, education, film, graphic design, information ergonomics, information science, information technology, information theory, journalism, linguistics, mass communications, media, pedagogics, photography, physiology, psychological information theory, semantic information theory, semiology, sociology, speech communication, television, trade language, visual arts, visual thinking, etc. The concept *information design* is usually concentrated on typography and graphic design of information materials. Infology can be viewed from various research angles. We can study parts of the communications process ("Communication") as well as various types of presentations ("Presentation"). Each "part" as well as each "type" can be divided into several sections.

As far as various aspects of verbo-visual messages are concerned, it is necessary to work from a holistic point of view in which the individual receiver is at the center.

Points in common
As the above presentations of the different research fields show, many of these fields will be seen to have points in common.

Data processing is studied in information science, information processing, and information technology. *Information searches in databases* are conducted in both information science and information processing. The concept *communications* is studied in information science, information theory, and infology. The *measurement* of information occurs in information theory, semantic information theory, and infology. *Perception* and *cognition* are studied in psychological information theory, information ergonomics, and infology. *Social developments* are studied in information technology and social information. Information *design* is a subject of interest in information ergonomics, infology, and social information. The *development of new media* is a subject of interest in information technology, social information, and infology.

This book deals mainly with the "visual" part of verbo-visual presentations.

CONTENTS

Author Index 341

VISUAL
INFORMATION

Chapter 1

COMMUNICATION

Technical developments have moved at a very rapid pace. Everything suggests that the pace of developments is likely to increase rather than decrease. New media like video, teletext, videotex, databases, and hypermedia all indicate that visual messages in different forms will become increasingly important in all kinds of communication.

Today computer-based interactive systems are used for training and learning in schools as well as in industry. The information society is already here. Attention must be devoted to issues concerning the production, transmission, presentation, and perception of verbo-visual information.

MEDIA AND REPRESENTATIONS

Communications between people have always been important. Aspects of our society are becoming increasingly intertwined, and the need for communications between people is increasing at a fast pace. We need to communicate in order to establish contacts with one another, to maintain and improve those contacts, to exchange information and views, and to develop ourselves and the society. If communication is to be possible at all, signals in some form must be transmitted, received, and deciphered. Both animals and people communicate with the aid of simple signals. The signals may be aural or visual. They can also consist of odors or tactile contacts and therefore act on our sense of smell and touch rather than on our hearing and vision. There is often an interplay between different signals or stimuli which coalesce into a unified whole. Simple signals usually elicit simple responses in the message recipient whose responses elicit responses from the original message transmitter, etc. Information systems of considerable complexity can arise in this way.

Communication models
Many information and communications theorists have devised models to explain the way the communications process operates. As early as 1948 Laswell put it this way:

communications are WHO says WHAT to WHOM via which CHANNEL and to what EFFECT. Then Shannon and Weaver (1949) proposed the following model, which illustrates the way information is passed from a sender to a receiver: A message is selected by an Information Source and incorporated by the Transmitter into a signal which is received by a Receiver and transformed into the message reaching the Destination. The signal can be influenced by noise.

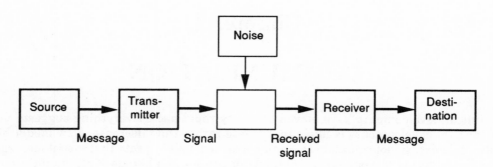

The Shannon and Weaver (1949) communications model.

We can be sure that people do not derive the same information from things they read, hear, or see. The meaning of any language, verbal or visual, is resident not only in words, lines, colors, etc., but in ourselves to a large degree. We have to learn to assign meaning to language symbols used. We have to learn the codes, and they differ

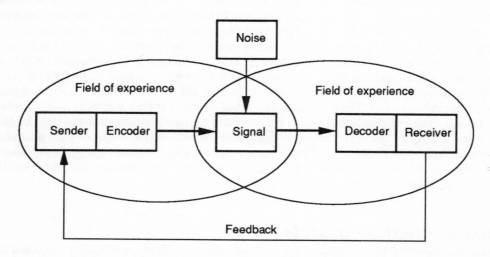

Schramm's (1954) adoption of the Shannon and Weaver communications model.

in different societies and in different cultures. Schramm (1954) used a model to show that there must also be some overlapping in the fields of experience of the sender and of the receiver for communication to take place.

Designers often produce material for information and instruction for their own counterparts, not for the people who actually need the information. This is because many designers lack basic knowledge about communication possibilities. Subsequent models have incorporated an increasing number of variables but often fail, in my view, in their treatment of perception processes.

In the production of information, a sender conveys information on a part of reality via a representation to an information receiver who, via sensory impressions, is able to obtain some perception of that reality. This perception may then evoke some response which affects the reality and/or creates some feedback to the original sender. The receiver's perception varies as a result of a number of factors, e.g., his current cultural and social status, the time and stage of his development, his mood, experience, memory, and other cognitive processes, such as creativity. Perception is divorced from the representation which, in turn, is divorced from the reality ($P \neq Rp \neq R$). Some of our sensory impressions give rise to "garbage" and some to learning. Learning is transferred to the memory by cognitive means. The cognitive variables exert an influence on subsequent perceptions and may also evoke inner perceptions and inner imagery.

"Noise" may intrude on various occasions and interfere with this process. Every "perception," such as a visual sensation, is actually composed of a large number of different sub-components which are aggregated into a single holistic impression. A

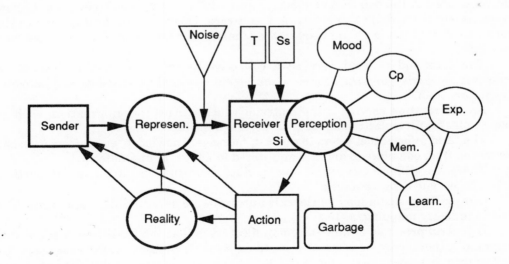

Pettersson's 1982 communications model. T = Time and stages of development, Ss = Cultural and social status, Represen. = Representation, Si = Sensory impression, Cp = Cognitive processes such as intelligence and creativity, Exp. = Experience, Learn. = Learning, and Mem. = memory.

representation, e.g., a visual, which is to be used to convey certain information, has a sender, one or more receivers and even a content, of course, a structure, a context, and a format. The visual is produced in a certain way with respect to various variables. The model shows that perception is different and never the same twice.

The content, the structure, the context, and the format influence the viewer's ability to perceive the picture. There is every reason to assume that the various picture variables play a very important role in our ability to read and understand pictures. A picture which is easy to comprehend provides good learning and memory retention. This makes it a better representation than a picture which the viewer finds difficult to comprehend.

So the task of the information producer is to select a representation in such a way that perception of the representation is optimized. This is a task with many different dimensions. Communications are successful when a receiver comprehends the message a sender has wished to convey to him or her.

People are being exposed to an increasing volume of "messages" from many different senders. The messages are transmitted from senders to receivers with the aid of different media. In all communications (even in mass communications), *many individuals are the recipients of the messages.*

Medium and message

In the 60s the famous media expert Professor Marshall McLuhan coined the expression "The Medium is the Message." This expression has given rise to considerable confusion. Now, in the 90s, it is often said "The Message is the Medium." Technology is the servant, and the message, the idea, is the master. This is said to be demonstrated by the fact that in 1980, for every dollar spent on A-V equipment, there were nearly three dollars spent on A-V software. However, the medium is not the message. A medium is an aid used in the transfer of information from a sender to a receiver.

The term aid is used here as a collective designation for the channel, or information carrier, and the processor/equipment required for encoding and decoding the information.

An information carrier is the material which carries the information, such as paper, plastic, film, electromagnetic waves, magnetic tape, etc.

The term information refers to content, message, knowledge, etc. Information can be moved from one place to another and stored in analog or digital form.

There are different types of media. Each has its own particular properties, advantages, and disadvantages.

Our existing media may be classified according to several different criteria. (See Media-industry mapping, p. 13.)

A general principle of human communication is that the likelihood of successful communication increases when a concrete reference is present. In the absence of the actual thing, the next best reference is a visual representation of the thing. A visual is a more pertinent reference for meaning than the spoken or written word. Visuals are iconic. They normally resemble the thing they represent.

A medium plus its contents is a representation (or even a re-presentation) of reality. Representations of reality can display varying structures, consist of a

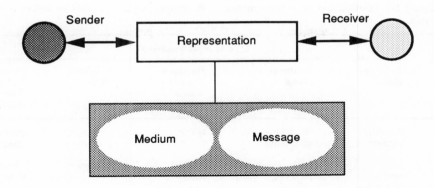

A representation (or re-presentation) is a medium plus its message/content.

number of different components, and be related to one another in different ways. Words and visuals, sound and visuals, or sound, words, and visuals are examples of components which can interact.

A message/content with a given design/form is conveyed by the sender to the receiver with the aid of a medium. The various media are undergoing comprehensive (technical) changes, changes in terms of production, duplication, stock-keeping, and distribution or presentation of contents. Some of these developments are proceeding in the same direction and working together. Others are on separate paths. Some are even counteracting one another.

Visuals used for information and in instructional message design are usually representations of our external reality. However, fine arts are sometimes representations of our inner reality, such as thoughts and dreams.

In a *redundant relationship*, the same information is conveyed via, e.g., words, sounds, and visuals and is therefore "superfluous." For example, subtitles can be added to a TV program so the action displayed on the screen is described by the words. This greatly enhances the educational impact of the program. A redundant relationship should be used in instructional message design.

In a *relevant relationship*, the information presented via, e.g., a text or sound supplements the information supplied in the visual. Visuals with a relevant relationship to a spoken or printed text can greatly enhance the text's informative effect and vice-versa.

In an *irrelevant relationship*, the information presented in various channels is completely independent of one another. In TV programs, for example, the picture sometimes deals with one aspect, the text with another, and the sound with a third. This makes it harder for viewers to make the most out of the program. Conflicts readily arise between a concrete visual event and abstract verbal information. When this happens, the concrete, readily accessible information assumes priority over the abstract information.

A *contradictory relationship* exists when the information in various channels conflicts. This is disastrous for an informative program.

Table showing the relationship of various media to structural complexity and to different types of representation.

Level of complexity	Type of representation				
	1-dimensional	2-dimensional	simultan. 1- and 2-dimensional	3-dimensional	simultan. 1-, 2-, 3-dimensional
low	acoustic signals	children's scribbling	teletext	stereo-picture	mirror-image
	text, spoken, & written (letters, telegrams, papers, books, telex)	still pictures, informative pictures, symbols	comics (text + cartoons + graphical symbols)	hologram	"living-visuals," sign-language, body-language
	dialogue, i.e., interactive text, spoken, & written (telephone)	still pictures, realistic pictures	videotex, (interactive text & pictures)	model	"living-visuals," ballet
	music, performed & written	still pictures, suggestive pictures, maps	filmstrips and slide series with sound	sculpture	"living-visuals," theater, conference
	stereo music, performed & written	still pictures, true-to-life analytical picture	exhibition	exhibition	holograpic film & TV in stereo & color
	radio theater in stereo	lexivision, complete co-ordination between text & image	film & TV programs	stereo picture & holograms with movement in image	reality
high					

Different media are capable of representing reality with varying facility owing to differences in their structure, the kind of representation involved and the content. The text (both spoken and written) is an example of a "one-dimensional" representation. It "flows" in a relatively fixed and often unambiguous form along a time axis. A still picture is "two-dimensional." Its interpretation is less constrained. A still picture can be interpreted in more than one way. We extract differing parts of the available information in it each time we view it. A stereo picture adds a third "dimension." Having a "one-dimensional" and "two-dimensional" representation at the same time, or even "one-dimensional," "two-dimensional," and "three-dimensional" representation, at the same time, is possible, even commonplace.

In the future, media also might be capable of representing smell, which would add still another dimension. Different media are also related to one another in regard to their level of structural complexity. The simplest form of a "one-dimensional" representation is a simple acoustic signal, such as a baby's cry. A higher degree of complexity is found in texts, interactive texts or dialogue, monophonic music, stereophonic music, and stereophonic radio theater with sound effects.

If text is likened to a flow along a time axis, then music can be likened to a multitude of streams flowing along the same time axis at the same time. Music is always structurally more complex than text but can, of course, be very simple in content. The greater the degree of structural complexity, the closer the representation approaches reality at a given time, in a given place, and in a given context. The accompanying table (p. 8) is an attempt to describe my view of the interrelationships of various media in a two-dimensional representation of a multi-dimensional reality.

Marsh (1983), however, uses another terminology. He points out that audible dimensions include: frequency, amplitude, complexity, duration, and localization. Then all representations should be considered "multi-dimensional."

The sender, like the information receiver, can be a person, a group, a company, an organization, or an authority. A distinction is often made between private media, group media, and mass-media. Each medium has its own particular properties. The selection of a suitable medium is important when informative material is to be produced.

Production of need-oriented information

When producing materials for information, instruction, education, or any other reason, we have to choose between different representations and between different media. Which representation would be best then? That question has many answers related to the needs and to the objectives. There are vast differences in a person's needs when s/he seeks information, general knowledge, diversion, entertainment, or leisure.

For entertainment and leisure, representations close to reality might be good choices. For instance, it could be exciting to "walk around" among the actors in a holographic film in stereo and realistic color. For information and education, too much realism in the representations would make it difficult or even impossible for the viewer or learner to identify the essential learning cues. On the other hand, too little realism would also be a poor choice. The information is inadequate. A moderate amount of carefully selected realism gives the best learning. Thus, a series of slides could be a better choice than a film in a specific learning situation. In addition, a few slides cost only a fraction of the cost of producing a film.

When a need for information is identified, the need can be satisfied as listed below:

• Carry out a problem analysis and find out what the problem really is and to whom it is a problem. Identify the characteristics of the receivers of the information.

- Carry out an analysis of the information requirement and find out just what the information is to cover.
- Frame the objectives as specifically as possible and express them in measurable terms.
- Select a suitable method and determine in which way or ways the objective should be attained.
- Select a suitable medium or identify which media are to be used.
- Prepare an outline of the contents. This will clarify the structure. The information production can then begin. Select, modify, or design new materials.
- Distribute the completed material to the users.
- Testing can result in the correction of the information, revision of the method and choice of medium, and identification of new information needs.

As far as the choice of medium is concerned, regard must be paid to the suitability of various media in every individual case. To be successful the sender has to know the medium and its unique possibilities. Advantages should be utilized, and disadvantages should be avoided.

MEDIA CONSUMPTION

Our media consumption will vary considerably depending on several different factors such as:
- cultural differences;
- socioeconomic factors;
- individual interests, which may cause large differences even between persons in the same family;
- different needs of education, entertainment, and information during various periods in a person's life;
- different usage of the media at home, in school, and at work;
- costs;
- technical developments;
- ease of use;
- competition with other activities; and
- competition with new media.

In the industrialized, cultural sphere, we are today living in mass-media societies. Every day we are bombarded with information via the media, at home, in school, on the job, and in the society in general. It is rather hard to avoid information and just as hard to obtain the "right" information, the information that we need at the right time. Audio, text, and visuals compete for our attention. It is possible that we miss the information in which we are really interested. In addition to radio, TV, books, newspapers, and magazines, vast amounts of information are distributed in the form of letters, advertising throwaways, posters, placards, stencils, photocopies, photographs, etc. We may "drown" in this "information flood." According to Key (1977) the average US adult is exposed to over 500 advertising messages daily, of which s/he consciously perceives around 75.

Already well established media will meet a lot of competition. Will people read books in the future? Will people listen to the radio? To follow these developments, the Swedish Broadcasting Corporation's Audience and Program Research Division (SR/PUB) conducts an annual survey on the way in which Swedes utilize different media on "an average day." As it turns out, people spend an average of more than five hours a day on mass-media consumption in Sweden. However, there is probably some overlapping in the figures. Other studies have shown, for example, that radio listening is largely a passive occupation. People sometimes listen to the radio while simultaneously reading a paper, for example. There are also wide individual differences in people's consumption habits. Five hours a day for mass-media consumption is anyhow a considerable amount of time in view of the fact that most people also hold down jobs, entailing time-consuming travels back and forth to work, and that they sleep anywhere from seven to ten hours a night. The average hours per day and night spent on major activities other than work by the urban US population in 1975 were as follows: sleep 7.8; leisure time 5.5; personal care 3.1; and family care 2.9 hours.

North American children may spend 11,500 hours in school during the period five to eighteen years of age. During the same time they watch TV at an average of 15,000 hours and listen to the radio, records (or CDs), and cassettes 5,000 hours. In the US people watch TV 31 hours a week and in Sweden 12 hours and 50 minutes a week. The corresponding figure for reading is six hours and six and a half, respectively.

Media market size

We can hardly talk about or define one single media market. Instead there is a vast amount of specialized markets or market segments. These are dependent on factors such as:
- populations and demographic data
- geographical and political situations
- cultural and socioeconomic factors
- languages
- trade and customs regulations
- the information economy
- technology trends
- different user groups and needs
- hardware, equipment and services, sales, rental
- software, production, distribution, sales, rental

A specific market may be considered very large for one medium but at the same time minor for another medium. Obviously, the characteristics and the economics of different media are extremely different. It may be worthwhile to produce a newsletter as an on-line database-service for a few hundred subscribers but not possible to produce a spectacular superstar movie for less than millions of viewers.

The activities needed to enhance the possible net profit per copy are different for various groups. For private media a solution may be to get more customers. For mass-market media the producers should get better margins. It might be forecasted that the information economy will take an increasing part of the total economy in the future.

Finance and business markets are time critical. Such services demand "real-time" communication. They may be available on demand or include an alerting service. Typically these services will be concerned with financial matters such as stocks and shares, commodity trading, etc.

Non-time-critical services will include a series of browsing and alerting services similar in purpose to newsletter-type publications. They may be supplied by such media as videotex, teletext, electronic mail, audio tape, and digital discs.

In-house publications such as manuals can be expected to be increasingly presented in electronic form, with greater interactivity and also quality of reproduction and presentation.

Professional markets have restricted and selective applications and specialized subject areas. Services are likely to grow out of existing requirements in answer to specific needs and will include provisions of specialist information and data, fast updating, current awareness, software packages, complex information retrieval, and research dissemination. The services may be provided by commercial umbrella information providers, professional organizations, or commercial publishers, and are likely to be mounted on host computers accessible via telecommunication networks, or supplied on portable machine readable files such as tapes and discs.

Education markets have a number of features which are important to communication media. One of the most important is the degree of interactivity which is offered between the teaching material and the user. Others include the variety of media and the ability to deliver the material where and when it is required.

Electronic media must be expected to provide an increasingly important supporting role. Typical services and products will include books with machine-readable sections, modular material, audio tapes and discs, video tapes and discs, mixed media productions, personal computer software, authoring languages to enable teachers to prepare their own material, and on-line computer-based training.

In further education, distance learning facilities are important. These will be provided by programmed learning and fault-finding routines, computer-based learning, television programs linked to other facilities such as software, simulation exercises, and tele-conferencing with tutors.

Consumer and leisure markets are expanding. One of the key marketing concepts in new media is to create products which will stimulate consumers into buying or renting the necessary hardware. The organization and networking facilities will differ from country to country.

Local or regional news and information services will emerge covering news stories, travel information, guidance on local authority services, advertising, entertainment, shopping, etc. Relevant media are videotex and cable TV.

Magazine-type services will focus on a collection of related topics and include information, entertainment, and advertising. Key features will be segmentation of the market, e.g., according to demographic or user needs; use of sound and moving pictures as well as text; creation of several products on the same theme but using different media; creation of multimedia products; coproduction with several types of organizations and sponsors; new ways of handling advertisements. Appropriate media will be videotex, cable TV, video tape, video disc, and magnetic and optical media for use with personal computers.

Computer games can be regarded as the leading edge in consumer displays and consumer involvement. The media which will be used include audio cassettes, floppy diskettes, plug-in memory, video tapes, video discs, optical discs and cards, videotex, and holograms.

Media-industry mapping

Several attempts have been made to make different kinds of "maps" or "models" of the media industry. These maps might be useful as tools for strategic planning for the information business. It is by far not easy, or even possible, to make one single map that covers all aspects of the media industry. Thus we have to work with a set of different maps at the same time. Such maps have been produced according to different criteria such as the needs of the users, time of delivery and number of receivers, growth of the information business, media evolution, and technical development (several other possibilities may still remain). A few systems will be briefly presented here.

We all have individual feelings towards media. Our media consumption depends upon factors such as interests and our *perceived need* for education, entertainment, information, and news. Our need for education, entertainment, information, and news can be visualized as areas partly covering each other. "Double" areas are the subject of special interest for publishers since these areas are most likely to attract more attention from consumers than other areas. Thus *edutainment* is education and entertainment. *Infotainment* is information and entertainment. *Infocation* is information and education. The BBC series about the life on earth by and with a noted naturalist is an example of a television program with elements covering all these needs.

News is handled differently in different cultures. In the US news includes a good portion of entertainment. In Japan news is more related to education. In Sweden news is related to information.

We have "fast" and "slow" media. We have "personal," "group," and "mass-media." In direct broadcasting, radio and television may reach a large number of receivers. Books and magazines may also reach many individuals, but much more time is needed. When Japanese researchers marked different media on a "time of delivery and number of receivers" map, they found new segments for development. Videotex and other new tele-communications media are developing fast to reach various market segments of between one hundred and one thousand customers.

At the Harvard University Center for Information Policy Research "the information business map" has been developed. The map is a rectangle in which the left side ranges from basic products like paper and file cabinets to delivery services of parcels and mail. The bottom side of the map ranges from plain paper to books. In the upper right corner we find financial and professional services. Thus all kinds of products and services related to the information business are placed on the map according to their conduit or content. The map is strikingly nice to look at. However, in my personal view, this model is not very easy to use in practical work.

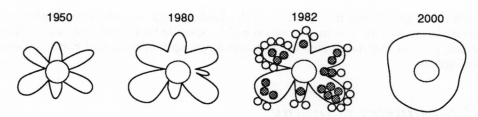

1950   1980   1982   2000

In 1950 we had live media (center), sound media, film media, broadcast media, models and exhibitions, graphical media, and telecommunications media (the "leaves in the mediaflower"). In 1980 video was a competitive medium (between film media and broadcast media). In 1982 several new technologies (grey circles) and completely new media (white circles) began developing. In 2000 most media will interact and partly overlap each other. We already have "multimedia."

Existing as well as future media may be mapped according to an evolutionary aspect. For many years the media situation was very stable, only expanding a little each year. In 1950 we had live media, sound media, film media, broadcast media, models and exhibitions, graphical media and telecommunications media (the "leaves in the mediaflower").

In the 1970s video developed into a competitive medium (between film media and broadcast media). At the same time the classical "borders" between the media groups began to dissolve. In 1982 several new technologies, most based on computers, and completely new media began developing. Demarcations are even less pronounced today, and most media will interact and partly overlap each other in the future.

Live media include:

Personal communication	personal body language, speech
Group communication	social body language, ballet, pantomime, theater, live music, conference, church, school

---

Sound media *can* be put into four groups based on the ways they can be used and the technology involved as shown below:

Products	Characteristics	Examples
1. Records	rotating disc with mechanical pickup	long playing record
	rotating disc with optical pickup	compact disc
	fixed disc with mechanical pickup	TAI-minidisc

2. Audio tape	soundwire	
	tape in open spool	
	compact cassette	Philips standard audio cassette
	mini cassette	
	cassette with endless loop	
3. Sound card	film base with magnetic layer	line reading
4. "Firm" memory	printed coding	EAN-coding
	computer (speech synthesis)	speaking toys speech output
	photographic audio disc	digital hi-fi

Film media may be two- or three-dimensional, still pictures, or moving pictures.

Products	Characteristics	Examples
A. *Two-dimensional*		
1. Still pictures	non-silver based	overhead transparency, slides, microfiche
	silver based	overhead transparency, slides, microfiche, panoramic, film strip, microfilm
2. Animated pictures	dynamic picture	overhead with overlay
	picture with movement	overhead with movement
	multi-projector show	multiple projectors
3. Semi-moving	program film	PiP (S-8), Bezeler (16)
4. Moving pictures	school and training films	single-concept, S-8, 16 mm
	movie theater	16 mm, 35mm, widescreen

B. *Three-dimensional*

5. Still pictures	Viewmaster, autostereo, chromatic stereo, polarized light
6. Moving pictures	chromatic film, polarized light

Broadcast media include both audio and television services. Examples are shown below:

Products	Characteristics	Examples
1. Radio	broadcast	national radio, local radio, narrow-casting, cellular radio
	communications radio	alarm, military, police, civil
2. Television	sound and picture	television, local TV, narrow-casting TV, interactive cable TV, closed circuit TV, direct broadcasting by satellite
	3D-TV	chromatic
3. Data		teletext, cable-text

Video media provide a high level of information content in a simple-to-understand form. Many of them include audio information. Because of the need to store a lot of information, a major characteristic is compactness of storage. Major examples are shown below:

Products	Characteristics	Examples
A. *Still pictures*		
1. Videotape		compact-cassette
2. Videosheet		Mavica
3. Video discs		optical pickup
4. "Firm" memory		pictures

B. *Moving pictures and sound*

1. Videotape	open spool video cassettes	1/2 in, 1-in., 2-in. angular search (U-matic,VHS, Beta, V-2000), Compact cassette longitudinal search (BASF, Toshiba)
2. Video disc	long-play	mechanical (TeD) magnetic disc (MDR) optical reflective disc (LaserDisc) optical transparent disc (Thomson CSF) capacitative disc without groove (VHD) capacitative disc with groove (SelectaVision)
	interactive	optical reading (Laser Disc, Thomson CSF)
3. "Firm" memory		video games
4. 3D TV		polarized light

Models and exhibitions offer a means of expression which is more accurate than many other media. Increasingly these can be seen to provide a total "experience." Different types and applications are shown below:

Products	Characteristics	Examples
1. Models	three-dimensional	sculpture, modelled items, globe, diorama
	multi-dimensional	robot, happening & events, simulation
2. Exhibitions	*fixed:* two-dimensional	exhibitions with pictures and text
	three-dimensional	pictures, text, sound, objects
	multi-dimensional	moving pictures

	moving:	
	two-dimensional	exhibitions with pictures and text
	three-dimensional	pictures, text, and sound, objects
	multi-dimensional	moving pictures
3. Holograms	fixed hologram	transmission-, reflex-, dichromatic holograms, and hologram with projected picture
	moving hologram	integral hologram, hologram film

Graphical media can be put into two groups: manually or personally produced; and manufactured media.

The *manually produced* graphical media include pictures, such as drawings, paintings, etchings, lithographs, textiles, signs, and text such as letters and handwritten manuscripts.

The *manufactured group* of graphical media has a wide range of products or services, as shown below.

Products	**Characteristics**	**Examples**
1. Serials	several times/week	morning papers, evening papers, business publications
	numerous times/year	weeklies, comics, journals, newsletters/bulletins
2. Books	periodical publications	yearbooks, almanacs, catalogues
	reference	dictionaries, directories, tables, encyclopaedias, statistics, indexes
	non-fiction	handbooks, biographies, travel guides, monographs,
	school and college textbooks	teachers' manuals, textbooks, workbooks, programmed instruction

	fiction	novels, anthologies of essays, poems
	comics	comic books
	children's books	baby, infant, teenage
3. Printed music		sheet music
4. Maps		atlases, gazetteer, wall maps
5. Separate pictures	two-dimensional	reproductions, posters, postcards
	three-dimensional	autostereo, chromic stereo
6. Printed matter	for distribution	booklets, brochures, reports, lists, manuals, circulars, printed articles
	for display	signs, menus, posters, decals, pamphlets
7. Security print		bills, shares, bonds, lottery tickets, coupons
8. Copying		electrostatic, diazo, thermal
9. Computer media		computer printouts

Telecommunications media are able to transmit a wide variety of information. Examples are:

Products	Examples
1. Sound	telephone conversation, teleconferencing, dial-up services, voice mail
2. Text	telegram, telex, teletex, facsimile, mobitex
3. Pictures	video teleconferencing, facsimile, TV-pictures
4. Data	datel, datex, telepak, teleshopping, telebanking, telesoftware, videotex

Computer media may be found as parts of the other groups, especially in the telecommunications group. Examples are:

computer print-outs, computer programs, computer conferences, artificial intelligence, expert systems, multimedia, computer games, hypertext, hypermedia, virtual reality, CD-ROM, CD-I, and Laser cards.

At present we can see a tremendous amount of work being done in technical laboratories all around the world. In the coming decades this will result in new techniques to produce traditional media, as well as in new media and in different kinds of new services. Especially interesting is the development of integrated digital tele-networks capable of transmitting sound, text, data, and pictures at the same time and in the same system. Various "technical development maps" or "time-scales" exist in different parts of the world.

NEW MEDIA

The amount of information being disseminated is increasing with unparalleled rapidity. At the latest turn of the century there were about 10,000 technical and scientific journals in the world. By 1970 the number had grown to 100,000, and this number is expected to increase tenfold by the year 2,000. By now no signs indicate a paper-less society, maybe a "less paper" society. Video discs, cable TV, satellite transmissions, videotex, computers, and other new media are due to increase the flow of information to even greater levels. Whole new "information industries" are being created.

For several years now, digital storage of more than 50 TV images has been possible on an ordinary compact audio-cassette. Other systems are much more efficient. Fifty color pictures can be stored with very good quality on one A6-size microfiche (10.5 × 14.7 cm). A stack of microfiche, 1 cm thick, can store more than 1,000 frames. However, a video disc with optical reading is capable of storing the text contents of 500,000 A4-size pages (21 × 29.5 cm; 10,000 million bits of information). Data are recorded by a laser beam which burns microscopically small holes in a disc. The disc is then read by a semiconductor laser and the information is on demand displayed on a CRT tube. Other optical video discs can store 90,000-100,000 stills for the TV-screen.

In the future, digital techniques will be employed in the recording as well as the editing and distribution of TV-programs. When digital techniques are introduced, a common world standard will be possible. Then the problems caused by the different TV-systems in use today, NTSC, PAL, and SECAM, will disappear. This will indeed facilitate international distribution of programs. However, in 1986 there were about 600 million TV-receivers in use in the world and the electronics industry was set up to manufacture conventional TV-sets. That means that it will take some time before the new technique will be in common use.

TV-screens might become the "spiders in the communication webs of the future." Some years ago there was only conventional broadcast television. Since then, however, a dozen different functions have been or are being introduced. So the TV-set will play a major role in the "pushbutton society" or rather the "voice recognition society" of the future and will only be employed to a limited degree for displaying traditional broadcast programs in the 1990s. This will heighten demands for more TV-sets and for large, flat color-TV-screens with stereo sound.

Current laser techniques make it possible to create three-dimensional images, holograms, enabling viewers to see "behind" image objects. These techniques are at about the same stage of development as photography was at the beginning of the century. Many people are aware of the dramatic developments in photographic and film techniques since that time. The development of holography will be equally dramatic, although more rapid in coming decades.

Studies in Japan have shown that the ratio between "utilized" and "available" information had fallen from about 40% in 1960 to about 10% in 1975. So 90% of available information was "wasted" from the sender's point of view. Today, the figure for "wastage" is probably even higher. We are rapidly heading for an information oriented society characterized by a need for selectivity in information consumption tailored to our individual needs instead of to the availability of large amounts of general, mass-produced/copied information. Computers with routines for intelligent searches of large amounts of information can be very useful and are probably essential.

Electronic publishing

At the end of the 1960s the "electronic revolution" was announced. The book was said to disappear and would very soon be replaced by new electronic media like video cassettes. During the first years of the 1970s publishing houses throughout the world were hit by severe crises followed by necessary re-organizations. At that time some people saw only threats. Others could see that the development of new media also could mean new opportunities as well as new risks. After more than 500 years the printed word is still alive and will certainly be so for a long time but together with other carriers of information and partly in other formats. We will experience "on-demand-publishing" when only the information needed at one specific occasion is copied or printed, for example by a laser printer linked to a computer. Most of the information needed can be read on the screen and might never be printed as a hard-copy.

In recent years, the concept "electronic publishing" has come into increasing use. However, the concept is not really very good. Like "traditional publishing," "electronic publishing" is far too vague, comprehensive, and ambiguous. Traditional publishing comprises publication of books, newspapers, magazines, maps, films, and AV material. Electronic publishing comprises the following media/forms of distribution:
1. Traditional ether media. Local, neighborhood, and network radio and TV.
2. "Special transmissions." Cable TV, pay-cable TV, coin-operated TV, satellite TV, viewdata, home fax.
3. Videograms and phonograms. Video cassettes, video discs, audio cassettes, phonograph records, CDs.
4. On-line databases and distributed databases, e.g., on CD-ROM.
5. Future media. "Electronic holograms," etc.

So publishing can comprise many different media with different properties and requirements. We should therefore try to express ourselves with greater stringency when discussing the subject of electronic publishing.

Video

Videogram is a collective designation for video cassettes and videodiscs, i.e., media for the storage and replay of TV programs at an optional time and place. The utilization of video cassettes can be said to comprise three main fields:

1. The recording of transmitted programs for subsequent replay.
2. Distribution and rental or sale of pre-recorded programs, such as movies for entertainment and education.
3. Program production.

In the beginning of the 1970s, expectations were high, especially in the electronic industry and from many producers of programs. However, changes in patterns of behavior are often slow. It takes time to develop a new medium.

For a number of years video developments progressed very slowly because of factors such as the multiplicity of incompatible technical systems, i.e., a cassette recorded according to one system could not be played on a VCR using another. Nor were the earliest VCR's particularly reliable. Playing time was also limited, in general, no more than one hour. Modern cassettes have playing times of several hours. The VHS cassette has become effectively the worldwide standard today, enabling the video industry to boom (the market for videocassettes is now larger than that for cinema attendance).

In 1980, there were no fewer than 70 different companies world-wide which manufactured 195 different kinds of video cassette recorders (VCR's). There were about 50 different systems for video discs. Most of these systems lack any real practical significance. But the numerous "major" and widely distributed systems often create practical problems for users since these systems are not compatible and the incorrect type of cassette or disc could be purchased.

Videodiscs offer new possibilities. As mentioned earlier, an optical video disc can store 90-100,000 stills to be presented at random on a TV-screen. It is possible to retrieve and display any one of these stills in a matter of seconds. Interactive videodiscs offer great possibilities for, e.g., education and information. The possibilities to produce adapted and individualized programming is almost unlimited. The possibility to have, e.g., all the paintings from the most famous collections in the world in all museums and all libraries is thrilling.

Teletext

For the past 20 years, experiments have been conducted in different parts of the world in which certain information stored in computer systems can be accessed from the home, company, agency, school, etc. The simplest of these experiments is teletext, sometimes called broadcast or one-way videotex. It is a one-way system for transmitting data from a data-base to TV sets with built-in decoders. The disseminator of information is able to reach several million sets with a limited number of messages (i.e., a few hundred "pages"), but these messages can be updated continually.

Teletext pages are transmitted by broadcasting or cable and can be viewed at any time. The digital data signals are stored on lines not utilized to form the ordinary TV image. An accessory with pushbuttons is used to "browse" until the desired information, e.g., a news summary, weather forecasts, or sports results is found. Waiting time in a teletext system comprising one hundred pages varies from a tenth of a second to 15 seconds with a mean of seven and a half seconds. When an entire channel is committed to teletext—which is easy in a cable TV network covering a total of 100 channels—the data base could hold up to 50,000 pages. Waiting time would then not exceed 30 seconds.

Teletext might develop into the TV-newspaper of the future with news as the most important programming. The role of daily newspapers and disseminators of news could be taken over by teletext to a large extent. A number of national systems have been devised for teletext. Experiments and services have been carried out in several countries. Britain was first off the mark with Ceefax from the BBC (1976) and ORACLE from ITV. The latter is a commercial radio and TV company.

Teletext is sometimes confused with "teletex"—minus a "t" at the end. "Teletex" is an interactive word processor linked to the Swedish data network and introduced by the National Telecommunications Administration in November 1981. Teletex, sometimes referred to as "supertelex," consists of terminal hardware, a teletex network, a number plan, and a teletex catalog.

Videotex

In contrast to our established media, videotex has no natural or clear-cut niche. Many standard products and/or services are threatened or can be augmented by videotex. One important application is in the distribution of messages, i.e., electronic mail. So postal authorities in many countries are interested in it. Videotex can be regarded as data traffic via telephone lines, so telecommunications and computer companies are equally interested. It is excellent for supplying various kinds of economic information. So banks are looking at it closely.

Videotex can currently be used to book tickets or make direct purchases of all kinds of goods and/or services in many countries. In the future, wholesalers may be able to eliminate retailers in a number of different trades. Videotex can also be viewed as a kind of electronic newspaper and/or book, so the medium has also attracted the attention of newspapers and book publishers. However, videotex can also be described as a kind of newspaperlike TV-service offering animation and attractive image quality. So TV companies are looking into it. Electronic games have proved to be the most popular videotex feature, so video game companies are interested. These are only a few of the fields covered by videotex. There are more. Videotex allows numerous information suppliers to store anything from a few "pages" to tens of thousands containing information in one or more computers. Many different users are able to conduct simultaneous searches for information of interest to them on any occasion. So salespersons in the field can always have access to absolutely fresh information on stocks, prices, delivery terms, etc. A person with specialist knowledge in a particular field can offer consultation service, newsletters, reports, etc.—all delivered via videotex systems to customers in different countries. National

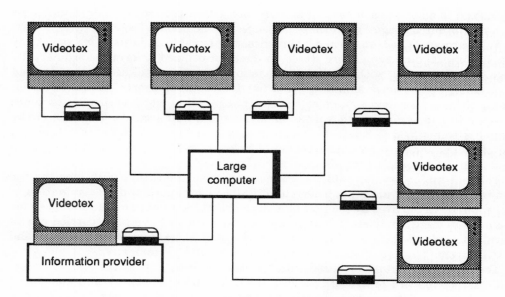

In a videotex system the signals are transmitted via ordinary telephone cables.

boundaries are no longer obstacles to the flow of information as was previously the case. By means of appropriate search routines, users can gain access to information in one or more data bases.

Since the signals are transmitted via ordinary telephone cables, the resolution of "pages" is necessarily limited. There are a number of different technical systems. Most of these systems can transmit text and very simple pictures. This works fine in the case of brief texts and various kinds of tabular information. A "page" on a TV screen has only 24 lines with 40 characters/line. This is a major limitation in many contexts. Compared to traditional graphical reproduction methods, text is difficult to read in all videotex systems.

The Swedish DataVision, like Prestel in England, Bildschirmtext in Germany, Telset in Finland, Teledata in Norway, etc., is a version of the same basic system and only the first step towards more sophisticated systems in the future. Both the Telidon system in Canada and the Captain system in Japan are examples of systems which already offer a wider range of options than the Prestel systems. *Prodigy* has been the most successful system to date in the USA. Digital telecommunications networks and digital TV sets will make it possible to use videotex in education. Future videotex systems should display the following properties: excellent image quality, animation, intelligent search systems, sound, and user friendly man-machine interaction.

An alternative to videotex is *audiotex*. With a digital telephone, it is possible to communicate with the computer and have messages delivered by synthetic speech.

Cable TV

Radio and TV reception at many locations in North America, Canada in particular, is often difficult because of the terrain. So companies began erecting television distribution aerials (often on mountain tops) in the 1950s. There were no serious copyright problems or difficulties since the TV programs were largely financed by advertising and regarded as a "natural right" by the public. TV distribution systems were ultimately improved. Since the TV programs were distributed via cable, the system was referred to as "cable TV." The first cables were only able to carry a single TV channel. But 6 to 12 channels were normal by 1970. Modern systems can now accommodate more than 100 TV channels.

The new systems offer channels showing movies, sports, news, weather reports, etc., in addition to the programs financed by advertising and transmitted by ordinary TV stations. This development has become possible, thanks to new distribution technology. A distribution chain may comprise the following:

A "wholesaler" owns program rights, such as Time Inc.'s Home Box Office (HBO) which broadcasts on two movie channels (24 hours a day, 365 days a year, on Eastern Standard Time and Pacific Standard Time) from its studio in Manhattan. Programs are transmitted by cable to the roof of a skyscraper. The programs are then beamed by microwaves to Long Island where they are relayed to a TV satellite. The signals are reflected by the satellite and picked up by thousands of parabolic antennas all over the U.S. and Canada. Local cable TV networks then operate as "retailers," decode and "clean up" the signals and deliver them to households subscribing to HBO. The "retailers" often offer several different entertainment channels without any advertising.

Cable TV systems will offer two-way communications in the next generation of videotex systems. Since image quality will be superior to the quality of present TV systems, the limitations imposed by the "mosaic images" in the present videotex systems when goods, services, and even information are ordered will be eliminated. Future cable TV systems will also offer extensive technical opportunities for advanced "remote education" programs.

Databases and multimedia

Optical media are being developed at a rapid pace. This is especially true of 12 cm optical *compact discs*. They can be viewed as "distributed databases." In the future they will probably capture a major share of the market from *on-line databases*, particularly in fields whose information does not require frequent updates. Compact discs are likely to attain widespread use in schools, universities, and other educational institutions, as well as for inhouse job training. A number of different systems with different characteristics are available. A few will be mentioned here.

CD-ROM, Compact Disc-Read Only Memory, is a CD disc for the storage of data (540–600 MB). It was announced in August 1983 and went on sale in the U.S. in 1985. One CD-ROM is capable of storing the text in several large encyclopedias, making this information available as a free-text database. Its capacity is equivalent to about 250,000 pages of typewritten text. One CD-ROM is capable of accommodating up to 15,000 simple line drawings while simultaneously storing all the requisite text information and procedures required for database searches. Today

CD-ROM is a viable technology attracting interest and investment worldwide. A variety of commercial products are already out on the market and more are coming at a steady pace.

CD-I, Compact Disc Interactive, is a CD disc capable of holding audio, images, text, and data. CD-I can store 10,000 hours of "synthetic sound," 384 hours of natural speech, 40,000 line drawings, 4,000 "TV quality" color frames or various combinations thereof. CD-I was announced in February 1986 and has been for sale since 1990.

DVI, Digital Video Interactive, is similar to CD-I and developed originally by the American company RCA and now available from Intel. Since one hour of digital storage of video information occupies 65,000 megabytes, DVI operates with advanced computerized image compression.

The development of different compact discs will open up fascinating, new opportunities to producers of, e.g., teaching aids. They will make it possible to create *"the total teaching aid"* encompassing text, sound, pictures, numerical information, *and* opportunities for various kinds of information processing in a single medium. A "total teaching aid" is a multimedia database (a hyper-medium) offering the user complete freedom in moving back and forth between verbal, numerical, visual, and audio information.

Originally, "multimedia" referred to the use of several different media at the same time. An example is a verbal presentation where the presenter uses slides and audiotape. Today "multimedia" refers to the use of several representations on a computer screen, or on several screens but controlled by a computer. It may be still or motion video, text, graphics, audio, and animation. The information is usually stored with digital technology on digital-based platforms.

Already we are seeing *virtual reality*, the display and control of synthetic scenes by means of a computer and peripherals, such as datagloves, helmets, and joysticks. Systems for virtual reality allow users to vicariously interact within "virtual worlds." For readings on virtual reality, see "Educational Technology Selected Bibliography Series," Volume Six (McLellan, 1992).

Mediateques

It is possible that our current libraries could be converted into mediateques in the future, i.e., places at which information can be sought. A mediateque could consist of a TV set/CRT display with decoders for teletext and videotex, a telephone plus a modem, a small computer with built-in memory, software for intelligent search routines, and one or more optical video disc players.

The computer makes it possible to "leaf" through 50,000 stills on one side of a single optical video disc. The same disc could also conceivably store more than two million videotex images. The system could offer an interesting combination of local and central storage of information. Absolutely up-to-date information in any of the world's various data bases could become accessible by means of a telephone link to the respective computer or by connection to a computer network. More stable and invariable information could be stored on optical video discs, magnetic discs or, to some extent, on magnetic tape. If a TV camera is added to the system, the user would be able to enter his/her own recordings of sound and moving pictures. Texts would be entered via the computer. A school could have a central mediateque with terminals in different classrooms.

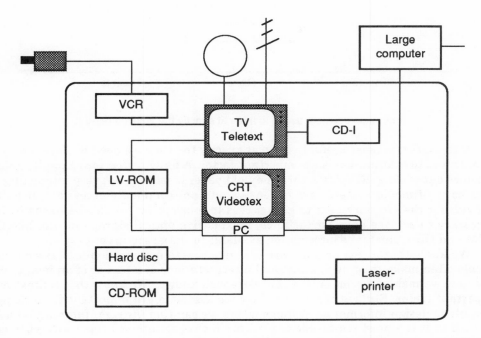

An example of a mediateque. It is possible to search for information in many different sources such as local databases on CD-ROM or CD-I. It is also possible to use on-line services. Print-outs can be made with the laser-printer.

FINDING INFORMATION

The possibility of finding some specific information is much higher when we are *interested* in finding that information. When we, for instance, browse through a newspaper, we will note those advertisements that we are interested in. In fact, we are seldom aware of the other advertisements in the paper. In an experiment, students taking a "Visual literacy-class" at the University of Stockholm were asked to write down the advertisements they could recall from the morning paper. Each year, only a few students could remember more than one or two advertisements so well that they could describe them in some detail.

It is not always obvious *where* to look for information. Using a systematic approach can increase the possibility of finding the information we are interested in. Our previous experience can also guide us to look in the right place. We are good at remembering information we can relate to concrete, spatial concepts. One example is books in a library. We might remember that there is an interesting passage of text below a picture of a Unicorn in a big, red book on the second shelf, close to the door.

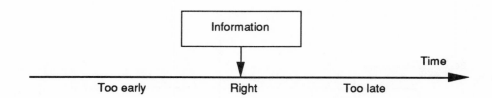

Information is most useful to have at exactly the time we need it.

Information is most useful to have at exactly the time we need it. Thus, *when* we have access to information is an important factor. A daily paper, for example, quickly becomes out-of-date. Reading a three-day-old paper is usually not very interesting. As long as multimedia systems are expensive and not commonly accessible, it will be difficult for the ordinary user to gain access to information when s/he needs it. It is necessary to explore how, for instance, inexpensive optical storage media, like CD-ROM and CD-I, can make information available for large groups of people.

We know that a text or a picture can give rise to many individual associations. People often make their own, individual interpretations of a text or of an image. Why and how we make associations are not very well known. We know that context is an important factor. Studies of why and how we associate are important for making it possible to design information systems where we can find *the right information when we need it*. It is almost impossible to predict which associations people will get in each specific situation. Thus there is an obvious risk that also multimedia-systems will be created according to traditional ways of structuring information for print media like books.

Computer-based information systems have made it potentially easier to find information, but there are also factors which can make it harder to find exactly the information we are interested in. One reason is that we associate words differently, and give words different meanings depending on the context in which they appear. An example of this can be found in research on visual literacy. The Swedish word "bild" (visual, picture, image) has *seven* different meanings in the Swedish language, and the word "färg" (color) has eight definitions. Thus it is quite apparent that one may find a lot of superfluous information when searching for research papers in a bibliographic database.

Furthermore, it can be almost impossible to know that we have found everything of interest to us after a search in a hypermedia or multimedia system. This is especially true for hypermedia systems, since the information we want might be located in many different nodes in the web. Therefore, we must scan every information item in the database to ensure that we have not missed any important information of interest. This is often impractical or impossible. Being able to execute search questions is thus desirable for hypermedia systems as a complement to browsing and navigation by pointing at various items in the display and clicking the right ones.

In addition, it is important that the producer of a multimedia information system carefully plans which information to communicate, and how to communicate it.

The amount of available information is growing every day. Modern research and development produce more information than ever before in our history. This growth

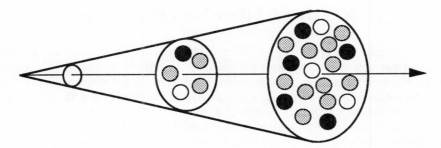

Information within different areas is increasing rapidly. The information cone is growing. Some information is very important to us (white circles), some is correct but not at all interesting (grey), and some information is wrong or even disinformation (black).

of available information can be described with a cone, the *information cone*, which is growing over time.

When a subject matter is new, it is easy to have an overall view of all available information. Fifteen years ago, one person could have a good grasp of topics like "optical media" and "multimedia." Today, however, it is almost impossible to know everything that is going on within these areas. As the amount of information grows and becomes easier and cheaper to store, the need for new ways of navigating and browsing increases.

Design and color signal different things. Typography and layout of text and pictures should be attractive and stimulate further reading (see Chapter 7). The graphic design should guide the reader and help her or him to access the information s/he needs. Graphical design for information has a clear focus on the primary message.

A good movie always starts with a clear presentation of the major elements of the story. The director knows that if the dramatic conflict is not clear, the story will appear meaningless and boring to the audience. Clarity is one of the most important principles of film making. The screen-writer must have a clear-cut idea of what the story is about, otherwise the resulting movie will be confusing. If the writer does not know the story, who does? A clear presentation of the subject matter is just as important in a multimedia system as in a movie. If the user does not understand right from the start what is going on, s/he can lose interest and/or get confused. Even though many multimedia systems are not centered around a dramatic story line, there is a need to state the purpose of the system clearly and to make it clear which information the user can expect to find, where it can be found, and how it can be found.

Whether we actually succeed in finding the information we need is dependent on how interested we are in finding it, where and when we look for the information, associations we make, graphical design, presentation technique, and our experience.

INFORMATION NAVIGATION

It is possible to distinguish between different categories of variables, or "dimensions," related to *navigation, browsing,* and *search* for information in multimedia systems, as well as in other information systems. Navigation is a goal driven search for some specific information, usually in a database or in a multimedia system. Navigation is a combination of visual, "human" browsing and computer based search. Browsing is a rather *ad hoc,* random way for a visual, "human," search for information. We can browse through information stored in a database in a way which is similar to browsing through a book, a newspaper, or an encyclopedia. Search is a systematic computer based search for information in a database using an exactly specified concept or search question. Pettersson and Kindborg (1991) discussed the following four dimensions:

1. *Type of search* and how to find information: from a regulated and restricted search to an unregulated and flexible search.
2. *Experience and perception* of information: from a directed and intended to a free and associative experience and perception.
3. *Structure and organization* of information: from linear positions in a defined order to non-linear positions in a flexible structure.
4. *Type of signs* and code-system for representation of information: from abstract alphanumeric characters, letters and figures to images.

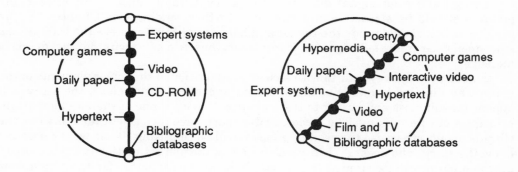

The "Type of search-dimension" (left) ranges from a regulated and restricted search (bottom white circle) to an unregulated and flexible search (top white circle). The "Experience-dimension" (right) ranges from a directed and intended (left white circle) to a free and associative experience and perception (right white circle).

Every specific representation, for example a film or a multimedia system, can be categorized by assigning a value for each of the above four dimensions.

The "Type of search-dimension" is based on man-machine interaction and restricted by systems design, technology, and computer software. Between the terminal points "regulated and restricted search" and "unregulated and flexible search," there are systems which can be characterized as hybrid systems. Bibliographic databases, hypertext, electronic encyclopedias, daily papers, video, computer games, and expert systems, can be used as examples for illustrating the "Type of search-dimension."

The "Experience-dimension" is based on the functions of human perception and our possibilities to experience the contents of the information. In many information systems, experience of information is somewhere between the terminal points "directed and intended" and "free and associative." Movies and TV-programs, video, expert systems, hypertext, daily papers, interactive video, hypermedia, computer games, music, fiction, and poetry can be used for illustrating the "Experience-dimension."

The "Structure-dimension" is based on the actual organization of the information. There are several hybrids of linear and non-linear organization of information. Videotex, videodiscs, hypertext, papers, hypermedia, interactive multimedia systems, and expert systems can be used for illustrating the "Structure-dimension."

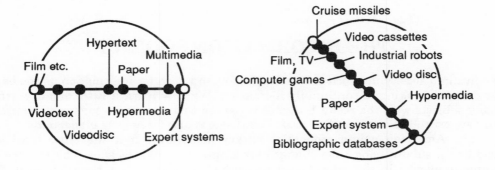

The "Structure-dimension" (left) ranges from linear positions in a defined order (left white circle) to non-linear positions in a flexible structure (right white circle). The "Sign-dimension" (right) ranges from abstract alphanumeric characters, letters, and figures (bottom white circle) to images (top left white circle).

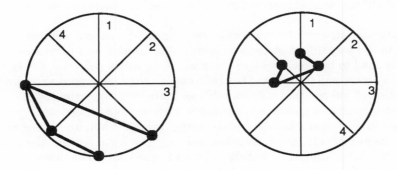

An information navigation diagram for bibliographic databases (left), and for interactive videodiscs (right).

The "Type of signs-dimension" is a "language-dimension" or "code-system" based on the signs used to represent the information with respect to storage, search, and display. Bibliographic databases, expert systems, hypermedia, papers, video discs, computer games, industrial robots, film and TV, cruise missiles, and future image databases can be used for illustrating this dimension.

An *information navigation diagram* showing the dimensions discussed above can tell us how different media are related to each other. The information navigation diagram can be used both for analyzing existing information systems, and for predicting the characteristics of future systems.

In an ideal information system it is easy to browse, navigate, and search for information. Such a system should have unregulated search, and free and associative experience, and make it possible to navigate in a non-linear structure. It should be possible to search using both images and alphanumeric characters.

THE INFORMATION SOCIETY

We live in a society in which the availability of and need for information as the basis for decision-making is continually increasing. We now learn a little about a great many subjects with the result that it is becoming easy to acquire comprehensive but very superficial knowledge. Our basic knowledge is also frequently inadequate.

The American media economist Parker has shown that the labor market's traditional subdivisions have changed strikingly in recent decades. The number of people employed in the information sector has risen from less than 5% of all the gainfully employed people in the U.S. in 1860 to more than 50% in 1980. The agricultural and industrial sectors have been the subject of extensive measures to improve efficiency measures. A number of measures aimed at making the service sector more efficient have also been implemented to some extent. For purely economic reasons, the same efficiency measures will also be introduced in the information sector. The number of people employed here will not continue to rise as quickly in the future. Nor will we be able to increase our information consumption very much in the future.

The information must be more effective. We must analyze the factors which are important to the way information is designed, distributed, and perceived. Previously, information used to be produced by people who frequently only had a very vague idea about the objective and function of the information they were producing. In the future the production of information will probably be more objective-oriented.

The production of a message commences with an idea occurring to someone with the need to convey information to a given target group. When an outline is ready, the generation begins of text, draft sketches, editing, graphical design, the production of originals, masters, and, ultimately, a given quantity. The sender produces a representation of reality. A representation is a medium with specific contents, i.e., a message. Other tasks for the sender are stock-keeping, distribution, marketing, advertising, selling, billing, bookkeeping, etc.

From writers to readers

Cave paintings, rock inscriptions, clay tablets, rune stones, church paintings, letters, and other hand-written material are all examples of unique documents conveying a direct message from the sender/writer/picture creator to the receiver/reader. However, these messages were sometimes intended for gods and other higher powers, not for people.

Text and pictures have been produced, distributed, stored, and utilized for thousands of years. The first "travel guides" were produced and sold as early as 2000 B.C. They were the Egyptian "Books of the Dead" which contained advice and information—in an integrated, lexivisual amalgam of text and pictures—on coping with the trip to the Kingdom of Death. They were completely hand-made rolls of papyrus and, thanks to their high price, only available to truly wealthy families. The trade in these books is reminiscent of the medieval Catholic Church's trade in letters of indulgence. Both phenomena are examples of what could be called profitable publishing. Duplicates were made in the most literal fashion imaginable by "middlemen," specially trained scribes and copiers who copied text and drawings, often repeatedly. The industrial production of books is a comparatively modern phenomenon. Despite the fact that books began to be printed more than 500 years ago, printing remained an exclusive and painstaking handicraft for many years. Gutenberg's bible was printed on 316 pages and took three years to make (1452–1455) in an edition comprising 200 copies. Some 170 of these copies were printed on paper and 30 on parchment. A total of 5,000 calf skins were required for the parchment versions. One goatskin was needed to cover each book.

Even at an early date, libraries of different kinds acquired major importance as "institutional middlemen" in the transmission of information from writers to readers. The first public library, Pisistratus, was founded more than 2,500 years ago (540 B.C.) in Athens. The first bookstore was opened, also in Athens, 140 years later (400 B.C.) Until the middle of the 19th century, bookstores often served as publishers, too, producing as well as selling books and other graphic products.

A great many people in different occupational categories are required for transmitting a message from writers to readers: people such as text and picture editors, graphic designers, typesetters, repro technicians, printers, bookbinders, stockroom staff, salespersons, order takers, bookstore employees, librarians, buyers, and administrators. The different steps involved in publishing are time-consuming and jointly represent a major expense. About ten percent of the price of a book, not including tax, usually goes to the author.

Electronic publishing could change this situation to some extent. It would reduce the distance between writers and readers. New opportunities for a dialogue could then develop in some instances.

Consequences of electronic publishing

There are a number of approaches to the field of electronic publishing. Depending on their frames of references, different people can interpret the same phenomenon in different ways.

The *user/reader* wants a fast, cheap, easy-to-use system. Disseminated information must also be presented in a clear and legible manner. A great deal of research

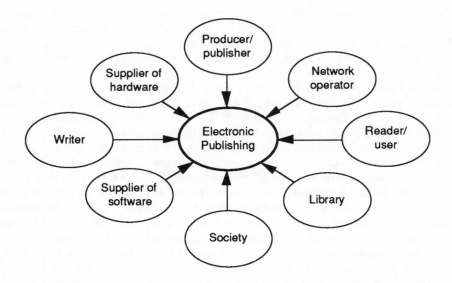

Different people will see a phenomenon such as "Electronic Publishing" in different ways.

and development is needed in this area. Poor legibility is currently fairly common, in e.g., videotex, thanks to the erroneous use of colors, for example.

The volume of available information is constantly expanding. This may make it even harder for people to find desired information.

The information *supplier/writer* is offered new opportunities for presenting her/his message. In the future, factual information, training, and entertainment will be processed in digital form throughout the entire production chain.

Writers and experts in different fields can generate their own texts and numerical tabulations in computers using programs for word processing, spread-sheets, and graphics. Artists can create their illustrations with computer-aided image processing systems. Photographers can use a video camera for recording video frames, stored as individual pixels, on magnetic discs.

The *producer/publisher* can "polish" basic material with typographical measures, editing, and information verification. The results of her/his efforts can then be stored (sometimes in versions especially tailored to different user categories) for convenient user access. Like a database operator and supplier of hardware and software, the producer must market her/his services and find a sufficient number of buyers for those services. Increasingly flexible systems are making it easier to reach groups with special interests in different parts of the world. The development of new technology and new media presents producers with exciting new options. An optically readable plastic card (about 3 x 2 inches) with 2 megabytes of onboard memory can store 800 pages of text, 2 hours of music, or 200 computer graphics frames. Once they

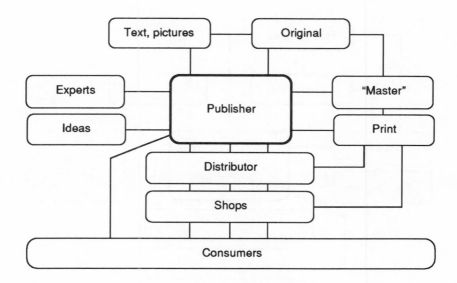

The traditional function of the information producer has been to coordinate people with ideas, experts on subject matters, writers, artists, designers, photographers, and others in the production of original, masters, and run. Traditional tasks have also been stock-keeping, marketing, distribution, accounting, etc. Reactions from the consumers give the information producer knowledge for new or revised editions, new runs, and even new products. The information/content is delivered by means of the most suitable media.

get into large-scale production, the cards should only cost about $1.50 each. Optical compact discs offer interesting prospects for the storage of large volumes of information.

Caxton, a British publisher of reference works, was already experimenting with putting reference volumes and image databases on videotex in the late 1970s. Grolier, an American publisher, was marketing on-line and videodisc versions of its reference works by the early 1980s, and CD-ROM versions (without pictures) by 1985. Twenty volumes of the *Academic American Encyclopedia*, containing 9 million words, are offered on a single compact disc (CD-ROM). A computer, a CD-ROM-drive, and suitable software make it possible for disc buyers to browse at will in this vast database.

An early Swedish publisher of reference volumes on CD-ROM was Esselte, which brought out its first CD-ROM encyclopedia in 1987. During the 1990s several multimedia encyclopedias will be published using CD-I and DVI technologies. These can be called "total information aids."

Traditionally publishers and booksellers have been working with books. Books are products. We can hold them in our hands. We can use them when we like and as often as we like. Regardless of the content, fiction or non-fiction, the book is still a product. Only a small part, say 10%, of what you have to pay for a book is the cost of the actual content. The rest is taxes, marketing, and production costs. In the future, products are gradually going to be replaced by "content-services," that is, services to

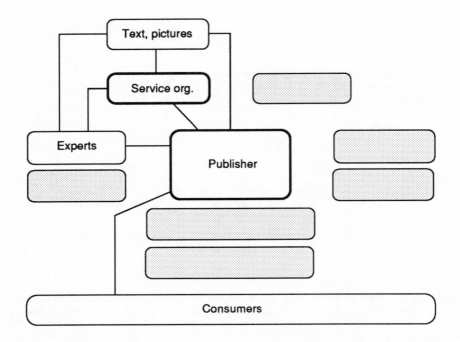

In the future information society with databases, cables, and terminals installed, it will be very easy for anyone with knowledge of a subject matter to "publish" certain kinds of information such as tables, manuals, reference books, dictionaries, etc. The consumers, the users of the system, can easily access the information they need.

give people the information, the knowledge, the news, or the entertainment they want to have in a specific situation.

When products gradually are replaced by "content-services," we will have a psychological type of problem. How much are people really willing to pay for something they cannot hold in their hands and keep in a physical representation? There is some experience from rental of video cassettes for entertainment. There is not yet much experience from the fields of information or education.

On-line databases are offered by different kinds of customers, such as the printing companies, publishing houses, computer manufacturers, and libraries.

Libraries will gradually improve their range of service by offering new media. Phonograms and, to some extent, videograms and on-line database searches are already available.

The OCLC (On-line Computer Library Center) is an interesting development. For example, the OCLC has a database holding more than ten and one-half million literature references and information on 166 million physical books, newspapers, and magazines at 7,000 libraries. The OCLC is developing full-text databases, based on, e.g., the aforementioned CD-ROM technique, with facilities to permit local write-out of hard copy if, when, and wherever needed.

Network operators must invest vast sums on the expansion and maintenance of their digital networks. In the future, networks will be capable of handling text, audio, video, pictures, and data.

Governments are commissioning an increasing number of studies to examine the need for control systems, ethical rules, and new sources of tax revenue. Copyright of and responsibility for factual information, i.e., data in constant need of change, processing and updating by many different people, are among the most difficult issues being addressed.

Changes in media consumption

It is unlikely that we will wish or be able to spend as much time on the media in the future as in the past. Economic trends suggest that there is unlikely to be any scope for major cost rises, in addition to inflation, for the mass-media in the next few years. So new media will have to compete with the media already in existence.

Now people all over the world are receiving far more audio-visual information than at any other time in history. And people working in audio-visual communications are striving to help people communicate, educate, train, and inform.

Media likely to decline in relative importance are letters, advertising throwaways, posters, certain books, newspapers, magazines, traditional AV media, radio, and television. Media likely to increase in relative importance are various telecom services, phonograms, videograms, CDs, teletext, videotex, cable TV, and satellite TV.

Media likely to predominate in the future are telecom services, videotex, cable TV, satellite TV, telefax, teletext, and various computer services. Most media will be under voice-actuated or image-actuated control, making it unnecessary to have complicated routines to enter information via keyboards.

TV, videograms, cable TV, satellite TV, CD-I, virtual reality, radio, and phonograms will be our most important sources of *entertainment*.

Teletext, cable TV, TV, and radio will be our most important sources of *news*.

Books, databases, and videograms with computerized search systems will be our most important sources of *knowledge and education*.

Videotex, databases, multimedia, books, and computerized reports, which are seldom printed in their entirety, will become our most important sources of *information*.

To summarize, I predict the following *long-range changes*:
1. A transition from products to services.
2. An increasing degree of segmentation.
3. Increasing flexibility.
4. Increasing competition for the individual consumer's time and money.
5. Gradual disappearance of demarcations between different media.
6. Development of new media and techniques through "hybridization."
7. Replacement of the different systems currently available by one international, integrated digital telecommunications system.
8. Development of a single world standard for TV.
9. Increasing copyright problems.

The introduction of new media

Before introducing new media, it might be a good idea to consider viewpoints from users, producers, originators, and society.

Users' viewpoints

Demand. Is there a demand for the new medium? Where? Why? For which categories? For which purpose is the new medium intended? Do other media offer the same or corresponding services? Which are the unique advantages of this medium that other media are lacking? How is the new medium adapted to reality?

Use. Is the medium easy enough to use? Does the user benefit in any way from using the new medium? How? Why? For how long will the medium serve its purpose? Will the media soon be "old-fashioned"? Is there a rapid technical development to be expected within the field that the medium represents?

Costs. Are the costs of the medium, when it is systematically used, higher than the costs of other media, which provide the corresponding information or experience? Is the cost a critical factor?

Producers' viewpoints

Demand. Is there a demand for the new medium? Where? Why? For which categories? For which purpose is the new medium intended? Do other media offer the same or corresponding services? Which are the unique advantages of this medium that other media are lacking?

Production. Can production be carried out within the frame of the present organization? By employees? By consultants? By "traditional" authors, drawers, photographers, and others? Must new personnel (competence) be recruited? Who? Why? Are special skills needed for production of originals? Which skills? Which time-schedule? Costs? Are special skills needed for production of masters? Which skills? Time-schedule? Costs? Are special skills needed for production of editions? Which skills? Time-schedule? Costs at different editions? Could the supply of raw materials be a critical factor? Are there any problems as to updating? Why? Time-schedule? Costs?

Stock. Is storage possible within the frame of the present organization? Is there a problem as to "perishables"? Costs?

Marketing. Can marketing be effected within the frame of the present organization? Is there any demand for special competence? Are there existing markets? Where? Which? How big? Can the users be reached through advertising? In which publications? Costs? Is it necessary to have an organization for direct selling? Is there a requirement for a special hardware? Is the necessary hardware available? Quality? Costs? Should the media be sold by the piece like certain products? Can you sell a "package" of hardware/software? Can you sell subscriptions? Is a high degree of price sensitivity to be expected? Are there "psychologically determined price levels" because of established price levels on similar services?

Distribution. Can distribution be carried out within the frame of the present organization? Costs?

Debiting. Can invoicing be made within the frame of the present organization? How do we charge? Costs?

Administration. Can the present organization be used for administration? Costs?

Investment/Financing. Does the new medium claim special investments? By which means is the medium financed? For how long will the medium serve its purpose? Will the medium soon be "old-fashioned"? Can you expect a rapid technical development within the field that the medium represents?

Copyright. Is the product protected as to copyright? Can the products be protected from being copied? Are there any great risks with regard to copying? Why? To what extent?

Statement of accounts. Are fixed payments to different originators advisable? Is a royalty account system appropriate? Can statement of accounts be made out to the originators within the present organization and with the present routines? Costs?

Profitability. Which profitability can be achieved and when? Are there other alternatives with better profitability?

Originators' viewpoints
Demand. Is there a demand for the new medium? Where? Why? For which categories? For which purpose is the new medium intended? Do other media offer the same or corresponding services? Which are the unique advantages of this medium that other media are lacking?

Income. What is the income? When is the money paid?

Production. Are there new creative possibilities? How will the working situation change? Do I actually need the producer? In what way? For what?

Copyright. Is the product protected as to copyright? Can the products be protected from being copied? Are there any great risks with regard to copying? Why? To what extent?

Viewpoints of the society
Value. What is the value with the new medium? To whom is it "good"? To whom is it "bad"? Why? Is the new medium likely to inflict any laws or ethical roles? Which? To what extent?

Tax. Is it possible to introduce new taxes? When? How much will it give?

Security. Will the new medium influence national security? Why? How much?

SCREEN COMMUNICATION

Today computer-based interactive systems are increasingly used for training and learning in schools as well as in industry. Graphics are combined with text. Videotapes and videodiscs may give high quality pictures. Voice input and output are also used. However, images used in most new media, like teletext, videotex, personal computers, and CAD/CAM systems, are often far too difficult to read and understand. Often combinations of colors are made in such a way that the actual information is more or less lost. Knowledge of traditional print design is usually not utilized.

Technical factors, programming factors, language factors, and contextual factors all influence the viewer's ability of perception, learning, and memory with respect to the function of the brain and the sensory organs. To achieve "good quality" man-machine interaction, we have to consider all these factors in a kind of "wholeness-perspective." To learn we must be able to hear, see and also understand the message.

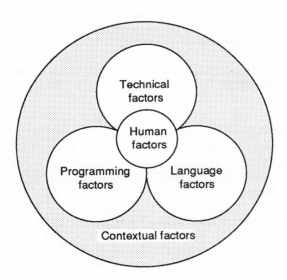

A model of man-machine interaction in a "wholeness-perspective."

In my view, it is no use to develop new, advanced systems and forget the aspects of the human factors. Such systems will never be successful in the long run.

In a printed material, such as a book, the table of contents and the index make it easier to find information according to one's wishes. When a person has read a page in a book, he or she may easily proceed to additional information by turning the page. Information stored in a computer system may be accessed in several different ways. The ease of use and the man-machine interaction are of vital importance. It is necessary to make the system as user friendly as possible by providing user support systems, standard function keys, and for example a possibility of full text search. Information and instructions should always be clear, consistent, concise, and simple. It seems to be very important that the user has full control of the system, i.e., with respect to reading rate when text is presented.

Compared with traditional graphic presentations, a presentation of information on visual displays is *very limited*. Still, information may be presented in many different ways. Obviously the use of color is important. Different "rules of thumb" will apply to different types of presentation. Information, the "content," might be represented as text, as numeric data, or as visuals.

Visual displays

Visual displays can be built in many ways. A color television set, an advanced color terminal, and a liquid crystal display all have very different characteristics. A television set is built to be watched at a distance of more than 120 centimeters. A computer terminal, however, is built to be used at a distance of 60 centimeters and has a much better picture quality. It also costs a lot more.

In discussions on technology, color is related to measurable amounts of light. In 1931 an international body called the Commission International de l'Eclairage (International Commission on Illumination), or CIE, defined standards of light and color. In this context color primaries are the basic color stimuli used for the synthesis of any color, by addition or subtraction. For color synthesis in a cathode ray tube (CRT) or a visual display unit (VDU), a range of colors can be produced by the additive combinations of a very limited amount of radiation. A color CRT is a vacuum tube, enclosing one or three electron guns for generating beams of electrons, a system for focusing the beam to produce a spot of visible light at the point of impact on the phosphorous screen, and for electric field deflection of the beam, suitable deflection electrodes. The thousands of small phosphorous dots are grouped into threes—called triads—with one dot emitting radiation that appears red, one dot emitting radiation appearing to be green, and the third emitting radiation appearing to be blue. Red, green, and blue are called the "three primaries," RGB. One lumen of white is given by 0,30 red + 0,59 green + 0,11 blue. Any two primary colors may be mixed to produce other colors. Red and green added can produce a range of hues around yellow. Green and blue produce a range centered on blue-green, while red and blue mixtures produce a red-blue range. The total number of colors that can be produced in a CRT depends upon the number of steps or grey levels obtainable for each phosphorous dot. Advanced systems are capable of producing up to 256 simultaneously visible color stimuli chosen from a palette of 16 million. However, in most cases only a few color stimuli are needed at the same time.

The uncertainties in the coordinates of colors are rather large as a consequence of the heterogeneous distribution and efficiency of the phosphorous over the screen, the defects in electron beam convergence, and the departures of the relations between the values of the color signals and the digital counts.

One consequence of additive combinations in color television is that characters presented in white (the three-color combination) are less sharp than those presented in yellow, blue-green, or red-blue (all two-color combinations). In a similar way, the latter colors are less sharp than red, green, and blue (pure colors). Sometimes color rims may be seen at the characters with two- or three-color combinations.

The additive combination starts in dark adding light to produce color. Thus, another consequence of additive combinations is that secondary color stimuli will always appear brighter than the primaries.

Luminance is a photometric measure of the amount of light emitted by a surface (lumen/steradian/sq.m.). Radiance is a radiometric measure of light emitted by a surface (watt/steradian/sq.m.). It should be noted that neither luminance nor radiance is the equivalent of brightness, which is the experienced intensity of light (bright-dull). In color displays it is very difficult to distinguish brightness from lightness (white-black). When the signal to the display is increased, the brightness of the total screen is increased. If a signal to a specific part on the screen is increased, the lightness of the area is increased compared to the total screen.

It is usually possible in a CRT to adjust the luminance, the hue, and the saturation. Like brightness and lightness, hue and saturation are also psychological dimensions. Hue is the basic component of color corresponding to different wavelengths. Saturation is most closely related to the number of wavelengths contributing to a color sensation. We should always remember that the production of color, by additive or subtractive methods, has nothing to do with the actual perception of colors.

In a CRT some 8,000 to 20,000 volts of tension are required to form an image on the screen. Screens with several colors even require up to 30,000 volts. The electrostatic field of the CRT is positively charged. Thus the person sitting in front of the screen is negatively charged and a strong field is created. The field affects the movement of dust particles in the air. Since the majority of the particles are positively charged, they are attracted to the operator. The rate of deposit can reach 10,000 particles per square millimeter of skin an hour. Thus skin and eyes become irritated. People suffering from allergies can experience extreme discomfort. The electrostatic field can be eliminated with the help of a grounded filter, mounted on the screen.

The electromagnetic field is created by the large magnets used to focus and direct the electron beam on the screen. The electromagnetic radiation consists of two components of which one can be shielded. It is not clear as to whether this radiation affects the adult human body unfavorably. However, it is known that this radiation might be injurious to unborn children when pregnant women work too many hours in front of the screen.

Color description systems

The relationship between hue, lightness, saturation, and brightness is very complicated. For practical use in art and in industry, several different systems providing numerical indexes for color have been developed. The most important ones will be mentioned here.

The Munsell System was introduced in 1905 and has been modified several times. The system consists of fixed arrays of samples which vary in hue, lightness (here called value), and saturation (here called chroma). The value scale ranges from white to black with nine steps of grey. Hue is represented by forty equal steps in a circle. The value and the hue are related to each other by a maximum of sixteen "saturation steps."

There are many theories about how perception of colors actually works. In 1807, Young proposed a trichromatic color vision system. In 1924, Young's theory was formalized by von Helmholz, who proposed hypothetical excitation curves for three kinds of cones in the retina, sensitive for red, green, and blue. In 1925 Hering based his "natural system" on man's natural perception of color that presupposes two pairs of chromatic colors blocking each other, red/green and blue/yellow. This model is the principle for the *Natural Color System (NCS)*, developed during the 1970s in the Swedish Color Center Foundation in Stockholm (Hård & Sivik, 1981).

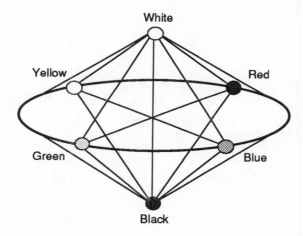

The NCS Color Solid with the six elementary colors. Yellow, red, blue, and green are all located on the circumference of the Color Circle. The color Triangle is any vertical sector through half of the NCS Color Solid, such as, e.g., white - blue - black - white.

From a perceptual point of view, Man perceives six colors as "pure." Black and white are achromatic colors. Yellow, red, blue, and green are chromatic colors. These six colors are called elementary colors. All colors that are not pure elementary colors have a varying degree of resemblance to several elementary colors. Thus every possible color can be described with a specific location in a three-dimensional model, a twin cone, called the "NCS Color Solid."

The chromatic elementary colors yellow, red, blue, and green are all located on the circumference of the Color Circle. Each quadrant can be divided by one hundred steps, thus describing the hue of a color. The color Triangle is any vertical sector through half of the NCS Color Solid. It is used to describe the nuance of a color, i.e., its degree of resemblance to white, black, and the pure chromatic color of the hue concerned (chromaticness).

When we want to describe a color using the color triangle and the color circle, it is done in the following sequence: blackness, chromaticness, and hue. For example, a color of 10 percent blackness, 80 percent chromaticness, and with a hue of Y7OR will have the notation 1080-Y7OR.

The NCS places emphasis on qualitative variation in the color sensation whereas the Munsell System is based on equally spaced visual scales. Both systems are based on surface colors.

In the *hue-lightness-saturation system (HLS)*, the hues are arranged as circles on the outside of a double cone resembling the NCS Color Solid (Murch, 1983). Hue specifications start with blue at 0° and then follow the spectral order around the circle. Lightness and saturation are defined as percentages from 0 to 100. The HLS system is easy to use for colors on the surface of the model. However, colors inside the model are difficult to define. As in the Munsell- and NCS-systems, brightness creates problems.

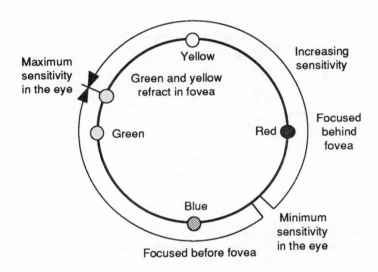

The NCS Color Circle combined with information on the eye's sensitivity.

The *hue-value-saturation system (HVS)* is a model that is rather similar to the NCS-system but utilizes another coding (Samit, 1983). Value is defined as the relative lightness. White has full value and black has no value at all.

In visual displays the color stimuli are specified by *red, green, blue (RGB)* values as discussed above. People who are specially trained can use the RGB proportions as a color description system. However, this is not possible for people in general.

The message on the screen
The message on the screen may consist of text, numeric data, and visuals.

Text

A presentation of text on a visual display depends on the type of characters used, the design of the information, the background, and also the content.

The *characters* may vary with respect to font, size, lowercase and uppercase letters, color, and contrast to the background. Legibility of the text depends on the execution of the individual character and the possibility for each one to be distinguished from all others. A lot of work has been conducted to create legible characters. Knave (1983) has given guidelines for the creation of characters. A minimum of ten to twelve raster lines per character is required. When characters are built by dots in a dot matrix, the characters will be round or square and not elongated. A dot matrix of seven by nine dots is often regarded as a minimum. The height of the characters should be a minimum of four millimeters for a viewing distance of sixty centimeters.

General *design rules* should be employed also in the design of screen displays. Thus material should be arranged and displayed so that it is easy to read, from top to bottom and from left to right.

A visual display design may vary with respect to spatial organization like headings, length of lines, justification, spacing, number of columns, number of colors at the same "page," and directive cues like color coding, twinkling characters or words, and scrolling text. Experiments (Pettersson *et al.*, 1984a) with 11,000 individual judgments of perceived reading efforts of text on visual displays were concluded as follows:

- Colors presented on color displays seem to be ranked in the same order as surface colors in traditional print media. Blue was most popular.
- When text is shown on a visual display, there is no easily read color combination. About thirty-five of one hundred and thirty-two combinations are acceptable.
- The best text color is black, which causes good contrast to most background colors.
- The best combination is black text on a white or yellow background.
- A text can be easy to read in any color, provided the background is carefully selected.
- The best background color is black, which has good contrast to most text colors.
- Reading efforts of color combinations are independent of the sex of the subjects.
- There was no difference between color blind (red-green) users and users with normal vision.

Inverse writing in various colors within a text may be used to achieve emphasis. Other possibilities may be a box around a paragraph or a change in font or size of letters.

Blank space in printed material increases cost, since more paper is required. Thus, it is not used often. However, color as well as blank space on a visual display is essentially free and might be used to increase readability. Full text screens in several colors are difficult to read and quite annoying. What about double spaced lines and/or spaces between columns? As stated above, it is possible to make rather clear statements with respect to the use of colors. However, it is not as easy to give guidelines for the other variables. Studies of attitudes to various variables (Pettersson *et al.*, 1984b) in the presentation of text on visual displays showed that subjects dislike fast scrolling text. Subjects seem to dislike more than three or four text colors on the same "page." They seem to consider color coding and/or twinkling text to be a good way to show that something is especially important. Subjects also seem to agree that text in uppercase letters is harder to read than normal text. Attitudes are indifferent to a few design variables. Thus text on every second line does not seem to make it easier to read than text on all lines. Higher characters do not seem to be easier to read than standard characters. Half lines do not seem to be better than full lines. A two-column layout does not seem to be better than a one-column layout. Other research suggest that margins should neither be narrow nor very wide.

The *background* may vary with respect to color and brightness. Good combinations of text and background colors always have a good contrast. Optimum contrast is often found to be 8:1 to 10:1. Most subjects prefer a positive image, i.e., dark text on light background with a minimum refresh rate of 70 Hz.

CLEA-research (Pettersson, 1984a) concerned with perceived reading efforts of text on visual displays and altering colors of the actual equipment found that the close *context* is really important for the perceived reading effort. The color of a terminal should be rather subdued. The best of ninety combinations were black text on a white screen with a dark grey terminal, closely followed by the context colors black, white, and light grey. It was also found that it is an advantage when the context color is the same as the color of either the color of the text or the background on the screen. The combination of context and text/background colors must match against each other. If they clash the reading effort increases.

Further experiments (*op. cit.*) with altering ambient light levels showed that this is of no or very limited importance for the perceived reading effort.

Numeric data

Computer graphics hardware and software have become widely available. In advertisements it is often stated that business graphics communicate the information effectively, thus being very useful. However, in real-life situations graphics often tend to be very poorly designed. Thus they may fail to improve the communication. Sometimes bad design might even make communication difficult or even impossible. Bertin (1967), Cossette (1982), McCleary (1983), and Pettersson (1983) all discuss the importance of individual design variables in visual language. However, these discussions are all based on research on traditional print media. Ehlers (1984) points out problems of legibility in business graphics. According to him, direction and pattern and texture of graphic elements appear to be important factors as well as color and size.

The CLEA-laboratory studies of *attitudes to different variables* in the presentation of information on visual displays (Pettersson *et al.*, 1984b) showed that subjects consider it easy to see the difference between vertical bars as well as between horizontal bars.

Further experiments by Fahlander & Zwierzak (1985) have shown that the greater the difference is between the color in a graphic presentation, the more distinct is our *perception of the border between the color spaces*. On *white* background the following color combinations are suitable to use: black combined with yellow, yellow-red, red, blue, green or the mixtures of red-blue (magenta), blue-green (cyan), and green-yellow. On *black* background the following color combinations are suitable to use: white combined with yellow-red, red, blue, or the mixtures of red-blue. On white as well as on black background the following combinations are suitable to use: yellow combined with red and blue, red combined with blue-green or green-yellow, red-blue combined with green or green-yellow.

Following this study Azoulay & Janson (1985) found that some colors used in business graphics have much higher *aesthetic values* than others. Blue, red, and green are liked the most.

In an effort to find some more detailed knowledge about our perception of business graphics, two comprehensive experiments were carried out with respect to *relationships between variables and parts of a whole* (Pettersson & Carlsson, 1985).

The findings, based on more than 2,300 individual assessments, were conclusive in the following points:

- Graphical information is very good in conveying a survey of a situation.
- When relationships between variables are presented, comparisons of lengths give the best results.
- When parts of a whole are presented, comparisons of areas can be used as well.
- Design of graphic elements is important to consider. Most available patterns are probably less good. Patterns should be subdued and not disturbing.
- Colors like blue, red, and green are liked very much but they do not improve our possibility of reading the message accurately.
- Different parts in graphic figures should have about the same luminance and radiance. The true differences between areas can be hard to see when shaded differently.
- When accuracy is needed, graphical information should be combined with actual figures.

"Choosing the Right Chart" ISSCO (1981) supplies 21 practical guidelines and pointers on effective chart design such as: "Make bars and columns wider than the space between them." In a study Ek & Frederiksen (1986) used the CLEA-equipment to find out about effective chart design. Forty subjects assessed the difference in size between two bars in a bar chart with six bars. The bars had one of three possible widths (1/60, 1/30, and 1/15 of the screen width). The distance between the bars had one of six possible values, from zero to more than twice the bar width. The bar charts were produced and displayed at random and always presented with blue bars on black background. The findings, based on 3,600 individual assessments, showed:

- The bar width has no influence on our perception of size.
- The space between bars has no influence on our perception of size.

This study confirmed earlier findings (with the perception of vertical lines). It can be concluded that *we can make screen design according to aesthetic appeal*.

Finally, it may be stated that *it is extremely easy to convey misleading information about statistical relationships by using misleading illustrations*. Those who are serious in their work should seek to avoid these mistakes.

Visuals

Our perception of visuals on visual displays are of course to a large degree dependent on the quality of the screen, especially when pie charts are used. European videotex terminals simply cannot reproduce a pie chart since the graphics resolution is only about 5,000 graphical elements. An ordinary television image consists today of about 250,000 image points or picture elements which vary with respect both to grey scale and color information.

Hayashi (1983) has reported on the development of High Definition Television (HDTV) in Japan. HDTV uses 1125 scanning lines and can contain five or six times more information than the present NTSC standard color television system with 525 lines. HDTV developments of flat plasma screens will also give increased technical possibilities for better perception of the visual information.

TEACHERS, STUDENTS, AND VISUALS

The concept "visuals in educational materials" can be considered from many points of view. We can assume that public agencies, politicians, teacher trainers, authors, editors, picture editors, graphical designers, artists, photographers, teachers, students, parents, journalists, and other opinion-makers can and often will entertain differing perceptions of the visuals employed in textbooks and teaching aids in modern schools. Many people can obviously belong to multiple categories. For example, a person could be a textbook author, teacher, and parent all at the same time. There must be major inter-individual differences within each group. In this section I will try to describe the way teachers and students perceive and use visuals in textbooks and teaching aids.

Visuals in textbooks and teaching aids
To commemorate the 500th anniversary of Sweden's first printed book, Åberg (1983) reviewed the Swedish people's reading habits in the first decades of the 20th century. At that time, school books were extremely popular, not the least with the parents of schoolchildren. In many families, textbooks were the only profane literature available.

There must still be children who love their textbooks but probably not with the same fervor. Society has changed dramatically since the turn of the century.

Textbooks and teaching aids have undergone rapid changes. Romare (1989) studied books on religion. She found that one primary school book on religion from 1945 had 25 visuals on its 288 pages, and one comprehensive school textbook from 1982 contained 114 visuals on 120 pages. Thus, the latter book had 11 times more visuals. Romare pointed out that wall charts were a fine complement to textbooks in the old days. Wall charts have now been superseded by slides, filmstrips, and overhead transparencies, but use of this material often requires extensive preparations by the teacher.

The visuals previously found in school textbooks were probably utilized in some active manner. Mulcahy & Samuels (1987) described the way visuals have been employed in American textbooks over 300 years. In their section on 19th century textbooks, the authors underlined the importance of illustration (page 24):

Illustrations, therefore, were considered central to the text rather than mere ornamental images on a page. Consequently, an important landmark in the history of illustrations occurred when these content area books in nineteenth-century America used pictures to explain scientific principles and to describe the world.

Gustafsson (1980a) studied the way textbooks were used in education in Sweden. In an appendix, Gustafsson (1980b) listed summarized descriptions of the activities occurring in 217 40-minute lessons. Thus, the material covered a total of 8,680 lesson-minutes in Swedish in grade 3, English in grade 6, science subjects in grades 7-9, working life orientation, electrotechnology, social science in high school, and English in adult education.

On the average, one-third of the lesson time was spent on "printed text material." This includes traditional textbooks as well as brochures produced as central A-V material. Lesson descriptions show that the visuals were only used in printed matter to a limited extent, on seven lesson occasions (3.2%).

The most common type of visual mentioned was the *overhead transparency,* employed on 13 lesson occasions (5.9%). Slides or filmstrips were also used a few times (1.3%).

No more than 1% of lesson time was devoted to *A-V material,* defined as "audio tape, film, filmstrips, etc." However, A-V usage concentrated heavily on 6th grade English and comprised audio tapes used for 12% of the lesson. "Audiovisual material" not especially produced for school use was listed separately and employed for a total of about 5.6% of lesson time, although with a heavy emphasis on "working life orientation" in which 21% of lesson time was spent on showing films and videograms, as well as some overhead transparencies and filmstrips. On the average, some form of visual material was employed in only every sixth lesson.

Sigurgeirsson (1990) has done a somewhat similar study on Iceland. Among other things he observed 667 lessons in 20 classes in 12 different schools. Sigurgeirsson noted that the use of textbooks is a very governing methodology. He found that no less than 70-90% of all teaching rely on the use of textbooks and various worksheets. Unfortunately, Sigurgeirsson did not make any notations about the use of the pictures printed in the textbooks.

Evans, Watson, & Willows (1987) found that teachers (in Canada) made very few direct references to illustrations in the classroom and that they provided little guidance on the educational functions that illustrations are thought to serve (page 93):

> Moreover, when questioned directly about their use of illustrations in teaching, most of the interviewees seemed not to have given the matter much serious thought. Beyond the decorational role served by pictures in the classrooms and the motivational/attentional role ascribed to textbook illustrations, it appears that the educational functions of illustrations are rarely articulated by teachers.

Visuals can always be interpreted in different ways (Pettersson, 1985, 1988, 1989). The intention of a visual is often to convey the simplest possible interpretation. However, different viewers often find meaningful and interesting connotations in a visual, even when these connotations are objectively absent. Aronsson (1983) discussed textbooks in Swedish for immigrants and pointed to the problem of establishing a common frame of reference (page 8):

However, books for beginners often depict objects without specifying any context, i.e., fragmentary depictions detached from any particular context.

The meaning of a visual often becomes clear when a teacher establishes some link between words and visuals in the course of a lesson. Aronsson explained the fact that visuals still work in language teaching as follows (page 12):

> One important reason appears to be the circumstance that the educational activity establishes a mechanical scanning pattern or some kind of visual dictionary in which each visual's meaning is fixed by various exercises and related to particular verbal expressions.

However, this argument assumes that the illustrations are employed in a very active way in education. This is not always the case. Comments made by teachers and students also suggest that visuals in textbooks are often disregarded. Many visuals obviously remain "unseen."

Teachers and students

Research in the area of reading indicates that the type of visuals that are used is an important variable in reading comprehension. However, this becomes less important in reality since most students do not attend to the visuals (Reinking, 1986; Pettersson, 1990). Nelson-Knupfer & Stock-McIsaac (1992) studied the effects of grey shades in instructional materials produced with desktop publishing software. Their results indicated that no group of subjects remembered very much of the graphics at all. Along with similar reading speed between the groups, the results supported earlier claims that readers do not really pay attention to visuals used in text.

Lingons (1987) studied the use of teaching aids in some schools in Stockholm. Among other things he asked teachers on these three levels to assess text and pictures in textbooks they were using in class. In total 157 teachers took part in the survey, 50 from junior, 50 from intermediate, and 57 from senior levels. With respect to all the pictures in the textbooks, many of the teachers (76%) felt that the images were good *but* that they often lacked relevant relationship with the text; 67% of the black-and-white photographs were assessed as relevant to the text. For color photographs the figure was 43%, for drawings 43%, and for maps 51%. On the average, these teachers answered that the pictures in every second textbook were not relevant to the text.

Elementary level (grades 1–3)

Lindsten (1975, 1976) studied different ways of acquiring knowledge in grade 3. Fifty primary school teachers and 224 students replied to different questionnaires. The activity "looking at visuals" was perceived in a positive light by both teachers and students.

Teachers felt that the most important properties of informative pictures are distinctness and realism. The visuals should be in color, realistic, and "sufficiently" large and distinct. When different picture sizes were rated, it was found that teachers displayed a definite preference for half-page visuals when the page size was A5 (about

15 × 21 cm), whereas students made no distinction between this picture size and a 3/4 page picture. Even if smaller sizes were acceptable to the studied groups under certain circumstances, larger pictures generally received higher ratings. All the teachers felt that size played a certain or major role in both informative pictures and pictures designed to stimulate. The picture subject was inherently important to the way students responded to the pictures. Certain pictures, such as a 12 × 7.5 cm picture containing numerous 90° angles (subject: "house"), could be reduced by a third without any significant drop in student ratings.

Most students, like most teachers, preferred photos to drawings. Drawings in color were preferable to drawings in black & white. Events were depicted better in a series of pictures than in a single picture. Students preferred watching a film or studying slides and charts to looking at visuals in textbooks.

Intermediate level (grades 4–6)

Lindström (1990) interviewed eight female, grade 4-6 teachers from different schools in central Sweden about their views on visuals in teaching aids. One starting point for the structured interviews, and follow-up questions, was a common textbook for grade 5 used by all the teachers in their classes. The subjects were able to select and refer to examples from the same material. But the views they expressed applied to grade 4-6 level textbooks in general.

The material set comprises a book in geography, science, and social studies, a book on history, and a book on religion. The first book contained 192 pages with about 50% visuals and 50% text. There was a total of 219 visuals, 135 of which were photographs (130 in color and 5 in black & white by 82 photographers) and 84 were drawings in color (by 10 artists).

As a rule, textbooks are selected by the teachers in each school. The overall impression and contents are the most important assessment criteria. Visuals and text are viewed as being of about equal importance. Teachers felt that visuals should have explanatory legends. All kinds of visuals are needed in all the subjects, but visuals should always have some link to (text) contents.

Color photographs showing what things look like, drawings as complements to photographs, authentic, historical pictures, and authentic pictures of works of art are examples of good visuals. "Fussy" overviews, abstract, obscure, ambiguous pictures, or pictures lacking the necessary facts are examples of poor visuals. Poor visuals display prejudice and attitudes in conflict with democratic principles. Pictures with merely a decorative function and "educational series" which fail to educate are other examples of poor visuals.

Teaching sometimes employs pictures as an introduction to some subject, as the basis of discussion, as inspiration for essay writing, and as factual material. Some pictures are considered completely superfluous and never used.

The number of pictures in textbooks has increased in recent years. However, this has not affected teaching. Teachers feel that textbook texts are dull and overloaded with facts. Textbooks are usually supplemented with other books, newspapers, slides, films, etc.

When Romare (1989) asked students how they viewed the use of visuals in books on religion their reply was right to the point: "They make homework shorter!" She subsequently noted (page 62):

Visuals must be carefully selected so they arouse curiosity and emotions, as well as convey knowledge. Visuals are essential to textbooks, but they must have something to offer when used/read. Knowledge and training in visual language are essential to the ability to read visuals. *The circumstance that teachers and students often skip visuals is often because of their inability to read visuals* (my italics).

Nyström (1990) gave 6th grade students a copy of a picture in one of their textbooks. The students then described the picture in very diverse ways and had greatly varying opinions about what the picture depicted. When asked whether their teacher had reviewed the picture in the classroom, 7 students replied "no," 11 "don't know," and 6 "yes."

Senior level (grades 7–9)

Backman, Berg, & Sigurdson (1988), all at the University of Umeå, studied the *"pictorial capability"* of comprehensive school students. The central issue was whether there was any difference in pictorial capability between 4–6th grade students and 7–9th grade students. Pictorial capability comprises both the *production* and the *reception* of pictures. The study comprised a total of 1,200 visual and verbal statements made by 240 comprehensive school students (grades 5, 6, 7, and 8 respectively). All the statements were evaluated by two of the authors, both teachers at the Department for the Training of Visual Arts Teachers at the University of Umeå.

The results showed that comprehensive school students possess very poor pictorial capability and that intermediate level students and senior level students did not differ significantly in pictorial capability. The students were all poor at both producing pictures and reading pictures. Only 5% of the students were able to produce a picture conveying information on the importance of red and green as traffic signal colors. Only 43% of the senior level students were able to supply a written description of the message conveyed by a series of instructive pictures. The authors concluded that visual arts teachers need to alter their approach to teaching and that the subject "visual arts" demands the same competent, cognitive processing as Swedish or mathematics.

Interview surveys

I performed two interview studies in the autumn of 1989: "Visuals in Textbooks; the Views of Students" and "Visuals in Textbooks; the Views of Teachers." Students and teachers anonymously selected choices in replying to questions on a form. A total of 128 students participated, i.e., 70 girls and 58 boys, plus 36 teachers, i.e., 13 women and 23 men. The subjects can be regarded as a random selection from several different schools. The students were all from senior level comprehensive schools. Four of the teachers taught intermediate level classes and 32 taught senior level classes. The studies failed to show any difference in perception between girls and boys or between women and men. The percentile distribution of answers in the two questionnaire studies is indicated below (figures rounded off). The studies comprised a total of 1526 answers from students and 412 answers from teachers.

Picture type

Students replied that their preferred picture type was "realistic drawings in color" (59%), "color photos" (26%), "line drawings" (8%), "black & white photos" (6%), and "maps" (1%). The teachers replied that they preferred "color photos" (44%), "realistic drawings in color" (36%), "black & white photos" (11%), and "maps" (6%). None of the teachers preferred "line drawings." As far as the teachers are concerned, the difference between color photos and realistic drawings may have been a coincidence. But the difference for students was considerable. In both groups, color was preferred far more often than black & white.

Most students (74%) replied that they read the legends for pictures in textbooks. The distribution of answers was as follows: "never" 0%, "occasionally" 27%, "usually" 58%, and "always" 16%. Most teachers (75%) reported that they usually instructed students to read the picture legends in textbooks. The teachers' replies were distributed as follows: "never" 6%, "occasionally" 44%, "usually" 19%, and "always" 31%.

Many of the teachers (75%) replied that they usually talked or asked questions about visuals in books. The distribution was: "never" 6%, "occasionally" 19%, "usually" 47%, and "always" 28%. However, students saw things differently. Only 29% replied that teachers usually talked or asked questions about pictures in books ("always" 5% and "usually" 24%). Most students replied "occasionally" (64%). Some students replied "never" (8%).

Homework

Teachers who assigned homework, i.e., all except one, usually asked questions about the contents of pictures: "never" 7%, "occasionally" 27%, "usually" 57%, and "always" 7%. When students had homework, only a few (6%) felt that they "always" learned something from the visuals. However, rather many students (37%) selected the "usually" alternative. Half of the students (53%) replied "occasionally." Some students replied "never" (4%). Many students and teachers felt that the textbooks they used struck a good balance between text and pictures. The textbooks had "about the right amount of drawings" (66% and 58%, respectively), "about the right amount of photographs" (69% and 84%, respectively), and even "about the right amount of text" (67% and 54%, respectively). About one-third of the students felt that there were "too few drawings" (31%), "too few photographs" (31%), and "too much text" (32%). Some students felt that there were "too many drawings" (2%), "too many photographs" (0%), and "too little text" (1%). Some teachers would have liked to see more text and drawings. One-third of the teachers (33%) felt that there was "too little text." Almost as many (28%) felt that there were "too few drawings." Some teachers (8%) felt that there were "too few photographs." Some teachers felt that there were "too many drawings" (14%), "too many photographs" (8%), and "too much text" (13%).

Students were not particularly happy with the layout of textbooks, i.e., the interplay between text, pictures, margins, and graphic design. About half of the students (46%) replied that the layout "made it easier to understand the contents." Half of the students (50%) replied that the layout "neither made it harder nor easier to understand the contents." A few students (4%) chose the third alternative, i.e., that the layout "made it harder to understand the contents." On the other hand, teachers were rather satisfied with the layout of textbooks. As many as 82% felt that the layout "made it easier to understand the contents." Some (12%) replied that the layout "neither made it harder nor easier to understand the contents." A few (6%) felt that the layout "made it harder to understand the contents."

Visuals and subjects
In the final assignment, students and teachers were asked to complete the following two statements: "I feel that visuals really are needed in [the subject(s)] ...." and "I feel that [the subject(s)] .... can get along fine without visuals." Many teachers replied "all subjects" and "no subjects," respectively. When teachers indicated particular subjects, most of their answers were similar to the answers submitted by the students. Some students (4%) failed to submit any answers to these questions, some students (11%) submitted multiple answers but most (85%) indicated one subject for each question. All the replies were counted. The replies showed that "... visuals really are needed" in the following: social science subjects (49%), visual arts (21%), science subjects (19%), languages (7%), and mathematics (4%). The following subjects "... get along fine without visuals": sports (31%), mathematics (29%), music (16%), languages (16%), handicrafts (5%), science subjects (3%), and visual arts (1%).

Visual arts in school
Since visuals are being employed to an increasing degree in an increasing number of contexts, the National Board of Education in Sweden proclaimed (Skolöverstyrelsen, 1980) that all teachers are responsible for providing instruction and training in the use of visuals and communications devices (page 30 and 72):

> "The ability to express oneself with the aid of a visual is a skill of benefit to many subjects.

> "Visuals have become important parts of the contents of many school subjects. So picture analysis should be a natural feature in all teaching."

However, most teachers appear to have insufficient training in the use of visuals in their classes. Teacher training programs do not touch on textbooks and other teaching aids to any great extent. Backman & Eklund (1989) found that Swedish teacher training in the subject visual arts for comprehensive school and high schools is spread out over the entire college program in the form of about 15 "picture and design units" in the old class teacher programs and in two visual arts departments. Backman & Eklund (1989) noted the following (page 26):

> From the autumn of 1988, the weight of courses on "visuals" or "visual arts" in teacher training varied considerably, i.e., 5, 15, 20, 60, and 80 points. It is obviously important for these courses, even if implemented in the correct manner, to reflect the same philosophy. "Visuals" is a narrow subject with no corresponding scientific discipline.

Some county boards of education examined comprehensive school education in the subject visual arts. Arvidsson & Engman (1989), both at the National Board of Education, wrote (page 2) that "The review showed that school leaders and teachers of subjects other than the subject visual arts were unaware of the goals of "visual arts" and the subject's evolution into an important communications discipline in our modern society." Somewhat later, Arvidsson & Engman observed (page 4):

> Research on the importance of visuals to our ability to observe, visually conceive and express ourselves touches on factors of major importance to thinking and human behavior. We should keep in mind that the visual is ascribed a role in stimulating both aesthetic and general creativity. Against this background, the importance of visual language to general teacher proficiency has been underestimated, as is also the case for the position of visual arts teaching in school.

Main points

Most of the views expressed by teachers and students in different contexts can be summarized in the following main points:

- Comprehensive school students have a very poor pictorial capability. They are poor at reading and understanding pictures. They are also poor at expressing themselves with pictures.
- Both students and teachers need to learn how to use visuals.
- We have to learn how to read pictures.
- Visuals in textbooks are used rather sporadically. Many visuals are "unseen."
- Visuals in textbooks are seldom used in an "active" manner.
- Visuals can always be interpreted in multiple ways. So legends are needed to explain what is important and to indicate how pictures should be interpreted.
- Visuals in teaching aids must evoke some response in the reader. For this to be possible, the reader must be able to discover the visuals, become interested in them, and read them in an active and selective way.

In view of the educational potential, limited use and high costs of informative pictures, there is every reason to continue studies, with the emphasis on:

- What steps can be taken so teachers and students really make proper use of the visuals in textbooks?
- How can teacher training be improved in respect to the use of visuals in teaching?

REFERENCES AND SUGGESTED READINGS

Åberg, Å. (1983). *Folket läste*. I H. Järv (Red.). *Den svenska boken 500 år*, 365–401. Stockholm: Liber.

Aronsson, K. (1983). *Verklighetens mångtydighet och pekbokens begränsningar. Om bild och begrepp i språkläromedel*. I L. Gustavsson och H. Hult. (Red.). *Text och bild i läromedel*, SIC 4, 7–24. Linköping: Universitetet i Linköping. Tema Kommunikation.

Arvidsson, H., & Engman, R. (1989). *Skolledarperspektiv på bildspråket i skolan*. Stockholm: Skolöverstyrelsen, Sk 89:8 / Specialinformation till skolledare.

Azoulay, B., & Janson, H. (1985). *Estetiska upplevelser av färger på bildskärm*. (Undergraduate thesis) Stockholm: University of Stockholm, Department of Computer Science.

Backman, J., Berg, T., & Sigurdson, T. (1988). *Grundskoleelevers produktion och reception av bilder*. Umeå: Umeå universitet. Institutionen för bildlärarutbildning. Rapport nr 7.

Backman, J., & Eklund, S. (1989). *Efter konferensen. Diskussioner och förslag.* J. Backman & S. Eklund (Red.). *Bilder, bildmedier, tänkande och kreativitet. Rapport från ett kulturpedagogiskt seminarium.* Umeå: Umeå universitet. Institutionen för bildlärarutbildning. Rapport nr 9, 22–27.

Baylor, J. G. (1989). Computer generated instructional graphics. In R. A. Braden, D. G. Beauchamp, L. V. W. Miller, & D. M. Moore (Eds.). *About Visuals: Research, Teaching, and Applications.* Readings from the 20th Annual Conference of the International Visual Literacy Association. Blacksburg: Virginia Tech University.

Bertin, J. (1967). *Semiologic graphique: Les Diagrammes, Les reseaux, Les cartes.* Paris: Moutin .

Burg, K. F., Boyle, J. M., Evey, J. R., & Neal, A. S. (1982). Windowing versus scrolling on a visual display terminal. *Human Factors, 24,* 385–394.

Cossette, C. (1982). *How Pictures Speak: A Brief Introduction to Iconics.* Paper presented at the 32nd International Communication Association Conference, Boston, May 1–5. Translated from French by Vincent Ross, Quebec.

Dillon, A., & McKnight, C. (1990). Towards a classification of text types: A repertory grid approach. *International Journal of Man-Machine Studies, 33,* 623–636.

Ehlers, J. H. (1984). *Problems in Legibility in Presentation Graphics.* CAMP/84, Computer Graphics Applications for Management and Productivity, Berlin Sept. 25–28. Proceedings: AMK Berlin.

Ek, G., & Frederiksen, M. (1986). *Utformning av histogram.* (Undergraduate thesis). Stockholm: University of Stockholm, Department of Computer Science.

Evans, M. A., Watson, C., & Willows, D. M. (1987). A naturalistic inquiry into illustrations in instructional textbooks. In H. A. Houghton & D. M. Willows (Eds.). *The Psychology of Illustrations: Vol. 2. Instructional Issues.* New York: Springer-Verlag.

Fahlander, P., & Zwierzak, A. (1985). *Gränstydlighet mellan färger.* (Undergraduate thesis). Stockholm: University of Stockholm, Department of Computer Science.

Gould, J. D., & Grischkowsky, N. (1984). Doing the same work with hard copy and the cathode-ray tube (CRT) computer terminals. *Human Factors, 26,* 323–337.

Grabinger, R. S. (1989). Screen layout design: Research into the overall appearance of the screen. *Computers in Human Behavior, 5,* 175–183.

Gustafsson, C. (1980a). *Läromedlens funktion i undervisningen.* En rapport från utredningen om läromedelsmarknaden. DsU 1980:4.

Gustafsson, C. (1980b). *Läromedlens funktion i undervisningen. Bilagedel.* En rapport från utredningen om läromedelsmarknaden. DsU 1980:5.

Hartley, J. (1987). Designing electronic text: The role of print-based research. *Educational Communications and Technology Journal, 35,* 3–17.

Hayashi, K. (1983). Research and development on high definition television. *SMPTE Journal, 3,* 178–186.

von Helmholz, H. (1924). *Physiological Optics. Vol. II.* (J. Southall Rochester, Trans.) New York: Optical Society of America.

Hering, A. (1925). *Grundzuge der Lehre vom Lichtsinn. Handbuch der gesamten Augenheilkunde.* (2nd edition, 3rd volume). Berlin.

Hård, A., & Sivik, L. (1981). NCS–Natural Color System: A Swedish standard for color-notation. *Color Research and Application, 6, 3,* 129–138.

ISSCO (1981). *Choosing the Right Chart. A Comprehensive Guide for Computer Graphics Users.* San Diego: ISSCO.

Key, W. B. (1977). *Subliminal Seduction.* New York: Signet.

Knave, B. (1983). The visual display unit. In *Ergonomic Principles in Office Automation.* Uddevalla: Ericsson Information Systems AB.

Kolers, P. A., Duchnicky, R. L., & Ferguson, D. C. (1981). Eye movement measurement of readability of CRT displays. *Human Factors, 23,* 517–524.

Laswell, H. (1948). The structure and function of communication in society. In L. Bryson (Ed.). *The Communication of Ideas*. New York: Harper & Brothers.

Lax, L., & Olson, M. (1983). NAPLPS Standard graphics and the microcomputer. *Byte 8, 7*, 82–92.

Lindsten, C. (1975). *Hembygdskunskap i årskurs 3, Att inhämta, bearbeta och redovisa kunskaper*. Lund: Liber Läromedel.

Lindsten, C. (1976). *Aktiviteter i hembygskunskap: Elevpreferenser i årskurs 3. En faktoranalytisk studie* /Activities in Science and Social Studies: Pupils' preferences in grade 3. A factorial study. Pedagogisk–psykologiska problem. Malmö: Lärarhögskolan, 310.

Lindström, A. (1990). Bilder i läromedel, lärarsynpunkter. Stockholm: Stockholms Universitet. Konstfack, Institutionen för bildpedagogik.

Lingons, B. (1987). *Rapporter från Stockholms Skolor. Läromedelssituationen i några Stockholmsskolor 1986/87*. Stockholms skolförvaltning 1987:4.

Marsh, P. O. (1983). *Messages That Work: A Guide to Communication Design*. Englewood Cliffs, NJ: Educational Technology Publications.

McCleary, G. F. (1983). An effective graphic "vocabulary." *IEEE Computer Graphics and Applications, 3, 2*, 46–53.

McLellan, H. (1992). *Virtual Reality: A Selected Bibliography*. Englewood Cliffs, NJ: Educational Technology Publications.

McLuhan, M. (1967). *Media. Människans utbyggnader*. Stockholm: Pan/Norstedts.

Mulcahy, P., & Samuels, J. S. (1987). Three hundred years of illustrations in American textbooks. In H. A. Houghton & D. M. Willows (Eds.). *The Psychology of Illustrations: Vol. 2. Instructional Issues*. New York: Springer-Verlag.

Murch, G. M. (1983). Perceptual considerations of color. *Computer Graphics World, 6, 7*, 32–40.

Nelson-Knupfer, N. & Stock-McIsaac, M. (1992). The effects of grey shades in instructional materials produced with desktop publishing software. In J. Clark-Baca, D. G. Beauchamp, & R. A. Braden (Eds.). *Visual Communication: Bridging Across Cultures*. Selected Readings from the 23rd Annual Conference of the International Visual Literacy Association. Blacksburg: Virginia Tech University.

Nyström, T. (1990). Bilder i läromedel. En jämförande studie av bildmaterialet i några läroböcker i historia från 1889–1984. Stockholm: Stockholms Universitet. Konstfack, Institutionen för bildpedagogik.

Parker, E. B. (1975). *Social Implications of Computer/Telecommunications Systems*. Program in Information Technology and Telecommunications. Report No. 16. Stanford University: Center for Interdisciplinary Research.

Pettersson, R. (1981). *Bilder Barn och Massmedia*. Stockholm: Akademilitteratur.

Pettersson, R. (1983). *Visuals for Instruction* (CLEA–Report No. 12). Stockholm: University of Stockholm, Department of Computer Science.

Pettersson, R. (1984a). *Visual Displays and Reading Effort* (CLEA–Report No. 20). Stockholm: University of Stockholm, Department of Computer Science.

Pettersson, R. (1984b). Numeric data, presentation in different formats. Presentation at the 16th Annual Conference of the International Visual Literacy Association, Baltimore, Nov. 8–11. In N. H. Thayer & S. Clayton-Randolph (1985). *Visual Literacy: Cruising into the Future*. Bloomington: Western Sun Printing Co.

Pettersson, R. (1985). Intended and perceived image content. Presentation at the 17th Annual Conference of the International Visual Literacy Association. Claremont. Nov. 1–2. In L. W. Miller (Ed.). (1986). *Creating Meaning*. Readings from the Visual Literacy Conference at California State Polytechnic University at Pomona.

Pettersson, R. (1988). Interpretation of image content. *ECTJ, 36*, 1, 45–55.

Pettersson, R. (1989). *Visuals for Information: Research and Practice*. Englewood Cliffs, NJ: Educational Technology Publications.

Pettersson, R. (1990). Teachers, students, and visuals. *Journal of Visual Literacy, 10*, 1, 45–62.

Pettersson, R., & Carlsson, J. (1985). *Numeric Data on Visual Displays* (CLEA–Report No. 30). Stockholm: University of Stockholm, Department of Computer Science.

Pettersson, R., Carlsson, J., Isacsson, A., Kollerbaur, A., & Randerz, K. (1984a). *Color Information Displays and Reading Efforts* (CLEA–Report No. 18). Stockholm: University of Stockholm, Department of Computer Science.

Pettersson, R., Carlsson, J., Isacsson, A., Kollerbaur, A., & Randerz, K. (1984b). *Attitudes to Variables on Visual Display* (CLEA–Report No. 24). Stockholm: University of Stockholm, Department of Computer Science.

Pettersson, R., Carlsson, J., Isacsson, A., Kollerbaur, A., & Randerz, K. (1984c). *Reading Efforts on Prints-outs* (CLEA–Report No. 21). Stockholm: University of Stockholm, Department of Computer Science.

Pettersson, R., & Kindborg, M. (1991). *Classification of Navigational Principles in Multimedia Systems.* Paper presented at the Multimedia Information, The Second International Information Research Conference 1991. July 15–18. Churchill College, Cambridge, U.K. Published in M. Feeney & S. Day (Eds.). *Multimedia Information.* London: British Library Research/Bowker Saur.

Rambally, G. K., & Rambally, R. S. (1987). Human factors in CAI design. *Computing Education, 11(2),* 149–153.

Reinking, D. (1986). Integrating graphic aids into content area instruction: The graphic information lesson. *Journal of Reading, 30(2),* 146–151.

Romare, E. (1989). Bildens betydelse i läroboken. En text–och bildanalys av religionsböcker från 1940–tal och 1980–tal. *Spov, 7,* 45–64.

Samit, M. L. (1983). The color interface, making the most of color. *Computer Graphics World, 7,* 42–50.

Schramm, W. (1954). Procedures and effects of mass communication. In B. H. Nelson (Ed.). *Mass Media and Education. The Fifty-Third Year-book of the National Society for the Study of Education. Part II.* Chicago: University of Chicago Press.

Shannon, C. E., & Weaver, W. (1949). *The Mathematical Theory of Communication.* Champaign, IL: The University of Illinois Press.

Sigurgeirsson, I. (1990). *The Use of Reference Materials, Other Books, Audio–Visuals and Educational Equipment.* Presentation vid konferensen Nordträff, 2–5 August 1990.

Skolöverstyrelsen (1979). *Bilder i gymnasieskoleundervisningen.* Stockholm: Rapport 1979–05–28.

Skolöverstyrelsen (1980). *Lgr 80. Läroplan för grundskolan. Allmän del. Mål och riktlinjer. Kursplaner. Timplaner.* Stockholm: Liber Utbildningsförlaget.

Wright, P., & Lickorish, A. (1983). Proofreading texts on screen and paper. *Behavior and Information Technology, 2(3),* 227–235.

Chapter 2

PERCEPTION

This chapter will examine some of the functions related to perception, learning, and memory of pictorial information. Several experiments and studies concerning interpretation of image contents are presented.

OUR SENSES

How do we receive information about the outside world? We can smell, taste, feel, listen, see, and examine our surroundings. We can also ask questions. Smell, taste and feeling are not as yet especially important factors to be considered in information production. So only aural and visual impressions will be the subjects of a discussion here.

Hearing

Sound is a subjective sensation of hearing, i.e., the sensory cells in the inner ear's hearing apparatus are stimulated. In objective terms, sound consists of longitudinal wave motions capable of acting on our hearing apparatus and thereby eliciting sound sensations.

Man is normally capable of perceiving sound waves at frequencies from 16 to 20,000 Hz. Sound waves lower than 16 Hz are referred to as infrasound, and frequencies higher than 20,000 Hz are referred to as ultrasound.

Sound intensity, i.e., the average rate of sound energy transmitted per unit of time and unit area which passes a plane perpendicular to the transmission direction, is an objective measure of sound intensity. It is usually measured in w/m^2 (watts per square meter). However, a psychologically based concept is necessary in order to designate the strength of sound waves striking our ears. The hearing range is the interval between the lowest sound intensity we are capable of perceiving, i.e., the auditory threshold, and the highest level we are able to tolerate, i.e., the pain threshold.

Vision

In subjective terms vision is a complex process which elicits a sense of vision, i.e., awareness of the stimulation of the eye's vision perception cells. In objective terms, light consists of electromagnetic waves (light "rays") capable of acting on our eyes and creating sensations of light and images.

Human vision is sensitive within a wide wavelength range. Visible light ranges from wavelengths of 400 nm (0.0004 millimeter), that is violet, to 770 nm, that is dark red. In between these extremes are blue, green, yellow, and orange. Green-orange (about 555 nm) lies in the region of the eye's greatest sensitivity. Sensitivity decreases markedly toward the red and violet ends of the spectrum.

Like sound waves, light waves are propagated in straight lines from their source. They can also be reflected, refracted, bent, and absorbed. The velocity of light in air is nearly 300,000 km/s. When light rays (usually parallel) from an object enter the eye, they are refracted in the cornea and lens and pass through the vitreous humor until they strike the retina. When the ambient light level is high, the light rays strike the macula lutea, the fovea, a small area of the retina which is rich in cones. Cones are the receptors which record colors.

The classical view is that each sensory organ picks up individual sensory impressions which are interpreted more or less individually. The retina's receptors are excited by light and respond by chemically converting a pigment, rhodopsin (visual purple). This conversion triggers impulses which are transmitted along the optic nerve to the brain's visual cortex. This takes only a few milliseconds. In the visual cortex the impulses are translated into a sensation of vision.

When light rays from an object are bent in the cornea and lens, an upside-down image of that object is formed on the retina. Very small children view the world as being upside-down. After a time, however, the brain somehow learns to process retinal images so that they are perceived to be right-side-up. Since we have two eyes, both pointing forward and with partially overlapping visual fields, we can assess the distance, both forward and laterally, between objects. It takes a certain amount of time for the eye to record light rays from an object, such as a painting. And it also takes time before we are capable of perceiving that object as an image. The eye has inertia. This inertia enables us to perceive motion. When we look at a person who is walking or running, the eye records a series of stills which ultimately blend into one another and form a moving image. This inertia also enables us to see motion in the stills which comprise a movie film or a TV image.

Nowadays, however, sensory organs are often described as sensory systems and the total energy flux striking them viewed as information about the surrounding world and about ourselves. The individual sensory organs receiving this information are not merely passive receptors but jointly constitute an active, exploratory system in which all the senses intimately interact, supplying us with an undergirded view of the world. So we are spared the task of having to consciously translate a myriad of individual sensory impressions into coherent perception.

According to Gibson (1966) the eye does not really operate like a camera. We are never conscious of the "stills" formed on the retina. We only perceive the external world they represent. The eye and head shift their attention constantly from one point to another in our surroundings or in a picture. Thus, our vision is an active, exploratory process. We usually concentrate our attention to interesting events within a narrow segment of our total field of vision.

Eye movements

Bergström (1974) noted that visual information on our surroundings is conveyed to the eye, a very imperfect optical system. Eyes never remain still. They tremble at a frequency of about 30-90 Hz. This serves to shift information of individual cells. The eye alters its fixation point constantly. It also makes constant small jumps.

We constantly "scan" the things we look at. By using complex instrumentation that allows the researcher to record exactly where in a picture a person is looking at any given moment, it is possible to study the way in which the gaze wanders over a picture, pauses and fixes on certain points (Buswell, 1925; Webb *et al.*, 1963; Zusne & Michels, 1964; Guba *et al.*, 1964; Berlyn, 1966; Leckhart, 1966; Gould, 1967, 1973; Yarbus, 1967; Mackworth & Morandi, 1967; Faw & Nunnaly, 1967, 1968; Fleming, 1969; Wolf, 1970; Noton & Stark, 1971a, b; Loftus, 1972, 1976, 1979; Antes, 1974; Hochberg & Brooks, 1978; Baron, 1980; Biederman, 1981; Nesbit, 1981; Pettersson, 1983a). The gaze never fixes on most parts of a picture. Only certain image elements capture our attention.

Yarbus (1967) found that fixation usually lasts for two to eight tenths of a second and that eye movements between eye fixations took from one to eight-hundredths of a second. So we normally view a picture by means of a large number of eye movements and eye fixations in rapid succession. The location of each fixation influences how a picture is interpreted and later remembered (Nelson & Loftus, 1980).

Yarbus (1967) found that instructions given prior to viewing determined what segments of the picture received the most attention. The pattern of eye movements and fixations is entirely different when our objective is to search for something in a picture. The things we wish to see in a picture have a major impact on the location of eye fixations. Where we look and why we look there determines what we see. *Global to local scanning* means that we notice the overall structure or figure first and then the details or informative areas (Printzmetal & Banks, 1977; Navon, 1977; Antes & Penland, 1981; Biederman, 1981). We quickly find out which details of a picture are the most informative ones and then we concentrate our attention to those parts. To get maximum impact from a visual, the writer or the presenter should introduce it before presenting it.

A number of scientists have found that pictures which are hard to interpret require more eye fixations than "easy" pictures (Webb *et al.*, 1963; Zusne & Michaels, 1964; Berlyn, 1966; Leckhart, 1966; Faw & Nunnaly, 1967, 1968; Mackworth & Morandi, 1967; Hochberg & Brooks, 1978).

Wolf (1970) determined that "difficult" pictures require more fixations up to a certain point. When a picture was extremely difficult, subjects tended to avoid looking at it or searched for a visual center. However, neither Baron (1980) nor Nesbit (1981) found any correlation between picture type and the number of fixations. But the two latter scientists did employ a different method in their studies than the authors mentioned previously.

Faw & Nunnaly (1967, 1968) also found that new pictures required more fixations than pictures with which subjects were already familiar. Movement or change in a picture or event also attracts attention and therefore causes many fixations.

Guba *et al.* (1964), Gould (1973), and Nesbit (1981) found a positive correlation between eye movements and intelligence. Highly intelligent subjects utilized more fixations than less intelligent subjects. Wolf (1970) discovered that highly intelligent

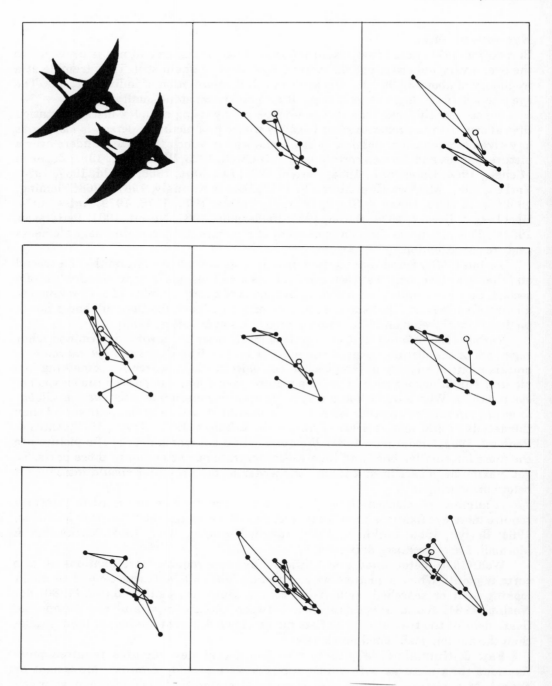

During experiments adult subjects looked at a drawing of two flying House Martins as indicated in the above analyses of eye fixations and eye movements. In each case the first eye fixation is marked with an unfilled circle. Each fixation takes about 1/5 of a second. In this case subjects got the instruction: "Tell me what you see!" It takes only a few seconds for adult subjects to recognize "two birds."

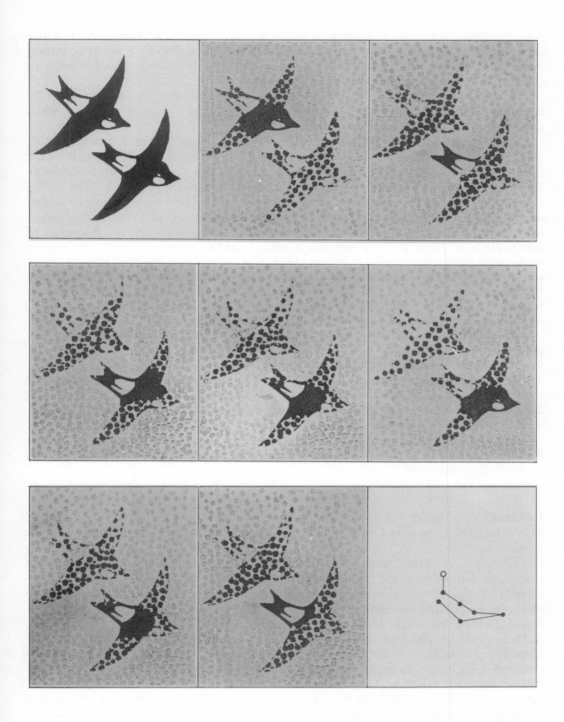

A model of the "stills" formed on the retina during different eye fixations. Eye fixations are rapid, usually four to six per second. We are never aware of the stills on the retina.

subjects displayed great flexibility in their "scanning patterns," irrespective of the stimuli, whereas subjects with low intelligence tended to display a static scanning pattern which was the same for different stimuli. Nesbit (1981) found a positive correlation between learning and the number of fixations.

Wolf (1970) suggested that eye movements can be employed as an index of visual learning. Eye movements supply information on where, how long, and how often subjects look at different parts of a picture.

Looking at pictures is a "natural" way of free exploring. However, *reading* a text needs to be very structured with several eye fixations on each line. The time for each fixation varies among individuals and different texts (Ekwall, 1977), with the average time for good readers between 1/4 to 1/6 of a second. It also takes from 1/25 to 1/30 of a second for the eye to move from one fixation to the next and sweep from the end of one line to the beginning of the next. In normal reading the text within foveal vision comprises an area of seven to ten letter spaces. At normal reading the angle of convergence is about 2^0. This means a reading speed of five to ten words per second or 300-600 words per minute. Lawson (1968) has established the physiological limit of reading as being a maximum of 720 words per minute. Ekwall (1977) calculated the maximum reading speed of the most efficient reader as being 864 words per minute under ideal conditions. Speed and eye movements during reading are dependent on the reader's perceived informativeness of the text.

The importance of eye movements can be summarized in the following five points:
1. Only certain image elements attract our interest.
2. The pattern for eye movements and fixations depends on what we wish to see or are told to see in a picture.
3. Informative parts of a picture attract more fixations than less informative parts.
4. Different kinds of pictures give rise to different kinds of fixations and intelligence and visual learning.
5. There is a positive correlation between the number of fixations and intelligence and visual learning.

Color-shape-color

The relationship between color and shape as stimuli has been studied by many researchers.

Otto & Askov (1968) found that the importance of these stimuli is related to the respective subject's level of development. For small children (three to six years), color stimuli have greater impact than shape stimuli. However, the reverse is true of older children; i.e., shape becomes more important than color. Modreski & Gross (1972) found that four-year-olds were better at pairing objects by shape than by color. Ward & Naus (1973) studied pre-school children and found that they were also better at identifying objects by their shape than by their color. MacBeth (1974) found that children from three to eight emphatically tended to sort colored paper by shape rather than by color, so shape is often more important to children than color. According to Keates (1982) the term shape is reserved for the spatial arrangement of geographical features. The apparently equivalent term "form" can only be applied directly to point or line symbols on maps. Form is an element in identification, whereas shape leads to recognition.

Itten (1971) maintained that shapes, like colors, have their own sensual, expressive value. The expressive qualities of shape and form must provide mutual support. All shapes characterized by horizontal and vertical lines belong to the square shape category; i.e., even the cross, rectangle, and similar shapes. The square is equivalent to the color red. The weight and opaqueness of red is related to the static, heavy shape of the square.

The triangle's pointed vertices suggest belligerence and aggression. All diagonal shapes in nature, such as the rhombus, parallel trapezoid, zigzag lines, and similar shapes, are counted as triangles. The triangle is the symbol of thought. Its chromatic equivalent is yellow.

Shapes circular in nature, such as the ellipse, oval, waves, parabola, and similar shapes, belong to the same category as circles. The chromatic equivalent of the unceasingly restless circle is blue.

In his comprehensive "symbols dictionary," *Symbol Sourcebook*, Dreyfuss (1972) described a large number of meanings for different, basic geometric shapes. These meanings varied considerably from one field to another. As far as the correlation between color and shape is concerned, Dreyfuss pointed out that the following tradition prevails: yellow-triangle, orange-rectangle, red-square, purple-ellipse, blue-circle, green-regular hexagon, brown-rhombus, black-parallel trapezoid, white-semicircle, grey-hourglass, silver-bi-concave, and gold-bi-convex.

Accordingly, one might well ask if there is any correlation between traditional perceptions and "natural" or spontaneous views of matches between shape and color. In order to shed some light on this matter, we performed two empirical studies, one devoted to the color-shape relationship and the other devoted to the shape-color relationship.

For discriminating of colors on maps, Keates (1982) found that three factors are important. In the first place, for hues which have a high lightness value (such as yellow) only a few differences in saturation are apparent. Conversely, for a dark blue or red, a larger number of perceptible differences can be made between maximum saturation and a neutral grey of the same value. Second, the perceptible differences in value (lightness) and chroma (saturation) are not symmetrical for different hues. In the third place, the ability to discriminate between different saturations of the same hue is strongly affected by the area of the image and by spatial separation.

Fine discriminations in saturation and lightness are only possible if there are no other color distractions. If other color elements, such as lines crossing the areas, are introduced, then the ability to distinguish slight differences in saturation or lightness is decreased.

Color-shape

A total of 118 upper-level comprehensive school students and 12 adults took part in a color-shape experiment. They were given an A4-sized sheet of paper on which the names of six colors, yellow, red, blue, green, white, and black, were printed in a random sequence. The subjects were asked to "draw the shape you feel best matches the respective name of a color." They had 15 minutes to complete this assignment. Subjects also supplied information on their age and sex. They produced a total of 780 visual statements on the correlation between color and shape.

The results clearly showed *that there was no natural, spontaneous, and un-ambiguous correlation between color and shape.* The color names used all gave rise to many different geometric shapes. In no instance did an anticipated, traditional shape predominate over other shapes. In three instances, the anticipated shape was not drawn at all. In the other three instances, the anticipated shape was only drawn in 2–3% of the visual statements.

The study disclosed a considerable spread in the way subjects develop associations with different natural phenomena, different objects, and different geometric figures. One or more subjects predominated for each color. Subjects related yellow primarily to the sun and other heavenly bodies, red to love and blood, blue to water and clouds, green to various kinds of plants, and white to clouds or snow and even, like black, to various geometric figures. Geometric figures delineated by straight lines were more common for white and black than was the case for "soft" figures. Rectangles, squares, and triangles were particularly common.

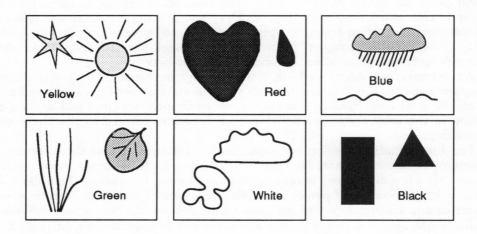

Examples of the most typical figures that the subjects made associations to when they were given a color name as stimulus.

The study also showed that there is no real difference between boys and girls, regarding associations between color and shape. Intra-group variations were greater than inter-group variations. One interesting finding was that students *perceived shape as a colored area*, only infrequently delineated by a line. Thus, yellow is a yellow area, red a red area, blue a blue area, green a green area, and black a black area. White is a white area delineated by a thin line (on white paper). Several students probably did not regard white as a color. Color was divorced from shape for subjects in the adult group. In this group, all colors, were delineated by a thin line (pencil, ball point, India ink).

Shape-color
A total of 157 upper-level comprehensive school students (not the same as those who participated in the color-shape experiment) were each given an A4-sized sheet of

paper on which six shapes, i.e., a square, star, "jigsaw puzzle piece," circle, triangle, and rectangle, were printed. Their task was: "Color the shapes on this page. Select the colors you feel are best suited to the respective shape." They had 15 minutes to complete this assignment. Subjects also supplied information on their age and sex. They produced a total of 942 visual statements on the correlation between shape and color.

The results clearly showed *that there was no natural, spontaneous, and un-ambiguous correlation between shape and color.* We sorted the visual statements on each page into the following color categories: yellow, orange, red, purple, blue, greenish blue, green, yellowish green, brown, black, white, grey, and "multiple simultaneous colors." No form had less than 11 of the 13 color categories. The most common colors were as follows:

Triangle: purple (14%), orange, blue, and green (each 13%).
Star: yellow (34%), orange (22%), and red: (12%);
Square: blue (32%), red (15%), and purple (14%);
Rectangle: green (16%), purple, blue, and brown (each 13%);
Circle: red (22%), purple and blue (both 15%);
"Jigsaw puzzle piece": red (22%), purple (20%), and green (16%).

In total, the most popular colors were blue (16%), red (15%), and purple (14%), followed by green (12%), yellow (11%), and orange (10%). The colors used least were brown (6%), black, and greenish blue (4% each), "multiple simultaneous colors" and grey (both 3%), yellowish green (2%), and white (0%). This color scale is in rather close agreement with previous studies of color preferences. Eysenck (1941) tabulated the results of experiments on color preferences. The results of evaluations made by more than 21,000 subjects produced the following ranking: (1) blue, (2) red, (3) green, (4) purple, (5) orange, and (6) yellow.

Movement and change

Movement or change in a picture or an event attracts our attention and therefore causes many fixations. Hubel & Wiesel (1962) found that many sensory cells in vision responded only very weakly to uniform light but very vigorously to changes in light intensity. This principle also applies to other sensory cells, i.e., the cells respond primarily to change. Sensory cells are also quickly exhausted. Acuity falls rapidly outside of the fovea. However, some information can be processed from peripheral vision. The gist of a picture can be understood after only a few fixations.

Gibson (1966), Moray (1970), and many of their successors (e.g., Edwards & Coolkasian, 1974) feel that movements detected in peripheral parts of our visual field automatically cause the eyeball to shift position to permit fixation of these movements.

It is possible for us to see the difference between several million color stimuli at simultaneous viewing. However, if not being seen simultaneously, the number we can identify is much smaller, maybe 10,000–20,000. It has been assumed that our perception of colors is a two-sided phenomenon. The discrimination capability represents our possibility to differentiate a figure from its background. It is strongly influenced by and dependent on contextual variables such as lighting conditions and other surrounding colors. The color identification capacity on the other hand makes us capable of interpreting "the quality" of the object we perceive. "Color constancy" is a tendency to judge objects as the same despite changes in illumination.

LISTENING AND LOOKING

Sensory organs jointly constitute a perceptual system which, in a natural environment, collects an enormous amount of superfluous information about this environment. In a natural environment, the sensory system normally supplies us with exhaustive, unambiguous intelligence about events occurring there. We are often unaware of the sensory channel(s) supplying us with information. We are merely aware of the external events, events which appear to be absolutely real and unambiguous. But in unnatural artificial surroundings, the brain often "translates" sensory stimuli in an attempt to relate them to its stored information about more familiar places, events, and times.

We are capable of successfully hearing and seeing things at the same time. We are also capable of simultaneously hearing different stimuli in either ear. However, we are incapable of simultaneously perceiving different stimuli aimed at the right and left eye, respectively. However, a stimulus may easily be perceived in different ways at different times.

Perception "laws"

The concept "perception" is a collective designation for the processes in which an organism obtains information on the outside world. We unconsciously make a constant effort to create some semblance of order in the impulses. Points, lines, areas, colors, tones, noise, heat, cold, touch, pressure, sound, etc., are integrated in such a way that they can be interpreted as a meaningful whole. A number of psychologists view these attempts to establish order as an innate faculty carried out in accordance with certain "laws."

Figure/ground. The contrast provided between the positive elements (figure) and the surrounding and negative space (ground or background) allows visual images to be recognized. This is the "theory of figure/ground."

Similarity. According to the "theory of similarity" or the "similarity law," we tend to group impressions on the basis of their similarity. Objects sharing similar characteristics such as color, shape, or size belong together. One black sheep in a flock of white sheep tends be noticed. This can be used for emphasis of a message.

The "similarity law." We tend to group elements that look alike. Here it is easy to see the similarity of size (left), the similarity of texture (middle), and the similarity of tone (right).

Proximity. According to the "proximity law," we also group objects and events on the basis of their proximity to one another. Objects near each other belong together. The eye tends to be attracted to groups or clusters rather than to isolates.

The "proximity law." We see four pairs of dots instead of just eight individual dots. Perception is organized.

Continuity. According to the "continuity law" or "theory of direction," we perceive a slow and gradual change in a stimulus as a single stimulus. Lines moving in the same direction belong together. Events which have a natural relationship to one another also give the impression of being continuous.

The "continuity law." We see this pattern as two lines crossing rather than as two angles joined together at their apexes. This is also referred to as "line of direction." Perception is selective.

Straight or curved lines tend to lead the eye along, and even beyond, the line. An arrow or a finger pointed at something leads your eye to it.

Closure. According to "theory of closure" or the "natural law," various stimuli form meaningful patterns. If a figure is incomplete, our minds will fill in the missing part. For instance, letters printed with damaged or broken type are typically seen as perfect or whole. A single dot on a paper has strong visual power to attract the eye. Two or more dots connect and are capable of leading the eye. Dots create the illusion of lines and areas.

The "natural law" or closure. Man has a need to make "wholes of units," in this case to connect the dots. Two dots suggest a line. Three dots suggest a triangle. Four dots may suggest a square. Several dots may suggest a circle.

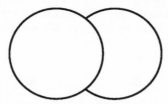

The "natural law" or closure. We see this pattern as one circle partially occluded by another. Even though there are many possibilities, this interpretation seems to be the natural one. Perception is influenced by expectations.

Common fate. According to the "common fate law," objects grouped in a particular way will be expected to change in conformance to this grouping. When change does not follow this pattern, the change is difficult to process.

Objective set. According to the "objective set law" some states are perceived more strongly than others. For example, two lines which almost form a right angle are perceived as a right angle.

Contrast. According to the "contrast law," we tend to array impressions which form natural opposites, thereby reinforcing one another, in groups. Usually there is a constancy of size, shape, color, and contrast in the perception of known objects. This is regardless of distance, angle, and illumination.

a _____
b _____
c _____

The "contrast law." A line (a) seems to be long when it is compared with a shorter line (b) but short when it is compared with a longer line (c). Perception is relative.

Previous experience. New impressions are dependent upon and interpreted against the background of our previous experience and learning, our attitudes and interests, our needs and feelings, and the prevailing situation. We direct our attention to things which are large, have bright color, move, deviate from the surroundings or from familiar patterns, things which arouse feelings and needs, and in which we happen to be interested in at the moment.

Subliminal reception

According to Dudley (1987), *subliminal* reception may be defined as the individual's ability to perceive and respond to stimuli that are below the "limen" or level of consciousness. Above it stimuli are called *supraliminal*. Dudley outlines four methods of subliminal stimulation:
1. a tachistoscope which flashes messages or pictures so rapidly that the viewer is unaware of their presence;
2. accelerated speech in low volume auditory messages;
3. embedding or hiding pictures or words in larger pictures or ornamental detail; and
4. suggestiveness, the image implying quite a bit more than a quick glance would indicate.

At an IVLA symposium in London in 1990, Ronald Sutton, at the American University, provided an extensive overview of research on subliminal reception. He concluded (p. 12), "In summary, it seems apparent that the phenomenon of subliminal reception is a scientifically demonstrated phenomenon. It is also apparent that there needs to be precise definition of what we mean when we use the term. It is equally clear that much of what is being claimed commercially as subliminal effects is not scientifically validated through carefully controlled independent testing and experimental replication. The reaction of the media to the phenomenon is often lacking in awareness of the problem and its history. Government forces, while wary of the hidden dimension involved, seem unable and unfitted to deal with the situation. In some areas the media educator and visual literacy practitioner have little role to play beyond being a concerned citizen and consumer; but in others, especially in the area of ad design and appeal on the basis of meaning through inference and implication, there is a great need for media awareness and visual literacy."

Choice of information

The average person speaks about 135 words per minute (Judson, 1972) and the fastest professional television or radio announcers speak about 150 to 160 words per minute. Our top reading speed is some 720 words per minute (Lawson, 1968). Text, spoken and written, is always linear and must be processed sequentially, word by word. It takes a long time to convey a verbal message. Non-verbal information, however, seems to be processed very fast. It only took a few seconds for adult subjects to recognize "two birds" when shown a picture of two flying House Martins.

The perception process is often assumed to consist of two stages. Information processing is tentative, fast, rough, and parallel in the first stage. It comprises all kinds of analysis, from physiological to cognitive processes. A number of different properties of a stimulus are identified simultaneously. In many instances, one such analysis is sufficient.

The second stage of the information analysis is conscious, demands attention, and is detailed and sequential. Various hypotheses about a stimulus are weighed against one another and tested. Information processing is more definite on this level.

Color blindness, or better yet "anomalies of color vision," is a condition in which certain color discriminations can not be made. It is much more commonly observed among men than among women, with estimates ranging as high as 8–10% of the male population. Only 1% of the female population has anomalous color vision. Most common is the failure to distinguish between red and green. Unfortunately, red and green are quite often used as discriminating symbols in our modern society.

In the torrent of information that bombards us, we have to select the information we want. So one of the main problems in advertising today is to reach people with the "message." In view of our limited capacity for handling simultaneous information, it is important to find out which factors determine the parts of the available information that will be processed. Which stimuli do we select and why? When we first look at a visual we only see that which is necessary to perceive and identify objects and events in a reasonable and meaningful manner. This is Gibson's "principle of economy" (Gibson, 1966).

According to Brody (1982) preference for a particular visual format does not necessarily result in increased learning. Yet, in the absence of more substantial data, information based on student preference has a meaningful role to play in affecting learning.

Getting and keeping a reader's attention may be improved by using different design variables such as color, changes in brightness, and varying the size of a particular pictorial subject. Keates (1982) notes that discriminatory responses to map symbols depend on contrast in form, dimension, and color. Attention-getting techniques are used extensively in advertising. Vogel *et al.* (1986) showed that it is undeniable that visual presentation support is persuasive. Presentations using visual aids were 43 percent more persuasive than unaided presentations.

The perception system strives to obtain clarity. If the system arrives at clarity, then clarity serves as a reinforcement, a reward. So our perception of an image depends on our previous experience, our mood, other pictures, text and sound, our personal interests, etc.

When we look at a visual, we also "see" different details in the visual on different occasions. So highly "saturated," information-packed visuals may have something new to offer even after having been viewed many times.

We have to learn to read and comprehend the content of an image. According to Salomon (1979), the process of extracting information from messages that are presented in any symbolic format involves mental activities. In order to match between the symbols and their referents in the learner's cognitive schemata, translation activities are needed. Such processes differ as a function of the symbolic systems used to convey the message. Tidhar (1987) studied children's understanding of the content in educational television programs. It was concluded that "Channel Dominancy," the degree to which either the visual or the auditory channel carries the brunt of information whereas the other channel provides compatible supportive information, was found to affect viewer's information processing in areas such as recall, comprehension, generalization, and inferential activity. Equivalence in verbal and visual information was found significantly superior to verbal or visual dominancy in its effect on spontaneous recall. Presentations characterized by visual dominancy or equivalence in verbal and visual information were found significantly more comprehensible than presentations characterized by verbal dominancy. Visual dominancy was revealed to have the highest positive effect on generalizations, followed by equivalence, whereas verbal dominancy presentations achieved the lowest generalization scores. The effect of channel dominancy on inferential activity interacted with the viewing condition: when viewers were exposed to the visual channel only, visual dominancy elicited a higher degree of inferential activity than the presentations characterized by verbal dominancy or equivalence.

We only see the things that affect us emotionally. Everything else is ignored. When we look at a picture, we first discover the cues we already recognize. We probably become more easily familiar with simple patterns than with complex patterns. Closed shapes are preferred to open shapes and fields. Once we have identified a few well-known shapes, we sometimes feel that we have "seen everything" and could well miss some valuable information.

Some structures will be perceived as reversible when it is hard to choose between figure and background. Reality and what we see at any given moment will always be separated and different. We will see different things at different occasions both with respect to reality and pictures.

The brain

Verbal languages have digital codification with combinations of letters and/or numbers representing contents (Elkind, 1975). There is no direct correspondence between groups of letters, words, and reality. Each meaning is defined and must be learned. In contrast to this, non-verbal languages have analogical codification with combinations of basic graphical elements (dots, lines, areas, and volumes) for likeness of a (concrete) reality (Pettersson, 1983b). Usually there is a correspondence with reality. Visuals are iconic. They normally resemble the thing they represent. Meaning is apparent on a basic level but must be learned for deeper understanding. Gombrich (1969) argues that no pictorial image gains the status of a "statement" unless an explicit reference is made to what it is supposed to represent. Barthes (1977) uses the term "anchorage" to describe the relationship of pictures to legends or other accompanying verbal language. Most pictures are capable of several interpretations until anchored to one by a caption.

The modern era of brain research began in the mid-1960s, when Dr. Roger Sperry and his associates published their findings regarding patients who were operated on to control life-threatening epileptic seizures (see Gazzaniga & Le Doux, 1978; Wilson, Reeves, & Gazzaniga, 1982; and Sinatra, 1986, for reviews).

According to some theories, the two halves of the brain are apparently specialized and function independently of one another. At the same time, however, either of the brain halves appears to be capable of assuming the functions of the other half. There is immense communication between the two halves. It has been estimated at six billion pulses per second.

Each half of the brain has its sensory perceptions, thoughts, feelings, and memories. Thus the left half of the brain is said to be mainly verbal, capable of speech, counting, and writing. It seems to be specialized in abstract thought, is analytical, logical, detailed, and sequential. The right half of the brain is said to be speechless but capable of concrete thought, perception of space, and an understanding of complicated relationships. It is said to be holistic, spatial, intuitive, and creative.

Most certainly there is a lot of cooperation between the two brain hemispheres. Dual processing modes of the hemispheres are beneficial to the human being.

According to Perfetti (1977) and Sinatra (1986), perception of linear representations, such as text, means a sequential, slow processing to compose and comprehend the content ("left brain activity"). Retrieval from verbal memory is a serial integration and sequential processing of auditory-motor perception systems (Sinatra, 1986).

According to Gazzaniga (1967) and Sperry (1973, 1982), perception of two- or three-dimensional representations means a parallel, simultaneous, holistic, and fast processing ("right brain activity"). Lodding (1983) concluded that the image memory and processing capabilities of the human mind are extremely powerful. Pirozzolo & Rayner (1979) suggested that *word identification* is a multi-stage process. Visual-featural analysis is carried out by the right brain hemisphere. Word naming and word meaning are processed by the left hemisphere. According to Sinatra (1986), the meaning of well-known phrase units may be accomplished without activating the auditory-motor speech system. This is said to be done by rapid interchange of information between the language center in the left hemisphere and its non-verbal representation in the right hemisphere.

Western societies have long placed a premium on the properties represented by a well-developed left half of the brain. The design of our intelligence tests is usually such that residents of urban areas consistently record higher scores on the tests than residents of rural areas; middle-class people record higher scores than blue-collar workers; and whites record higher scores than blacks. However, one study recently showed that Australian aborigines were dramatically superior to white Australians in solving test problems when these problems were designed so that the right half of the brain had to be brought into play in order to solve the problems. So intelligence is linked to culture and cannot be defined with numerical values. The right half of the brain is said to be more developed than the left half of the brain in boys. With girls it is the opposite. At school children receive a good training of the left part of the brain. After a few years boys catch up with girls with respect to the development of the left half of the brain and remain superior with respect to the right half of the brain. All children should be able to develop both parts of their brains at school. More right-brain activities like drawing, handiwork, and rhythm exercises are needed.

Our Western society is dominated by the written word and is extremely quadrangular. It is a society in which bureaucrats occupy quadrangular cells in such a way that creative and intellectually lively people are perceived as disturbing and disruptive features of the prevailing order. New ideas are effectively stifled. This leads to stagnation, industrial crises, and a breakdown of the social fabric.

It is conceivable that some of the fantastic success noted by the Japanese in the field of electronics and computer technology is due to the circumstance that the Japanese, since time immemorial, have lived in a "pictographic" society and therefore think differently than we do in Western cultures.

However, the development of new media will lead to a shift in our media consumption in the coming decades from "reading" and "listening" to "looking," i.e., in our consumption of "entertainment," "information," "education," and "news." Future generations are likely to grow up in a picture-dominated society, rather than in a text-dominated society. The unrestrained consumption of TV and video programs by children may lead to a drastic change in our cultural life and our perception of culture, human values, and ethical norms. Even today we already know that the viewing of TV entertainment containing repetitious violence has an influence on our attitudes so that violence becomes more acceptable to us. This could lead in turn to antisocial attitudes and asocial or even criminal behavior. We are faced by the prospect of major changes in our media consumption. Yet we still know relatively little about visual language. It is important for society to make resources available to facilitate our transition from text-orientation.

Picture perception

Three-dimensional images, like sculptures, can be viewed from almost an infinite number of points, not just front, back, and two sides, but 360° vertically, horizontally, and all the points in between. When we look at sculptures, we create our own individual impressions and perceptions. A single sculpture, made by one of the great masters, is like a rich encyclopedia of aesthetic experience. We can look endlessly at Michelangelo's "Rondanini Pietà," Rodin's "The Thinker," or Moore's "Reclining Figure," and find many new aspects to appreciate. It is also known from several experiments that also two-dimensional images are perceived in many different ways by various subjects (Pettersson, 1985, 1986b). Even simple line drawings evoke many associations. Vogel *et al.* (1986) showed that image-enhancement intended to improve interpretation of image content sometimes got in the way of the message. They concluded that image-enhancement graphics should be used selectively and carefully. When in doubt, they recommended, plain text should be used. Limburg (1987) pointed out that receivers have even more ambiguity or semantic diversity with visual images than with most expressions of written language with its manifold meanings. Lodding (1983) reported on the problems with misinterpretations of icons used in computer systems. However, he concluded that people find a naturalness in dealing with images either as an aid to or, in some circumstances, as the sole means of communicating.

Commissioned by the Director's Guild in honor of its 50th anniversary (1986), the film "Precious Images" was a gift to the American movie audiences. This short film consists of a 6-1/2 minute assemblage of classic moments from 469 favorite movies, past and present. Some moments linger for a few seconds but many are as short as eight frames (1/3 of a second) averaging 20 frames (less than a second). It is a strange experience to see this film. The carefully chosen images retain their meaning and emotional impact and trigger your memory.

Experiments

In several experiments subjects have been given different assignments. Thus subjects have been asked to name image contents, to describe image contents, to index image contents, to write legends, to assess image contents, to create images, to complete a story, to illustrate a story, to produce informative materials, to produce information graphics and to describe picture context. Results from these experiments, based on more than 77,000 verbal and visual statements from 2,500 subjects, confirm the theory of a dual stage perception. It is suggested that different assignments cause perception and image interpretation on different cognitive levels.

To name image contents

When Snodgrass & Vanderwart (1980) asked 219 subjects to name 260 simple line drawings with concrete image contents such as "a doll," "a finger," and "a trumpet," they found that 80 percent of the pictures were given the anticipated answers.

In one study (Pettersson, 1986b), 80 adult subjects were shown five illustrations. These concrete image subjects showed "two house martins in flight," "a young tadpole," "a squirrel with a nut between its front paws," "a gnawed spruce cone," and "a bird nesting box." In the following pages, these drawings will be referred to as "the five illustrations." Subjects were asked to describe the content of each image. All subjects answered with very concrete and directly content-related, descriptive words. A total of 400 words were used. Usually two or three different words were used for each picture. The mean value was 2.8. The frequency for the most common word was high. The mean value was 60.5.

One of the five illustrations ("two house martins in flight") had been used in a previous study of eye-movements (Pettersson, 1983a). Within one or two seconds ("immediately"), subjects recognized the concrete image content ("two birds" or "two flying birds") in the picture. This had also been true of other eye-movement experiments, for example, Potter & Levy (1969).

These results all indicate that there is an *image interpretation mode* in which the "whole" and "immediate" concrete contents of an image are perceived.

Intended and perceived meaning of icons

In 1988, a study was conducted under my leadership by CLEA at Stockholm University of the way subjects perceived the meaning of *icons*, i.e., symbols employed in computer programs (N. Scüsseleder and Å. Troedsson). The study comprised empirical experiments with two groups, each comprising 48 subjects. The task of subjects in one group was to supply oral descriptions of 38 icons in commercially available computer programs for the Macintosh computer. Subjects in the other group listened to program manual definitions read aloud to them and were then asked to point to the respective icon. In both instances, the experiments were performed in random sequence. So the statistical material encompassed 3,648 statements.

The results showed *that there was a very considerable difference between the interpretation of icons by subjects and the intended meanings*. Not a single icon was correctly interpreted by all the subjects in either of the two sets of experiments. Only 10.5% (4) of the icons were correctly interpreted by at least 75% of the subjects. Only 23.7% (9) of the icons were interpreted correctly by at least 50% of the subjects.

As expected, results were better when the task was to relate icons to their verbal definitions. Here, 47.4% (18) of the icons were correctly interpreted by at least 75% of the subjects; 63.2% (24) were correctly interpreted by at least 50% of the subjects. So the range of *association options was greatly restricted when verbal descriptions were available*.

Griffin & Gibbs (1992) asked U.S. and Jamaican subjects to identify 48 symbols. It was expected that subjects would easily recognize and identify the symbols. This was, however, not the case. A "difficulty index" of .45 indicates that U.S. subjects recognized less than half of the symbols correctly. For the Jamaican subjects, it was even lower, .25.

To describe image contents

Subjects have been asked to make descriptions of the contents of images (Pettersson, 1985, 1986b). In one case, 80 subjects (other than those mentioned above) made brief descriptions of ten pictures, all intended to convey abstract image contents. Only some (12.5%) of these 800 descriptions contained the anticipated "key words." Each picture was described with several different descriptive words. The 80 subjects utilized 1,406 words which can be regarded as "key words." For each picture the number of different key words ranged from 31 to 51 with a mean value of 37.6. The four most common key words for each picture accounted for half of all the key word designations (51%). Most of the designations were only mentioned once or a couple of times.

In subsequent experiments, 80 subjects have made detailed descriptions of "the five illustrations." These descriptions comprised 15 to 300 words. Here too, a large variety of descriptive words were used. Mean values were between 59 and 119 words.

To index image contents

Copies of "the five illustrations" were also subsequently given to 125 other subjects. Subjects were given the following task: "These five pictures are to be filed in a picture archive. Write one or more index words for each picture."

In this case, subjects answered with 40 to 51 different index words for each picture with a mean value of 43.6. A total of 1,034 words were used. The words expressed in the first study were always the most common in this test. On the average they account for some 48 percent of all the words used as index words for each picture. The three most common index designations for each picture accounted for half of all the index designations (52.5%). Most of the designations were only mentioned once (51.8%) or twice (17.4%). Concrete, descriptive designations dominated. Thus this study confirms the findings from the previous study with brief descriptions.

The suggested index words can be organized into various hierarchic structures with abstract and concrete words, as well as synonyms and near synonyms. Several of the words that were used clearly show that the images have been carefully studied.

These results all indicate that there is an *image interpretation mode* in which details and the abstract contents in an image are perceived.

To write legends

Ten pictures were shown subsequently to some 80 students taking a course in visual communication. The students were asked to compose legends which were (1) positive and reinforced image contents, (2) negative and weakened image contents, and (3) neutral and neither reinforced nor weakened image contents. Subsequent reviews of the legends (appr. 2,100) and also discussions in class showed that picture legends clearly have an ability to affect our perception of the image content. Actually *the legend has a very great impact on our image perception.* It might be said that *to a large degree readers see what they are told to see in an image.* This is also shown in eye-movement studies (Pettersson, 1986c).

To rank and rate images

Experiments with rankings and ratings of pictures (Pettersson, 1984) showed that picture readability is positively correlated with both aesthetic ratings and assessed usefulness in teaching.

In order to study children's preferences regarding image shapes, the author had a realistic black-and-white drawing made of house martins in flight against a grey background. The image was reproduced in eight different croppings and in sufficient quantities to permit comparison of all the image shapes in pairs. Each pair was mounted on a sheet of paper inserted in a binder. The visuals differed only in the shape of the image background. In one version there was no tint block; i.e., the drawing was a "free shape" on white paper. The other shapes were oval, round, square, video format, horizontal rectangle, vertical rectangle, and triangle. The 28 possible image pairs were mounted and numbered at random. A total of 30 girls and 35 boys from 10 to 12 years of age then told an interviewer at a private session which image pairs they liked best (a total of 1,764 possible choices). The results were analyzed with the aid of a binomial normal distribution test and disclosed a significant preference for the "soft" image shapes.

On the whole, the following rankings were obtained: (1) oval; (2) and (3) video format and "free" shape; (4) and (5) round and square; (6) low rectangle; and (7) and (8) high rectangle and triangle.

On another occasion, 36 girls and 39 boys aged 8 to 12 ranked five pictures placed at random on a table. The picture was a realistic drawing in color depicting "oyster catchers in a lake-shore meadow." Each picture had a different cropping; i.e., oval, round, video format, rectangular, or square, with the subject at the center. The same procedure was used in this experiment as with the pictures of house martins. In both studies, all the pictures had the same image area (69 cm^2). Statistical analysis (homogeneity test, utilizing the hypothesis that rankings of different image shapes are equally distributed) of the children's rankings of image shapes showed that they displayed a significant preference for the "soft" image shapes.

Both experiments clearly showed that children, on these occasions and with the subjects chosen, definitely preferred "soft" images to images with rectilinear framing. The results suggest that the use of more "soft" pictures in our textbooks might be justified.

The latter experiment with children was repeated in London in the spring of 1980 using pictures of both the house martin and the oyster catcher and with both black and white children of the same ages as in Sweden. There was no difference between black and white children. However, a difference was noted between boys and girls. The girls preferred "soft" image shapes to a greater degree ($p < 0.05$).

On a subsequent occasion, I had 79 adults (12 women and 67 men), participants in a Scandinavian audio-visual conference, rate the two image subjects in all the croppings except for the "free" shape. Ratings were made on a scale of 1 to 5 (very poor—very good). The pictures were projected on a screen in a conference room. Each picture was displayed to all participants for 12 seconds. The "soft" image shapes were always rated higher than the images framed by straight lines ($p < 0.05$); however, the differences were not as pronounced as with the children.

To assess image contents

In one study (Pettersson, 1985) 46 "senders" as well as 80 "receivers" assessed image contents. Results showed that for seven out of ten pictures there was a significant difference between the intended and the perceived image content. The above pictures were all mounted on cardboard paper in the A3 format (29.7 × 42.1 centimeters). In a follow-up study, slides were made of the five drawings. These slides were then shown to and rated by 113 adult subjects at the UREX image laboratory in Finland.

In the first study, a semantic differential scale was used. The verbal ratings "very poor," "rather poor," "neither poor nor good," "rather good," and "very good" were supplemented with a numerical value from zero to one hundred. For practical reasons, a Likert scale ("very poor," "rather poor," "rather good," and "very good") had to be used in the second study. Thus results from the two studies are not exactly and immediately comparable. However, these two studies show a remarkable similarity of results. In both cases pictures were rated very much the same. In this case it can be concluded that *content was more important than format.*

Weidenmann (1989) studied underevaluation of pictures. In an experiment, 206 male undergraduates rated the "perceived quality" of five materials on leadership. The five versions were:
1. text;
2. text with "imagination instructions";
3. text with pictures and no instructions;
4. text with pictures and picture-oriented instructions; and
5. text with pictures and imagination instructions.

The "illustrated text with picture-oriented instructions" group rated the material more positively with respect to the following dimensions: comprehensibility, concreteness, attractiveness, and memorability. The three groups with instructions in their texts each rated the material lower in scientific "seriousness" than did the two other groups.

After two weeks 159 subjects received a questionnaire concerning main ideas and details of the text. Results showed that the "illustrated text with picture-oriented instructions" group recalled significantly more main ideas and details of the text than did all other groups. The differences among the other four groups were statistically equivalent. It can be concluded that an underevaluation of pictures can be compensated for by explicit picture-oriented instructions. *Pictures need legends.*

To create images

In four different experiments, art and design students in Sweden have been assigned the task of making pictures according to various instructions (Pettersson, 1984, 1985, and 1986b). These experiments resulted in a variety of pictures (almost 600). There is no doubt that an intended content can be expressed using many different images. It is also quite clear that different people perceive and depict a given text in widely differing ways. *Content is more important than format.*

In visual language, non-meaningful basic elements (dots, lines, and areas) are put together into shapes which are combined into syntagms or sub-meanings (Pettersson, 1987). Syntagms can be part of complete meanings which in turn can be sub-meanings to other complete meanings. The basic elements can be put together in different ways, thus forming different images.

In an experiment, subjects were given three sets of basic elements. They were given the assignment "Combine the basic elements on each piece of paper into an image." The efforts resulted in 165 pictures. According to image contents, the pictures were grouped in various categories. Contents comprised groups like eye, cat, bird, face, animal, person, and also abstract ones. The basic elements had been produced by taking original pictures apart electronically. The elements were mixed in a new way and some got new orientations before they were printed out in hard-copy formats. It can be concluded that *a given set of basic elements can be combined to form various completely different images.*

The same subjects were also given a picture in which they were asked to use white ink and eliminate one hundred dots without changing the image contents. They all succeeded. Results fully confirmed earlier findings (Pettersson, 1986d). We can delete, add, or shift information in an image without drastically affecting perception of image contents.

To illustrate a story
It is interesting to study the pictures in different editions of fairy-tale books (or movies). Different artists all have their individual styles of work. They also have their own ideas of what to select and how to emphasize interesting contents. It is an obvious fact that our perception of a story is very much dependent on the illustrations that are selected. In one experiment an organization, Illustratörcentrum, for illustrators in Sweden, gave their members a short story by a well-known author (Illustratörcentrum, 1990). A total of 57 artists created illustrations to the text. All the pictures were quite unique. In fact there were almost no similarities at all between the different images.

To produce informative materials
In one experiment (Hellspong *et al.*, 1987) groups of students at the University of Stockholm were assigned the task of producing informative materials in different versions. After production, senders as well as receivers assessed all the 29 versions of information materials according to the 0–100 semantic differential scale. Results showed that there were major differences between intended and perceived levels of quality for the four examined variables "text," "visuals," "graphic design," and "total impression." The average level of intended quality was higher than the perceived levels (m = 22.5), i.e., *the senders rated their material more favorably than the receivers.* Perceived quality was better than intended quality only in about 15 percent of all 116 group assessments.

To produce information graphics
IFRA Institute (in Darmstadt, West Germany) organized a workshop "Infographics" (Nov. 29–Dec. 1, 1988). Twenty journalists, artists, and graphic designers from different newspapers participated in the workshop. They worked in eight groups with two to three persons in each. All groups had computer equipment and they worked with the same theme.

The workshop was concluded with evaluations of the information graphics that had been produced. Copies of all graphics were distributed to all groups together with evaluation forms. Each graphic was assessed according to ten different criteria. A combined five grade numeric and verbal scale was used: 1 = not satisfactory, 2 =

satisfactory, 3 = rather good, 4 = good, and 5 = very good. The ten criteria were: 1 = legibility of text, 2 = legibility of image, 3 = foreground (should be clear and distinct), 4 = background (should not be disturbing), 5 = text-image connections (should be clear), 6 = location of places and/or events, 7 = documentation of facts and/or explanations, 8 = presentation of statistics, 9 = editorial comment/s, and 10 = overall aesthetic value.

Results showed that *all criteria were assessed in a subjective way*. In fact most of the grades were used for all criteria. This was true for all graphics. The eight graphics form three categories. One graphic has a concentration at the high end with 80 percent of ratings good and very good. The contrary is true for two graphics. They have a concentration at the low grades with 80 percent of ratings not satisfactory and satisfactory. The remaining five graphics have an even distribution of grades or a weak concentration at the middle of the scale. It can be concluded that *subjects have different opinions about information graphics*.

Describing picture context

In communications, the sender is anxious for different receivers to perceive her/his message in the same or at least in similar ways. But this is seldom the case. Major discrepancy between the sender's perception and the individual receiver's perception is very common (Pettersson, 1989). A picture always represents a *choice* among several alternatives. A picture represents a "frozen" slice of time. Something is always going on *around, before,* and *after* a depicted event.

In one experiment (Pettersson, 1989), adult subjects were asked to draw pictures depicting events in the enclosed field around six small and simple illustrations. They were also asked to draw pictures depicting the events they considered to take place "before" two and "after" two pictures. Subjects also wrote explanatory captions. The subjects drew a total of 378 pictures and wrote the same number of captions. As expected, subjects had very definite and differing opinions about what was probably going on around particular pictures and about events prior to or after a depicted situation.

This experiment has been repeated (Pettersson, 1991) with four of the original pictures ("cat," "dog," "boat," and "cloud"). The first two of these pictures refer to the question of *around*. The other two refer to the questions of *before* and *after* respectively. The results of this experiment confirmed the results from the first study.

For the first assignment, 120 subjects drew an average of 49 different depictions of the picture's contextual events. On the average, 24 different motifs were drawn by more than one subject. The most common motif was selected by an average of 16 persons. Most subjects (71%) ignored the inner frame when depicting context. However, the inner frame was utilized as significant image element in the composition of 69 pictures. The inner frame was then incorporated as, e.g., a window, painting, poster, book page, aquarium, or cinema screen, to mention just a few. Context therefore governed the size of the original motif.

Regarding the second assignment, 120 subjects produced an average of 29 depictions of events preceding and following each picture. On the average, 18 different motifs were drawn by more than one subject. The most common motif was selected by 18 persons. The results showed far closer agreement between the subjects' perception of events "before-after" than of events "around." The latter produced fewer motifs (29 vs. 49). In addition, the most common motif was represented in more

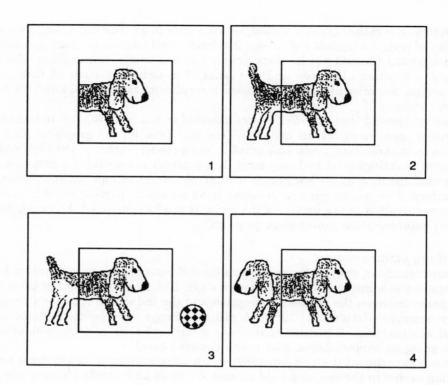

Example. Assignment: Supplement the picture (1) by filling in the information you feel should be between the inner and outer frames. Write an explanatory caption. Three examples of results of "around" the framed image, (2) only a behind, (3) the dog plays with a ball, and (4) mirror, half dog to the left.

pictures (24 vs. 18). However, the number of motifs drawn by more than one subject was about the same for both assignments (16 vs. 18).

The results show that the subjects have treated the visual information in a conscious and analytical manner. The results suggest that each subject placed available information in a wider, expanded, "personal" context. All the interpretations were realistic and about equally credible. We are apparently capable of sensing far more information than is explicitly displayed in a given picture. Adult perception tends to be holistic rather than detail-oriented. No one, except the original picture creator, can state with absolute certainty what is *really* going on around a particular picture's events or what *really* happened before or after the situation depicted in a selected picture. All the subjects still expressed opinions about circumfluous events on their drawings. They also tended to feel that their particular interpretations were the correct ones.

Pictorial capabilities

Backman, Berg, & Sigurdson (1988) researched pictorial capabilities of comprehensive school students. They wanted to know if there is any difference in the pictorial capabilities of intermediate level vs. senior level students in the Swedish compulsory, comprehensive school. Pictorial capability comprises the *production* and *reception* of visuals. Differences between the pupil categories can be expected with respect to (1) the production of visuals, (2) the analysis of visuals, (3) the perception of visuals, and (4) the communication of visuals. Empirical studies with a random selection of sixty 5th, 6th, 7th, and 8th year students respectively, i.e., a total of 240 subjects, participated.

For *picture production* the assignment was to produce a picture showing sky, mountains, forest, a lake, a house, a field, a meadow, a fence, and two trees. The subjects were supplied with paper, a pencil, brushes, and eight colors (80 min.). The use of tools, the number of colors, color mixing, perspective, and areas was evaluated.

For *picture analysis* the assignment was to submit answers to questions about the way a picture had been made (40 min.). The presence of comments on shapes, color, figures, composition, and technique was evaluated.

For *picture perception* the assignment was to submit a written description of everything the test picture conveyed (40 min.). The presence of comments on emotions, imagination, associations, and events was evaluated.

Picture communications was divided in two parts. For *production* the assignment was to produce a picture which supplies information about the significance of red and green as traffic signals (40 min.). Communications was evaluated as unequivocal, not quite unequivocal, or incomprehensible. For reception the assignment was to write down the message conveyed by a series of instructive pictures (40 min.). Whether the student understood fully, partially, or not at all was evaluated.

The study comprised a total of 1,200 visual and verbal statements submitted by 240 comprehensive school students. All the evaluations were performed by two of the authors, both teachers of method at the Department for the Training of Visual Arts Teachers at the University of Umeå.

The students displayed very poor pictorial capabilities. They were poor at producing pictures and in reading pictures. Only 5% of the senior level students were able to produce a picture which supplied information on the importance of red and green as traffic signals. Only 43% of the senior level students were able to supply a written description of the message conveyed by a series of instructive pictures.

The results showed that the two comprehensive school categories did not display any significant difference in pictorial capability.

The teaching of visual arts does not live up to the expectations teachers should have on the basis of existing curricula. There is probably a very considerable need for further training of teachers of visual arts. The authors concluded that teachers of visual arts must adopt a new approach. The subject "visual arts" demands the same competent, cognitive processing as, e.g., English, Swedish, or mathematics.

To understand diagrams

Lowe (1992) studied how experts and non-experts processed information provided in weather maps. The results indicated fundamental differences between the way diagrams were represented mentally by the experts and non-experts. The nature and extent of these differences indicated that the non-experts lacked a suitable basis for processing the diagrams in a way that would help them learn about the discipline. Their mental representation was impoverished, fragmentary, and mainly based upon superficial visuo-spatial characteristics of weather map diagrams' pictorial constituents. The non-experts' mental representation was limited to the particular diagram under consideration and lacked the scientists' highly interrelated and hierarchical structure between different types of information. The research showed that the task of processing diagrams may not be as different from the task of processing other types of presentation as might be supposed. Individuals lacking experience in a discipline will have a limited capacity to make effective use of diagrammatic presentation. Diagrams cannot be regarded simply as an alternative form of presentation that is easier to process than drawings and photographs.

Perceptual constancy

A country's flag is often its most prominent national symbol. The flag is devised according to a specific pattern with specific colors and proportions. There are usually very strict rules about the times when the flag may be hoisted and lowered. Children quickly learn to recognize their country's flag. This is evident in the spontaneous drawings made by children in different countries. Yet even though most people learn to recognize their country's flag at an early age, they would probably still be incapable of supplying an exact description of the flag's appearance. But we are still capable of recognizing our flag when we see it, irrespective of the way wind may change its shape or weather conditions alter its apparent colors. Perceptual constancy generally prevails for flags and many other symbols. In our mind's eye, objects tend to retain their shape, size, brightness, and colors, irrespective of the distance, angle, or lighting conditions from/in which we view them.

In another experiment under my leadership, Paukstadt (unpubl.) used an A4-sized paper to which a blue-yellow-blue strip was glued. The strip had the same colors and width proportions (5:2:9) as the Swedish flag and was equivalent to less than 4% of the area of a normal flag. The blue-yellow-blue strip inspired 91 students (65%) to think of the Swedish flag. The other 50 students in the study (35%) thought of no less than 27 different subjects. The results showed very clearly *that even a highly deformed flag symbol was often capable of generating associations with the national symbol.* There is a large degree of perceptual constancy.

Approaches to picture perception

There are many approaches to picture perception. Based on the theory of linear perspective, invented during the Renaissance, Gibson (1971) defined picture perception as *a stimulus-driven process* in which information is picked up from optical arrays. The opposite view is held by Gombrich (1969) and Gregory (1978). While seeing a picture *the viewer constructs a meaning* based on experience and expectations. From this receptionist position neither the readers nor the message remains the same. Meaning exists only for a moment within each individual reader. Another approach to picture perception is based on semiotics and symbol theory (Goodman, 1976). Intentionalism suggests that meaning is embedded in the message by a producer, leaving the reader to discover and unfold it. From this perspective meaning exists independent from the reader. For an intentionalist a painting means what the artist says it does. For a receptionist the painting does not mean anything until the reader says it does (Muffoletto, 1987). Boeckman (1987) makes a clear distinction between drawings and paintings, which have "signs" and photographs which have "recorded perceptional stimuli." "Before photography was invented there were two modes to learn about reality. Perception processing stimuli of the surrounding reality on the one hand and communication processing signs on the other. Now we have something in between: "Recorded perception stimuli which are not reality but not signs either." And for Arnheim (1974) picture perception is a matter of responding to basic forms such as gestalt laws. An important point of Arnheim's is that visual perception includes the same behaviors that we commonly consider only as matters of cognition or thinking. A "percept" is a building block of visual thinking and as such is analogous to the cognitive function of a concept.

Some researchers suggest that information is represented solely in the form of propositions. Images are said to be recorded into propositional format by a series of transformations (Pylyshyn, 1973, 1979). Others suggest more complex systems in which a variety of storage formats co-exist in an interlinked manner (Anderson, 1978, 1983; Wender, 1989).

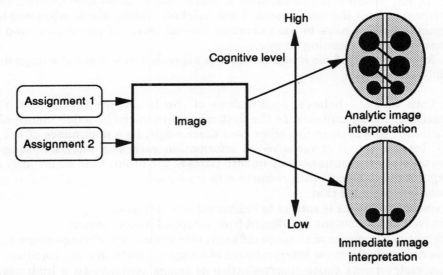

An image is interpreted in different ways depending on the assignment. An immediate image interpretation is handled on a low cognitive level. An analytic image interpretation needs high cognitive level activities.

The perception process is often assumed to consist of two stages. A fast overview is followed by a conscious analysis. When we first look at an image we only see that which is necessary to perceive and identify objects and events in a reasonable and meaningful manner. This is Gibson's "principle of economy" (Gibson, 1966).

Simple line drawings accompanied by various assignments caused very different reactions in subjects. It is obvious that the different assignments have caused perception and image interpretation on different cognitive levels. It may be suggested that image interpretation on low cognitive levels follows these steps:
1. The subject looks at the image. A few rapid eye fixations are made.
2. The information is handled as a "whole" in parallel, simultaneous, tentative, rough, holistic, and fast processing.

3. A "wholeness interpretation" occurs, recognition, and meaning of the image content is formed very quickly—"immediately."
4. This interpretation is expressed by the use of a very limited number of words.

It may also be suggested that image interpretation on high cognitive levels follows these steps:
1. The subject looks at the image. A few rapid eye fixations are made.
2. The information is handled as a "whole" in parallel, simultaneous, tentative, rough, holistic, and fast processing.
3. A "wholeness interpretation" occurs, recognition and meaning of the image content is formed very quickly—"immediately."
4. Certain details in the image attract more eye fixations.
5. The information is processed again, maybe several times, detail by detail. The process demands attention and is sequential.
6. Our verbal memory is activated in a search for suitable expressions. Various hypotheses about the image content are weighed against one another and tested. Segmented codes have to pass through several levels of recognition and interpretations before meaning occurs.
7. The interpretation of the image contents is expressed by the use of a large number of different words.

In both cases, I believe, both halves of the brain are involved in the interpretation of image contents. In the first case there might be a dominance of right brain activity. However, in the other case there might be a dominance of left brain activity. Interpretation of verbo-visual information such as a television-program is likely to take place simultaneously in both parts of the brain. *How we actually create meaning is an area where much research still is needed.*

It can be concluded that:
• All visual experience is subject to individual interpretation.
• Perceived image content is different from intended image content.
• Different assignments may cause different interpretations of image contents.
• Some assignments cause interpretation of image contents on a low cognitive level.
• Some assignments cause interpretation of image contents on a high cognitive level.
• Even simple pictures may cause many different associations.
• A given set of basic elements can be combined to form completely different images.
• The design of a picture can be changed a great deal without any major impact on the perception of the image contents.
• Content is more important than execution or form.
• Picture readability is positively correlated with both aesthetic ratings and assessed usefulness in teaching.
• Legends should be written with great care. They heavily influence our interpretation of image content.
• To a large degree readers see what they are told to see in an image.
• There seems to be no major difference between gender in interpretation of image contents.
• Students display poor pictorial capabilities.
• Most subjects have their own ideas on how to finish a story.

- There are major differences between intended and perceived levels of quality in informative materials.
- We must learn to read image content.
- How we actually create meaning is an area where much research still is needed.
- Guidelines to visual artists will usually not lead to destruction of creativity.

Pictorial style preferences

Like a text, a picture can be produced in various styles. Illustrative or artistic pictorial style can be defined as the mode of expression employed by an artist in interpreting pictorial content. Sloan (1971) discussed four pictorial artistic styles: photographic, representational, expressionistic, and cartoon. *Photographic style* was defined as a colored photograph of the subject. *Representational style* was defined as an artist's rendition of the subject which conforms to the subject in its true form. *Expressionistic style* was defined as an artist's rendition of the subject which leans heavily towards abstraction. *Cartoon style* was defined as an animated caricature of the subject. These four artistic styles form a realistic to an abstract continuum.

Literature on preferences for pictorial artistic styles fall into three primary groups; studies in which subjects selected a preferred picture from a series of pictures, in isolation from any accompanying text; studies in which subjects selected a picture which they felt best illustrated accompanying text; and studies in which subjects were asked to supply verbal reasons for their picture preferences. Several researchers (e.g., Rudisill, 1952; Lam, 1966; Sloan, 1971; Lindsten, 1975, 1976; Myatt & Carter, 1979) concluded that children preferred realistic art styles. However, Ramsey (1982) concluded that primary age children preferred photographic as well as cartoon art styles, when they selected pictures in isolation from text. According to Pettersson (1990), teachers as well as children regarded color photographs showing what things look like, drawings as complements to photographs, authentic, historical pictures, and authentic pictures of works of art as examples of "good visuals." "Fussy" overviews, abstract, obscure, ambiguous pictures, or pictures lacking the necessary facts were regarded examples of "poor visuals." Poor visuals display prejudice and attitudes in conflict with democratic principles. Pictures with merely a decorative function and "educational cartoons" which fail to educate are other examples of poor visuals. And Lucas (1977) reported that fifth grade children preferred "impressionistic" art with legends and photographic art with biography.

Like Sloan (1971) and Lucas (1977), Ramsey (1989) concluded that children equate highly realistic art styles (photographic and representational) with text content which depicts reality and real-life situations. Ramsey also found that children were very consistent in equating the more abstract art styles (expressionistic and cartoon) with imaginative, "pretend" or "make-believe" literature. Rank scores for the pictorial styles for 173 subjects were photographic (1.08), representational (2.01), expressionistic (3.16), and cartoon (3.75). Even children as young as first grade are visually literate in the interpretation of artistic style. According to Ramsey, children like to read about real-world subjects illustrated with full-color photographs, and they like to read about imaginative subjects illustrated with cartoons. This research suggests a complex interaction between children's perceptions of artistic style and their selection of style to accompany specific literary forms. Ramsey suggests that children employ pictorial artistic style as a yardstick for measuring the reality or fantasy of accompanying content material. Artistic styles may therefore give children various "pre-understandings" of the text contents.

Message design

Seeing pictures, a movie, or TV program clearly seems to be an active process. Some of the retina's 125 million sensory cells record the light impulses by chemical conversion of visual purple, signals are transmitted to the cortex, and the cortex converts the signals into a sensation of vision. In the case of movies and TV programs, dialogue, music, and sound are additional effects which are transmitted by the auditory apparatus to the brain, where they are incorporated into a unified perception of the total information. We must never commit the error of confusing still pictures, movies, or TV programs with reality. They are only representations and always render a subjective, selective view of reality. According to Fleming & Levie (1978) "Instructional Message Design" refers to the process of manipulating, or planning for the manipulation of, a pattern of signs and symbols that may provide the conditions for learning. It is assumed that practitioners in this domain can be more effective if they make use of appropriate generalized research findings from the behavioral and cognitive sciences. Fleming & Levie (1978, 1993) provide generalizations and express them as several hundred "principles" for instructional message design.

A general principle of human communication is that the likelihood of successful communication increases when a concrete reference is present. In the absence of the actual thing, the next best reference is a visual representation of that thing. A visual is a more pertinent reference for meaning than the spoken or written word. Visuals are iconic. They normally resemble the thing they represent.

A medium plus its contents is a representation (or even a re-presentation) of reality. Representations of reality can display varying structures, consist of a number of different components and be related to one another in different ways. Words and visuals, sound and visuals, or sound, words, and visuals are examples of components which can interact.

Some general principles of information message design to be used in the production of information and instruction may be given on the basis of different research results:
- Introduce novel or unexpected events at the start of instruction.
- Inform learners of expected outcomes.
- Recall relevant prerequisite information.
- Present only relevant information.
- Organize content and present "organizers."
- Progress from simple to complex.
- Provide prompts and cues.
- Vary information presented.
- Present examples and non-examples.
- Provide appropriate practice.
- Provide immediate feedback or knowledge of results.
- Review and repeat.

A *cognitive model*

Salomon (1984) points out that there is a widespread naive preconception about pictures as "easy media." Most people are convinced that pictures require only a small amount of invested mental effort to be understood. Weidenmann (1988) points out that a learner may quickly get an illusion of full understanding of the content or message in an image, and may stop the information processing after only a short glance. When the picture is combined with a text, s/he will concentrate on the part of the message that is perceived as the more informative. Text is generally perceived as a better medium than film for communication of to-be-learned content (Katz, Blumler, & Gurevitch, 1974; Kosbiech, 1976; Salomon, 1984). Weidenmann (1988) suggests that similar preconceptions may also exist about text vs. printed pictures.

An outline of a cognitive model to clarify differences between the concepts "see-look-read" and "hear-listen" is presented in the two illustrations below (pages 90, 91). The model should be viewed as a theoretical device, based on empirical findings and extensive research on eye movements and fixations as summarized above, clearly showing that we are capable of perceiving picture contents in many different ways .

A single fixation of a picture is sufficient to enable us to recognize it subsequently among other pictures. If we, e.g., go shopping in a department store, we are *virtually unaware* of the large number of advertising pictures/messages and background music to which we are exposed in the store. Everything merges into a kind of "noise." We probably only process most of the stimuli in this noise on a superficial level. We see and hear but do not look or listen. When we listen to the radio while engaged in some other simultaneous activity, such as cooking a meal, fixing a punctured tire, or glancing through a newspaper, we are aware of words, music, and images.

Looking at a picture consumes more mental energy and demands a higher cognitive level than merely seeing a picture. Visual impressions are conducted from the sensory to the short-term memory, i.e., operative memory. We only become aware of the information which succeeds in passing through the brain's filtering system. Most of the information disappears after a while.

When we, e.g., study material in books or on TV, we process that material actively. We *read* texts, *listen* to music, and *read* pictures. Perceived information is processed, sorted, and stored in certain parts of the brain's long-term memory. Many fixations of a picture are required for people to recall it subsequently and, e.g., be able to describe it.

Conscious analysis of linguistic messages, such as texts, music, and pictures (e.g., research), probably demands an even greater consumption of mental energy and a higher cognitive level. The brain actually uses about one fifth of our daily consumption of energy.

The most demanding processes are those leading to the creation of text, music, and pictures. Creative people have often described the mental effort which is often associated with creativity. The model assumes the existence of a dynamic relationship in which we consciously and unconsciously switch cognitive levels.

Our sensory organs respond to changes in our environment. We are normally capable of resolving changes with a gradient greater than about two percent. But we adapt to slow, gradual changes and often fail to notice them. So our senses are normally in the resting state but have a rapid response capability. In the corresponding manner, we are unable to remain on the highest cognitive levels for more

Cognitive level

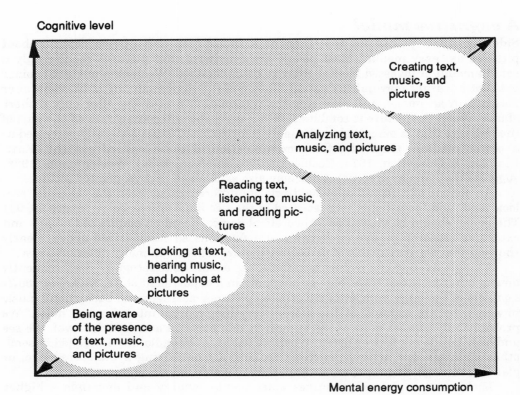

The relationship between cognitive level and mental energy consumption in different activities.

than relatively brief periods of time, since this would otherwise be too enervating and lead to some form of mental "cramp." Like a pike lurking in the reeds or a cat poised outside a mouse hole, we know what our surroundings look like. When changes occur in those surroundings, we are capable of responding rapidly and powerfully by activating our bodies both in physical and mental terms. Sometimes, everything goes according to plan. The pike gets a minnow, the cat gets its mouse, and we find the information we are looking for. At other times, efforts may fail. A predator may miss its prey, and we may spend a great deal of time and energy gathering information which turns out to be useless.

No clear distinctions can be made between the cognitive levels discussed here. But there are probably major differences between individuals due to cultural, social, and personal factors. So the model should not be interpreted too literally. However, it can be employed to elucidate the fact that there are major differences between the concepts "see-look-read" and "hear-listen." Active reception of linguistic intelligence comprising text, sound, or pictures, individually or in concert, always requires exertion. Reading and listening are mentally and physically exhausting. Uninteresting or poorly designed material reduces our interest in the subject described by that

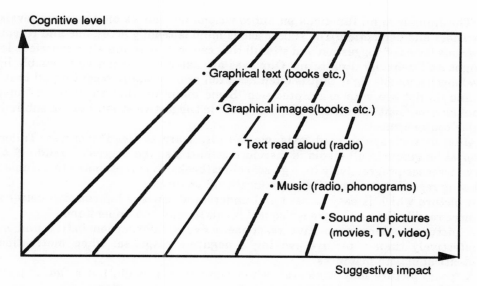

The relationship between cognitive level and suggestive impact for different kinds of representations. Suggestive impact increases as the cognitive level increases. Writing a text may have a greater suggestive impact than viewing a completed film or TV program. Creative involvement in the making of a movie or TV program may have a very considerable suggestive impact and evoke powerful emotions.

material. So the sender of a message should strive *to design text, music, and pictures in the most attractive, relevant manner possible* so receivers are encouraged to process the message on the highest possible cognitive level.

This should be the case irrespective of whether the "message" involves "information," "entertainment," "education," or "news." The principles apply irrespective of the medium involved, although different media transmit messages from senders to receivers in completely different ways.

Compared to a book, an interactive computer programs, phonograms, films, TV, and videograms have a highly manipulative effect on receivers. Message contents change continuously in a predetermined manner with respect to subject selection, time, and space. The receiver's active efforts to seek information are therefore largely disabled. A reader can "digest" the textual and visual contents of a book at a self-selected pace. In a structured information context, the reader is able to process information in about the same way as in a "natural" situation.

The aforementioned discussion could conceivably explain why pictures have such an impact and a much greater ability to influence us than a text. Children are more easily frightened by *watching* an act of violence on TV than by *reading* about the same act in a book or in a newspaper. This is because things we see appear to be more "real" than things we merely read about and because a higher cognitive level is required for reading than for seeing. Many scientists, such as Tröger (1963) and Noble (1975), have shown that small children are incapable of actively processing the contents of and understanding contexts in a TV or video program. This is something most parents of small children have also experienced.

The human mind functions on subconscious as well as on conscious levels of awareness and perception. The subconscious mind is readily accessible and receptive to various forms of suggestion and stimuli that can influence and alter conscious level thought and behavioral patterns. Our eyes are extremely sensitive to visible light wavelengths, visible light that is often not even seen, visually recording all that we see and do not see with exact precision. Some maintain that there is an "unseen visual environment" which can and does provide suggestive stimuli to the subliminal level of consciousness.

Just as we learn to read texts, we can also learn to "read" pictures. Tailoring pictorial language in all media is therefore essential so the degree of "reading" difficulty increases progressively in, e.g., school textbooks. It is reasonable to assume the following regarding informative and educational pictures:

- A picture which is easy to read and understand conveys information better and more readily than a picture which is difficult to read and understand.
- A picture evoking a positive response conveys information better and more effectively than a picture evoking a negative response, when motivation is identical in both instances.
- A "poor" picture may work well when motivation is high, but a "good" picture would then work even better.
- An easily read picture can be assumed to have a greater functional, communicative impact than a picture which is difficult to read.

LEARNING AND MEMORY

We receive a lot of information about the outside world. We ultimately learn to interpret and "read" different coded messages such as those contained in, e.g., text and visuals.

Learning

The first learning experience of a child is through tactile awareness. In addition recognition includes smelling, hearing, and tasting in a rich, immediate environment. However, these senses are quickly distanced by the ability to see, to recognize, to understand, and to remember visual impressions. What we see is very important for our experience and perception of the world. Seeing is direct and effortless. Making and understanding visual messages is natural to a point. However, effectiveness in visual literacy can only be achieved through learning. And the ability to read and understand pictures is learned. This learning takes place more rapidly in a culture where pictures are used and seen frequently. Pictures reinforce our knowledge when they are close to the real experience. Most people have a preference for visual information.

Learning must always be an active process. Just sitting passively and receiving information is not a particularly effective learning method. It must not be assumed that "disseminated" information is the same as "received" information. In language teaching, it has been found that a foreign word has to be repeated an average of 34 times before it has been learned. Learning should take place in a natural situation to the greatest possible extent.

An old teaching principle states that you should first tell your students what you plan to tell them. You then tell them what you wanted to tell them. Afterwards, you tell them what you have just told them. An old Chinese proverb states the following:

> *That which I hear, I forget.*
> *That which I see, I remember.*
> *That which I do, I understand.*

These old observations from reality have been confirmed by a number of different studies. We now know with great certainty that representations, such as text and pictures, sound and pictures, or sound, text, and pictures with redundant or relevant relation provide the basis for much better learning than sound, text, or pictures alone. We also know that representations with irrelevant or contradictory commentaries make for poorer learning than sound, text, or pictures alone.

The ability to recognize stimuli develops with age. Children of all ages recognize visual stimuli better than auditory stimuli. Learner characteristics such as age, gender, culture, prior knowledge of the subject matter, scanning habits, and visual and text processing abilities affect learning abilities. We all develop our individual behaviors while we are learning. The expression "learning style" refers to these individual preferences. These preferences concern our environment, like sound, light, temperature, moisture, and design of the room, our emotions, and our sociological, physiological, and psychological situation. Numerous scientists, such as Gardner (1983), Jung (1964, 1965, 1971), and Thurstone (1937), have discussed learning styles. Hanson (1988) identified four basic learning styles. The *sensing-thinking learner* prefers instruction that focuses on facts and especially on the physical manipulation of tangible objects. S/he likes to know exactly what is expected in each situation. The *sensing-feeling learner* prefers instruction that focuses on personal values and support for one another. The *intuitive-thinking learner* prefers instruction that focuses on the meanings and relationships of data. S/he likes problems that require logic analysis and reasoning. The *intuitive-feeling learner* prefers instruction that allows for personal exploration of a subject or content of personal interest.

One dimension of the concept cognitive style is "field independence" and "field dependence" (Messick, 1970). In comparison to field dependents, the field independents are less dependent upon external stimuli to bring order to their experiences (Witkin *et al.*, 1962). Subjects' level of field independence can be determined by their relative performances on the Group Embedded Figures Test (GEFT) as defined by Jackson, Messick, & Myers (1964).

We receive and process information from our sensory systems in various ways. Preferences for different kinds of information or "modalities" do exist. Thus people may have visual, auditory, kinesthetic, and/or tactual modality. Some people have a mixed modality.

In the US it has been found that 30 percent of elementary school children have visual modality, 25 percent have auditory modality, and 15 percent have kinesthetic modality. The remaining 30 percent have a mixed modality (Duffy, 1983).

Children with *visual modality* rely very much on seeing things and on their internal visualization. They learn by seeing, they are "visual learners." Thus these children remember faces rather than names. They must take notes and write down verbal information if they need to remember it. Visual modality children are very quiet. They can not listen for a long period at a time. Visual learners have vivid imagination. They think in images and visualize in components and details rather than the whole. Visual learners are not particularly responsive to music.

Children with *auditory modality* rely very much on hearing and verbalization. They learn by hearing, they are "auditory learners." Thus these children remember names rather than faces. They learn from verbal directions and descriptions. They think in sounds. Auditory modality children talk a lot. They like to hear their own voices. Auditory learners miss significant details in pictures. However, they may appreciate a work of art as a whole. They favor music.

Children with *kinesthetic and/or tactual modality* rely very much on their movements and muscular involvement. They learn by doing and remember what was done rather than seen or heard. Imagery is not important, nor pictures. Kinesthetically oriented children prefer sculptures which they can touch. When communicating these children use a lot of bodily expressions. They respond to music by physical movements.

Children with mixed modality strength learn from visual, auditory, as well as kinesthetic and tactile stimuli. According to Bagget (1989), elements coming from different modalities can become parts of the same concept. For example, the name of an object, what it looks like, and the actions one performs on it can be included in a single concept. In a dual media presentation, visuals should be in synchrony with verbal or precede them by up to seven seconds. Bagget found that college students comprehend information in a film just as well when visual and verbal elements are presented simultaneously, as when they are presented sequentially, doubling study time.

It is important to consider these various learning styles when we are producing materials for information and instruction. Such materials should have a good balance between verbal and visual messages and maybe also suggestions for practical, hands-on-exercises.

Bertoline, Burton, & Wiley (1992) discuss three primary stages of "Visual Learning." These steps are (1) visual cognition, (2) visual production, and (3) visual resolve. Visual cognition includes, (1) visual perception, the ability to mentally comprehend visual information; (2) visual memory, the ability to mentally store and retrieve visual information; and (3) visualization, the ability to mentally create and edit visual information. Visual production includes, (1) externalization; the ability to create and edit visual products throughout a design process; (2) transmission, the ability to communicate information through visual products; and (3) reception, the ability to comprehend responses to visual products. Visual resolve includes the ability to comprehend the termination of a design process.

A verbal response to visual stimuli or a visual response to verbal stimuli requires a transformation from one modality to another. Research concerning the effects of verbal as well as visual modalities shows that children pay more attention to visual than to verbal information. Zuckerman *et al.* (1978) found that children tend to be more accurate in recognizing visual than auditory segments in television commercials. Hayes & Birnbaum (1980) showed pre-school children cartoons in which the audio track either matched or mismatched the visual information. In both cases children had a higher retention of the visual than of the auditory information. Pezdek

& Stevens (1984) found that when children had to choose which of two incompatible channels to process, they preferred the video channel. The auditory information sustains attention and facilitates comprehension. Pezdek & Hartmann (1983) found that video without sound reduced comprehension among pre-school children. Rolandelli *et al.* (1985) concluded that children used the auditory component of television to direct attention to important visual information, as well as to process auditory, especially verbal, content.

Dwyer (1978, 1982-3) and his associates have conducted more than 200 studies on the effects of pictures on the learning of factual information. The studies are based on a 2,000 word text and various sets of illustrations of the human heart. A variety of formats such as booklets, television, and slide-audiotape presentations have been used. Pictures have been found helpful in identifying the parts of the heart, e.g., when visual discrimination is needed. It has also been concluded that line drawings generally are most effective in formats where the learner's study time is fixed and limited. More realistic versions of art work however, may be more effective in formats where unlimited study time is allowed.

Keller & Burkman (1993) provide several design principles that apply to visual communication. Hannafin & Hooper (1993) provide a comprehensive overview of "Learning Principles."

Memory

Common to all the phases of the analysis performed on incoming information is the need to store the signals for varying lengths of time so that the information processing can be carried out. The processes which carry out this information storage are referred to in psychological terms as "memories."

Norman & Rumelhart (1975, p. 17) state that 'The fact that a person 'perceives images' when recalling perceptual experiences from memory does not mean that information is stored within memory in that way. It only implies that they are processed as images." Pylyshyn (1973) argues that pictures cannot be stored as complete point-to-point representations, because both the processing and the storage for each would be enormous, and therefore overload both the sensory system and the brain. There are many models seeking to explain the function of our memories (see Sinatra, 1986, and Levie, 1987, for reviews). One way of viewing memory functions is based on information processing in several steps.

The first of these steps is the sensory memory which carries out the storage of stimulus information on the peripheral level, i.e., far away from the brain. An example of sensory memory is the biochemical processes in the eye. The visual cells there possess some inertia and function therefore as a kind of memory. The sensory memory normally stores information for one half to one second (vision). Loftus, Shimamura, & Johnson (1985) showed that for one tenth of a second as much information can be extracted from this sensory memory icon as from the picture itself. The iconic memory (vision) and the econic memory (hearing) are closely related to the sensory memory. These memories precede the integration of signals from various sensory systems.

After being processed in the iconic memory and the econic memory, some information is passed on to the short-term (or operative) memory (STM) where it is only retained for a brief period of time, i.e., not more than one to two seconds. A number of complex operations are carried out here during solution of problems. But the short-term memory has severe capacity limitations. Any information to be retained in this memory must be repeated every few seconds, otherwise it will be lost.

Information which has entered the short-term memory can proceed through a filter (reception) which selects the information to be passed on. Once this filtration has taken place and certain information units have been assigned priority over others, these priority units are given access to a P system (register) with a limited memory capacity. This is the point at which a person becomes aware of the stored information. All other non-priority information disappears, normally forever if it is not re-transmitted to the filter when the filter is able to accept the traffic. The filter scrutinizes the information received from the outside world and identifies the special properties of this information. When the information involves aural signals, the filter notes whether the signal is strong or weak. When visual signals are involved, the signal is scrutinized for information on color, size, any movement, etc.

The information which passes the P system can proceed in different ways. The information can be stored in a long-term memory (LTM). This is what normally happens with the knowledge we do not need for the moment. This long-term memory then affects the selection filter so the filter makes selections related to previous experience. The long-term memory is what most people mean when they refer to "memory." The long-term memory has carrying contents, episodic memories (i.e., recollections of events, feelings, experiences, etc.), words, pictures, concepts, etc. The short-term and long-term memories are actually theoretical models which cannot be related to any activity pattern or any particular anatomical structure in the human brain. The distinction made between the STM and LTM is probably too clear-cut.

Information can also be passed on to an "output system" which emits signals to the muscles which are to carry out a given act. The information can be switched back from the P system to the reception or to the short-term memory. The information can also get lost.

Comparisons are sometimes made between the human brain and a computer. However, the brain differs in many ways from a computer. As a rule, a computer must be able to process considerably more information than a human in any given situation, since the computer program is unable to distinguish between important and unimportant information. The machine is therefore incapable of ignoring any information the way the human brain constantly does. This is one of the reasons why a person's ability to process sensory information is far beyond the capability of even giant computers, even though the individual processing steps are carried out much faster in a computer than in the human brain, about one million times faster. The dual-code memory model (Paivio, 1971, 1978) proposes a verbal system specialized for processing and storing linguistic information and a separate nonverbal system for spatial information and mental imagery. These systems can function independently but are also interconnected. Other memory models include a single-code approach. All information is coded as abstract propositions. Complex cognitive processing of information involves the use of both visual and auditory cues. According to cue information theory (Adams & Chambers, 1962), information that is shared between channels facilitates learning. Cues that occur simultaneously in auditory and visual channels are likely to be better recalled than those presented in one channel only. Drew & Grimes (1985) showed that close coordination between audio and video improved audio recall of television news and that redundancy aided story understanding.

Several researchers, such as Nickerson (1965), Shepard (1967), Standing, Conezio, & Haber (1979), and Paivio (1971), have shown that subjects are capable of accurately identifying previously seen pictures. Haber (1979) felt that our ability to recognize pictures can be described as virtually "perfect." Over a five-day period, Standing (1973) showed subjects 10,000 slides and found that they were able to recognize 83% on a later occasion. According to Potter & Levy (1969), a person only needed to look at a picture for 1–2 seconds in order to be able to recognize it among other pictures viewed on a subsequent occasion. A child's inability to assign a name to a previously seen picture could be because picture contents were unfamiliar or because the subject's distinguishing features were depicted with insufficient clarity. A child may thus recognize a picture subject but have no idea what to call it.

Loftus (1972) felt that the number of fixations are decisive to our ability to recall a picture. He found that pictures studied by subjects several times were remembered much better than pictures studied ("fixed") less often. Brigthouse (1939), Haber & Erdelyi (1967), and Haber (1979) studied how much subjects actually remembered of picture contents. They found that much more time was needed for people to remember pictures than to merely recognize that they had seen them before. Christianson (1990) showed subjects a series of pictures with emotionally charged, neutral, and unusual contents. The experiments disclosed that the subjects concentrated their attention on the central aspect of a depicted event, i.e., the thing that surprised them when they viewed an emotionally charged or unusual event.

The fixations can be guided and determined by a picture legend or by a spoken commentary. Meaningful material is learned more easily and remembered longer than meaningless material. Thus, we are normally forced to make a continuous selection from the information which constantly bombards us. According to Paivio (1971), the image is centrally important in facilitating long-term retention, at least for adults. Many people have experienced how looking at old photographs in a forgotten album can result in a dramatic flow of memories. Paivio (1983) showed that our memory for pictures is superior to our memory for words. This is called the *"pictorial superiority effect."* It is also known that memory for picture-word combination is superior to memory for words alone or pictures alone (Haber & Myers, 1982).

By the mid-1970s, it was well-established that children's immediate, factual recall of simple fiction was improved when picture content was completely redundant with prose content (Levin & Lesgold, 1978). More recent reviews (Levie & Lentz, 1982; Levin, Anglin, & Carney, 1987) substantiate the Levin & Lesgold conclusions.

Levin *et al.* discuss different functions of pictures used in prose. According to them, four functions are "text-relevant." These are called representation, organization, interpretation, and transformation functions. Illustrations are representational when they serve to reinforce the major narrative events in the text and "tell" the same story, i.e., are redundant with the text. Representational pictures add concreteness to the prose since memory for pictorial materials is better than memory for verbal materials. Illustrations are organizational when they provide a framework for a text. They add coherence to the prose since memory for organized

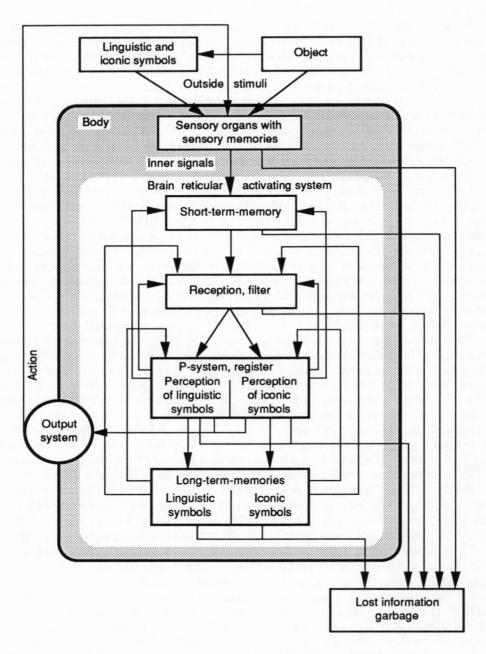

A suggested model for the perception of linguistic and iconic symbols.

materials exceeds memory for unorganized materials. Illustrations are interpretational when they clarify passages in the text that are difficult to understand. Interpretational pictures add comprehensibility to the prose since materials that are initially well understood are remembered better than materials that are more poorly understood. Illustrations are transformational when prose content is re-coded into concrete form and related in a well-organized context. These pictures provide readers with a systematic means of retrieving the critical information. Transformational illustrations are designed to impact directly on readers' memory.

After a meta-analysis of results from some 100 experiments on functions of pictures used in prose, published in 87 separate documents, Levin *et al.* concluded that all types of text-relevant pictures facilitate learning from reading prose. There was an increasing learning effect from representational pictures ("moderate"), organizational and interpretational pictures ("moderate to substantial") to transformational pictures ("substantial"). It was also concluded that when illustrations are not relevant to the prose content, no prose-learning facilitation is to be expected. On the contrary, there can be a negative effect.

Pressley & Miller (1987) reviewed experiments concerning children's listening comprehension and oral prose memory. They concluded the following ordering of conditions with respect to their potency for affecting children's learning of prose: sentences only < sentences + single incomplete picture (i.e., partial picture) < sentences + two incomplete pictures < sentences + complete pictures.

Conveying redundant information through both linguistic and iconic symbols facilitates information processing, reduces error and information loss, and increases the amount of information that learners can recall. Linguistic and iconic symbols make it possible for the learners to alternate between functionally independent, though interconnected, and complementary cognitive processing systems. *In conclusion,* results from several experiments show that *when content is the same in visual, audio, and print channels, learning is maximized.*

A number of techniques are available for improving memory. Buzan (1977) discussed, e.g., special *memory systems* that establish links between or exaggerate the image of things to be recalled. The mere act of making a special effort to remember may suffice to improve memory capacity. According to Kossllyn (1975) more details of a mental image of an object are remembered when the object is imagined next to a smaller object. Thus the relative size of a part of an image may affect our ability to remember and recognize it.

Modern systems for computer-aided design make it possible to actually display a similar kind of "inner images" on a screen or on paper with the help of a plotter before the object itself actually exists. It is often possible to rotate the screen image of the object and study it from all possible angles. It is often also possible to "take the object apart."

Many people, of all ages, have had accidents bringing them close to death and subsequently described death or near-death experiences they had just before losing consciousness. These experiences often encompass a large number of wide-ranging images of events throughout their lives, flashing past in a rapid, sometimes chaotic succession. They may even recall people, places, and events from their earliest years. Buzan (1977) suggested that people may well remember everything that has ever happened to them but are normally unable to access this information.

Witness psychology is the branch of applied psychology that studies the reliability of testimony and the mechanisms contributing to the distortion of perceptions and the recollection of events. The reliability of testimony depends on many factors, including circumstances at the time of an event, the witness's emotional state and memory function, etc. Some witnesses find it easy to remember events accurately and in great detail. The memory of other witnesses may be faulty. They sometimes fill in memory blanks unconsciously so a memory still seems correct to them. Such a witness might then be convinced that she/he is supplying highly accurate information, even when it is highly inaccurate. According to Christianson (1990), witnesses often change their recollections to conform with descriptions supplied by other witnesses or information in the media. This is a subconscious process that is independent of whether an event was emotionally charged or banal.

There seem to be people who have perfectly accurate memories but without conscious awareness of memory as an activity to be experienced. These people are individuals who function on an unconscious wavelength of instinct which functions independently from memory or thought in the conscious sense of awareness.

Intellectual development

When a person attempts to copy a drawing made by someone else, he or she generally simplifies the subject so that it increasingly assumes simple, basic geometric shapes such as circles, rectangles, and triangles. When small children begin to make pictures of their own, the circle is generally their first definable area, followed by the square and then the triangle. The external contours of an image and its "total shape" are probably very important to the way we perceive image content. Segall, Cambell, & Herskovits (1966) pointed out that one of the most striking things about a photocopy is its rectangular shape and its white frame. These properties may very well have an effect on and interfere with our perception of the image subject itself.

My own study of the image creativity of children (Pettersson, 1979) showed, among other things, that the paper's edge, the corners in particular, attracted the children's attention. This influence was apparent in one-third of the pictures made by children from two to seven. Yarbus (1967) and many other scientists have shown that we only fix our attention on certain elements of a picture's image, so it is possible that the corners of rectangular and square pictures are distracting to small children reading a picture. The corners may demand attention which should be conferred on image content. An ideal picture should probably be oval with blurred edges; i.e., the image should emerge from the background, about the way Gibson (1966) described our perception of "selected visual fields." Pictures in our books and newspapers have not always been rectangular and square, and we can find interesting differences in different cultures. Today, we live in an age increasingly dominated by television. Children may ultimately expect all images to have the same format as a TV screen.

Amen (1941), Mackworth & Bruner (1970), and a number of other authors have commented on the tendency of young children to become absorbed in details of a picture at the expense of the whole. Elkind, Koegler, & Go (1964) found that children are generally unable to switch attention voluntarily from parts to whole until they are about nine years old.

The ability of children to decipher the contents of a picture is governed by their mental development, previous experience, and social circumstances. According to Piaget, chronological age is the most important factor in a child's mental development. He described four stages of that development:

1. The sensory-motor period (0 to 2 years) ;
2. The pre-operational period (2 to 6 years) ;
3. The period of concrete thought processes (7 to 12 years); and
4. The period of formal or abstract though processes (from 13 years).

Miller's (1956) initial review of short-term memory research, "The magical number seven, plus or minus two: Some limits on our capacity for processing information," related to items like brightness, color, digits, hue, length, letters, loudness, pitch, size, and taste. Subsequent studies by Case (1974, 1975), Pascual-Leone & Smith (1969), and Bazeli & Bazeli (1992) have come to similar conclusions. They also found clear differences over age groups with children having an increasing capacity until reaching adult levels in the middle teen years. Bazeli & Bazeli (1992) provide rules of thumb for this increasing capacity (p. 44). "As a rule of thumb second graders ought not be asked to handle new information that contains more than two or three steps or components at one time, fourth graders no more than three or four, seventh graders no more than four or five, and high school students no more than five or six. Presentations of new information ought to include combinations of visual and verbal media, but teachers should be careful to limit simultaneous multi-media presentaion of information; they appear to be more distracting than helpful to some students."

Noble (1975) analyzed the way in which children of different ages perceive the content of TV programs and found very wide differences between children in the different stages of development. Children from 2 to 6 tended to either strongly like or dislike what they saw. They had difficulty in distinguishing between internal and external experiences, i.e., between imagination and reality, and felt involved in and able to influence events in TV programs. They are unable to comprehend how different aspects of an event may be interrelated and therefore view TV programs as a succession of mutually unrelated happenings.

According to Goldsmith (1987) most children, in cultures where pictures are a regular feature of the environment, are "pictorially literate" by the time they are about 8 or 9. However, Barufaldi & Dietz (1975) found that most of the children between grades 1 and 6 performed better in observation and comparison tests when using real, solid objects as opposed to pictures of the same objects.

When children acquire the ability to carry out reversible thought processes in the third stage of their development, they begin to respond systematically to concrete stimuli in their surroundings. Their world of thought is no longer restricted to the present, and it becomes possible for them to foresee events and understand relationships. At the beginning of this stage of development, the children concentrate on special events in a TV program, but they gradually begin to understand the plot. Children from 11–12 are only capable of understanding the concrete, physical behavior of the TV performers, not the emotions supplying the motivation for a given action. From about the age of 13, children begin to be capable of dealing with logical thought processes on an abstract plane. Only at this stage do they acquire the ability to understand the indirect symbolism often found in movies and TV programs.

Illustrations in materials for use with children under thirteen should be strictly relevant to the text. Younger children can not ignore incidental illustrations. If pictures do not help, they will probably hinder the understanding of the content.

Noble found that TV producers could accurately predict what children would like, but not what children would understand.

Social circumstances, in addition to chronological age and intelligence, play an increasingly important role in the ability of children to understand the events in a TV program.

Various studies have shown that middle-class mothers talked and discussed things with their children to a greater extent than working class mothers. In Noble's view, therefore, we can expect to find similar differences regarding TV programs. The socialization process in middle-class children means that these children tended to receive more encouragement in understanding the programs.

Tröger (1963) felt that children first have to learn to comprehend individual pictures before they can comprehend the plot of a movie. A basic requirement here is that the children really are capable of distinguishing between an object and a picture of that object. Only after this is possible is a child mature enough to deal with various subjects on an abstract level. Tröger suggested that children do not achieve picture comprehension until they reach the age of about six. Comprehension of movies is therefore only possible after this age.

Tröger defined the following stages in movie comprehension:
1. The child attains picture comprehension, i.e., the ability to distinguish between an object and a picture of the object.
2. The child comprehends individual scenes in a movie. But these scenes are not perceived as being related to prior and subsequent scenes.
3. The child begins to comprehend the interrelationship of individual scenes.
4. The child begins to comprehend all the relationships in the film.

Tröger's view is in close agreement with Piaget's and Noble's with the exception of age level. Actually, children probably attain facility in picture comprehension at a much earlier age than six, possibly as early as three years.

In Tröger's view, children under seven perceive movie reality differently than adults. Even here Tröger described four stages of development which arise in chronological order but at different ages for different children, depending on their development in other respects:
1. The child lacks movie comprehension and views a movie realistically.
2. The child views a movie as a reproduction of reality, i.e., the events on the screen have really happened. The photographer just happened to be passing and made the movie.
3. The child perceives the movie as possible reality, i.e., they understand that the movie was made but that the events in the movie could actually happen in reality.
4. The child perceives the movie as selected and processed reality. Not every adult reaches this stage.

In the United States, TV programs made for children are basically designed in the same way as programs for adults. In programs such as Sesame Street, for example, children see a series of rapid and varied scenes which are frequently unrelated to one another. Children's programs in Sweden are better tailored to children's prerequisites. The former Soviet Union was even more advanced in this respect. The state-run Soviet TV company produced programs for five age groups: up to the age of 7, 8–10, 11–14, 15–18 and over 18 years of age. The former Eastern Bloc countries have amassed considerable know-how about the way TV programs should be designed to suit different age groups. However, less is known about this subject in the West.

Results indicate that visual languages exists, at least for three-, five-, eight-, and twelve-year-olds, and that these languages are apparently more efficient than verbal languages in memory tasks. A verbal response to visual stimuli or a visual response to verbal stimuli requires a transformation from one modality to another. The ability to transform from verbal to visual modality develops more rapidly than the transformation from visual to verbal modality. As previously noted we may have one kind of memory for pictorial material and another for linguistic material. Pictorial stimuli are stored as images and not as words. The stimuli cannot be recalled without extensive cognitive efforts to retrieve the stored image, transform it into words and then verbalize those words.

Reynolds-Myers (1985) suggests that we put the theories of Piaget (1968), Bloom (Bloom *et al.*, 1956), and Gagné (Gagné & Briggs, 1974) together to be able to meet the principles of visual literacy.

Basic assumptions of Piaget's theory:
1. The ability to think and reason occurs in developmental stages through which individuals progress in an invariant order.
2. These stages are dependent upon several interacting factors: physical maturation, experience, social transmission, and equilibration.
3. Although the stages develop in a fixed order, individuals move from one stage to another at different ages.
4. An individual may function in one stage for some bodies of knowledge, while he functions in a different stage for other bodies of knowledge.

Basic assumptions of Bloom and Gagné:
1. Desired learning outcomes can be described and classified into levels of learning.
2. A higher class of learning subsumes all lower levels of learning.
3. Instruction can be designed to allow the learner to develop the desired level of learning.

However, before we can do this we must refine the means of testing for learning. At the present time, most learning is measured or assessed through verbal means.

Illusions

One and the same stimulus can easily be perceived in different ways on different occasions. A very famous example of this is the Necker cube. It is perceived in one of two ways. There are many examples of "transformation" pictures of this kind. Some artists have become specialists in making pictures which can be perceived in different ways.

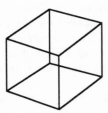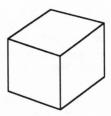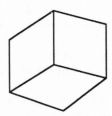

The Necker cube left and the two ways we can perceive it.

This figure is "impossible." The depth ambiguity means that the eye is unable to obtain all the information necessary to locate all the figure's parts. The brain becomes unable to determine how to interpret the image.

We often think we see things which are not really there. The black lines here are interpreted by many viewers as forming the word "word." An illiterate person would be unable to interpret the lines as forming a word.

We often have difficulty in interpreting simple relationships. For example, horizontal lines are often perceived as being shorter than equally long vertical lines.

Open and light forms are perceived as being larger than closed and darker forms of the same shape.

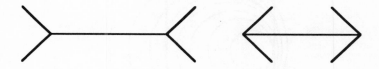

The left figure seems to have a longer horizontal line than the right figure (Müller-Lyer's illusion).

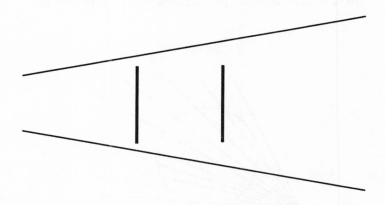

The left vertical line seems to be longer than the right vertical line (Ponzo's illusion).

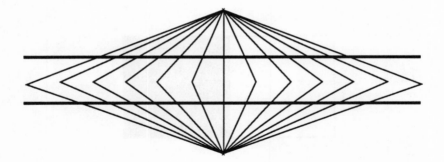

Intersected straight lines no longer appear to be straight but bent or serrated (Wundt's illusion).

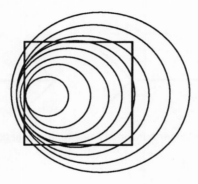

These intersected parallel lines no longer appear to be parallel.

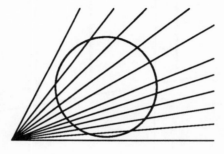

An intersected circle no longer appears to be a circle.

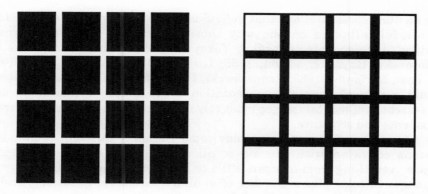

In regular patterns like these, the areas in the intersections of the white and black lines look grey. The total black and, respectively white area must be considerably larger than the white and, respectively, black area for this phenomenon to arise.

Changes in scale produce an illusion of elevations or depressions in a figure.

When the brain analyzes new data, it automatically adds or subtracts information in an effort to obtain a "sensible" interpretation of that data.

INNER IMAGES

When we look at a visual or at an object, this obviously results in a perception; we create an inner visual image or a mental picture. Visualizing is the ability to form mental pictures. However, we do not require external stimuli to create inner images. It is enough to think about a specific object, a visual, a person, or an event. So inner images arise both when we look at things and even in our thoughts and dreams. Inner images can therefore represent both "external reality" and "internal reality."

The mental representations that individuals generate for tasks are considered to have powerful influence on the way those individuals process external task information they encounter (Anzai & Yokoyama, 1984; Chi, Feltovich, & Glaser, 1981; Kotovsky, Hayes, & Simon, 1985; Larkin, 1983; Lesgold *et al.*, 1988; Voss, Greene, Post, & Penner, 1983; Romiszowski, 1993). Unlike a physical representation of a visual, a person's mental representation is not directly available for scrutiny. Thus researchers of mental images must rely upon inference in order to characterize its components and structure.

The perception of inner images may comprise many different combinations of impressions conveyed with the aid of all our senses. Our inner images may encompass everything from abstract stills to highly realistic, moving, three-dimensional images in color plus a number of auditory, olfactory, gustatory, and tactile sensations.

Inner images can be described to other people through the medium of drawings, paintings, models, sculpture, etc., as well as with words alone and without any physical representations.

In my view, there are two main types of inner images: primary visual imagery and secondary visual imagery.

Primary visual imagery

Gibson (1966) rejected the concept of the retinal image as a picture. We are never conscious of the process in which rays of light reflected from some object enter the eye, are refracted by the eye's cornea, lens, and vitreous humor, and strike the retina. These optical *retinal "images"* are continuously translated into signals sent through both optic nerves to the visual centers in both halves of the brain. There, *primary visual imagery*, i.e., our perception of vision, is created in the brain's visual centers. This imagery is subsequently stored in our memory. So primary visual images are the result of external stimuli.

Most people define the term "visual imagery" as something seen or experienced, roughly synonymous with the term *"memory"* (see below).

Secondary visual imagery

In contrast to primary visual imagery, *secondary visual imagery* is mainly the product of internal stimuli. External stimuli can and do initiate secondary visual imagery. Memories and thoughts (including dreams) are secondary visual images.

Memories

A memory (see the subsection "Memory" earlier in this chapter) is a mental image enabling us to visualize an object, event, or particular situation. In some way, we retrieve and "activate" a copy of this visualization stored in our long-term memory.

Thoughts

Thoughts are visual representations that arise when we think. According to Blakeslee (1980), the American mathematician Hadamard (1945) found that distinguished mathematicians often avoid thinking in words. Instead, they employ visual imagery in their creative work. Hadamard reports that Albert Einstein once remarked that certain characters and more or less distinct, reproducible, combinable, consciously evoked images are the physical units that apparently serve as elements in the thought process. Blakeslee (1980) pointed out that even Aristotle, the father of formal logic, was aware that thoughts are dependent on images. In De anima (Eng. = On the soul), he wrote: "Thinking is impossible without some inner images. The process is the same when a person thinks as when a person draws a diagram."

Creative people sometimes witness that they are able to create with very few if any conscious thought processes. While design decisions are constantly being made, the design process is so fluid that thinking merely gets in the way. The McKim diagram (see below) explains the fluid dynamic that occurs without conscious awareness or thought.

Geisser (1992) pointed out that we need words for logical reasoning. She concluded that a propositional/linguistic representation system is a necessary condition for logical inference. "Images, or pictorial representaions, can at best play a limited, heuristic role in logical reasoning, and more generally in the processing of thoughts. A pictorial/visual representation system, whatever its role in general cognitive processes may be, is a poor substitute for the verbal/linguistic system as a vehicle of logical reasoning" (p. 181).

In my view, there are several different kinds of mental images: "fantasy images," "self-images," and "target images."

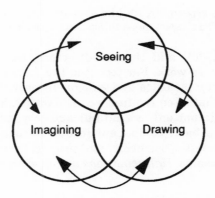

In *Thinking Visually* Robert H. McKim (p. 8) illustrates the interactive nature of seeing, imagining, and drawing with a figure of this kind. The three partly overlapping circles symbolize the idea that visual thinking is experienced to the fullest when seeing, imagining, and drawing merge into active interplay. The visual thinker utilizes seeing, imagining, and drawing in a fluid and dynamic way, moving from one kind of imagery to another.

Fantasy images

Fantasy is an imagined, generally pleasant, event or object. We create *fantasy visual images* by juxtaposing previously acquired combinations in new ways. Using our imagination, we can generate mental visual images of things we have never seen nor experienced. Fantasy fulfills a wish or satisfies a desire whose ultimate origin is subconscious. According to Freud, our fantasies may be conscious, like daydreams, preconscious, such as cancelled plans, or subconscious, like proto-fantasies. A daydream is a flight from reality in the form of wishful thinking. During a daydream, we are aware that events in our thoughts are distinct from events in the material world.

Conscious and preconscious fantasies are formed under the influence of subconscious fantasies. We utilize previous experiences and knowledge in a process in which we may well activate long-term memory, retrieve "copies" of visual elements, such as dots, lines, areas, shapes, patterns, etc., to the perceptive and cognitive level, and test different combinations in new ways. We form new inner images. Thus, imagining the existence of fantasy animals composed of body parts and properties taken from a number of real creatures previously known to us is quite feasible. This type of imagery represents an abstract "inner reality" and needs to have nothing in common with ordinary, everyday "external reality."

Fantasy is creative, enabling us to experience new and meaningful totalities. The gift of fantasy varies considerably from one person to another. Some people claim to lack any fantasy at all, but no one is ever wholly without some fantasy. In children, the borderline between fantasy and reality may be very diffuse. A child may be completely convinced that s/he saw a real lion in a closet or a tiger strolling in the garden. Such a child is not consciously lying.

Authors sometimes claim to "see" their characters on some "inner screen" on which events are displayed. The Swedish detective story writer Gösta Unefäldt noted the following in an interview in the Dagens Nyheter newspaper (p. 33) on December 2, 1984 (in translation):

> When I'm sitting at my typewriter, it's like having a screen in front of me on which all the action unfolds. The characters do things, and I just describe their behavior.

Other authors, film, TV and theater directors, etc., have supplied similar descriptions of their creative work. Far too often the activities of creative people are thought to be motivated by pleasure and enjoyment only. Truly creative activity is extremely difficult work that often requires years of dedication and different struggle.

Fantasies can include not only visual but auditory, tactile, and other sensory experiences. Fantasy is a basic component in our culture. It can be expressed in numerous ways, i.e., in artistic, scientific, and practical creativity, games, illusions, daydreams, and (sleep) dreams. *Hallucinations* are an extreme form of fantasy.

Self-images

A *self-image* or *ego image* is the view a person has of her/himself on a particular occasion. This view usually differs in many respects from the view held by other people. A person may regard her/himself as rather fat (self-image), prefer being slim (target image) but actually have a normal build (objective image). *Self-confidence* is a measure of how positively we view ourselves.

Closely knit groups, such as a football team, a teenage gang, a religious sect, or a political extremist group, may strive to create a very considerable common identity. Common views and values, similar actions, clothing, uniforms, hairstyles, badges, symbols, etc., enhance the feeling of affiliation. Group members often acquire a definite "collective self-image." Companies, public agencies, and different kinds of clubs always have some kind of *collective self-image*. Employees, members, and supporters usually have a "we" outlook, i.e., some shared perception of the organization's identity.

Target images

A *target image* is the image a person forms about her/his future in life. Dreams, visions, hopes, or fears are decisive to a person's involvement in preparations for her/his future. Ingvar (1975) noted (p. 56) that our perception of the future is highly important to us (in translation):

> The memories we have, our experiences, the knowledge we acquire in life, are governed by the vision we have of the future.

A *positive target image* is the *ideal image* ("ego ideal") people form about themselves, their goals for personal development, i.e., things they would like to become and actively strive to achieve. For example, politicians often see themselves as victors in a future election. Many successful athletes see themselves as winners on top of the winner's stand. They repeatedly perform mental "dry runs" of a future contest/game, polishing their imagined performance each time. This kind of "mental training" may be as demanding and strenuous as real physical training.

REFERENCES AND SUGGESTED READINGS

Adams, J., & Chambers, R. (1962). Response to simultaneous stimulus of two sense modalities. *Journal of Experimental Psychology, 63,* 125–198.

Amen, E. W. (1941). Individual differences in apperceptive reaction: A study of the response of preschool children to pictures. *Genetic Psychology Monographs, 23,* 319–385.

Anderson, J. R. (1978). Arguments concerning representations for mental imagery. *Psychological Review, 85,* 249–277.

Anderson, J. R. (1983). *The Architecture of Cognition.* Cambridge: Harvard University Press.

Antes, J. R. (1974). The time course of picture viewing. *Journal of Experimental Psychology, 108,* 62–70.

Antes, J. R., & Penland, J. G. (1981). Picture context effects on eye movement patterns. In D. F. Fisher, R. A. Monty, & J. W. Senders (Eds.). *Eye Movements: Cognition and Visual Perception.* Hillsdale, NJ: Lawrence Erlbaum Associates.

Anzai, Y., & Yokoyama, T. (1984). Internal models in physics problem solving. *Cognition and Instruction, 1,* 397–450.

Arnheim, R. (1974). *Art and Visual Perception: A Psychology of the Creative Eye.* Berkeley, CA: University of California Press (rev. ed.).

Backman, J., Berg, T., & Sigurdson, T. (1988). *Grundskoleelevers produktion och reception av bilder.* Umeå: Umeå Universitet. Institutionen för bildlärarutbildning. Rapport nr 7.

Bagget, P. (1989). Mixing verbal, visual, motoric elements in instruction: What's good and what's not. In R. A. Braden, D. G. Beauchamp, L. V. W. Miller, & D. M. Moore (Eds.). *About Visuals: Research, Teaching, and Applications.* Readings from the 20th Annual Conference of the International Visual Literacy Association. Blacksburg: Virginia Tech University.

Baron, L. J. (1980). Interaction between television and child-related characteristics as demonstrated by eye movement research. *ECTJ, 28(4),* 267–281.

Barthes, R. (1977). The rhetoric of the image. In *Image, Music, Text, Essays.* Translated by S. Heath. London: Fontana.

Barufaldi, J. P., & Dietz, M. A. (1975). Effects of solid objects and two-dimensional representations of the objects on visual observation and comparison among urban children. *Journal of Research in Science Teaching, 12,* 127–132.

Bausell, R. B., & Jenkins, J. R. (1987). Effects on prose learning of frequency of adjunct cues and the difficulty of the material cued. *Journal of Reading Behavior, 9,* 227–232.

Bazeli, F. P., & Bazeli, P. T. (1992). Instructional implications of visual and verbal short-term memory capacity differences among children. In J. Clark-Baca, D. G. Beauchamp, & R. A. Braden (Eds.) *Visual Communication: Bridging Across Cultures.* Selected Readings from the 23rd Annual Conference of the International Visual Literacy Association. Blacksburg: Virginia Tech University.

Beitl, D. (1962). Das Bilderleben im frühen Kindesalter. *Jungenliteratur, 8,* 440–461.

Benson, P. J. (1985). Writing visually: Design considerations in technical publications. *Technical Communications Journal,* 35–39.

Bergström, S. S. (1974). *Varseblivningspsykologi.* In B. Allander, S. S. Bergström, & C. Frey. *Se men också höra.* Stockholm.

Berlyn, D. E. (1966). Curiosity and exploration. *Science, 153,* 25–33.

Bertoline, G. R., Burton, T. L., & Wiley, S. E. (1992). Technical graphics as a catalyst for developing visual literacy within general education. In J. Clark-Baca, D. G. Beauchamp, & R. A. Braden (Eds.). *Visual Communication: Bridging Across Cultures.* Selected Readings from the 23rd Annual Conference of the International Visual Literacy Association. Blacksburg: Virginia Tech University.

Biederman, I. (1981). On the semantics of a glance at a scene. In M. Kubovy & J. R. Pomerantz (Eds.). *Perceptual Organization.* Hillsdale, NJ: Lawrence Erlbaum Associates.

Blakeslee, T. R. (1980). *The Right Brain: A New Understanding of the Unconscious Mind and Its Creative Powers.* New York: Anchor Press: Doubleday.

Bloom, B. S., Englehart, M. D., Furst, E. J., Hill, W. H., & Krathwohl, D. R. (1956). *A Taxonomy of Educational Objectives. Handbook I: The Cognitive Domain.* New York: Longman.

Boeckman, K. (1987). *The sign structure of realistic images.* Paper presented at the IVLA Symposium Verbo-Visual Literacy: Research and Theory. Stockholm, June 10–13.

Bogert, J. (1989). Designing visuals to complement the message. In R. A. Braden, D. G. Beauchamp, L. V. W. Miller, & D. M. Moore (Eds.). *About Visuals: Research, Teaching, and Applications.* Readings from the 20th Annual Conference of the International Visual Literacy Association. Blacksburg: Virginia Tech University.

Brigthouse, G. (1939). A study of aesthetic apperception. *Psychological Monographs, 51,* 1–22.

Brody, P. (1982). Affecting instructional textbooks through pictures. In D. H. Jonassen (Ed.). *The Technology of Text.* Englewood Cliffs, NJ: Educational Technology Publications.

Buswell, G. T. (1925). *How People Look at Pictures.* Chicago: University of Chicago Press.

Buzan, T. (1977). *Make the Most of Your Mind.* London: Colt Books Ltd.

Case, R. (1974). Strictures and structures: Some functional limitations on the course of cognitive growth. *Cognitive Psychology, 14,* 287–302.

Case, R. (1975). Gearing the demands of instruction to the developmental capacities of the learner. *Review of Educational Research, 45(1),* 59–87.

Chi, M. T. H., Feltovich, P. J., & Glaser, R. (1981). Categorisation and representation of physics problems by experts and novices. *Cognitive Science, 5,* 121–151.

Christianson, S-Å. (1990). Vad minns vi av en fasansfull upplevelse? *Forskning och Framsteg, 1/90*, 14–19.

Cronholm, M., Rydin, I., & Schyller, I. (1979). *Samspel mellan TV och barns lek, moral och bildmognad.* Stockholm: SR, Publik-och programforskning Nr. 1–79.

Dessoir, M. (1913). Uber das Beschrieben von Bildern. *Zeitschrift für ästhetik, 1913, 8*, 440–461.

Drew, D. G., & Grimes, T. (1985). *The Effect of Audio-Visual Redundancy on Audio and Video Recall in Television News.* Paper presented at the annual meeting of the Association for Education in Journalism and Mass Communication (68th, Memphis, TN, August).

Dreyfuss, H. (1972). *Symbol Sourcebook.* New York: McGraw-Hill Book Company.

Dudley, S. E. (1987). Subliminal advertising: What is the controversy about? *Akron Business and Economic Review, 18*(2), 6–18.

Duffy, B. (Ed.) (1983). *One of a Kind. A Practical Guide to Learning Styles 7–12.* Oklahoma State Department of Education.

Dwyer, F. M. (1971). Color as an instructional variable. *AV Communication Review, 19*, 399–413.

Dwyer, F. M. (1978). *Strategies for Improving Visual Learning.* State College, PA: Learning Services.

Dwyer, F. M. (1982–83). The program of systematic evaluation—a brief review. *International Journal of Instructional Media, 10*, 23–39.

Edwards, D. C., & Coolkasian, A. (1974). Peripheral vision location and kinds of complex processing. *Journal of Experimental Psychology, 102*, 244–249.

Ekwall, E. (1977). *Diagnosis and Remediation of the Disabled Reader.* Boston: Allyn and Bacon.

Elkind, D. (1975). We can teach reading better. *Today's Education, 64*, 34–38.

Elkind, D., Koegler, R., & Go, E. (1964). Studies in perceptual development II: Part-whole perception. *Child Development, 35*, 81–90.

Eysenck, H. J. (1941). A critical and experimental study of color preferences. *American Journal of Psychology, 54*, 385–394.

Faw, T. T., & Nunnaly, J. C. (1967). The effect on eye movements of complexity, novelty, and affective tone. *Perception and Psychophysics, 2*, 263–267.

Faw, T. T., & Nunnaly, J. C. (1968). The influence of stimulus complexity, novelty, and affective value on children's visual fixation. *Journal of Experimental Child Psychology, 6*, 141–153.

Fleming, M. (1969). Eye movement indicies of cognitive behavior. *AV Communication Review, 17*, 383–398.

Fleming, M., & Levie, W. H. (1978). *Instructional Message Design.* Englewood Cliffs, NJ: Educational Technology Publications.

Fleming, M., & Levie, W. H. (Eds.) (1993). *Instructional Message Design* (2nd ed.). Englewood Cliffs, NJ: Educational Technology Publications.

Gagné, R. W., & Briggs, L. J. (1974). *Principles of Instructional Design.* New York: Holt, Rinehart, and Winston.

Gardner, H. (1983). *Frames of Mind: The Theory of Multiple Intelligence.* New York: Basic Books.

Gazzaniga, M. (1967). The split brain in man. *Scientific American, 217*, 24–29.

Gazzaniga, M. S., & Le Doux, J. (1978). *The Integrated Mind.* New York: Plenum Press.

Geisser, M. J. (1992). Logical reasoning: Without pictures ... not without words. In J. Clark-Baca, D. G. Beauchamp, & R. A. Braden (Eds.) *Visual Communication: Bridging Across Cultures.* Selected Readings from the 23rd Annual Conference of the International Visual Literacy Association. Blacksburg: Virginia Tech University.

Gibson, E. J. (1969). *Principles of Perceptual Learning and Development.* New York: Meredith Corp.

Gibson, J. J. (1950). *The Perception of the Visual World.* Boston: Houghton Mifflin.

Gibson, J. J. (1966). *The Senses Considered as Perceptual Systems.* Boston: Houghton Mifflin.

Gibson, J. J. (1971). The information available in pictures. *Leonardo, 4,* 27–35.

Glynn, S. M., Britton, B. K., & Tillman, M. H. (1985). Typographic cues in text: Management of the reader's attention. In D. H. Jonassen (Ed.). *The Technology of Text: Principles for Structuring, Designing, and Displaying Text. Volume 2.* Englewood Cliffs, NJ: Educational Technology Publications.

Goldsmith, E. (1987). The analysis of illustration in theory and practice. In H. A. Houghton & D. M. Willows (Eds.). *The Psychology of Illustrations. Vol. 2. Instructional issues.* New York: Springer-Verlag.

Gombrich, E. H. (1969). *Art and Illusion: A Study in the Psychology of Pictorial Representation.* Princeton, NJ: Princeton University Press.

Goodman, N. (1976). *Languages of Art: An Approach to a Theory of Symbols (2nd ed.).* Indianapolis, IN: Hacket Publishing .

Gould, J. (1967). Pattern recognition and eye movement parameters. *Perception and Psychophysics, 2,* 399–407.

Gould, J. (1973). Eye movement during visual search and memory search. *Journal of Experimental Psychology, 98,* 184–195.

Gregory, R. L. (1978). *Eye and Brain (3rd ed.).* New York: McGraw-Hill.

Griffin, R. E., & Gibbs, W. J. (1992). *International Icon Symbols: How Well Are Macro Symbols Understood?* Presentation at the 24th Annual Conference of the International Visual Literacy Association, Pittsburgh, Sept. 30–Oct. 4.

Guba, W., Wolf, W., deGroot, S., Knemeyer, M., Van Atta, R., & Light, L. (1964). Eye movements and TV viewing in children. *AV Communication Review, 12,* 381–401.

Haber, R. N. (1979). How we remember what we see. *Scientific American, 222,* 104–115.

Haber, R. N., & Erdelyi, M. H. (1967). Emergence and recovery of initially unavailable perceptual material. *Journal of Verbal Learning and Verbal Behavior, 6,* 618–628.

Haber, R. N., & Myers, B. L. (1982). Memory for pictograms, pictures, and words separately and all mixed. *Perception, 11,* 57–64

Hadamard, J. (1945). *The Psychology of Invention in the Mathematical Field.* New York: Dover Publications.

Hannafin, M. J., & Hooper, S. R. (1993). Learning principles. In M. Fleming & W. H. Levie (Eds.). *Instructional Message Design: Principles from the Behavioral and Cognitive Sciences* (2nd ed.). Englewood Cliffs, NJ: Educational Technology Publications.

Hanson, J. R. (1988). Learning styles, visual literacies, and a framework for reading instruction. *Reading Psychology: An International Quarterly, 9,* 409–430.

Hartley, J. (1987). Designing electronic text: The role of print-based research. *Educational Communications and Technology Journal, 35,* 3–17.

Hartley, J., Bartlett, S., & Branthwaite, A. (1980). Underlining can make a difference— sometimes. *Journal of Educational Research, 73,* 218–223.

Haubold, M. (1933). *Bildbetrachtung durch Kinder und Jugendliche.* München.

Hayes, D. S., & Birnbaum, D. W. (1980). Preschoolers' retention of televised events: Is a picture worth a thousand words? *Development Psychology, 16, 5,* 410–416

Hellspong, L., Melin, L., Pettersson, R., & Propper, G. (1987). *Intended and Perceived Content in Informative Materials.* Paper presented at the IVLA Symposium Verbo-Visual Literacy: Research and Theory. Stockholm, June 10–13.

Hinkel, H. (1972). *Wie betrachten Kinder Bilder?* Steinbach-Giessen.

Hochberg, J., & Brooks, V. (1978). Film cutting and visual momentum. In J. Senders, D. Fisher, & T. Monty (Eds.). *Eye Movements and the Higher Psychological Functions.* Hillsdale, NJ: Lawrence Erlbaum Associates.

Hubel, D. H., & Wiesel, T. N. (1962). Receptive fields, binocular interaction, and functional architecture in the cat's visual cortex. *Journal of Physiology, 160,* 106–154.

Ibison, R. A. (1952). *Differential Effects on the Recall of Textual Materials Associated with the Inclusion of Colored and Uncolored Illustrations*. Unpublished doctoral dissertation. Indiana University, Bloomington.

Illustratörcentrum. (1990). 57 illustrationer till en novell av Niklas Rådström. *Svart på Vitt, 1.*

Ingvar, D. (1975). *Att minnas-att komma i 'håg'*. I David H. Ingvar (Red.). *Att minnas. Aspekter på minne och glömska*. Stockholm: Bonniers, 37–57.

Isaacs, G. (1987). Text screen design for computer-assisted learning. *British Journal of Educational Technology, 18,* 41–51.

Itten, J. (1971). Färg och färgupplevelse. Stockholm: Norstedt.

Jackson, D. N., Messick, S., & Myers, C. T. (1964). Evaluation of group and individual forms of embedded figures measures of field independence. *Educational and Psychological Measurement, 24* (2), 177–192.

Jonassen, D. H. (1982). *The Technology of Text: Principles for Structuring, Designing, and Displaying Text. Volume 1.* Englewood Cliffs, NJ: Educational Technology Publications.

Judson, H. (1972). *The Techniques of Reading* (3rd ed.). New York: Harcourt, Brace, Jovanovich.

Jung, C. G. (1964). *Man and His Symbols*. New York: Dell.

Jung, C. G. (1965). *Memories, Dreams, and Reflections*. New York: Vintage Books.

Jung, C. G. (1971). *Psychological Types*. Princeton, NJ: Princeton University Press.

Katz, E., Blumler, J. G., & Gurevitch, M. (1974). Utilization of mass communication by the individual. In J. G. Blumler & E. Katz (Eds.). *The Uses of Mass Communications: Current Perspectives on Gratifications Research*. Beverly Hills: Sage.

Katzman, N., & Nyenhuis, J. (1972). Color vs. black-and-white: Effects on learning, opinion, and attention. *AV Communication Review*, Spring, 16–28.

Keates, J. S. (1982). *Understanding Maps*. London and New York: Longman.

Keller, J., & Burkman, E. (1993). Motivation principles. In M. Fleming & W. H. Levie (Eds.). *Instructional Message Design: Principles from the Behavioral and Cognitive Sciences* (2nd ed.). Englewood Cliffs, NJ: Educational Technology Publications.

Kintsch, W. (1974). *The Representation of Meaning in Memory*. Hillsdale, NJ: Lawrence Erlbaum Associates.

Kosbiech, K. (1976). The importance of perceived task and type of presentation in student response to instructional television. *AV Communication Review, 24,* 401–411.

Kossllyn, S. M. (1975). Information representation in visual images. *Cognitive Psychology, 7,* 341–370

Kotovsky, K., Hayes, J. R., & Simon, H. A. (1985). Why are some problems hard? Some evidence from Tower of Hanoi. *Cognitive Psychology, 17,* 248–294.

Krugman, H. (1965). The impact of television advertising: Learning without involvement. *Public Opinion Quarterly,* 349–356.

Krugman, H. (1966). The measurement of advertising involvement. *Public Opinion Quarterly,* 583–596.

Krugman, H. (1967). Brain wave measures of media involvement. *Journal of Advertising Research,* p. 11.

Krugman, H. (1977). Memory without recall, exposure without perception. *Journal of Advertising Research, 17,* 7–12

Lam, C. (1966). Pupil preference for four art styles used in primary reading textbooks. *Grade Teacher, 37,* 877–885.

Lamberski, R. J. (1972). *An Exploratory Investigation of the Instructional Effect of Color and Black and White Cueing on Immediate and Delayed Retention*. Master's Thesis, The Pennsylvania State University.

Larkin, J. H. (1983). The role of problem representation in physics. In D. Gentner & A. L. Stevens (Eds.). *Mental Models*. Hillsdale, NJ: Lawrence Erlbaum Associates.

Lassen, N., Ingvar, D., & Skinhöj, E. (1978). Brain function and blood flow. *Scientific American, 239,* 62–72.

Lawson, L. (1968). Ophthalmological factors in learning disabilities. In H. Myklebust (Ed.). *Progress in Learning Disabilities (Vol. 1)*. New York: Grune and Stratton.

Leckhart, B. T. (1966). Looking time: The effects of stimulus complexity and familiarity. *Perception and Psychophysics, 1*, 142–144.

Lenze, J. S. (1990). Serif vs. san serif type fonts: A comparison based on reader comprehension. In D. G. Beauchamp, J. Clark-Baca, & R. A. Braden (Eds.). *Investigating Visual Literacy*. Selected Readings from the 22nd Annual Conference of the International Visual Literacy Association. Blacksburg: Virginia Tech University.

Lesgold, A., Rubinson, H., Feltovich, P., Glaser, R., Klopfer, D., & Wang, Y. (1988). Expertise in a complex skill: Diagnosing x-ray pictures. In M. T. H. Chi, R. Glaser, & M. J. Farr (Eds.). *The Nature of Expertise*. Hillsdale, NJ: Lawrence Erlbaum Associates.

Levie, W. H. (1987). Research on pictures: A guide to the literature. In D. M. Willows & H. A. Houghton (Eds.). *The Psychology of Illustration: Vol. 1. Basic Research*. New York: Springer-Verlag.

Levie, W. H., & Lentz, R. (1982). Effects of text illustrations: A review of research. *ECTJ, 30*, 195–232.

Levin, J. R., Anglin, G. J., & Carney, R. N. (1987). On empirically validating functions of pictures in prose. In D. M. Willows & H. A. Houghton (Eds.). *The Psychology of Illustration: Vol. 1. Basic Research*. New York: Springer-Verlag.

Levin, J. R., & Lesgold, A. M. (1978). On pictures in prose. *ECTJ, 26*, 233–243.

Lidman, S., & Lund, A-M. (1972). *Berätta med bilder*. Stockholm: Bonniers.

Limburg, V. E. (1987). *Visual "Intrusion": A Two-Way Street in Visual Literacy*. Paper presented at the IVLA Symposium on Verbo-Visual Literacy: Research and Theory. Stockholm, June 10–13.

Lindsten, C. (1975). *Hembygdskunskap i årskurs 3, Att inhämta, bearbeta och redovisa kunskaper*. Lund: Liber Läromedel.

Lindsten, C. (1976). *Aktiviteter i hembygdskunskap: Elevpreferenser i årskurs 3. En faktoranalystisk studie. (Activities in Science and Social Studies: Pupils Preferences in Grade 3. A Factorial Study.)* Pedagogisk-psykologiska problem (Malmö, Sweden: School of Education), Nr. 310.

Lindsten, C. (1977). *Bilder i hembygdsboken: Elevpreferenser i årskurs 3. En faktoranalystisk studie. (Pictures in the Science and Social Studies Book. Pupil Preferences in Grade 3. Factorial Studies.)* Pedagogisk-psykologiska problem (Malmö, Sweden: School of Education), Nr. 312.

Locatis, C. N., & Atkinson, F. D. (1984). *Media and Technology for Education and Training*. Columbus, OH: Charles E. Merrill Publishing Company.

Lodding, K. (1983). Iconic interfacing. *Computer Graphics and Applications, 3(2)*, 11–20.

Loftus, G. R. (1972). Eye fixations and recognition memory for pictures. *Cognitive Psychology, 3*, 521–551.

Loftus, G. R. (1976). A framework for theory of picture recognition. In R. A. Monty & J. W. Senders (Eds.). *Eye Movements and Psychological Processes*. New York: John Wiley.

Loftus, G. R. (1979). On-line eye movement recorders: The good, the bad, and the ugly. *Behavior Research Methods & Instrumentation, 11*, 188–191.

Loftus, G. R., Shimamura, A., & Johnson, C. A. (1985). How much is an icon worth? *Journal of Experimental Psychology: Human Perception and Performance, 11*, 1–13.

Lowe, R. K. (1992). *Scientists' and Non-scientists' Mental Representation of Scientific Diagrams*. Ph.D. Thesis. Murdoch University. Perth, Western Australia.

Lucas, F. D. (1977). Fifth-grade children's preferences for illustrations in middle grade basal reading materials. *Dissertation Abstracts, 38*, 3270–3271.

MacBeth, D. R. (1974). *Classificational Preference in Young Children: Form or Color*. Chicago: National Association for Research in Science Teaching. (ERIC Document Reproduction Service No. ED 092 362).

Mackworth, N. H., & Bruner, J. S. (1970). How adults and children search and recognize pictures. *Human Development, 13,* 149–177.

Mackworth, N. H., & Morandi, A. J. (1967). The gaze selects informative details within pictures. *Perception and Psychophysics, 2,* 547–552.

MacLean, W. (1930). A comparison of coloured and uncoloured pictures. *Educational Screen, 9,* 196–199.

Matsushita, K. (1988). *A summary version of the Comprehensive Report on Hi-OVIS PROJECT Jul.'78–Mar.'86.* Tokyo: New Media Development .

Mayer, R. (1969). *A Dictionary of Art Terms and Techniques.* New York: Crowell.

McKim, R. H. (1980). *Thinking Visually: A Strategy Manual for Problem Solving.* Belmont, CA: Lifetime Learning Publications.

Messick, S. (1970). The criterion problem in the evaluation of instruction: Assessing possible, not just probable, intended outcomes. In M. C. Wittrock & D. E. Wiley (Eds.). *The Evaluation of Instruction: Issues and Problems.* New York: Holt.

Miller, G. A. (1956). The magical number seven, plus or minus two: Some limits on our capacity for processing information. *Psychological Review, 63, 2,* 81–97.

Modreski, R. A., & Gross, A. E. (1972). Young children's names for matches to form-color stimuli. *Journal of Genetic Psychology, 121, 2,* 283–293.

Moore, J. F., & Moore, D. M. (1984). Subliminal perception and cognitive style in a learning task taught via television. *British Journal of Educational Technology, 15,* 3, 22–31.

Moray, N. (1970). *Attention.* New York: Academic Press.

Muffoletto, R. (1987). *Critical Viewing-Critical Thinking: Reading the Visual Text.* Paper presented at the IVLA Symposium on Verbo-Visual Literacy: Research and Theory. Stockholm, June 10–13.

Myatt, B., & Carter, J. (1979). Picture preferences of children and young adults. *ECTJ, 27,* 45–53.

Navon, D. (1977). Forest before trees: The precedence of global features in visual perception. *Cognitive Psychology, 9,* 353–383.

Nelson, W. W., & Loftus, G. R. (1980). The functional visual field during picture viewing. *Journal of Experimental Psychology: Human Learning and Memory, 6,* 391–399

Nesbit, L. L. (1981). Relationship between eye movement, learning, and picture complexity. *ECTJ, 29(2),* 109–116.

Nickerson, R. S. (1965). Short-term memory for complex meaningful visual configurations: A demonstration of capacity. *Canadian Journal of Psychology, 19,* 155–160.

Noble, G. (1975). *Children in Front of the Small Screen.* Beverly Hills, California: Sage.

Norman, D. A., Rumelhart, D. E., & LNR Research Group. (1975). *Explorations in Cognition.* San Francisco: Freeman.

Noton, D., & Stark, L. (1971a). Scanpaths in eye movements during pattern perception. *Science, 171,* 308–311.

Noton, D., & Stark, L. (1971b). Eye movements and visual perception. *Scientific American, 225,* 34–43.

Nugent, G. C. (1982). Pictures, audio, and print: Symbolic representation and effect on learning. *ECTJ, 30 (3),* 163–174.

Otto, W., & Askov, E. (1968). The role of color in learning and instruction. *Journal of Special Education, 2,* 155–165.

Paivio, A. (1971). *Imagery and the Verbal Process.* New York: Holt, Rinehart, & Winston.

Paivio, A. (1978). A dual coding approach to perception and cognition. In H. L. Pick, Jr. & E. Saltzman (Eds.). *Modes of Perceiving and Processing Information.* Hillsdale, NJ: Lawrence Erlbaum Associates.

Paivio, A. (1979). *Imagery and Verbal Processes.* Hillsdale, NJ: Lawrence Erlbaum Associates.

Paivio, A. (1983). The empirical case for dual coding. In J. C. Yuille (Ed.). *Imagery, Memory, and Cognition.* Hillsdale, NJ: Lawrence Erlbaum Associates.

Pascual-Leone, J., & Smith, J. (1969). The encoding and decoding of symbols by children: A new experimental paradigm and a neo-Piagetian model. *Journal of Experimental Child Psychology, 8,* 328–355.

Perfetti, C. (1977). Language comprehension and fast decoding: Some psycholinguistic prerequisites for skilled reading comprehension. In J. Guthrie (Ed.). *Cognition, Curriculum, and Comprehension.* Newark, DE: International Reading Association.

Pettersson, R. (1979). *Bildkreativitet, en pilotstudie.* Stockholm.

Pettersson, R. (1982). Cultural differences in the perception of image and color in pictures. *ECTJ, 30(1),* 43–53.

Pettersson, R. (1983a). Factors in visual language: Image framing. *Visual Literacy Newsletter,* 9 and 10.

Pettersson, R. (1983b). *Picture readability.* Rapport till VI:e Nordiska konferensen för Masskommunikationsforskning, Volda, 1983.

Pettersson, R. (1984). Picture legibility, readability, and reading value. In A. D. Walker, R. A. Braden, & L. H. Dunker (Eds.). *Enhancing Human Potential.* Readings from the 15th Annual Conference of the International Visual Literacy Association. Blacksburg: Virginia Tech University.

Pettersson, R. (1985). Intended and perceived image content. Presentation at the 17th Annual Conference of the International Visual Literacy Association. In L. W. Miller (Ed.). *Creating Meaning.* Readings from the Visual Literacy Conference at California State Polytechnic University at Pomona.

Pettersson, R. (1986a). Picture Archives. *EP Journal.* June 2–3.

Pettersson, R. (1986b). Image–word–image. Presentation at the 18th Annual Conference of the International Visual Literacy Association. Madison, Wisconsin, Oct. 30–Nov. 2. In R. A. Braden, D. G. Beauchamp, & L. W. Miller (Eds.). (1987). *Visible & Viable: The Role of Images in Instruction and Communication.* Readings from the 18th Annual Conference of the International Visual Literacy Association. Commerce: East Texas State University.

Pettersson, R. (1986c). See, look, and read. *Journal of Visual Verbal Languaging.* Spring, 33–39.

Pettersson, R. (1986d). Properties of pixels. *EP Journal.* December 2–4.

Pettersson, R. (1987). *Linguistic Combinations.* Paper presented at the IVLA Symposium on Verbo-Visual Literacy: Research and Theory. Stockholm, June 10–13.

Pettersson, R. (1989). *Visuals for Information: Research, and Practice.* Englewood Cliffs, NJ: Educational Technology Publications.

Pettersson, R. (1990) Teachers, Students, and Visuals. *JVL, 10.*

Pettersson, R. (1991). Describing picture context. Presentation at the 23rd Annual Conference of the International Visual Literacy Association. Washington, Oct. 9–13. In J. Clark-Baca, D. G. Beauchamp, & R. A. Braden (Eds.). *Visual Communication: Bridging Across Cultures.* Selected Readings from the 23rd Annual Conference of the International Visual Literacy Association. Blacksburg: Virginia Tech University.

Pezdek, K., & Hartmann, E. (1983). Children's television viewing: attention and comprehension of auditory versus visual information. *Child Development, 51,* 720–729.

Pezdek, K., & Stevens, E. (1984). Children's memory for auditory and visual information on television. *Developmental Psychology, 20(1),* 212–218.

Piaget, J. (1968). *Barnets själsliga utveckling.* Stockholm:Liber.

Pirozzolo, F., & Rayner, K. (1979). Cerebral organization and reading disability. *Neuropsychologia, 17,* 485–491.

Potter, M. C., & Levy, E. I. (1969). Recognition memory for a rapid sequence of pictures. *Journal of Experimental Psychology, 81,* 10–15.

Prawitz, M. (1977). Varför förstår du inte vad jag säger, när jag hoppar, skuttar och målar? In G. Berefelt (Ed.). *Barn och bild.* Stockholm: AWE/Gebers.

Pressley, M., & Miller, G. E. (1987). Effects of illustrations on children's listening comprehension and oral prose memory. In D. M. Willows & H. A. Houghton (Eds.). *The Psychology of Illustrations. Vol. 1.* New York: Springer-Verlag.

Printzmetal, W., & Banks, W. P. (1977). Good continuation affects visual detection. *Perception and Psychophysics, 21,* 389–395.

Pylyshyn, Z. W. (1973). What the mind's eye tells the mind's brain: A critique of mental imagery. *Psychological Bulletin, 80,* 1–24.

Pylyshyn, Z. W. (1979). Imagery theory: Not mysterious—just wrong. *Behavioral and Brain Sciences, 2,* 561–563.

Ramsey, I. L. (1982). The influence of styles, text content, sex, and grade level on children's picture preferences. *The Journal of Educational Research, 75,* 237–240.

Ramsey, I. L. (1989). Primary children's ability to distinguish between illustrative styles. *JVL, 9(2),* 69–82.

Reynolds-Myers, P. (1985). Visual literacy, higher order reasoning, and high technology. In N. H. Thayer & S. Clayton-Randolph (Eds.). *Visual Literacy: Cruising into the Future.* Readings from the 16th annual conference of the International Visual Literacy Association. Bloomington: Western Sun Printing Co.

Rolandelli, D. R., Wright, J. C., & Huston, A. C. (1985). *Children's Auditory and Visual Processing of Narrated and Non-narrated Television Programming.* Paper presented at the Annual Meeting of the International Communication Association.

Romiszowski, A. J. (1993). Psychomotor principles. In M. Fleming & W. H. Levie (Eds.). *Instructional Message Design: Principles from the Behavioral and Cognitive Sciences.* Englewood Cliffs, NJ: Educational Technology Publications.

Rudisill, M. (1952). Children's preference of color versus other qualities in illustrations. *Elementary School Journal, 52,* 444–451

Salomon, G. (1979). *Interaction of Media, Cognition, and Learning.* San Francisco: Jossey-Bass.

Salomon, G. (1984). Television is "easy" and print is "tough": The differential investment of mental effort in learning as a function of perceptions and attributions. *Journal of Educational Psychology, 76,* 647–658.

Schallert, D. L. (1980). The role of illustrations in reading comprehension. In R. J. Spiro, B. C. Bruce, & W. F. Brewer (Eds.). *Theoretical Issues in Reading Comprehension: Perspectives from Cognitive Psychology, Linguistics, Artificial Intelligence, and Education.* Hillsdale, NJ: Lawrence Erlbaum Associates.

Segall, M. H., Cambell, D. T., & Herskovits, M. J. (1966). *The Influence of Culture on Visual Perception, an Advanced Study in Psychology and Anthropology.* Indianapolis: Bobbs-Merrill.

Shepard, R. N. (1967). Recognition memory for words, sentences, and pictures. *Journal of Verbal Learning and Verbal Behavior, 6,* 156–163.

Sinatra, R. (1986). *Visual Literacy Connections to Thinking, Reading, and Writing.* Springfield, IL: Charles C. Thomas.

Sloan, M. (1971). *Picture Preferences of Elementary School Children and Teachers.* Ann Arbor, MI: University Microfilms.

Smerdon, G. (1976). Children's preferences in illustration. *Children's Literature in Education, 20,* 17–31.

Snodgrass, J. G., & Vanderwart, M. (1980). A standardized set of 260 pictures: Norms for name agreement, image agreement, familiarity, and visual complexity. *Journal of Experimental Psychology: Human Learning and Memory, 6/2,* 174–215.

Spangenberg, R. (1976). Which is better for learning? Color or black and white? *Audio Visual Instruction, 21(3),* 80.

Sperry, R. W. (1973). Lateral specialization of cerebral function in the surgically separated hemispheres. In F. J. McGuigan & R. A. Schoonever (Eds.). *The Psychophysiology of Thinking.* New York: Academic Press.

Sperry, R. W. (1981). Changing priorities. *Ann. Rev. Neuroscience, 4,* 1–15.

Sperry, R. W. (1982). Some effects of disconnecting the hemisphere. *Science, 217*, 1223–1226.

Standing, L. (1973). Learning 10,000 pictures. *Quarterly Journal of Experimental Psychology, 25*, 207–222

Standing, L., Conezio, J., & Haber, R. N. (1970). Perception and memory for pictures: Single-trial learning of 2500 visual stimuli. *Psychonomic Science, 19 , 99*, 73–74.

Sutton, R. (1990). *Subliminal Reception and Visual Literacy.* Paper presented at the IVLA Symposium on Verbo-Visual Literacy: Mapping the Field. London, July 10–13.

Thurstone, L. L. (1937). *Psychological Tests for a Study of Mental Abilities.* Chicago, IL: University of Chicago Press.

Tidhar, C. E. (1987). *Verbo/Visual and Print Interactions in Television Presentations: Effects on Comprehension Among Hearing and Hearing-Impaired Children.* Paper presented at the IVLA Symposium on Verbo-Visual Literacy: Research and Theory. Stockholm, June 10–13.

Tröger, W. (1963). *Der Film und die Antwort der Erziehung.* München: Basel Reinhardt.

Vogel, D. R., Dickson, G. W., & Lehman, J. A. (1986). Driving the audience action response. *Computer Graphics World,* August.

Voss, J. F., Greene, T. R., Post, T. A., & Penner, B. C. (1983). Problem solving in the social sciences. In G. Bower (Ed.). *Psychology of Learning and Motivation.* New York: Academic Press.

Waller, R. (1987). *The Typographic Contribution to Language: Towards a Model of Typographic Genres and Their Underlying Structures.* University of Reading, Department of Typography & Graphic Communication.

Ward, W. C., & Naus, M. J. (1973). *The Encoding of Pictorial Information in Children and Adults.* Princeton, New Jersey: Educational Testing Service. (ERIC Document Reproduction Service No. ED 085 073).

Webb, W. W., Matheny, A., & Larson, G. (1963). Eye movements and a paradigm of approach and avoidance behavior. *Perceptual and Motor Skills, 16*, 341–347.

Weidenmann, B. (1988). Der flüchtige Blick beim stehenden Bild: Zur oberflächlichen Verarbeitung von pädagogishen Illustrationen. (The Careless View in the Case of Standing Picture.) *Zeitschrift für Lernforschung, 16, 3*, 43–57.

Weidenmann, B. (1989). When good pictures fail: An information-processing approach to the effect of illustrations. In H. Mandl & J. R. Levin (Eds.). *Knowledge Acquisition from Text and Pictures.* Amsterdam: Elsevier.

Wender, K. F. (1989). Mental models for spatial knowledge. In A. F. Bennet & K. M. McConkey (Eds.). *Cognition in Individual and Social Contexts.* Amsterdam: Elsevier.

White, J. (1987). *New Strategies for Editing and Design.* Presentation at Trialog 87, Stockholm.

Wilson, D. A., Reeves, A., & Gazzaniga, M. S. (1982). "Central" commisurotomy for intractable generalized epilepsy: Series two. *Neurology, 32*, 687–697.

Witkin, H. A., Dyk, R. B., Faterson, H. F., Goodenough, D. R., & Karp, S. A. (1962). *Psychological Differentiation.* New York: John Wiley.

Wolf, W. (1970). *A Study of Eye Movement in Television Viewing. Final Report.* Columbus: Ohio State University. (ERIC Reproduction Service No. ED 046 254).

Yarbus, A. (1967). *Eye Movements and Vision.* New York: Plenum Press.

Zuckerman, M., Zeigler, M., & Stevenson, H. V. (1978). Children's viewing of television and recognition of commercials. *Child Development, 49*, 96–104.

Zusne, L., & Michaels, K. (1964). Nonrepresentional shapes and eye movements. *Perceptual and Motor Skills, 18*, 11–20.

Chapter 3

LITERACY AND VISUAL LANGUAGE

There are many different kinds of languages. In this chapter special attention is paid to characteristics of visual language. Its functions, levels of meaning, properties, and structure are discussed.

Combinations of different kinds of languages are used in mass communication. Yet little is known about the effects of various linguistic combinations. Some linguistic designations are suggested. Different verbo-visual representations are presented.

It is concluded that different linguistic combinations must be studied in detail before optimum combinations can be found for various purposes, such as education, information, and entertainment.

LANGUAGE

According to Skinner (1957), language is a *behavior which is learned by habit.* Children imitate adults until they learn the language spoken by them. On the other hand, Eriksson (1986) cites Chomsky (1959) who argued that language is not "a set of habits." Instead, the development of language is a continuous and creative process working in concert with the surrounding. The brain develops *verbal proficiency* making it possible for Man to formulate and understand an infinite number of sentences. This view has been supported by the findings of a number of scientists after Chomsky (e.g., Slobin, 1973; Littlewood, 1984).

According to semiotics, all cultural processes may be seen as communication processes (Eco, 1971). Thus, there are different languages, such as spoken, written, and visual languages. Lotman (1973) suggested that any system used as a means of communications between people can be regarded as a language. Cochran (1987) concludes that humans cannot transfer ideas whole and intact from one person to another. Human communication depends upon an interactive series of successive approximations presented in metaphors. She finds "languaging" useful in directing attention to the actions of people as they share their own ideas, listen to others, or learn from technologically produced sights and sounds. There are many approaches to language and language classification systems. Twyman (1982) pointed out that while linguistic scientists distinguish between spoken and written language, graphic designers distinguish between verbal and pictorial language. From a design point of view, written, printed, or displayed texts or *verbal graphic language* are important components of visible language. Examples of poor design which hinder the comprehension of text contents are far too commonplace.

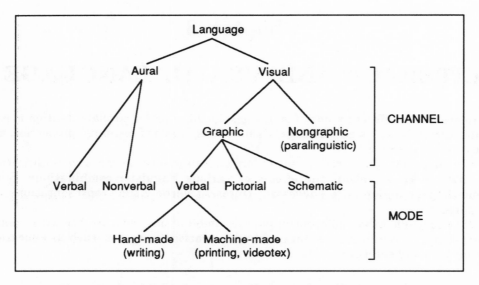

Twyman's (1982) language model devised to accommodate the approaches to language of linguistic scientists and graphic designers. Reproduced by permission of the author.

However, if the linguistic representation (e.g., the medium and its content) is placed at the forefront, another approach is natural. In this model, linguistic differentiation is based on the form of the messages: words, sounds, images, and other forms. Thus, *verbal language* has spoken (aural), written (visual), and tactile categories; *audial language* comprises sound effects, music, and paralinguistic sounds (all aural); *visual language* has symbols, pictures, and paralinguistic visual expressions (all visual); and *other language* is based on smell, taste, touch, etc. This latter approach is used in this book.

Languages differ in their ability to express concepts with precision and flexibility. Physics, chemistry, and mathematics, for example, employ *non-ambiguous* symbol and equation languages. In verbal and technical descriptions, the language of specialists must be as unambiguous as possible. Languages such as these can only be understood by people with the appropriate specialized knowledge. Normal prose is often open to multiple interpretations, i.e., it is *ambiguous*. Fiction and poetry in particular offer abundant opportunities for individual interpretations. Pictures are normally ambiguous too.

In the animal world various body signals supply most of the communications between individuals. Animals send messages by displaying parts of their bodies in various ways. Message receivers "respond" with equivalent displays or movements.

Bees have developed an advanced "language." After returning to the hive, a bee can perform a dance informing other bees about, e.g., the location of a source of food.

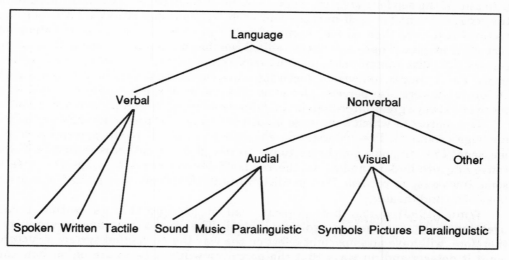

Language model based on the form of representation. The model can be broken down into additional sub-categories.

Body language and paralinguistic and extralinguistic signals are also important in Man. Some scientists suggest that body language accounts for up to half, or more, of all our communications with others. By the time we are adults we are all highly sensitive to the tiniest changes in expression, gesture, posture, and bodily adornment of our companions. We acquire this sensitivity through intuition rather than analysis. If we took the trouble to make a more analytical study of body appearances, we could become even more sensitized to them, and could avoid some of the pitfalls into which our intuition sometimes leads us (Morris, 1985).

Many movements and gestures can be interpreted without ambiguity in a given cultural community but not outside that community. In some societies, for example, the raising of an eyebrow, consciously *or* unconsciously, designates surprise. Or shrugging the shoulders designates indifference. But confusion and misunderstandings can occur before visitors to foreign cultures learn to understand the body language prevailing there.

Our body language is partly instinctive, partly learned and imitative (e.g., Fast, 1971). An interesting fact is that bilingual persons change their body language, gestures, and eyelid movements when they switch (spoken) languages.

Brun (1974) gives many examples of sign languages. We can see examples of "formal" signs almost every day. Deaf people are often very skilled in using their highly developed and structured visual verbal sign language. Other less sophisticated kinds of sign languages are used by, e.g., umpires in sporting events, traffic policemen, people directing airplanes on the ground, etc. Further examples are the sign languages used in making radio and television programs or movies.

Thousands of alternatives are available to a sender wishing to transmit a rendition of some reality to receivers. Senders always utilize a "filter" and quality checks before selecting one of the many available text and picture options. The choice is based on the sender's *subjective opinions*. She/he selects the option believed to be the most efficient for each purpose and each transmission situation. The selected pictures/texts are then edited in one of many ways for the purpose of enhancing reception impact. Thus, a selected, edited version of reality is transmitted to receivers. In mass communications, message reception can be affected in countless ways. For example, television reception may range from very bad to very good. Different viewers also perceive the same text and/or image in different ways, since there are always great inter-individual differences in perception (Pettersson, 1986b).

The context in which a message is seen can convey a "pre-understanding" of the message's contents. Pre-understanding is vitally important to our perception of any message. The language we choose to use in any given situation is in itself a device conveying pre-understanding to the reader/listener/viewer. Message response is sometimes easy to predict. This predictability is often heavily exploited in movies, television, and theater.

Winn (1993) notes that a great deal of perceptual organization occurs preattentively, not under cognitive control. The way a message is organized, therefore, will have an important effect on the way the perceptual system structures what it detects and, in ways that the perceiver will not be aware of, on how that information is interpreted.

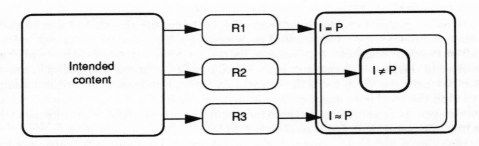

A large number of different representations, texts, and/or pictures are always possible. The representations convey identical (R1), acceptable (R3), or discrepant (R2) perceptions (P) of the intended content.

There is no unambiguous verbal or visual language. In a closed, homogeneous cultural group, "ordinary" pictures and texts probably give rise to similar interpretations and perceptions of a specific reality, single object, event, message, or content. However, we do not know the magnitude of the individual "tolerance ranges" in which different texts and pictures generate *reasonably identical perceptions*. One representation may produce accurate perception of content by one person but a completely different perception by another person. Perception of a given text/image by a random receiver in exactly the manner intended by the sender is extremely unlikely. Senders, though, do not often require identical perception of transmitted messages by all receivers. A large number of approximate interpretations may suffice. A well-written explanatory and elucidating caption can enhance understanding of the content. One study (Melin, 1986a) of student perception of texts and pictures in lexivision (i.e., openings in a book where documentary and analytic pictures and descriptive texts interact) showed that pictures were better at expressing contrast and specification and that texts were better at expressing logical relationships such as cause and effect. Some lexivisual presentations utilize the respective advantages of text and image.

VERBAL LANGUAGES

Usually we understand what we are saying. We know what we mean. However, we can never be sure that other people perceive our verbal messages as we have intended. On the contrary, people perceive and depict a given message in widely differing ways (Pettersson, 1986b).

Spoken languages

Many animal species are capable of communicating with the aid of sounds. The messages they convey often express simple concepts, such as hunger or repletion. These acoustic messages are usually sent to individual(s) of the same species. However, the noisy cries emitted by a crow to "warn" the flock are actually a form of "mass communication" rather than personal messages.

One of the simplest forms of communication between humans, the crying of an infant, is to some degree specific for that specific individual. Parents often quickly learn how to understand the meaning of different kinds of acoustically similar crying. They can also distinguish their own child's crying from the crying of other infants. After some time the child acquires linguistic facility, enabling it to express a wide range of needs and emotions.

More than 2,000 languages and countless dialects have long been said to exist. However, Gunnemark & Kenrick (1985) claim that there are probably 5,200 living languages, certainly no less than 4,500 and possibly as many as 6,000. Tens of thousands of years ago, our ancestors were able to communicate with one another by means of some linguistic expressions. Over the millenia, language ultimately evolved into Man's most important means of expression.

Man is the only terrestrial species to acquire a language in the true sense of the word. However, the ability to form concepts is not unique to the human brain. Primates and several lower animals are capable of entertaining general, picture-based concepts. Concepts probably form in their brains in a similar way as in Man's brain. Several scientists in the U.S. have succeeded in teaching chimpanzees to communicate by means of visual sign language. Chimpanzees can deal with more than 100 words and display linguistic creativity, i.e., they are independently able to form new, logical word combinations. To a certain extent, their language has a grammatical structure. Previous attempts to teach apes to learn a language probably failed because they involved efforts to teach apes to speak, despite their anatomical inability to produce human language sounds.

Even very primitive societies often have advanced languages providing scope for great expressiveness. These languages sometimes contain many subtle terms for concrete concepts.

A pioneer in the field of semiotics, Ferdinand Saussure, divided the phonologic components of language into their smallest, non-meaningful parts, i.e., phonemes. Phonemes are basic units of sound. When combined, they form units with meaning. A language's smallest meaningful grammatical unit is referred to as a morpheme. Morphemes are combined to form syntagms (Fredriksson, 1979), i.e., words, phrases, sentences, and complete texts. Spoken and written languages are formed from a limited number of phonemes (usually 20–40). These phonemes can be inter-combined in a limited number of ways. We can make a distinction between individual language, i.e., speech, and super-individual language, i.e., the language itself. When we speak and write, the phonemes, morphemes, and syntagms we use must follow one another in a particular sequence if our messages are to be understood. Language is consequently hierarchic and linear.

The term "spoken language" is almost always taken to mean direct, informal verbal language. A sender and a receiver share a highly interactive communications situation. This situation offers immediate feedback and opportunities for explanations and corrections. However, the situation is highly transient and impossible to rehear/resee. On the other hand, the spoken word in technical media lacks any interactive component to facilitate communications. TV, though, does have limited, sender-controlled or simulated interaction. These media all lack immediate feedback but are non-transient, at least in principle, and their messages can be played back. Speech conveyed by technical devices depends on the quality of the reproduction technology employed and even on factors such as cost. Speech reproduction devices often clip higher frequencies, thereby impairing reception conditions for the listener and conveying speech less adequately than direct conversation.

This all means that the reception conditions of the spoken word conveyed by technical media are similar to the reception conditions of the printed word. The sender must plan her/his message carefully. She/he must practice cognitive clarity and avoid ambiguity—both acoustically and optically. As is the case for the printed word, the language used by broadcast media for recurrent messages, such as weather forecasts, can be rationalized and formalized.

Dahlstedt (1979) predicted that the verbal language used in media would not only develop on its own terms but even exert an impact on the spoken language as a whole. The media probably do have a leveling effect on the spoken language and thereby contribute to the disappearance of dialects. As a result of its wide-ranging coverage, the language of broadcast media tends to become a national standard to a greater extent than direct conversation. As is the case for the written language, the language of broadcast media is tailored to be understood by a wide range of listeners/viewers with widely varying backgrounds. This development is bound to retard new language development, since the use by message senders of old and familiar phraseology maximizes the likelihood of message comprehension by receivers.

Written languages

To be considered verbally literate, one must learn the basic components of a written language: the letters, words, spelling, grammar, and syntax. Just a few basic elements and a set of principles is actually enough to create an almost infinite number of expressions. Most people can learn to communicate with written language. Many develop their own personal styles. Man's ability to communicate was greatly enhanced when knowledge and information began to be stored with the aid of simple pictures and, subsequently, symbolic characters a few thousand years ago. *Pictographic languages* ultimately evolved in different cultures. They initially depicted objects and events as realistically as possible. These early pictograms were drawn with a stick in sand or clay, or on the wall of a cave with a piece of charred wood or bone. Ultimately, people began depicting abstract concepts, largely religious or magic in nature, using pictograms to represent concrete objects. Pictograms of concrete objects were often combined to designate some abstract concept or thought. The pictograms became increasingly stylized and evolved into simple symbols or characters. Each character was equivalent to one or more concepts and came to represent a word. The Chinese language is an example of a living pictographic (ideographic) language in which each character represents one or more words. Other pictographic languages have developed in other ways. *Alphabetic* languages and alphabets evolved when characters designating words began to be used to represent the initial sounds of words.

The utilization of written languages, composed of individual letters, provided the bases for mass storage of knowledge and information and for communications between people at a great distance from one another in terms of both time and space. Most alphabetic written languages evolved from the Phoenician language which appeared around 1200 B.C. The wide-ranging sea voyages undertaken by the Phoenicians spread their language to many places. It reached the Greeks in 800–900 B.C. They added vowels to the Phoenician alphabet, which only consisted of consonants, and began writing from left to right instead of right to left. Many languages have alphabets based on the Greek alphabet, including the Latin of the Romans. Latin, in turn, has given rise to the alphabets employed in most modern written languages in Western countries. They use only a few dozen characters to represent thousands of words and concepts.

English is often said to contain no less than 750,000 words. Many languages are closely related. However, Japanese is an example of an interesting and extremely complicated language which is probably unrelated to any other tongue. Words borrowed relatively recently from Chinese and European languages (English in particular) have been adapted to the Japanese phonetic system, but many of them remain recognizable. In Japanese many inflections share the same explicit significance but differ in implicit meaning, depending on the prevailing social and other circumstances.

Japanese script is highly complex. It is said to comprise about 48,000 different characters, *kanji*, designating different words. Each kanji character can be written in three different fonts and has two or often more meanings, sometimes as many as 15–20. Combining different kanji characters can create a large number of new words and concepts. In elementary school, children learn the 996 most important kanji characters. About 1,850 kanji characters are used in the basic set employed in daily newspapers. A few thousand more are used on special occasions. Few Japanese are able to read and write more than 10,000 kanji characters. The older generation frequently complains that "the schools just aren't teaching children to read well anymore." This might be true, but Japanese children must spend a lot of time and effort on learning to read and write, since their language is so difficult. In addition to kanji, Japanese has *kana*, a 48-character syllabic language. These characters are used in two versions, *katakana* and *hiragana*. Kana writing is used for various inflective elements and for the phonetic writing of, e.g., borrowed words.

Typographic communication

Waller (1987) points out that the writer's text is different from the reader's text. In conventional book-publishing systems, the writer deals with a document that becomes progressively more formal as production processes develop: rough notes become typescript, typescript becomes galleys, galleys become pages, pages become chapters, and chapters become a book. Traditional printing methods require the writer to make most significant decisions in relation to a manuscript and type specification. The reader, on the other hand, sees only a finished product, which is expected to betray little of the complexity and difficulties of the writing process. Printed texts may vary from their original manuscripts with respect to letter-forms, line length, line endings, page breaks, page size, spelling, spacing, punctuation, etc., and even the use of words.

```
Writer ——————————— Writer's text . . . . . . . . . . Imagined readers
                              |
                              |
                              |
Imagined writer . . . . . . . . . . . Reader's text ——————————— Readers

      Topic                    Artifact                   Access
    structure                  structure                 structure
```

Waller's (1987) generic model of typographic communication (p. 178). Each of the three stages in the communication relationship—writing, production, and reading—determines an underlying functional constraint on the typographer. In Waller's model, they are termed *topic*, *artifact*, and *access structure*. The management of their combination is called *conventional structure*.

As desktop publishing systems are getting more common, this situation might change. In personal publishing the writer is responsible not only for the content of the text but also for the editing and the graphic design. The writer's text and the reader's text will be the same. The writer may very well know his or her own subject matter but will have to also learn at least some of the traditional skills of the editor and of the graphic designer.

```
Writer ——————————— Text ——————————— Readers
```

In personal desktop publishing the writer's text is the same as the reader's text.

Communication is vastly more efficient and effective if it follows a plan instead of being a miscellaneous list of sentences or paragraphs. People remember more and read information more quickly when it is logically organized with a plan than they do when the same information is presented in a disorganized, random fashion. Text structure is important, even at the sentence level.

Traditionally, most texts are presented in a linear or rather in an interrupted linear fashion. Thus, the writer exercises strong control over the reader's use of a document. The readers have few alternatives. They will basically have to accept the way the content is presented. Non-linear presentations represent much weaker control of the reading process from the writer. Examples of non-linear presentations are lists, tables, linear branching, matrixes, and, of course, all kinds of visuals.

According to Jonassen (1982) the literature related to the design and organization of text can be divided into two large categories: (1) internal textual structuring and (2) external textual structuring.

Internal textual structuring refers to the techniques used to organize, sequence, and provide an internal framework for helping readers understand the prose content. These techniques include signalling the text structure by using organization, verbal cueing, introductions, topic sentences, transitions, pointer words, and summaries.

External textual structuring refers to the techniques used to structure text with linguistic, spatial, and typographic cues. These techniques include the use of blocked text, horizontal lines to divide blocks, italicized text, and bold text.

Graphic design for information can and should be used to facilitate the reader's ability to find the desired information quickly, easily, effectively, and reliably. Thus it is possible to use the various "perception laws" (see Chapter 2) to create guidelines for graphic design.

Verbal languages have digital coding using combinations of letters, marks, and numerals to represent content. There is no direct correspondence between groups of letters, words, and reality. Each meaning is defined and must be learned (Elkind, 1975).

In English we use 26 letters in two versions. In a plain, running text most letters are in lower case: abcdefghijklmnopqrstuvwxyz, but all letters also appear in upper case: ABCDEFGHIJKLMNOPQRSTUVWXYZ. We use punctuation marks like these: ,.;:!?"( )/&%+-=><*, and numerals like these: 1234567890. This small number of individual characters can be combined in almost infinite numbers of meaningful permutations. Many words can be formed and arrayed in sentences and texts with completely different meanings. There is a wide carry-over of letter shapes and typefaces from one language to another. Thus the same letters can be used to form meaningful words in many different languages.

Elkind (*op. cit.*) points out that the properties of letters are limited. A letter has a given position in an alphabet, it has a name, it is represented by one or more sounds, and it is used in a context.

To achieve optimum legibility it is known that the technical quality of type should be high. Letters can be hand-written or they can be created on machines such as typewriters, dot-matrix impact printers, laser printers, or typesetters. Machine-created characters, *type*, are well-formed, and consistent in their size and style.

Traditionally, type was the old wooden or metal cast of letterforms. The individual pieces of type were put together and locked up into forms. Then the type was coated with ink. Sheets of paper were placed on the type, pressed with a roller, and then removed. Each sheet of paper then contained an impression, an image, made from the real type.

The use of physical letterforms was replaced by a system that used photographs of the letters' images. Today photo-typesetting machines work with digital images of characters. They work with a very good resolution and create high quality typography.

Laser printers use digital image or type that is stored in the memory of the machine. An image of a completed page is built up on a photo-sensitive drum, using a laser beam, and transferred to a piece of paper passing through the machine. Laser printers work with much better resolution than dot-matrix printers but with much lower resolution than photo-typesetters. They are, however, easy to handle for the layman and relatively cheap.

The purpose of page assembly software is to allow the desktop or personal publisher to assemble a publication in much the same manner as in traditional production. This kind of software allows you to move elements such as texts, images, and lines about on a page and paste them almost anywhere.

A printed message

Written or printed verbal messages basically consist of a number of characters such as those used here, i.e., a mixture of letters, spaces, punctuation marks, and sometimes even numerals. Most letters are lower case, but upper case letters occur from time to time.

aaaaaaaaaaaaaaaaaaaaaaaaaaaaaaaaaAAbbbbbbbbbbccccdddddddddddddddeeeeeeeeeee eeeeeeeeeeeeeeeeeeeeeeeeeeeeeeeeeeeeeeeeeeffffffffffffffffggggggggggggggggghhhhhh hhhhhhhhhhhhhhhhhhhhhhhiiiiiiiiiiiiiiiiiiiiiiiiiiiiiikkklllllllllllllllllllmmmmmmmmmm mnnnnnnNnnnnnnnnnnnnnnnoooooooooooooooooooooooooooooooooooopppppppppqrrr rrrrrrrrrrrrrrrrrrrrrssssssssssssssssssssssssssstttttttttttttttttttttttttttttTTTTtttttttttttttttttttttuuu uuvvwwwwwwxxxxyyy-,,,,,,,......

The 431 characters above can be combined in many different ways. Here is one ...

t b ni si oN fo fo fo oros tao tuo, adn ae are. iss acn orf tis the lge eth hTe thp topo ckba byoed. bgtod esey infef fomr frm frae,om frnaom eh htad heiad eaflt, lsreft le-hft lirine pdoart rehst ene seoen sch thateil tha iel thsatan tahin, wieng an,ogle. btlt apck heotuse otgther. rgihht right tmrin ihagflht heioa uhse htitwe inws. wAings dgea tasil eexpt muar mbtin fortked aebotve halves, hg her little strAong upfper. boaymote toncm botltom execept lihdig oliqe iaonl dinal oards, exwtea wnding peog erigorst edshaed

... not a very successful example. It looks like a genuine text, but no combination of characters represents any intelligible concept. There are much better ways of combining the characters in the original example. These characters can easily be used to form both short and long words. Here is an example with more than one hundred real words of successively increasing length.

a a a a A A s an as at be in is is No of of of or so to to and are can for its leg the the the the the the the the the The The The The top top back body body eyes fine form

form from from from from head head left left left line part rest seen seen such tail tail tail than thin wing angle black house other right right flight house white wings wings detail except martin martin forked above halves higher little strong upper bottom bottom except gliding oblique diagonal diagonal towards extending posterior wedgeshaped-,,,,,,,,......

These words can, in turn, be combined to form meaningful sentences.

A house martin in flight A house martin seen at an oblique angle from above is gliding so its body forms a diagonal from top left to bottom right The wings form a strong diagonal from bottom left to top right The tail is a little higher than the head The wedgeshaped wings the upper halves of the head the back and the forked tail are black The rest of the body is white except for a thin line extending from the tail towards the posterior part of the left wing No other fine detail such as eyes or leg can be seen -,,,,,,,......

The addition of punctuation marks at appropriate points make the text much more cohesive.

A house martin in flight.
A house martin, seen at an oblique angle from above, is gliding so its body forms a diagonal from top left to bottom right. The wings form a strong diagonal from bottom left to top right. The tail is a little higher than the head. The wedge shaped wings, the upper halves of the head, the back and the forked tail are black. The rest of the body is white, except for a thin line extending from the tail towards the posterior part of the left wing. No other fine detail, such as eyes or leg, can be seen.

Many other words could be formed and the new words arrayed in sentences and texts with completely different meanings. It is easy to conclude that a text retains its content even when type size is changed. Here are several examples of the same text in different sizes (character size is designated in typographical points—p).

A house martin in flight (9 p)
A house martin in flight (10 p)
A house martin in flight (12 p)
A house martin in flight (14 p)
A house martin in flight (18 p)

Individual characters can be designed in many different ways. Here are a few examples of the same text rendered with different fonts.

A house martin in flight (Times 12 p)
A house martin in flight (Helvetica 12 p)
A house martin in flight (Geneva 12 p)
A house martin in flight (Courier 12 p)
A house martin in flight (Chicago 12 p)

Each type font is usually available in different versions. Here are some examples of the same text with different versions of the same font.

A house martin in flight (12 p, normal)
A house martin in flight (12 p, italic)
A house martin in flight (12 p, bold)
A house martin in flight (12 p, bold, italic)
A house martin in flight (12 p, outline)

So type size, fonts, and font versions can be combined in many ways. However, these options should normally be used sparingly and only a few different versions utilized in a text. Verbal characters also retain their meaning even if rotated in different directions or if turned upside down as in this example.

A house martin in flight

A mirror-reversed text (written from right to left, below) can also be read.

A house martin in flight

The contents of a verbal message are *relatively independent of its form*. However, its readability is strongly influenced by its design or topology. The basic rule is quite simple, that the most common type sizes are easier to read than uncommon sizes. The combinations employed most frequently in newspapers and books have the greatest readability. Characters may neither be too small, nor too large. In the first case we can not read them. In the other case we can only have a few words on each line. The optimum line length seems to be about 40 characters and spaces. Aspects such as margin width, the number of paragraphs, number of columns, the number of lines per page, and the line width are also important to our ability to read text.

Reading the text

The text should be readable, legible, and well worth reading. *Readability* in this context can be defined as the degree of linguistic difficulty, i.e., the sum of the linguistic properties of a text which make it more or less accessible to the reader.

The two factors which best designate the linguistic comprehensibility of a text are sentence length and the proportion of long words. An easily comprehensible text is characterized by short sentences, short words, and simple sentence structure. Other variables which affect the comprehensibility of text are the vocabulary's degree of abstraction, the number of syllables in words, the commonness of words used, the choice of subject, the subdivision into paragraphs, the prevalence of clauses, headings and sub-headings, line length, inter-line distance, illustrations, the size of letters, the relevance of the text to the reader, and the page size. The index of readability (LIX) is calculated as follows:

- Count the number of words in the text.
- Count the number of words with more than six letters.
- Count the number of sentences.
- Divide the number of long words by the total number of words and multiply the product by 100. This yields the average word length (WL).
- Divide the number of words by the number of sentences. This yields the average sentence length (SL).
- WL + SL = LIX.

20–30	=	simple text, suitable for children's books
30–35	=	literature
35–45	=	moderately difficult text, weekly magazines
45–50	=	popular science subjects
50–55	=	difficult text, trade literature
55+	=	extremely difficult text

The concept of *legibility* refers to a text's external properties. These are properties such as letter size, inter-line distance, line length, the distance between letters, the number of letters per line, the distance between words, the typographic style, the subdivision into paragraphs, headings, headings in the margin, the layout, color of the printing ink and paper, the paper quality, etc. These different external properties have not been found to have a drastic effect on legibility as long as the text is presented within the framework of variation normally found in contemporary books. Some general principles for legibility can be noticed (see Chapter 7).

The text should be *well worth reading*. This designates the properties of the content of a text and is very dependent on the reader's degree of interest. Each group of readers selects reading material on the basis of personal preference. Studies of readability have resulted in lists with reading suggestions for various age groups.

Interplay of words and visuals

As seen earlier, pictures may have various functions. For example, pictures are very good at conveying information about what objects really look like. Text, however, is very good to use when, e.g., logical relations will be expressed. Visuals used to be a kind of special feature in books and still are in far too many situations. The illustrations in the laboriously copied books from the Middle Ages can often be compared to paintings in a museum or windows in a church. The illustrations in the manuscripts even had frames of genuine gold in many cases. For hundreds of years, visuals often remained extra features with a rather limited connection to the text. In the last century, textbook visuals were often placed vertically to provide better use of page space, or an already existing illustration, e.g., a wood-cut was sometimes used. It was not unusual that one picture was used to depict, e.g., several different persons or several different towns. Visuals were often a kind of "painting" with little or no real interaction with the text. In most books, pictures served primarily as an artistic supplement to the text. However, visuals have been used in a more intentional way in non-fiction books. As early as the Middle Ages, some secular texts were illustrated.

Medical science demanded a knowledge of herbs. Plant recognition was aided by clear and analytical drawings as early as the 5th century. Color, when used, was true to life. Each illustration had a text under it giving the characteristics of the herb and its medical use. However, copies made from earlier manuscripts, rather than from living plants, ultimately transformed the illustrations into stylized forms very different from botanical reality.

Visual stories with only brief text occur in many situations. A surprising variety of the frame shapes and juxtapositions is shown. One of the most impressive visual stories was made as a textile. The *Bayeux Tapestry,* 70 meters long, uses 79 consecutive scenes to depict the story behind the Battle of Hastings in 1066.

In manuscripts it was easy to put words and visuals anywhere on a page. The skills of integrating words with visuals were gradually developed. In Europe, the ability to print images on paper was achieved during the 14th century. The *block book* contained text that was written by hand and printed images. These printed images invariably included some form of captions or texts. When moveable type was introduced during the 15th century it was possible to produce books in larger quantities. This was the beginning of a cultural revolution. There followed a dramatic growth in the quantity and quality of books and other printed documents like maps. Informative drawings developed. However, the new technology impaired the possibilities for integration of words and visuals.

In more modern times, the first one to really show how visuals and words could interplay was the bishop Johannes Amos Comenius of Moravia (later a part of Czechoslovakia). His illustrated textbook, *Orbis Sensualium Pictus* (The Visible World in Pictures), was first published in 1658. Comenius presented information on the world and on mankind in closely related pictures and words. The 150 illustrations, copper cuts from his own drawings, had numbers referred to in the text. In some later editions the text was printed in four different languages. This book was widely used in both Europe and America for over 150 years. The first American edition was published in 1810, with texts in Latin and English. *Orbis Sensualium Pictus* is generally considered to be the first illustrated schoolbook. Comenius emphasized the importance of the senses in learning. His famous illustrated alphabet, combining letters, pictures, and "sounds," and found in the opening pages, has later been adopted by many authors of ABC-books. In *Orbis Sensualium Pictus* the illustrations are actual teaching devices and not merely ornaments on the pages. Comenius preceded Diderot's picture-volumes and the visualized fact books of today.

The first truly American textbook, *The New England Primer*, originally published in England around 1683, contained small and rough woodcuts, illustrating the alphabet. This book also contained numerous pictures to help the child memorize the text. Comenius' findings after this time gradually were more or less forgotten or not practiced and "reinvented" only recently.

Visuals should be incorporated directly into the text. It is usually a mistake to put illustrations in an appendix to a report. Today, words and text usually interact nicely with visuals in information and instructional message designs. The systems for desktop publishing make it possible for the author to integrate words and visuals to aid communication. To get maximum impact from a picture it should be introduced in the text. Each picture should also have its own legend.

Substantial research has clearly shown that learning efficiency is much enhanced when words and visuals interact and supply redundant information. The improvement sometimes exceeds sixty percent and averages thirty percent.

VISUAL LANGUAGES

It has probably always been natural for Man to express himself or herself by means of visual messages. Since the beginning of mankind we have been using body languages and different kinds of signs for communication.

Prehistoric Man made murals and rock inscriptions with mythological meaning. In everyday life, people probably made drawings on the ground to show the location of game for their food. Simplified images ultimately evolved into characters, letters, and numerals.

Pictures helped Man communicate long before we had written languages for our messages. Our children make pictures, they draw and paint long before they learn to read and write.

For 20,000 years we have had murals. For about 2,500 years we have had rock inscriptions. For about 700 years we have had framed paintings and put them on our walls as pieces of art. For more than 500 years we have had printed illustrations in books. We have had photos for 150 years, films for 90 years, electronic pictures for more than 40 years, and computer images for more than 20 years. Electronic "live-pictures" last only for one twenty-fifth of a second, but they can be stored for example on videotape or videodisc.

Nowadays, pictures are to be found almost everywhere. They differ in character. It is not possible for every one to stand out on every occasion. People "drown" in a flood of general "pictorial noise," a kind of mental pollution of the environment. Visuals can be classified according to several different criteria, such as sender, receiver, content, execution, format, and context, and even according to criteria such as function, use, and the means of production, etc. Thus, there are many possibilities for classification. However, one and the same visual can and will be classified in different ways at the same time, depending on the criteria applied in each case. Often the boundaries between different groups partially overlap each other.

Visual literacy

Sutton (1992) compared *information literacy, media literacy,* and *visual literacy.* In the USA, a National Forum on Information Literacy was established in 1989. The background was that information is expanding at a very rapid rate. The American Library Association defined information literacy as follows: "To be information-literate, a person must be able to recognize when information is needed and have the ability to locate, evaluate, and use effectively the needed information."

Everyone appreciates the need to learn the meaning of words. We also have to learn to read and understand the meaning of visual information and the different components of visual language. Heinich *et al.* (1982) discussed the concept of visual literacy and offered the following definition (p. 62): "*Visual literacy* is the learned ability to *interpret* visual messages accurately and to *create* such messages. Thus interpretation and creation in visual literacy can be said to parallel reading and writing in print literacy." In my opinion, this is a very good definition of visual literacy. The definition reflects the perspective that visual literacy is a concept in which particular skills, knowledge, and attitudes can be taught and learned which enhance our abilities to communicate in a variety of visual forms. Several years ago I read and obviously assimilated this definition, and later used the same definition in the first edition of this book (Pettersson, 1989) without a proper reference to these authors (my apologies). There are, however, several other definitions of visual literacy.

However modern the term visual literacy is, it is not a new idea. Discussions about using images go back far in history. Some ancient philosophers used images for visual communication. In anatomy and medicine, Aristotle used anatomical illustrations. In mathematics, Phythagoras, Socrates, and Plato used visual images to teach geometry. Leahy (1991) pointed out that Aristotle had formed the conceptual idea that certain elements of visual grammar are necessary to visual composition and appeal. Aristotle provided a seminal notion that art and visual literacy theorists Arnheim (1969, 1986) and Dondis (1973) further refined.

After the first conference on visual literacy was held in Rochester, USA, Debes (1969, 1970) agreed to write the first definition of visual literacy. Since then several researchers interested in the concept have developed their own viewpoints, opinions, and definitions. Many have discussed the concept with reference to her or his own, personal background. Thus individual researchers have placed emphasis on many different aspects of visual literacy. There has been a large amount of disagreement concerning "what visual literacy really is." It is quite clear that it is extremely difficult to describe with words a concept that is primarily non-verbal. Definitions have varied from very narrow to very broad and of various complexity. Some definitions of visual literacy are provided by theoreticians and some by practitioners, especially by those involved in teaching. Some researchers, like Cassidy & Knowlton (1983), and Suhor & Little (1988), have more or less rejected the whole concept.

Theoretical framework
Several researchers have defined visual literacy from various theoretical viewpoints. According to Schiller (1987), the theoretician's analytical methods have pressed the trend of defining visual literacy toward "genericism." Debes' original definition from 1969 reads (p. 26): "Visual literacy refers to a group of vision competencies a human being can develop by seeing and at the same time having and integrating other sensory experiences. The development of these competencies is fundamental to normal human learning. When developed, they enable a visually literate person to discriminate and interpret the visible actions, objects, and symbols, natural or man-made, that he encounters in his environment. Through the creative use of these competencies, he is able to communicate with others. Through the appreciative use of these competencies, he is able to comprehend and enjoy the masterworks of visual communication."

Another early definition was presented by Dondis (1973) in her book *A Primer of Visual Literacy* (p. 182): "Visual literacy implies understanding, the means for seeing and sharing meaning with some level of predictable universality. To accomplish this requires reaching beyond the innate visual powers of the human organism, reaching beyond the intuitive capabilities programmed into us for making visual decisions on a more or less common basis, and reaching beyond personal preference and individual taste."

The "universality" Dondis calls for is actually *insight*, which is the highest goal of education. Contrary to the misconceptions of some people, being *visually literate* does not at all require a person to be an artist, skilled in drawing, painting, or film making.

Ausburn & Ausburn (1978) focused their attention on developing skills and understandings. They provided this short definition (p. 293): "Visual literacy can be defined as a group of skills which enables an individual to understand and use visuals for intentionally communicating with others."

Obviously, visual literacy requires an interest in developing one's communication skills using visual media, including body language. Braden & Hortin (1982) suggested a definition which avoids the use of much potentially controversial terminology and introduces the concept of thinking in images into the definition. They wrote (p. 169): "Visual literacy is the ability to understand and use images, including the ability to think, learn, and express oneself in terms of images." The Braden and Hortin approach is similar to that of McKim (1980a, 1980b). McKim suggested that visual thinking is carried on through the employment of three types of visual images—those we see, those we imagine, and those we draw. The "McKim diagram," consisting of three partly overlapping circles (see page 109), explains the fluid dynamic that occurs without our conscious awareness or thought. The circles symbolize the idea that visual thinking is experienced to the fullest when seeing, imagining, and drawing merge into active interplay. The visual thinker utilizes seeing, imagining, and drawing in a fluid and dynamic way, moving from one kind of imagery to another.

Hortin (1982) noted that while the concept "visual literacy" had been popular since 1969, no substantial theory of visual literacy had yet been developed. So far most of the visual literacy researchers had discussed various practical aspects of visual literacy and teaching of visual literacy. This is in fact still the case.

Griffin & Whiteside (1984) argued that theory should stimulate practical applications and they suggested that visual literacy should be approached from three different perspectives (p. 74):

1. *Theoretical perspectives*, which incorporate the philosophical, psychological, and physiological aspects of learning.
2. *Visual language perspectives*, which incorporate a receiver-oriented approach committed to helping people become visually literate by effectively relating to visual stimuli.
3. *Presentational perspectives*, which incorporate a presenter-oriented approach, the improving of the communications process through design of visual stimuli.

Reynolds Myers (1985) postulated the following four "Principles of visual literacy theory" (p. 48):

• Visual languaging abilities develop prior to, and serve as the foundation for, verbal language development.
• Development of visual languaging abilities is dependent upon learner interaction with objects, images, and body language.

- The level of visual language development is dependent upon the richness and diversity of the objects, images, and body language with which the learner interacts and upon the degree of interaction.
- The level of visual language development is facilitated by direct learner involvement in the process and equipment used to create objects, visual images, and body language.

On a theoretical basis Sinatra (1986) connected visual literacy to thinking, reading, and writing. He pointed out that visual literacy becomes the basic literacy in the thought processes of comprehending and composing which underlie reading and writing. The non-verbal components of visual literacy are the real "basics" in literacy learning. Sinatra suggested the following definition of visual literacy (p. 5): "Visual literacy is the active reconstruction of past visual experience with incoming visual messages to obtain meaning." The active reconstructive nature of our thought processes means that as visual information is presented to our brains, it is modified and interpreted in the light of what information already exists there. Piaget (1963) maintained that the sources of thought are not to be found in any verbal language but in the non-verbal, visual-motor reconstruction performed by the very young child during its first two years of life.

Considine (1986) argues that visual literacy attempts to account for both an input and an output set of processes. Thus visual literacy is said to refer "to the ability to comprehend and create images in a variety of media in order to communicate more effectively." And visually literate students should be able to produce and interpret visual messages. Since visual literacy is a *process* requiring the ability to *send*, *receive,* and *process* visual messages effectively in order to participate in two-way communications, visually literate individuals have to develop a variety of proficiencies.

Schiller (1987) noted that all the different viewpoints of visual literacy show that every visual medium has its own characteristic form. Thus there are clearly different visual literacies, and there are different skills to be learned in terms of their characteristic techniques and methods of expression. As a consequence we should rather concentrate on more limited concepts, such as, for example, computer-literacy, film-literacy, video-literacy, and television-literacy. It might actually not be possible to create one single definition of the broad concept of visual literacy.

Braden (1987) identified three "domains" of visual literacy:

1. Visualization, described as "aspects of vision in the human process of thinking and communication." In this domain Braden included elements such as visual syntax, visual design, visual expression, and visual thinking.
2. The "theory–research–practice trilogy as it applies to visual literacy." Here are elements such as instruction, design, communication, and persuasion.
3. Technology, including the effects of technological developments, upon the other two domains of visual literacy. Here Braden included electronics and television, computers, and reprographics.

Clark-Baca (1990), Clark-Baca & Braden (1990), and Braden & Clark-Baca (1991) have dealt with the complexity of various definitions. Clark-Baca's Delphi Study (1990) involved input from 52 "experts in the field of visual literacy." The final round yielded 167 statements which were identified as constructs that define, describe, or elaborate upon visual literacy. These statements can be seen as an "index to the field." Braden & Clark-Baca (1991) propose "a conceptual map which would serve as a graphic organizer of visual literacy constructs" (p. 156).

Curriculum and teaching issues

Some researchers and practitioners have provided definitions of visual literacy with emphasis of the holistic success of the use of visual literacy techniques in producing a visual message, in art, in everyday life, and in teaching. When Cochran (1976) asked delegates at a media leadership conference to define the term "visual literacy," the 62 definitions indicated that 52 different phrases were used to define the adjective "visual" and that three major meanings evolved for the word "literacy," as a group of competencies, as a process or method of teaching, or as a movement. All the delegates agreed that visual literacy was used to refer to three major diverse categories: human abilities, teaching strategies, and the promotion of ideas.

Esdale & Robinson (1982) argued that visual literacy should be integrated across all curricular areas in an effort to both expand ability and to prevent categorization which could limit learning and use of visual literacy skills. Lacy (1987) concludes that visual literacy is a communication skill like verbal literacy. She defined visual literacy in the following way (p. 46): "It (visual literacy) can be defined as the ability to identify, analyze, interpret, evaluate, and produce visual messages. A visually literate person has acquired skills in gathering information from such straightforward visual messages as another person's body language. Or from complicated visual images that are combinations of new technologies like video, computer, and enhanced photography. And visually literate persons can both mentally image and communicate to others by producing a visual message themselves."

Schiller (1987) developed a diagram attempting to show the input/output model of human perception and expression suggesting how the different literacies have developed from the abstractive processes of symbolic and imagic expression. He noted that every image is an aesthetic abstraction with a depictive capacity. This capacity ranges from highly abstract, such as printed letters of the alphabet, to exacting isomorphism, such as realistic paintings. Schiller claimed that in all the imaginative visual arts, the *composition* is the fundamental unit—and that *composing* is the fundamental process. He stated that: "It is in providing a deeper understanding of this process that visual literacy can offer education a pathway into the future that can begin to focus on the knowledge most worth knowing" (p. 282). In an attempt to give teachers and administrators the sense of a new direction, Schiller offered the following definition of visual literacy (p. 276): "Visual literacy is an ability to interpret by means of trained perceptual capacities feelings, ideas, and information; and to communicate them imaginatively with compositions created via a diversity of visualizing mediums."

Official definitions

The International Visual Literacy Association, IVLA, was established as a non-profit association incorporated in the State of New York in 1968 to provide a multi-disciplinary forum for the exploration, presentation, and discussion of all aspects of visual communication and their various applications through visual images, visual literacy, and literacy in general. IVLA serves as the organizational base and communications bond for professionals from various disciplines who are interested in visual literacy. Other concerns are to encourage the funding of creative visual literacy projects, programs, and research, and to promote and evaluate projects intended to increase the use of visuals in education and communications in general.

IVLA provides us with the following four "official definitions" of visual literacy (printed on leaflet, 1989):
1. a group of vision competencies a human being can develop by seeing and at the same time having and integrating other sensory experiences;
2. the learned ability to interpret the communication of visual symbols (images), and to create messages using visual symbols;
3. the ability to translate visual images into verbal language and vice versa;
4. the ability to search for and evaluate visual information in visual media.

It is quite clear that visual literacy is a broad and interdisciplinary concept including bits and pieces from several "established fields" as presented below.

Visual literacy is reported to be related to many different areas:

Area	Selected references
advertising	Besser, 1987
aesthetics	Metallinos, 1991
art	Arnheim, 1969, 1986
art education	Pettersson, 1991
art history	Garoian, 1989
audiovisual media	Cochran, 1976
brain research	Sinatra, 1986
business presentations	Griffin & Whiteside, 1984
child development	Ausburn & Ausburn, 1978
communication	Wisely *et al.*, 1989
computer science	Ragan, 1988; Pettersson, 1989
curriculum	Martinello, 1985; Miller, 1987; Ragan, 1988; Robinson, 1991
education	Dondis, 1973; Muffoletto, 1984; Evans *et al.* 1987; Miller, 1987; Pettersson, 1991
ethics	Limburg, 1988
film	Miller, 1989
graphic design	Hardin, 1983; Pettersson, 1989
illustrations	Levie & Lentz, 1982
infology	Pettersson, 1989
information technology	Braden, 1987; Pettersson, 1989
instruction	Levie, 1978
journalism	Barnhurst & Whitney, 1991
learning	Dwyer, 1978
library science	Good, 1987
media	Cochran, 1976; Lloyd-Kolkin & Tyner, 1990
perception	Haber & Myers, 1982: Metallinos, 1991
philosophy	Leahy, 1991
photography	Oudejans, 1988; Pettersson, 1989

phototherapy	Krauss, 1984; Weiser, 1984
psychology	Moore, 1988
reading	Levin & Lesgold, 1978; Sinatra, 1986
teaching	Rezabek, 1990
television	Becker, 1987; Johnson, 1988; Robinson, 1988; Barry & Leaver, 1989,
thinking	McKim, 1980a, 1980b; Braden & Hortin, 1982
video	Hobbs, 1989; Williams, 1988
visual communication	Dondis, 1973
visual learning	Dwyer, 1978

Functions

From a theoretical point of view, a visual can possess many different functions and effects or combinations of functions and effects. Thus, a distinction can be made between *symbols* and *pictures* .

In western civilizations a symbol is usually something which "represents" something (Lee, 1959). We "apply" words to things or names to persons. These "signs" stand for the things to which they have been applied. However, Agrawal *et al.* (1987) pointed out that in the context of the ancient Indian civilization the symbol is not a representation. A symbol is a concretization of reality having intrinsic power of its own. It is a part within the whole belief system, and a link between the past, the present, and the future.

Signposts, traffic signs, and labels are examples of symbols. They are unambiguous by convention. *We agree and decide on their meaning.*

All pictures are *representations* of reality. The "reality" of a printed page does not exist in real life, other than on the page. As is the case for other kinds of representations, pictures are always open to different interpretations by different people at different times. Some pictures are open to many interpretations, others to only a few. Cochran (1987) distinguishes between actual events/objects, iconic representations, and arbitrary representations. Examples of iconic representations are film and TV-images, still photographic pictures, and realistic art work. Symbols, signs, computer graphics, and words are all examples of arbitrary representations. Here no cues from actuality are left.

Wileman (1993, p. 12) provides a good illustration of different ways to represent an object. He shows a continuum ranging from concrete to abstract. *Pictorial symbols* are photographs and drawings. *Graphic symbols* are image-related graphics, concept-related graphics, and arbitrary graphics. *Verbal symbols* are verbal descriptions and nouns/labels.

Many papers have been published outlining the various functions of illustrations (e.g., Duchastel, 1978; Duchastel & Waller, 1979; Holliday, 1980; Levie & Lentz, 1982; Levin, Anglin, & Carney, 1987). All papers include the functions of attracting *attention* to and creating interest in a given material or in a given subject. The material may be "appealing to the eye" (Duchastel, 1983; Levin, 1981); motivate a person to pick up, browse through, and read the text (Duchastel, 1978, 1983); and making reading more enjoyable (Duchastel & Waller, 1979). Evans, Watson, & Willows (1987) noted that the attentional role of illustrations is highlighted in teacher's manuals and teacher's editions of a variety of textbooks.

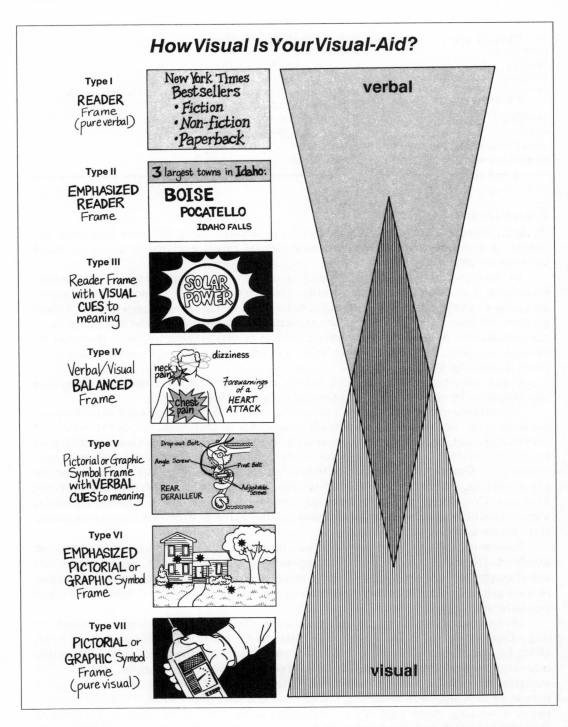

Wileman (1993, p. 19) shows a way to organize the relationship of verbal and visual images, with different functions, along a continuum. This verbal/visual continuum is called the degree of visualization. Reprinted by permission of the publisher.

Visuals are perceived much more rapidly and readily than text. Visuals explain things and illustrate appearance. In many instances, pictures provide a much better overview and understanding of a subject than words. Visuals are great at designating spatial orientation, time and magnitude relationships, etc.

Pictures may be *cognitive* and convey knowledge and information to the reader or viewer. They can facilitate learning from a text by enhancing comprehension and memory. Pictures can be used, e.g., for instructing, exemplifying, identifying, or providing variation, authority, or information as a supplement to text and sound. Pictures are often used for content that is important, hard to understand, and new.

It should be remembered that *pictures can have a negative effect*. At some point illustrations move from being engaging motivators to engaging distractors. When too many pictures are used, readers may ignore many of them. It should also be noted that children's preferences for illustrations differ widely from those of adults (Rudisill, 1951–1952). The inability of children younger than thirteen to ignore incidental images means that effects are unlikely to be neutral: if the pictures do not help, they will probably hinder. *Illustrations should be strictly relevant to the text*.

Pictures can be *affective* and provide readers with entertainment and reinforce an experience both positively and negatively. They can trigger associations and influence emotions and attitudes, especially in movies and TV. Pictures can be used to persuade, to flatter, tease, shame, scare, and seduce the audience (Zakia, 1985). In advertising and television, pictures may carry subliminal messages. Ads for liquor or cigarettes, for example, sometimes use sexual symbols.

Pictures can be *compensatory*, making it easier for poor readers to comprehend, learn, and recall things they read in a text (Duchastel, 1978). The purpose of realistic pictures is normally to exemplify or illustrate something (Melin, 1986a).

Aronsson (1983) maintained that visuals employed in teaching aids for immigrants could conceivably play a major role in culture transfer.

Visuals may have a purely decorative purpose and be used for beautifying or adorning something (Selander, 1988).

In addition to purely realistic visuals, there are also visuals that can be described as "metaphoric." They exemplify and depict some linguistic metaphor. Visuals of this kind are not symbolic in any semiotic (Jacobson, 1976) or art science sense (Berefelt, 1976). Melin (1986b) noted that metaphoric pictures are particularly abstract and therefore intellectually demanding.

In various ways, pictures often have important *social functions* in the home, at school, in organizations, and in society. *Picture creation* is more important than the visual results in certain instances. Some pictures may not have any or only a limited function once created. Modern cameras which automatically set the exposure, focus the lens, and advance the film have made it possible for anyone to take pictures. More than 90% of all Swedish families own at least one camera. Two thirds of the population make a movie or take still photographs at some time during any year. Millions of amateur photographs are the result. The advent of lightweight, portable VCR equipment has opened up new horizons for non-professional creators of moving pictures.

Illustrations can also be used to break up longer blocks of text and make the pages more appealing. Pictures may also have a generally *decorative effect* and be used to improve our environment. However, cognitive and decorative functions should never be confused or mixed.

Winn (1993) concludes that pictures play many roles in instruction. It is therefore necessary to know precisely what a picture's function is intended to be before it is designed.

An empirical study

From 1986–1991, about 180 Swedish students took the course "Visuals for Information" given by the author at Stockholm University. During these courses, students worked on individual assignments comprising a number of different tasks that, after completion, were reported and jointly discussed in class sessions. In one of these assignments, students were asked to make an attempt at evaluating the senders' intentions for visuals published in newspapers, magazines, books, brochures, etc. The assignment's wording was as follows:

> Look for visuals clearly showing that the sender had one or more definite intentions. Cut out these visuals and paste them onto sheets of paper. Then describe the sender's (presumed) intention(s) for the visuals!

The 238 visuals used were mainly clips from newspapers, magazines, and brochures. Visuals copied from a book were selected only in a few instances. One interesting observation was that only 1–3 visuals of the 30–40 visuals discussed at each session were identical, i.e., selected by more than one student. These "duplicates" were not included in the statistics below. The image functions discussed above were all mentioned by the students. Clearly, the students saw visuals as performing a great number of functions.

Advertising

In many instances (121 visuals, 51%), students felt that the sender's intention was to induce receivers to take a stand *for* some person or issue. This obviously applied to visuals in ads but also concerned visuals in editorial text to some extent. The visuals were to: sell products (30), sell a lifestyle (19), sell services (12), convey or create associations (8), convince viewers about something (6), create needs (3), arouse interest (3), create a need for travel (3), create a debate (2), induce fascination (1), create an opinion (1), show a product as attractive (2), create trust (2), capture attention (3), arouse attention (3), entice people to buy (3), entice people to see a movie (1), arouse emotions about someone (6), make viewers react (4), induce viewers to take certain action (3), motivate (1), pose questions (1), activate (1), induce belief in the future (1), create interest in preserving the environment (1), and gloss over reality (1).

Propaganda

In some instances (26 visuals, 11%), students felt that the sender's intention was to induce receivers to take an active stand *against* some person or issue. These visuals were to: frighten people into greater awareness (8), shock (3), provoke (3), illustrate starvation (3), illustrate violence (2), create irony (2), illustrate oppression (2), show detest for politics (1), show detest for war (1), and show detest for environmental pollution (1).

Information

In some instances (71 visuals, 30%), students felt that the senders were attempting to convey *objective information* about something. These visuals were to: convey factual information (11), illustrate factual circumstances (8), document (7), instruct (5), illustrate the text (4), inform (4), supply information on what something looked like (4), convey feelings (4), convey culture (2), demonstrate (4), explain (3), explain statistics (2), explain a text (3), prove (2), be cognitive (2), compensate for text shortcomings (2), educate (1), illustrate advantages (1), clarify (1), and clarify complex processes (1).

Entertainment

In some instances (12 visuals, 5%), students felt that senders were attempting to provide *entertainment*. The visuals were to: entertain (7), amuse (3), and make us laugh (2).

Decoration

In some instances (8 visuals, 3%), students felt that senders used the visuals as *adornment* or *decoration*. The visuals were to: be aesthetic (2), decorate (4), adorn (1), and beautify the page (1).

Selection of visuals

Results from several experiments show that learning is facilitated and maximized when visual, audio, and print media contain the same information. In normal situations, the addition of visual embellishments has not been found to enhance the learning of information which is only conveyed in printed form. The presence of text-redundant visuals will neither help nor hinder the learning of information given in the part of the text without illustrations. Some picture editors admit that some of the pictures they use in textbooks are only there to "stimulate" the reader, to have "a life of their own," or merely to provide a "breathing space" within the text. Such uses seem dubious. Many illustrations (often without legends) in contemporary textbooks appear to serve no useful purpose whatever. It is even possible that certain types of illustrations, incorporated to "stimulate" the reader's imagination and interest, could instead have a heavily governing effect which stifles the imagination and diverts interest from the information and knowledge the author wishes to convey.

Interviews with editors, art directors, and designers from major Swedish publishing houses showed that they, in the selection of visuals for reference books and textbooks, often ask themselves questions such as the following:

- Does the picture depict the right thing?
- Is the presentation of the subject satisfactory?
- Is the picture technically acceptable?
- Is the picture aesthetically satisfactory?
- Is the picture "flexible," i.e., will it work with different formats?
- Will the picture fit into a given area?
- Will the picture fit in with the other pictures on the same page?

In practice, many editors, art directors, and designers find that *procurement time, availability,* and *image clarity* are the most important considerations in making their *subjective* choices among possible visuals. Evans, Watson, & Willows (1987) interviewed editors, art directors, and designers from nine major Canadian publishing houses. They concluded (p. 90): Our interviews confirm Dwyer's (1972) summary that the selection and inclusion of illustrations in textbooks appear to be based on "subjective feelings of the designer about what is best, the accessibility of raw information, the availability of materials, the cost, the attractiveness of the finished product, and the availability of a ready market" (p. 16).

Evans, Watson, & Willows (1987) noted that the attention-getting and motivational aspects of illustrations in textbooks seemed to predominate among teachers. They made very few direct references to illustrations in the classroom, and they provided little guidance in the educational functions that illustrations are thought to serve.

Preference for a particular visual format does not necessarily result in increased learning. Yet, in the absence of more substantial data, information based on student preference has a meaningful role to play in affecting learning from information materials and instructional texts. All other things being equal, we should provide formats which are preferred by the viewer, thus making the text more attractive, and hopefully more motivating.

Selection of artistic style for visual materials, then, should not be an arbitrary decision, but always a conscious one.

Visuals cost money, often quite a lot of money. But in many situations a "good" picture need not cost more than a "bad" picture! Spending a lot of time on the visualization process and on sketches (usually a less expensive process than the cost of originals, "masters," and printing runs) may therefore be worthwhile.

Levels of meaning

Visual languages differ just as do spoken and written languages. The codes used in visual language differ in different cultures as well as in many sub-cultures. Even within a western mass-media country like the U.S., visual codes differ in different parts of the country, in different socioeconomic groups, etc. Visual languages have their own "grammars," syntaxes, etc., just like spoken and written languages. To a limited extent, some of the factors involved in the grammar and syntax of visual languages are known. However, most of this linguistic work still remains to be done. One obvious problem is the lack of simple and general systems for classifying visual messages.

In contrast to spoken and written languages, pictures have no general, distinguishing elements which are not bearers of information. Visual languages have analog coding. Visuals are iconic. They normally resemble the thing they represent. The simplest components in a picture, i.e., its *basic elements*, are dots, lines, and areas which can be varied in a great many ways. A dot may vary in size, shape, color, value, grain, position, and context. A line may be varied with respect to its starting point, length, direction, curvature, shape, thickness, evenness, points of changes, printing, color, value, grain, brightness, orientation, terminus, and context. An area can be varied with respect to size, "emptiness," shape, color, value, grain, texture, shaded, non-shaded, grey scale, color combinations, brightness, and context. Three-dimensional pictures also possess *volume* in different forms. Basic graphical elements are sometimes meaningful, sometimes not. The number of ways in which the smallest image components can be inter-combined is unlimited, and the importance of certain combinations varies from one picture creator to another.

So basic picture components are not equivalent to the phonemes in spoken and written languages. If there were some kind of "visual phonemes," it would be possible for people to learn to draw and paint in about the same way they learn to read a text. In a picture, the basic image components—dots, lines, and areas—form *shapes* which form *visual syntagms* or sub-meanings. These components interact to form complete meanings in stills, picture series, or moving pictures.

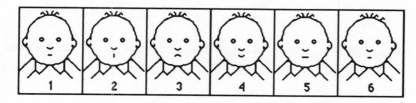

In a pictorial presentation, a dot or a line may have widely varying meanings. Here, execution influences content. To illustrate this, six copies were made of a simple drawing. Figure 1 was left unchanged. The mouth was changed in figures 2–5 by the addition of small lines which completely altered our perception of the illustrations. In Figure 6 a small line was added to the hair, but this addition has no effect on our perception of the illustration.

In visual language, a small dot is usually a meaningless or non-significant image element, such as one of many halftone dots, but it could also be a syntagm, such as an eye in a cartoon-face. Or it may even have a complete meaning, such as a ball in midair. It all depends on the situation depicted. So like written and spoken languages, visual language has numerous but varying levels of meaning.

Dots, lines, and areas can be put together in many ways resulting in different contents. Changes of the basic elements will result in different images, sometimes of great and sometimes of minor importance.

Non-significant basic elements (dots, lines, and areas) are arrayed into shapes which form syntagms or sub-meanings (here an eye).

Here is an example with eight black areas.

These areas can be combined in many different ways. Here is one example ...

... not particularly successful. No combination of characters corresponds to any intelligible concept. The picture gets no concrete image content. There are better ways of combining the characters in the original set. In the following example, the elements are combined to form a bird, a house martin in flight:

Simple image elements, such as those used to depict this house martin, can be rotated, turned upside down, and re-combined to form a series of completely different but still intelligible representations of real concepts:

Contrary to the situation with verbal messages, the contents of a visual message are highly dependent on its shape. Size variations for example are only possible within certain limits. The image can be made rather small ...

... or rather large, but will then not convey the same message.

There is an optimum size for every pictorial subject. This size can only be established by trial and error. In this instance, the small version is probably too small and the large version needlessly large.

If two different sized pictures of objects such as house martins are placed next to one another, one is perceived to be near the viewer and one farther away. Or the birds are perceived as being of different sizes. Maybe one bird is adult and the other still a baby bird. Or maybe the two birds belong to different species.

Visual signs do not retain their meaning in the same way as verbal signs when rotated and turned in different directions. Turn the page in different directions and see in what way the impact of the pictures change. Also, the actual placement on the page, the layout, is important.

Above is an "upside-down" mirror image. Here the house martin is ascending to the right and not descending to the right, as in most of the previous pictures. This picture supplies the viewer with the same basic information about the bird's appearance but completely different information about the bird's actions.

In this "side-ways" mirror image the house-martin is apparently descending to the left. Again the image contains the same basic information as the original image about the bird's appearance but completely different information about the bird's actions.

Cossette (1982) claims that it is possible to build an iconic "alphabet." He identified six families of basic graphic sign elements, which he called *graphemes*, e.g., "visual phonemes." Each of these graphemic elements is part of one of six continuum families: tallness, value, grain, color, orientation, and form. The same variables were discussed by Bertin as early as 1967. Each grapheme signifies nothing in itself. A spot is nothing but a spot. Together with other graphemes the spot may be contextually enriched to a unit of iconic significance, an *iconeme*. In a photograph of a man, one iconeme can be an arm, a leg, the head, and so on. By analysis of an image, it is possible to identify the iconemes which are important to the information content and identify the *key syntagm*, the "meaning nucleus" of the visual. By editing, eliminating, or adding certain iconemes the effectiveness of an image can be altered.

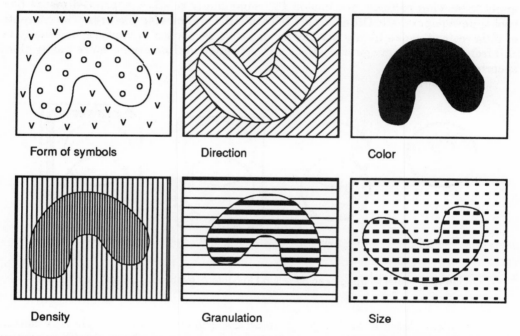

Examples of visual variables in the form of areas on a map, based on Bertin (1967), and Baudoiun & Anker (1984).

In my view, the Cossette graphemes represent *qualities* more than visual phonemes. Graphemes would instead be dots, lines, and areas, since they all can vary more or less with respect to tallness, value, grain, color, orientation, and form. Anyhow, they are all *variables in the visual language*.

According to Bertin (1967) and later Baudoiun & Anker (1984), a graphic language used on maps consists of visual variables. The most important variables are form (of symbols), directions, color, density, granularity, and size of symbols. Each variable can be a dot, a line, or an area.

The way in which different variables are combined has greater importance than how the variables are comprehended. Using too many visual variables at the same time makes map reading more difficult. When several variables are used simultaneously the hierarchy of visibility is important. The largest symbols are always perceived first. Size is more important than form and color.

Structure

The structure of visual language is formed by different image variables which jointly influence our interpretation of images. Image variables can be subdivided into four main categories: *content, graphic execution, context*, and *format*.

Variables related to image *content* are the degree of realism, the amount of detail, objects, time, place, space, events such as "action," humor, drama, violence, etc., time displacement, parallel action, metaphoric descriptions (symbolic actions), the relevance and credibility of the contents, comparisons and statistics, motion, sounds such as speech, music, sound effects, and emotions. Some of these variables apply to moving pictures in films or TV. Some apply to stills in printed media like books, newspapers, etc. Others apply to both stills and moving pictures. The contents of pictures can evoke highly positive or negative responses in viewers, especially in children. Visual language can affect our attitudes and emotions more easily than speech and text.

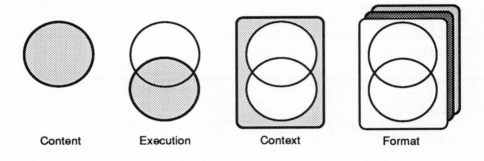

| Content | Execution | Context | Format |

Variables in visual language can be related to content, execution, context, and format.

Variables related to an image's *graphic execution*, form, or art style may consist of image factors and image components. They are composed of non-significant image elements, such as dots, lines, and areas in different combinations. Examples of image factors and image components are image type, i.e., whether images are drawings, paintings, photos, computer-generated visuals, etc., brightness, light, shape (external shape, external contour), size (image, subject, depth), color (color, hue, grey scale), contrast, emphasis, composition (organization, centers of interest, balance), perspective (depth, depth-of-field, image angle, image height), technical quality, symbols, signs and code signals in the image, pace, speed change (slow, fast), editing, zooms in and out, panning, visual complexity, and visual effects.

A picture has both an *internal* and an *external context*. I regard factors inside the medium as "internal context." In books internal context is the interplay between text and illustrations, the interplay between illustrations and layout. Movies and TV programs have sound with speech, music, and sound effects plus visual and audio metaphors. Some computer programs contain advanced animation with interaction between text, images, and even sound. I regard the entire communications situation, i.e., senders and their intentions for the picture and receivers and their circumstances (e.g., time available), as external context.

The choice of *format* is of major importance to our perception of image contents. Our perception of a picture (such as a photograph) changes when we view it as a paper print, transparency projected on a white screen, as a computer image, etc. If you watch a film on TV, cable TV, or VCR at home alone, your perception of the film is very different from your response when you watch the same film on a wide screen with hi-fi sound in a cinema full of people. In analogical technical systems, letters and numerals are represented by defined "type" (a, b, c, ...). Pictures consist of lines and halftone dots. In digital systems, image elements are mathematically defined either as intersections of coordinates and vectors providing direction or as "pixels," i.e., small rectangular image components.

As an example of the interplay between different variables, let us consider an ordinary deck of cards. It consists in fact of 52 (or 54) different visuals. Regardless of the suit, cards with small values, such as one to six, are usually "very easy to read." It only takes one or a few glances for a card player to know which one of the 52 cards he or she has been dealt. Cards with values from seven to 13 contain more information and can be classified as "easy to read." However, pictures of jacks, queens, and kings are sometimes harder to read and distinguish from one another, depending on their design and execution complexity. Cards of the same numeric value, e.g., four, differ in their execution with respect to the symbols for the four suits. They differ in content. Different decks of cards can differ in design and execution. Thus, e.g., the king of spades looks different in different decks, but the king always represents the same content. A card seen together with other cards is seen in different contexts. The value of one card (or of any other visual) is different, then, for the player (or for the user) in different contexts.

It is also possible to describe how the variables in visual language are related to each other using a three-dimensional model, a pyramid. In the model all the "corners" are related to all the other corners. In a similar way, all variables are related to all other variables.

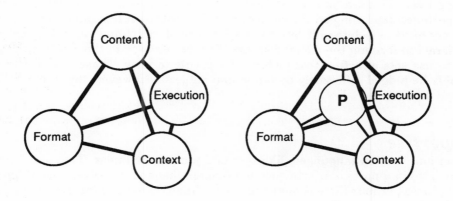

Variables in visual language can be related to content, execution, context, and format. This model illustrates the close relationships of all the different groups of variables (left). All variables in visual language will influence our **Perception** (right).

In a study of picture readability (Pettersson, 1983a), 15 experienced "visual design experts" in Sweden were asked to rate the importance of each of 21 individual visual language factors to the total readability of a picture. They indicated their ratings on a questionnaire with a semantic scale from "very slight importance" to "very great importance." The results suggest that it is very difficult to rank the variables. Only a few of the variables were regarded as being of very slight or very great importance. A number of respondents noted that in their view the variables varied in importance depending on the context. Thus, a variable may be very important in one context but of only slight importance in another.

The same task was later given to 25 students in the USA. The results from this rating suggest that it is difficult to rank the variables and that the variables vary in importance. In these model experiments the number of subjects was limited. In an attempt to get more information, copies of a somewhat extended and partly different questionnaire were sent to members of IVLA, International Visual Literacy Association, who distributed them among their students. In this case a semantic differential scale which combined verbal statements with numeric values (0–100) was used. This scale has been successfully used in several studies (e.g., Pettersson *et al.*, 1984). The use of numeric values makes it possible to calculate mean values.

The idea was to collect information from several different cultures and compare the results. Questionnaires were sent back from Canada, Holland, Japan, United Kingdom, United States, Sweden, and Switzerland. An analysis of more than one hundred answers shows enormous variations between individual subjects. For most of the 24 variables there is a difference of 70–80 points with mean values ranging from 58 to 76, corresponding to "great importance." Standard deviations were also very high (15–22).

In this study it is not possible to find any certain differences between the opinions of subjects in different countries. Basically the study supports earlier findings and shows that people have very different ideas about the importance of various aspects of visual language to the readability of a picture. However, on average, all variables are "important." Several subjects also noted that variables varied in importance depending on the content and the context. A few subjects noted that it was very hard to isolate and rate the importance of individual variables, since they all interact in forming the visual message. Future research in this field will probably have to use sets of actual test pictures for people to view. These test pictures will probably be judged differently by individual subjects. However, there might also be cultural differences.

Properties

Spoken and written languages, like text and music, are linear. They must be read (listened to) in a particular sequence to be comprehended. However, visual language is two-, three-, or four-dimensional and can be "read" by letting the eye scan a picture or sculpture in many different ways. Time is an important dimension, not only in film and TV, but also in still pictures. Our "decoding" of an image, and our subsequent perception of it, may vary considerably with respect to which of the visual cues we see first. Studies of eye movements have shown that we often scan pictures in search of simple shapes providing structural simplicity. Missing information is filled in by the brain so a logical and "complete" visual impression is created. Influenced by our reading habits, people in western countries often scan pictures from left to right.

In comparison to a written text, a visual contains an infinite amount of information (Pettersson, 1985a). By selecting and utilizing different parts of a picture's information on different occasions, we can experience completely new and different perceptions when we re-see a picture in new contexts. Like other languages, pictures consist of coded messages that are comprehensible in a given social context and in a given age. For example, we often find it difficult to interpret the messages in pictures from unfamiliar cultures and ages. "Modern art" puzzles its public who has not yet learned to decipher the new codes. The reader (viewer) always has greater freedom in interpreting a visual message than a verbal message. Pictures almost always convey multiple messages. Extraneous messages may compete with the messages the sender regards as significant and important. So pictures always incorporate some ambiguity and numerous "correct" interpretations, although not always a picture creator's intended or anticipated interpretation. The way in which a picture is interpreted depends to a great extent on the reader's code in relation to the sender's code. Studies of intended vs. perceived image content give clear evidence that there are major differences between intended and perceived image content.

There are many ways to depict even the simplest object. Many pictures are appropriate to and representative of a given designation, such as "Easter," "Christmas," "flowers," "children," "horses," "dogs," "cats," "cards," etc. The depiction of, e.g., "Jesus Christ" and "Buddha" is commonplace in the classical art of the respective religions. The number of pictures capable of depicting a concept declines as the degree of descriptive detail increases. Many pictures may be regarded as "visual synonyms." A message may always be expressed in different pictures. A picture will always be interpreted in different ways. Thus, it may be concluded that pictures used in information and instructional materials always should have captions to guide understanding of the content.

As far as ambiguous pictures are concerned, there is often a major difference between their *denotation*, i.e., their literal meaning, and their various *connotations*, i.e., their associative meanings, and their *private associations*.

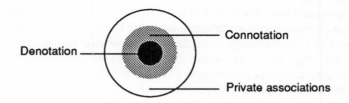

Each complete meaning can be interpreted in different ways by various persons. We can define fields of denotation (center), connotations (middle), and private associations (outer area).

By, e.g., exaggerating perspective, deforming shapes, making symbolic use of colors, etc., a picture creator can easily create works which evoke extra associations in viewers. This is in fact the very idea behind an artistic picture. However, the *informative picture* should not be open to different interpretations. The picture's message should then be the message intended by the person/agency commissioning the picture.

The total amount of information presented varies considerably in different media. A typed A4-sized page can hold up to 2,500 characters, whereas a TV image consists of 250,000 pixels whose color content and grey scale can be changed 25 times a second. By editing a text we can reduce the number of words required to convey a "content." The amount of information in synthesized (computer-generated) speech can sometimes be reduced by up to 99% without obliteration of message comprehension. A number of graphic elements in pictures can also be reduced without any major impact on content. We can *delete, add,* or *relocate* information. Graphic elements which constitute boundaries between different image elements are more important to our perception of the image than other graphic elements. In principle, it should be possible to delete a rather large number of *non-significant* elements in, e.g., a photograph. As long as some of the *significant* picture elements are retained, we can still get some idea of the image content. So *image design can be changed a great deal without any major change in the perception of image content.*

Image design can be changed a great deal without any major change in the perception of image content. In this example one hundred pixels were successively changed.

Since the brain fills in missing information and, in certain instances, attempts to make the best possible interpretation of a given stimulus, certain significant graphic elements can also be deleted from images. Missing lines in cartoons can sometimes be as important as the lines actually used. Employing about the right amount of graphic elements and finding the right visual balance are characteristics of skilled and experienced artists, photographers, and graphic designers. Inadequate information results in an inadequate picture. Excessive information results in visual overload, making a picture hard to interpret. There is an optimum trade-off for each content and application.

The graphic execution of a visual can be measured by objective as well as by subjective methods. The content can only be measured by subjective means. Each content has an execution, and each execution has a content. The variables in visual language have both functional and suggestive properties. *Functional properties* are related to cognitive factual information in contents, execution, and context. *Suggestive properties* are related to emotions, conceptions, aesthetic perception, tension, fright, etc. The choice of format also comprises a large measure of emotional content.

Functional properties predominate in symbols. They are also more important than suggestive properties in "informative," "information-dissemination," or "educational" pictures, since their task is to convey certain knowledge, information, etc., in the simplest and most effective manner possible.

The objective of an "information-dissemination" picture is also to convey certain emotions and arouse the viewer's interest and involvement (e.g., regarding conditions in other countries or in past times).

Suggestive properties are more important than functional properties in "artistic" pictures. Art is not primarily a question of objects. It is actually a visual language for dissemination of ideas and experiences that are difficult to put across in words. Irrespective of the sender's intentions, different receivers may respond in an emotional manner to a picture with mainly functional properties. In the corresponding manner, some viewers may respond unemotionally and functionally to pictures with predominantly suggestive properties.

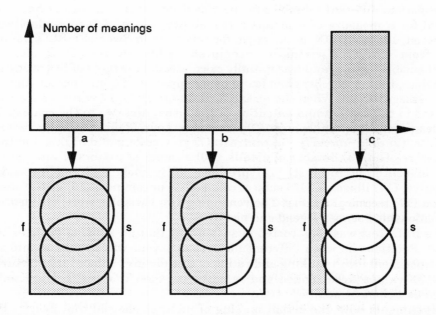

A symbol (a) usually has only a denotation and very few connotations and private associations. It is unambiguous. All other visuals have one or more connotations and private associations. They are more or less ambiguous. In realistic pictures (b), used in information and instructional message design, functional properties are more important than suggestive properties. In a suggestive picture (c), like a painting, the reverse is true (f = functional properties and s = suggestive properties).

Picture readability

All sighted people are capable of "looking at" a picture. But people can also learn to "read" pictures the same way they learn to read words. The language of pictures used in all media should be tailored to reader perceptions. For example, the degree of reading difficulty should gradually increase in textbooks intended for different school grades. It is reasonable to assume the following regarding pictures designed to convey information and knowledge:

- A picture that is easy to read and comprehend conveys information more readily than a picture that is hard to read and comprehend.
- A picture that evokes a positive response conveys information more effectively than a picture that evokes a negative response when motivation is identical in both instances.
- Even a "poor" picture will work when viewer motivation is high, but a "good" picture would then work even better.

Cermak & Craik (1979), however, found that if learners perceive a task as more demanding, they tend to process the material more deeply and are better able to remember the main ideas and details in a text. Weidenmann (1988) found some support for this relationship in his research on the effectiveness of pictures.

In view of our understanding of the importance of the way a picture is executed with respect to different variables in the visual language, the author has devised a proposal for a measure of a picture's readability, i.e., a picture readability index (Pettersson, 1984a) (BLIX, an acronym for this term in Swedish). BLIX values may range from 0, i.e., a virtually incomprehensible picture, to 5, i.e., a very comprehensible picture, and was initially calculated on the basis of the rating of up to 19 variables, that researchers had found being important for information and instructional message design. When the research started in 1979, 17 variables were directly connected to the content and execution of the visual and two to the context. The 17 variables were: (1) external shape, (2) external contour, (3) size, (4) color versus black and white, (5) color intensity, (6) contrast, (7) grey scale and darkness-lightness, (8) degree of realism, (9) number of details, (10) number of centers of interest, (11) location of center of interest, (12) presence of symbols and reading aids, (13) perspective, (14) illusions, (15) subject common or uncommon, (16) size of main subject, and (17) technical quality. The remaining two variables were: (18) legend, and (19) relationship between legend and picture.

The BLIX-test was constructed in such a way that all kinds of pictures could be indexed. Relations between different pictures or layout was not taken into account here. Experiments with ranking and rating of test-pictures showed that pictures with high BLIX-values were ranked and rated better than those with lower values by children as well as by adults.

Experiments with the actual making of pictures showed that despite detailed instructions on the execution of the visuals, there was still plenty of scope for individual creativity. It was also shown that informative pictures drawn so that their BLIX-ratings were high (more than 4.5) were to a large extent rated as aesthetically pleasing, rated as "suitable" or "very suitable" for teaching, and did not take more time to make than pictures with lower BLIX-ratings. Instructions on the execution had to be followed if reliable and satisfactory results were to be obtained.

BLIX must not be an end in itself. There is always a risk associated with index values, since they can be interpreted as absolute values. BLIX actually represents the average difficulty or ease with which a picture can be read. It also yields some very valuable information and detailed knowledge on the importance of individual picture variables. The ability of the receiver to study the contents of a word-picture message is likely to increase considerably if the word-picture is designed with this in mind.

Knowledge of picture readability, i.e., our total ability to interpret and understand a visual message in terms of our *perception of the content, execution, and context of the visual,* enables us to make a visual description. A visual description is a description in words and outlines of a visual which does not yet exist. The accuracy with which the intentions of the instructor are carried out can subsequently be checked, at least in part, by means of picture analysis, i.e., an evaluative description of a visual, and partly by means of various practical tests. The results of these tests lead to a revised visual description which leads to another still more effective material for information or instruction, etc., in a spiraling process of feedback interaction.

The BLIX-analyses gave as a result a revised BLIX-rating-scheme that may be used as a practical tool in design of materials for information and instruction:

Revised BLIX-rating-scheme

Questions   *Yes/No*
1. (a) Color picture: The picture is executed in a true-to-life color.
   (b) Black & white picture: The contrast and gray scale in the picture are clear.
2. The picture has a shape other than a square or a rectangle or covers an entire page.
3. The picture has a legend which is brief, easy to understand, and deals with the picture.
4. The picture is unambiguous and not too "artistic."
5. The picture has a dominant center of interest at or near its optical center (middle of the picture) and few details which can be regarded as distracting.
Total number of yes answers.   _____

The total number of "yes" answers provides a direct value for picture readability in which 0 = "a virtually incomprehensible picture," 1 = "very hard to read," 2 = "hard to read," 3 = "neither hard nor easy to read," 4 = "easy to read," and 5 = "very easy to read."

Picture quality

A question such as "what is good or poor picture quality?" may seem trivial. But there is no widely accepted definition for "picture quality," nor any unambiguous or sufficiently comprehensive measure of this parameter.

Any visual produced to convey information or knowledge must obviously contain the information to be conveyed. Such a visual's content, execution, context, and format elicit a response, a perception, and possibly subsequent learning and memory. The information producer should produce representations in such a way that perception, on the average, is optimized.

The sender of a message must define the objectives for each picture used. What emotions and information should the image convey? Who is the receiver? And in which medium will the visual be distributed? Correspondingly, the receiver (viewer) should attempt to identify the sender's intentions. Which emotions and information are conveyed by the picture? Who is the sender? What are the picture's apparent objectives?

Which pictures are "good" and which pictures are "bad"? In this context, "good picture quality" can be defined as the degree of coincidence between the sender's and receiver's subjective perception of the picture and the reality (external or internal) represented by the picture.

According to this definition, the concept "picture quality" is related to the entire communications process, encompassing both sender and receiver, representation and reality.

A "good" visual has a high level of picture quality. It is well worth reading and is executed so as to be legible and readable and be displayed in an optimum context in an appropriate format. The visual should convey information without ambiguity. It should be stylish and attractive, and is often, but not necessarily, also aesthetically pleasing.

A "poor" visual has a low level of picture quality. It displays poor legibility and poor reading value. It conveys information poorly, is seldom aesthetically pleasing, and often ambiguous. Dwyer & Dwyer (1989) point out that "the value of different types of visual illustrations is not a valid assessment of instructional effectiveness; that is, pleasing visuals may not be of great instructional value" (p. 122).

Reading value is governed by picture variables related to picture contents.

Legibility is governed by the functional properties of picture execution.

Readability is governed by the functional properties of picture variables. A picture's *aesthetic value* is the aggregate effect of all picture variables.

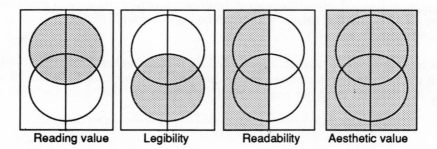

Reading value   Legibility   Readability   Aesthetic value

A visual is well worth reading and has a high reading value when the content is interesting to the reader from a functional and/or from a semantic point of view. The legibility is mainly dependent on the execution of the visual. The readability is mainly dependent on the functional properties of the visual. The aesthetic value of a visual is a combination of all the different variables.

Measuring picture properties

There are several ways of "measuring" picture properties. These "tools" can be used before the original is finished, before the technical production, and after the actual publication of the images.

Before the original

A picture description can be drawn up on the basis of our knowledge of man's ability to interpret and understand a visual in terms of perception, contents, execution, context, and format. A "picture description" is a depiction in words and sketches of a visual that does not yet exist.

Before technical production
Draft versions and also alternative versions of information materials may be tested to determine whether or not the visuals are attractive and appealing, communicate the intended information or message, and are acceptable to the intended audience.

OBS and Reading value ratings
Larssen & Skagert (1982) employed two "preview tests" in order to assess reader response to as yet unpublished advertisements. A simple interview test provides a good forecast of future OBS (observation) and reading value ratings. The two central questions were (p. 28): "(1) If you encountered this ad in a newspaper, would you stop to look at it? (2) If you encountered this ad in a newspaper, do you think you would read any of the text in it?" When numerous subjects respond affirmatively, an ad can be expected to receive high OBS and reading value ratings. The opposite is also the case, i.e., if numerous subjects respond negatively.

Utility/Originality rectangle
The second preview test entailed assessment of ads according to the concepts "utility" and "originality." First, the extent to which the reader derived any benefit from reading or taking a closer look at an ad was rated. The rating scale ranged from "no utility" to "great utility." The degree of execution originality was then assessed. Ads with positive originality and great utility (field 1 in the "utility/originality" rectangle) were usually subsequently rated as "good ads" by readers. Publication of an ad with negative originality and little or no utility (field 4) is virtually pointless.

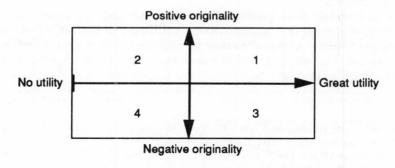

The "utility/originality" rectangle.

Redundancy/Information
Berefelt (1976) suggested that experience grows in steps in the power field lying between events previously observed and not observed, between the familiar and unfamiliar, and between banality and originality. The greater the amount of information supplied (the less the redundancy), the greater the amount of energy needed by the information recipient in order to register and comprehend the new data. Berefelt used a horizontal line with maximum redundancy and maximum (new) information as the line's theoretical end points to describe registration and processing of stimuli. Maximum redundancy elicits complete familiarity with the material, e.g., a picture. Maximum information elicits a total inability to comprehend the signals.

Our perception of different pictures probably falls between these two extremes. Berefelt assigned seven proportionally spaced perception positions from an infinite number of possible positions on the line. These perceptions, from a high degree of redundancy to a high degree of information, were referred to as "boring" (unpleasant), "neutral," "harmonious" (pretty?), "fascinating" (nice), "interesting" (exciting), "neutral," and "irritating" (unpleasant).

A picture creator who is very familiar with her/his target group can easily ensure that redundancy/information in a picture is on a level relevant to the picture's aim. The redundancy factor provides the picture creator with an opportunity to relate viewer perceptions to picture contents.

Redundancy / Information / Communicative impact

A refinement of Berefelt's ideas could result in a model that also includes consideration of the communicative impact of pictures. Our perception of a picture probably affects the picture's communicative impact. Pictures found to be boring or irritating are likely to have poor communicative impact. However, a picture perceived to be "wonderfully fascinating" is bound to be very good in communicative respects. The fact that the communicative impact of a given picture may differ for different people must obviously be kept in mind. Different people also respond to the redundancy factor in different ways depending on, e.g., previous experience, social factors, and cultural circumstances. For these reasons, plus the fact that identification of the degree of both redundancy/information/communicative impact may be difficult, the model may be unsuitable for use in practical work.

Interest / Perception

In a world in which it is becoming increasingly difficult to avoid unsolicited information and, at the same time, increasingly difficult to find information we really wish to find, our interest in material may be decisive to the way in which we perceive that material. Interesting material arouses our emotions to a greater extent than material we regard as boring.

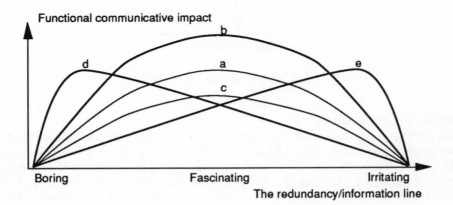

The redundancy/information/communicative impact model (a). The communicative impact of a given picture may differ with different people (b and c in this example). Different people also respond to the redundancy factor in different ways (d and e in this example).

The degree of interest can be described with a rating between "no interest at all" and "maximum interest." So the interest factor is one way to define the viewer's relationship to picture contents. When interest is zero, our emotional response is negative or, possibly, indifferent. Emotional response increases as the interest factor increases and becomes increasingly positive. However, a given picture may evoke different emotional responses in different people, even when they share a common degree of interest in the picture. Different people also perceive the interest factor in different ways. As is the case with the Redundancy/Information/Communicative impact model, the Interest/Perception model may be hard to use in practical work.

The Legibility/Reading value rectangle

A picture can also be rated according to legibility and reading value. First, the extent to which the picture is readable for the intended reader is rated. Does the picture have considerable reading value and interest or does it have poor reading value and little interest? The picture's legibility is then rated. Is the picture distinct and easily read, or is it indistinct and difficult to read with a view to its execution? An informative picture with positive reading value and legibility is probably "very good." A picture is "good" if it is readable but difficult to read. The picture is "bad" if it has limited reading value and is easy to read but "very bad" when it has poor reading value and is also difficult to read. Initial experiments suggest that a preview test of this kind could prove to be very useful.

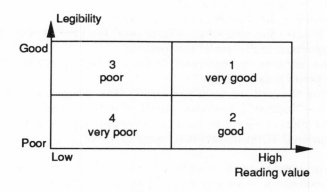

The "Legibility/Reading value" rectangle.

After publication

A picture analysis, i.e., a descriptive rating of a picture, and various practical tests can be carried out to determine whether or not an information disseminator's intentions are accurately realized. The results of these tests can be used for revision of the picture description which, in turn, could result in even more effective informative material.

Picture analysis

A picture analysis can comprise a description and, possibly, a rating of picture language, contents, execution, context, format, medium, distribution method, sender, receiver, objectives, etc. Different sets of questions can be used in picture analysis depending on the objective of the analysis. The following questions may be useful in a brief, general analysis:

- *Visual language.* Is the visual language clear and distinct? Is the visual language adopted to the culture and to the audience? Is the picture's "meaning nucleus" obvious? Does the picture contain a lot of insignificant information?
- *Content.* What is (are) the subject(s) in the visual? Is (are) the subject(s) easy to understand? What are the relationships of the different subjects? Is one part of the picture dominant over the others and why? Is the picture a typical or a non-typical example of the subject? What is the degree of realism and detail? What is the degree of credibility? How are motion, time, sound, and emotions expressed?
- *Execution.* What type of visual is it? Is the subject large and clear? What is the shape, size, color, and contrast? How is the composition in terms of organization, centers of interest, and balance? What are the depth, picture angle, and picture height? What is the technical quality like? Does the picture have symbols and explanatory words?
- *Context.* What is the context? Is there a legend, texts, other pictures, or sound in connection with the picture? How is the layout done?
- *Picture readability.* What is the picture readability index?
- *Medium.* In which medium is the picture used? Is the picture used in mass-media, in group media, or in personal media?
- *Distribution.* How is the distribution organized?
- *Sender.* Who is (are) the sender(s)? Who is (are) the producer(s)? Are the views of the sender important to the use of the picture?
- *Receiver.* Who is (are) the receiver(s)? Do the receivers form a homogeneous group? Is the group small or large?
- *Aims.* Why has the picture been produced? Has the picture been produced for advertising? Are "hidden" intentions imbedded in the image?
- *Impact.* Is the picture likely to have an effect on learning, human feelings, attitudes, or opinions? What impact is it likely to have?

The various preview tests can also be transformed into true readability tests. The results of these tests can also lead to revised picture descriptions.

Goldsmith (1980, 1984, 1986) offers an analytical model for illustrations. Her model consists of twelve elements which are formed by the interaction of four visual factors with three levels of communication. The four visual factors are: *unity*, which refers to a single image; *location*, the spatial relationships between two or more images within a single picture; *emphasis*, the hierarchical relationships between images; and *text parallels*, the relationship between text and picture. The three levels of communication are: *syntactic*, which does not assume any recognition or identification of images; *semantic*, which concerns the basic recognition of an image; and *pragmatic*, which reminds us that readers will differ in age, sex, education, and so on.

- *Syntactic unity.* An acknowledgment that an image exists. A minimum requirement is that the bounds of each image should be discernible.
- *Semantic unity.* The identifiability of an image.

- *Pragmatic unity.* The characteristics of the viewer can work for or against recognition of an image.
- *Syntactic location.* Depiction of depth with the use of converging lines, etc.
- *Semantic location.* Known size of an object can indicate depth.
- *Pragmatic location.* The experience of the viewer is needed to resolve ambiguous details.
- *Syntactic emphasis.* Cues for attracting and directing the attention of the viewer.
- *Semantic emphasis.* The human face is of universal interest and attracts attention.
- *Pragmatic emphasis.* Various instructions may influence our perception of the image. This aspect also includes special interests of viewers.
- *Syntactic text parallels.* The physical/spatial relationship between pictorial and verbal signs.
- *Semantic text parallels.* Distinguishing features of an object that serve to identify that object correctly. The matching of word and image.
- *Pragmatic text parallels.* The interpretation of the message by the viewer.

Peterson (1984) has worked on an analysis of comic strips and has proposed the following model based on a semantic approach:
- An analysis of the storyline. Which hidden values do the figures represent? How are conflicts presented in the story? How are conflicts resolved? Are any myths created?
- An analysis of picture structure and meanings on both denotative and connotative levels. When characters conveying meaning are interpreted, both internal and external context are taken into consideration.
- An analysis of the importance of balloon texts.
- A study of the location of emphasis in the communications process.

This should lead to identification of the comic strip's function, e.g., to be poetic or challenging. How is imagination employed? In an emancipative, compensatory, or power-confirmative manner? Which attractive properties do the pictures have? Fascinating, aesthetic shapes? Do they play on any particular emotions, needs, or dreams? Which dialectic relationships prevail between the strip's design and receiver context?

Values and attitudes

Semantic differential scales in which the sender and/or receivers report how positively or negatively they respond to a given picture in overall terms or with respect to individual picture variables can also be employed in measuring how "good" or "bad" a picture is.

Semantic differential scales can comprise general attitude toward a picture (Bad–Good), aesthetic value (Ugly–Pretty), reading value (Uninteresting–Interesting), technical quality (Poor–Good), legibility (Hard to read–Easy to read), educational value (Slight–Great), and credibility (False–True). The combination of verbal *and* numerical scale steps makes possible statistical calculations of mean values, standard deviations, and confidence intervals. This makes the method suitable for large groups of subjects.

Observations
Producers of visuals for information may benefit from observing how receivers and "actual users" use information materials in normal situations. Observers could also interview "members of the audience" about how, why, and when they use visuals.

Pictures and the "total teaching aid"

The development of different compact discs will open up fascinating new opportunities to producers of teaching aids. They will make it possible to create "the total teaching aid" encompassing text, sound, pictures, numerical information, *and* opportunities for various kinds of information processing in a single medium. A "total teaching aid" is a multimedia database offering the user complete freedom in moving back and forth between verbal, numerical, visual, and audio information. This will enable children (and adults) with all kinds of modalities, i.e., verbal, visual, kinesthetic, or mixed modalities, to actively seek and find information which is actively transformed into experience and knowledge. In supplying answers to assignments or writing reports, students will have easy access to the necessary background information. They will also be able to retrieve suitable examples, i.e., "quotes" from the individual databases, and incorporate them into their own presentations. Numerical information in tables, for example, can be processed and presented as bar charts, curves, or pie charts providing a better overview. A teaching aid could also contain different kinds of computer-based educational games and the like.

Kindborg & Kollerbaur (1987) point out that the use of graphical interfaces has made computers easier to use for people who are not computer experts. Visualization of system status and of on-going processes has enhanced the user's understanding of how various computer-based tools work and can be used. The Dynabook system (Goldberg & Kay, 1977) and the desktop metaphor of the Xerox Star system and its successors, including the Macintosh series of computers, are well known examples of graphical user interfaces (or GUIs). One reason for their success is that the visual presentation techniques employed communicate the model of the system to the user in a clear way. In addition, interaction with a graphical interface is often considered to be stimulating and fun. In fact it is easy for a child to learn to use graphical interface computers like the Apple Macintosh.

Most graphic products can only display a rather limited number of pictures depicting a situation. However, an optical/electronic system is capable of storing an extremely large number of pictures which need not be cropped as severely as "print published" pictures. So the user has a greater opportunity to utilize picture information as a "resource," "information bank," and retrieve information that is relevant and of interest on any given occasion.

A stored image is much larger than the image displayed on the screen. Only the central part is displayed. The entire picture can be viewed by scrolling the screen image up or down or to the side. Horizontal and vertical rulers with cursors outline the position of each displayed image window.

Here, electronic media are completely superior to all traditional media. For economic reasons, a book cannot contain multiple versions of a picture with different croppings. The sender's perception of what is important is the deciding factor in the choice of the picture selected for publication. With use of the "total teaching aid" the user of the system, the learner, can decide what is important to her or to him.

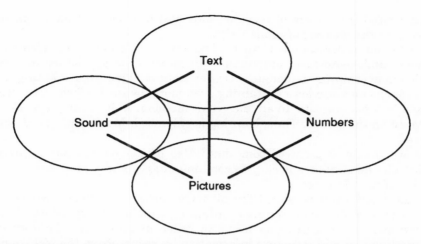

Search options in databases with verbal, numeric, visual, and audio information. There are always four ways to proceed. The user can remain in the same database or switch to any of the others at ease.

How can an image be processed? Modern, computer-based systems for processing graphical images offer wide-ranging opportunities for simple editing and *manipulation* of image contents. In addition to changing scale, the user can change projection, crop or expand, reduce, delete, modify, move, turn, supplement, isolate, or combine various image elements. Pictures can be stored as object oriented descriptions, in bit-mapped form, or as a combination of same.

Computerized image processing offers incredible opportunities. However, copyright laws and ethical rules make free use of these opportunities impossible. Manipulation or counterfeiting of image contents are condemned.

What happened before and after the displayed picture? Picture sequences depicting various events can be stored instead of individual pictures. Animation, with the option of freezing each component image, could be used. By the use of advanced computerized image compression, it will also be possible to show live sequences.

Entire picture sequences can be stored. This supplies information on "before" (picture to the left) "now" (picture in the center), and "after" (picture to the right).

Among traditional media, this technique is used with great success in comic strips. Comics are usually examples of presentations where text and pictures are highly integrated. Producers of teaching aids and producers of encyclopedias may learn a lot from the creators of comic strips.

How can you understand a picture? Pointing at different image elements opens one or more windows to other databases with information on picture contents. This information may comprise explanatory text or additional pictures. Pointing at a word in the text opens new windows containing even more detailed information, etc. Sound can be used in some contexts. In an "electronic dictionary," for example, spoken words are displayed on the screen. Thus, learning is enhanced. Music and sound effects can also be used.

How are text and pictures combined? Use of the windowing technique and electronic "clippings" makes it easy to combine images and text or parts of texts in the creation of new documents.

Are additional levels possible? The displayed picture is a basic picture. It can be stored with several different overlays containing supplementary information in the form of various symbols, such as terms in different languages. This gives us an opportunity to adapt and structure information by rising above the picture plane. In certain instances, the user can also descend below the picture plane.

Examples of windowing. Only the window frames are shown. Here the text is indicated.

Developments currently are very rapid. New products and new systems are released all the time. We can be sure that *databases of the future* will offer completely new options of very considerable interest.

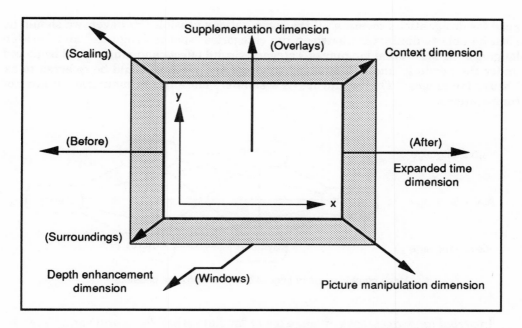

Databases of the future will offer completely new options. Pictures get new dimensions.

LINGUISTIC COMBINATIONS

Different combinations of linguistic expressions are usually employed in mass communications. For example, a textbook or newspaper generally utilizes both the printed words *and* pictures. A TV program employs words *and* images *and* sounds such as music. Interesting effects can be produced by the combination of various linguistic expressions, thereby heightening interest and attractiveness. We get more interested in the material and pay attention to it. The results of several experiments show that learning is maximized when the contents of visual, audio, and print channels are on the same level (cf. Levie & Lentz, 1982, for a review). Conveying information through both verbal and visual languages makes it possible for learners to alternate between functionally independent, though interconnected, and complementary cognitive processing systems. The cited categories yield numerous ways of combining spoken and written language, sound effects and music, symbols and pictures when producing representations of reality. We have no designations for most of these combinations, and the designations we do have are often misleading. *AV* or *audio-visual* are common designations illustrating the problem. You never know exactly what is meant by the term "AV." It may refer, e.g., to the use of slides *or* to slides with audio cassettes. The slides may contain images with pictorial content *or* images with verbal content *or* both. Braden & Beauchamp (1986) make a distinction between "reader slides" and "picture slides."

More distinct, specific designations are necessary to any serious discussion of linguistic expressions and different kinds of representations. There is no practical need for designations covering all the combinations possible. However, we should at least be able to distinguish between the categories "spoken language" and "written language" in the "verbal languages" category. Sound effects and music could be placed under the heading "audial language." Symbols and pictures could be referred to as "visual languages." This would leave a smaller, more easily managed number of combinations.

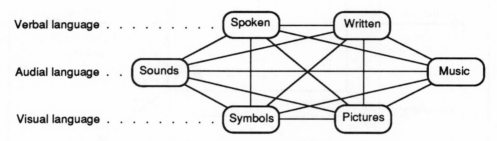

Verbal language . . . .

Audial language . .

Visual language . . . .

Many combinations of linguistic expressions are possible.

In *verbal languages,* spoken language or "audial verbal" (or "aural verbal") can be designated ***oral.*** Written language or "visual verbal" or "graphic-verbal" may be designated as ***lexigraphic.*** Combinations of these may be referred to as ***oral-lexigraphic.*** Examples of such representations are texts recited in a theater, radio program, or on audiotape.

In *audial languages* both sound effects and music are ***audial*** (or aural). Examples may be found in radio programs and audio tapes.

In *visual languages* both symbols and pictures are ***visual.*** Symbols are used, e.g., for traffic signs. Pictures can be found almost everywhere, usually in combination with verbal and/or audial languages. Paintings, drawings, and other objects of art often stand alone. (Paralinguistic visual expressions are not discussed here.)

Combinations of *verbal language + audial language* can be designated ***audio-verbal.*** This designation can be used in describing representations on radio, audio tapes, records, and compact discs.

Verbal language + visual language can be designated ***verbo-visual*** and subdivided into ***oral-visual*** (e.g., a filmstrip with a spoken commentary) and ***lexi-visual*** (frequently found in books, magazines, and other printed matter).

Audial language + visual language can be designated ***audio-visual.*** Many artistic slide-tape shows and multi-image presentations employing images, music, and sound effects belong to this category.

Verbal language + audial language + visual language may be designated ***verbo-audio-visual.*** Motion pictures, television, and video programs belong to this category. Audio-visual or verbo-visual films, TV shows, and video programs are also possible and sometimes necessary.

However, this theoretical model may not be practical to use in everyday life. Based on how the *verbal information* is presented to the receivers, we can distinguish between two forms of verbo-visual information. We *read* text in lexi-visual representations, and we *listen to* speech in audio-visual representations (the term audio-visual is used here in the traditional sense as a designation for sounds and visuals).

When we receive a verbo-visual message, it may be audio-visual, lexi-visual, or multi-visual. We usually are rather quick to form a mental pre-understanding, which influences our perception of the message. We do expect to find different kinds of contents in a newspaper, a business magazine, a book for small children, a textbook in chemistry, a non-fiction book about dog care or gardening, in the news or in the weather reports on TV, etc. It may in fact be rather hard to bypass such pre-understandings and reach to the "real or true" understanding of the message.

When we see a realistic picture we expect to find an informative real-world story content. When we see a cartoon we expect to find a narrative text and an imaginative content.

A page in a textbook should always be designed as a fully integrated verbo-visual message. To achieve harmony and avoid conflicting interpretations and confusion, it is important that the verbal and the visual parts of the message are created in corresponding "styles" and kinds of content. We usually see the pictures before we read the text (Lidman & Lund, 1972). A *heading* to a text gives the reader a preunderstanding of the contents of that specific text.

In many situations pictures may function like "headings" to the text, helping the reader to form pre-understandings. As seen earlier, an image is interpreted in different ways depending on the assignment. An *immediate image interpretation* is handled on a low cognitive level. An *analytic image interpretation* needs high cognitive level activities. When we see pictures on a printed page, we obviously very quickly make up a mental pre-understanding of the style and kind also of the text as well as a pre-understanding of the *complete message* on that page or in that program. We may decide not to read the text at all and leave the page. If we decide to read the text, then reading the text and reading the picture make it possible to create an understanding of the verbo-visual message contents.

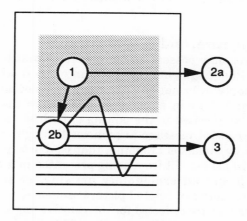

We look at the picture (1) and form a pre-understanding of the verbo-visual message. We decide either not to read the text (2a) or to read the text (2b). Reading the text and the picture makes it possible to create an understanding of the verbo-visual message (3).

Lexi-visual representations

Information materials often consist of text. Probably no other instructional device leads to more consistently beneficial results than does adding pictures to a text. There can be no doubt that pictures combined with texts can produce strong facilitative effects on retention and learning. These effects prove to be valid for a broad range of texts, pictures, learner characteristics, and learning tasks (Levie & Lentz, 1982; Levin & Lesgold, 1978).

Text and pictures must both be easy to read as well as complement and reinforce one another. Informative words need pictures, and informative pictures need words. It is very important that we use verbal and visual representations in an optimal way.

Interplay of text and graphic design

It is not enough for text to be well-edited, easy to understand, and interesting. Text must also have a *typography* facilitating its legibility. Headings, sub-headings, main text, legends, boxes, summaries, etc., must be clearly distinguished from one another. This must be accomplished in a purposeful, structured way. For example, the intermixing of an excessive number of fonts, point sizes, and typefaces in the same document should be avoided. As a rule, a little space left between different text categories can contribute to the creation of a harmonious, functional product.

Reference material, such as telephone catalogs, dictionaries, etc., are examples of highly structured information. Here, a carefully thought-out, functional layout can facilitate the reader's ability to find the desired information quickly, easily, effectively, and reliably.

Interplay of text and pictures

A picture without a caption has no or almost no informational value. A picture is too ambiguous on its own. A picture caption must describe the picture and guide the reader to the interpretation the informer wished to convey to the reader.

Interplay of text, picture, and graphic design

Both words and pictures may possess an emotive force that is not easily foreseen. A number of different value judgments could slip into a text when the purpose of the text was merely to supply information. The reader's emotions could be aroused by seemingly insignificant details in a visual or nuances in the wording of a text. So sufficient effort must be invested in the editing of both texts and pictures. Interest can be focused on the central message in pictures through careful picture selection and editing, primarily by means of cropping, that is, deleting nonessential portions. Sometimes different visuals benefit from being presented in a group. This may be the case for a photograph and an explanatory drawing, or several photographs or drawings forming a mini-series or related picture sequence.

When texts and visuals are collected for informative pages and spreads, "message transmission" must be a central consideration. This kind of "information layout" differs from a "decoration layout" in which purely aesthetic aspects are allowed to predominate.

Cartography

The preparation and production of maps is called cartography. The product of a cartographer's efforts is a mathematically defined depiction of a reality based on measurements. Maps describe reality and shed light on a number of conditions, such as terrain, political subdivisions, the prevalence of certain types of soil, minerals, etc. The utilization of variations in shape and color creates map symbols that provide a picture of the reality they represent. A carefully processed map contains more information per square inch than any other form of printed information.

Infography

A particular message is sometimes presented through the purposeful integration of text, pictures, and graphic design into clearly delineated and structured areas, i.e., a functioning whole. This design, i.e., the execution of verbo-visual information, is sometimes referred to as *infography*. The result of this work is a product called *information graphics, infographics,* the *"third language,"* or just *"graphics."* This infographic product is often interspersed with text and visuals in an information layout. Information graphics are informative and may be entertaining. They aid communication, enabling better understanding and comprehension. Information graphics are attention-getters when they appear on a page in a newspaper. They may improve readability and increase retention. In the past, information graphics were produced by hand—a tedious work process. Today most information graphics are produced with computers. Ideas can be tested in less time and good solutions may be found. In the case of newspapers, information graphics can be the key to attract new readers and to hold on to old readers.

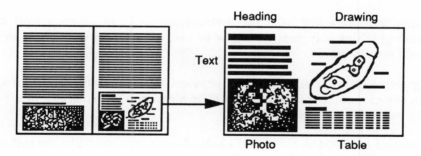

An information graphic is a "functioning whole." It has both text and visual(s). In this example, an information graphic is used in a book as an illustration.

Information graphics provide the reader with a rapid and easily grasped overall view of a message and are therefore highly suitable as an introduction to and summary of a subject. However, conventionally illustrated text is better for analysis, discussion, and study of details. So information in graphical media can utilize text, pictures, information graphics, and graphical design in conveying its message.

We should note that the word "graphics" can be used for completely different concepts:

1. One or more art forms in which copies can be made on paper or the same original.
2. Activity involving the printing of the written word.
3. Integrated presentation of text, pictures, and graphical design, in, e.g., the daily press, information graphics.
4. The technique of presenting data in the form of figures on a video display screen.

Objectives

Information graphics can be classified according to different criteria, such as objectives, medium, size, and time for production. One specific graphic may very well belong to several of these groups. We can produce information graphics in order to achieve several different objectives.

Content graphics or *everyday graphics* are used for information about the content in packages, e.g., with food.

Decorative and *artistic graphics* can also be found in both newspapers and television. Even though informative graphics can be both decorative and aesthetically attractive, the informative function always predominates. So purely decorative and artistic graphics are not information graphics.

Explanatory graphics depict the ways things were, are, or will be, for example, the weather. These graphics range from simple drawings to complex combinations of drawings, maps, and photographs.

Expo graphics are used at exhibitions and trade fairs. A subject matter is presented using verbo-visual technique and the real objects. The graphical information may aid understanding of how the real objects can be used.

Instruction graphics are used for instructions, e.g., in instructional manuals. Instruction graphics may deal with how to use, e.g., a machine or how to prepare, e.g., a meal step by step.

Locating graphics are used to give the physical location of an event or of an object. Based on one or more maps, movements of an object can be explained. Maps are often also included in other kinds of graphics.

News graphics are used to convey all kinds of news that are fit to see rather than to read as a printed story. News graphics are found in, e.g., newspapers and some magazines, and also on television.

Presentation graphics depict facts and are often used for different types of statistical tabulations. A graph or chart can be integrated into a symbolic image to heighten impact and identify the subject. Presentation graphics are often used for "business presentations." They are often called *business graphics*.

Signal graphics are small-scale graphics used to add impact and visual relief to a text.

Media

We encounter information graphics in many different media. In *graphical media* (books in particular), information graphics are often referred to as *lexivision* or lexi-visual information. In the corresponding manner, *lexigraphy* is a special version of infography for lexi-visual presentation of text, pictures, and information graphics in graphical media and computer media. Graphics are called *reference book graphics* in reference books and *dictionary graphics* in dictionaries, encyclopedias, etc.

Time for production

The American national daily newspaper USA TODAY has been a pioneer in the field of *news graphics* and has acquired imitators in many different countries. "News graphics" is a summarizing designation for several somewhat differing forms of information graphics. Due to available time for production, news graphics can be divided into several groups:

Business graphics are found in computer programs and newspapers. Business graphics is a general designation for information graphics that present economic and statistical data, for example: "the production of crude oil over the past five years."

Daily graphics is generally produced against tight deadlines. News must be published in the next edition or in the next TV news slot.

Feature graphics is a general designation for information graphics which describe more timeless subjects, such as popular science. Here, the producer may have several weeks or even months to create the copy and acquire the photographs.

Planned graphics is the designation for information graphics which the editors of news graphics have a few days to produce. This provides more opportunities for checking facts and more carefully thought-out execution.

Weather graphics are information graphics describing what the weather has been like and how it is likely to be according to available forecasts. The colorful weather graphics in USA TODAY have inspired a large number of dailies to introduce information graphics.

Audio-visual representations

Oral presentations can be planned and executed in different ways according to a number of factors, such as objective, target group, presentation duration, the time available for preparations, and the availability of various aids. The objective of an oral presentation may well be the most important factor. The objective could be, e.g., to teach, inform, convince, argue on behalf of something, or change the attitudes of listeners. A presentation may be aimed at different groups of listeners, such as pre-school children, students in elementary school, high school, colleges or universities, or different groups of adults, as in further training programs for teachers, just to mention a few examples. The oral presentation must always be on a level commensurate with the needs and interests of listeners. An oral presentation may last from a few minutes to several hours. The amount of time spent on preparations may range from nothing to weeks or months. A speaker or teacher usually employs some kind of aid, such as a chalkboard, flip-chart, overhead projector, slide projector, film projector, or VCR.

Speech and body language

The speaker must constantly strive to maintain close contact with individual listeners in order to insure that the information is reaching the mark and being understood. Listeners cannot back up and review oral information in the same way that they can with printed information. So every presentation should commence with an overview of the content to be discussed and conclude with a summary of the content. This will enable readers to obtain the best possible grasp of the total message. Including time for questions is also often appropriate.

Speakers transmit visual impressions. For students, teachers constitute "living pictures." This is because speakers employ body language in addition to oral language. Continuous contact between teacher and students can be sustained solely with the "speech" of body language. Body language reflects a person's emotional state, attitudes, and personality. It discloses whether a speaker is happy, pleased, angry, annoyed, confident, uncertain, truthful, or lying. Children, and even adults, are often highly sensitive to messages conveyed with body language. So a speaker's glances, gestures, mimicry, posture, arm and leg movements, and presentation method can serve to reject or confirm her/his oral message. Some experts claim that body language is often more important than the words in an oral presentation. Ringom (1988) wrote as follows (p. 29, in translation):

> Most of the research reports I have studied indicate that words only account for about 10%, intonation about 17%, and body language (i.e., mimicry, eye, ear, and leg movements, and posture) about 73% in a communications process.

Body language is both instinctive and something we mimic and learn. A given gesture often means different things in different cultures. We convey facts with words but emotions and values with our bodies. So people are usually unable to "lie" with their body language. We listen more emotionally than intellectually.

Keller & Burkman (1993) note that the enthusiasm of an instructor or speaker can stimulate positive motivation among students.

A sensitive speaker can learn to use her/his gestures, movements, facial expressions, and articulation for punctuating, underlining, clarifying, and enhancing the vitality of her/his words. The choice of clothing can also convey fairly detailed information. This is especially the case for markers and symbols associated with particular groups of people.

A speaker must always be easily visible. So a speaker should avoid being hidden behind a rostrum so only her/his face and part of the trunk are visible. The ability of a speaker to move freely in front of her/his audience is also an advantage. A speaker must be able to see listeners in order to maintain contact with them. So making an effective presentation in a dark room in which the speaker is standing in a spotlight is extremely difficult.

Speech and demonstrations

Exemplification of an oral presentation with demonstrations using relevant objects or events is almost always beneficial to audience comprehension of a speaker's message. Demonstrations can arouse the audience's interest, reinforce message perception, and improve audience ability to comprehend a message. Giving the audience a chance to examine and touch an object or experiment with and influence a course of events is even better. The playback of brief, authentic sound illustrations can easily enhance a sense of reality or create a particular mood.

Speech and stills

A speaker unable to exemplify her/his message with real objects should employ visuals instead. Stills can be used to supply structure and an overview, provide concrete examples, approach reality more closely, show what something really looks like, create interest, reinforce a message, or summarize a presentation. We should use visuals as *actively* as possible. People remember things they've seen more readily than things they've heard. Speakers should describe, explain, and ask questions about visuals. It is not enough just to show the pictures in a rapid pace without any comments.

Stills can comprise text, tables, graphics, maps, different kinds of diagrams, and, naturally, drawings and photographs. We should avoid visuals containing excessive detail. Do not use visuals needlessly! The visuals used should be relevant to the context and make a genuine contribution. They should also be easily grasped. In an oral presentation, listeners have few opportunities for detailed study of a visual at a comfortable pace. The visual is usually displayed at a considerable distance and at a point in time selected by the speaker. So a visual employed in an oral presentation should be designed differently than a printed picture in a book. In oral presentations, each visual should only depict a single object, idea, or trend. Multiple visuals should only be displayed simultaneously in direct comparisons, e.g., of different objects or events. When a series of pictures is used, it is important for the subjects to be depicted on the same scale to prevent viewer confusion.

Wileman (1993) shows a way to organize the relationship of verbal and visual images along a continuum, the verbal/visual continuum, or the degrees of visualization. The continuum is represented by seven types of visuals, ranging from purely verbal to purely visual. The seven types are Reader Frame, Emphasized Reader Frame, Reader Frame with Visual Cues to Meaning, Verbal/Visual Balanced Frame, Pictorial or Graphic Symbol Frame with Verbal Cues to Meaning, and Pictorial or Graphic Symbol Frame (pure visual). Please see visual on page 142.

Whenever visuals are displayed, the speaker always runs the risk of losing contact with the audience. Suggestive visuals can easily create a number of associations that deflect the audience's thoughts away from the subject of the presentation. However, the speaker can pave the way for improved audience comprehension of a subsequent visual by disclosing in advance what the visual depicts. The audience will then find it easier to identify important picture content and select a relevant interpretation. When a picture is shown, viewers need some time to interpret and understand its contents.

The speaker must never be positioned so she/he blocks the audience's view of a visual.

It is always important that projectors are placed in stable positions. Small movements of the projector will cause large "jumps" of the projected image.

Overhead transparencies

Overhead (OH) transparencies can only be projected with an overhead projector, and room illumination (at least illumination near the screen) must be reduced. To prevent image distortion, the top of the screen must usually be tilted forward. The projector should be put at such a distance from the display screen that the complete image is projected on the screen. If parts of the image fall on the wall, outside the screen, this may be quite disturbing. It is also very important that the whole image is in focus. Dirt on the transparency, on the lenses, or on the screen is also disturbing and makes the real image less effective.

The overhead projector should only be on while projecting a transparency. A visual should not be displayed any longer than it takes to explain its contents.

A composite overhead can be formed with a basic transparency and add-on transparencies prepared in advance. However, successively exposing parts of a transparency by removing, e.g., obscuring pieces of paper, is usually unsatisfactory (although a common practice, even by many visual experts). Adult viewers could be distracted by the picture's dark areas and begin wondering about the hidden information instead of giving their full attention to the presentation.

Many speakers use text transparencies, or "word-visuals," containing key words in attempting to supply an overview, clarify, reinforce, and summarize complicated arguments. These texts must then be brief and concise. They must also be easy to read. For good legibility, characters should be large, distinct, and boldface, never less than 5-6 mm high when projected in a room the size of a normal classroom. Larger rooms require larger character sizes. Normal text, containing both upper-case and lower-case letters, is easier to read than texts using only upper-case letters. Overhead transparency texts should usually consist of black characters on a light background. Text transparencies are a useful adjunct for a speaker but are sometimes very boring to an audience.

Slides

It is not enough that a slide be well-designed and have a high technical quality. It should also be projected and used in a correct way. A room must be properly darkened for the most advantageous projection of mounted slides and filmstrips, unless equipment is available for back projection, i.e., projection from the rear onto a matte-glass screen. A slide's subject should appear against a black background.

Text slides should only be used to a limited degree. Texts should be light (white or yellow) on a dark background (e.g., black or dark blue). Many color combinations are hard or even impossible to read.

Wall charts

Wall charts, mounted *photographs*, some *posters*, picture *collages*, wall *maps*, and roller blind-type maps are usually excellent teaching aids, provided they are relevant to the context and large enough for the audience to see distinctly. These visuals can be mounted on a wall or, for small groups, placed on a table. Only use one visual at a time unless different visuals are to be compared. Remove any unneeded visuals so they do not distract the audience.

Using a *flannel board* and flannel board visuals always demands preparations. But this presentation form can be be rather effective, especially when the audience consists of children.

An *episcope*, i.e., a device capable of projecting opaque originals, such as text and visuals on paper, or small objects, is used sometimes, although not very often anymore. The episcope can be used for projecting any kind of text or visual, such as material printed in books and newspapers. There is then no need for special overhead transparencies or slides. A room must be very dark for effective projection of episcope images. Speakers can write or make simple drawings on a conventional blackboard (although not often black anymore) or a more modern version, the flip-chart, in a small locale with full room lighting. Complex drawings should be prepared in advance of the oral presentation.

Speech and moving pictures

Events that are hard to illustrate with stills and difficult or hazardous experiments can be depicted with the aid of moving pictures, i.e., film, video, computer animation, or TV. A brief example only lasting a minute or two may suffice. Video is an excellent aid. A speaker can conveniently introduce the appropriate moving sequence at exactly the moment when it has the maximum impact. Sequences can also be repeated one or more times if necessary.

Information in pre-recorded presentations, like films, is conveyed by various combinations of different audio-visual presentations, i.e., words and text, audio illustrations and sound effects, stills and moving images in color or black & white.

All "traditional" information and teaching programs can be used in a "linear" way. Programs can be produced using cinematic or video techniques. They can be distributed as film prints, video cassettes, or video discs in various formats. Programs can also be distributed as broadcast TV programs or as satellite and/or cable TV transmissions.

Assessments of speakers

For some time, Griffin (1990) has studied oral presentations with focus on the speakers, the "senders" in the communications process. Griffin asked 272 managers, attending Penn State University's Executive Management Program, to make assessments of their own performances. Speakers were given printed forms with questions. For each question each speaker marked one of several alternative answers. This study was repeated by myself with 70 subjects in Europe and in the US, but now with the focus on the listeners, the "receivers" in the communications process, and the questionnaire was edited to fit the new groups of subjects.

Apart from personal information about the listener, the questions covered the following topics:
– What is the "average" length of the presentations you listen to?
– Do the speakers normally use visuals (visual support) when they make their presentations?

- What visual medium do speakers rely on most frequently when they make their presentations?
- Who prepares the visuals?
- What appear to be the most frequent purpose for the presentations?

Griffin (1989) defined four categories of visuals used in business presentations: word visuals, graphs, diagrams, and maps. *Word visuals* are predominantly lists of words which provide textual support to the presentation. In some cases pictures or other icons may accompany the word visuals. *Graphs* are defined as numerical arrays in pictorial form. They consist of line, column, bar, or pie graphs as well as a variety of special-purpose graphs. *Diagrams* are defined as visual representations of flow, direction, or procedure to be followed in the completion of a process. *Maps* are defined as diagrammatic representations of geographic area. Maps represent a growing category of visualization because new computer graphic software is available to produce several types of maps.

There is a difference between the speakers and the listeners with respect to the assessments of the average length of presentations. The listeners say that they have listened to many more long presentations (38%) than the speakers say they have delivered (13%). The listeners say that they have listened to fewer short presentations (10%) than the speakers say they have delivered (16%). This may indicate that listeners have a feeling that presentations tend to last long. Speakers, however, quite often declare that they need much more time to explain what they want to say. Thus, *it is possible that speakers underestimate and listeners overestimate the average length of a presentation.*

When speakers are asked if they normally use visual support when they make their presentations, more than 1/3 of them answered "always." Listeners, however, have another opinion. Less than 1/10 of the listeners gave the same answer. And many more listeners (67%) than speakers (38%) answered "sometimes." This is in good agreement with a study of the use of visuals in textbooks and teaching aids (Pettersson, 1990a). Far more teachers (28%) than students (5%) answered "always" on similar questions. Obviously, *presenters have a tendency to overestimate their own use of visuals.*

In the spring of 1990 I attended several international conferences in Europe as well as in the USA. Several aspects regarding the actual presentations were noted on specially designed forms with questions covering the following topics, partly corresponding with the study by Griffin (1989).
- Length of presentation.
- Visual medium used.
- Number of visuals for each medium and type of content.
- Average quality of execution of visuals.
- Average legibility of words on visuals.
- Average quality of actual presentation, AV-showmanship.
- What appears to be the purpose of the presentation.

A total of 114 presentations lasted for about 46 hours. No less than 83% of the speakers used some kind of visuals in their presentations. On average these speakers used .62 pictures per minute, adding up to a total of 1,464 pictures.

Most of the speakers (57%) used about half an hour for their presentations. The second length category was 15 minutes (26%). Only a few presentations were shorter than 15 minutes or longer than 45 minutes.

Overhead transparencies were used by 52% of the speakers. Slides were used by 28% of the speakers. The speakers used a total of 810 overhead transparencies and 612 slides. Thus, it is clear that speakers on average used far more slides in a presentation (19.7) than they used overhead transparencies (13.7). In the two previous studies, overhead transparencies were the most common visual medium, whereas 17% of the speakers used no visual support. Video was used by 5% of the speakers and 1% used computer generated visuals.

By far the most common type of content was word visuals (52%), followed by diagrams (23%), and graphs (14%). On average, pictorial images were not so often used (9%), nor maps (1%), or cartoons (1%). However, here a clear distinction can be seen between slides and overhead transparencies. In both categories, word visuals were the most common type (44% and 59%) followed by diagrams (24% and 22%). Pictorial images (16%) were the third group in the slides category and the sixth group (2%) in the OH category. Graphs (16%) were the third group in the overhead transparency category and the fourth group among the slides (13%). In both categories maps and cartoons were seldom used.

Griffin (1989) attended 32 business and engineering presentations. In total the presenters used 610 visuals. He found similar relationships among types of visual contents; word visuals (54%), diagrams (15%), graphs (11%), and maps (1%). A category "other" (19%) was an inclusive category including pictures of products and people, etc., probably rather equivalent with "pictorial images" in this study. Griffin concluded that *presenters appear to over-use the technique of word visuals* and clog the visual communication channel with excessive information.

With respect to the *average quality of execution* of visuals used in the presentations, about one third of the visuals were considered "very good" (5%) or "good" (27%). Most visuals (67%) were not acceptable, with 4% "very bad," 15% "bad," and 48% "neither bad nor good."

With respect to *legibility* of the words on the visuals, less than one third of the visuals with words were considered "very good" (4%) or "good" (25%). Most visuals (70%) were not acceptable, with 8% "very bad," 17% "bad," and 45% "neither bad nor good."

With respect to the average quality of the actual presentation, *AV-showmanship*, about one fourth (27%) of all the presentations were considered "very good" (4%) or "good" (23%). Most presentations (73%) were not acceptable, with 7% "very bad," 13% "bad," and 53% "neither bad nor good." Quite often it is obvious that *speakers are aware of the poor quality of their visuals*. Comments of this kind are not at all unusual in business presentations:
– I know that you cannot read this text ...
– Unfortunately you may not be able to see this ...
– I will read the text for you, since it is too small/blurred/indistinct ...
– You do not have to read this ...
– The copying machine is in a poor condition ...
– Please excuse my handwriting ...

It is, however, more and more common that speakers simply ignore the poor quality of their own visual materials! This is obviously a rather rude attitude to the audience.

As in the previous studies the most common purpose of the presentations is "to inform" (90%). The second most common purpose is "to persuade" (6%), followed by "to motivate" (4%), and "to entertain" (1%).

Multi-visual representations

This heading refers to the interplay between lexi-visual and audio-visual presentations. Two types of presentations belong to this category: interactive systems and simulator systems. Words and visuals can be combined in different ways in each category.

Systems for computer-generated visuals are being used to an increasing degree for presentations. Computer-generated visuals can be displayed with the aid of a TV projector or with an overhead projector accessory. Computer-controlled, interactive programs or databases designed for information and education can be used "interactively." We are already able to create "total information material." This material comprises text, sound, visuals, numerical information, and facilities for processing the information in different ways. Total information material is a "multi-representational database" offering the user complete freedom in shifting back and forth between verbal, numeric, visual, and audio information. A computer program sometimes controls film projectors, VCR's, video disc players, or other technical equipment. This then becomes a multimedia presentation worthy of the name.

Total information material offers people with all kinds of modalities, i.e., verbal, visual, kinesthetic, or mixed, to perform their own active searches for information that, when found, can be actively transformed into experience and knowledge. For example, students can easily access the background information needed for a school assignment or paper. They can even retrieve and "cut out" appropriate examples, i.e., "extracts" from individual databases, and "paste" and incorporate them into their own presentations. The text and picture extracts can then be edited. Numerical information in, e.g., tables can be processed and presented as bar diagrams, curves, or pie charts supplying a better overview.

CURRENT RESEARCH

Infology can be viewed from various research angles. We can study parts of the communications process ("Communication") as well as various types of presentations ("Presentation"). Each "part" as well as each "type" can be divided in several sections. Thus "mapping the field of infology" may result in the following structure:

Communication

The communications process
    A holistic view
    Social aspects
    Noise
The sender
    Framing a verbo-visual message
    Producing an original, master, and
    edition
    "Sending" a verbo-visual message
The representation
    Analyzing a verbo-visual message
    Studying the relationships of the message
    Studying the development of new media
The receiver
    Receiving a verbo-visual message
    Understanding a verbo-visual message
    Reacting to a verbo-visual message

Presentation

Lexi-visual representations
    Manual productions
    Technical productions
Audio-visual representations
    Oral presentations
    Recorded representations
Multi-visual representations
    Interactive systems
    Simulator systems

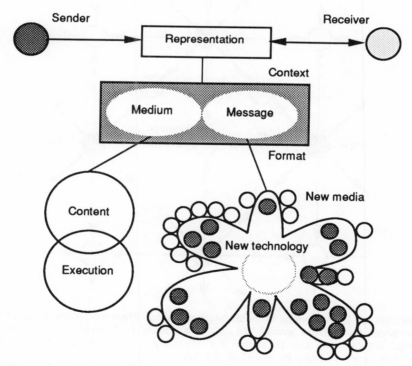

A representation is a medium with its specific message. The message has a content as well as an execution. Different media are undergoing comprehensive changes. The illustration at the bottom right shows various media groups. The circle in the middle represents live media. At the top is sound media, followed by film media, video media, broadcast media, models and exhibitions, graphical media, and telecommunications media. Several new technologies (grey circles) and completely new media (white circles) exist.

Communication

Infology encompasses studies of the way a representation should be designed in order to achieve optimum communication between the sender and the receiver. Thus, some studies are concentrated on the communications process as such, some on the sender, some on the receiver, and some on the representation.

The communications process

In the information society, people are being exposed to an increasing volume of "messages" from many different senders. The messages are transmitted from senders to receivers with the aid of different media. In all communications (even in mass communication), many individuals are the recipients of the messages.

We know that both texts and pictures can be interpreted in many different ways. As far as information is concerned, text, and pictures should therefore convey the same message/contents so as to reduce the number of potential interpretations and increase the learning effect. Captions are needed to "tie down" one of many possible interpretations of pictures.

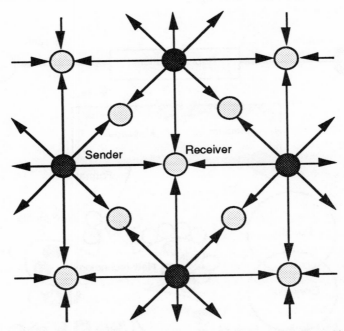

Many individuals are the recipients of messages from many different senders. How do we receive information about the outside world? We can smell, taste, feel, listen, see, and examine our surroundings. We can also ask questions. We ultimately learn to interpret and "read" different coded messages, such as those contained in, e.g., text.

This part, "the communications process," covers three areas: a holistic view, social aspects, and noise. There are several different questions at issue within each of these areas.

1. A holistic view
- Study the communications process: sender–representation–receiver.
- Create a terminology for research on verbo-visual messages.
- Study the intended vs. the perceived contents. How should a presentation be designed for optimum impact?
- Study the development of information science.
- Study the development of information technology.
- Study the development of information theory.
- Study the development of the information society.

2. Social aspects
- Study how verbo-visual messages influence democracy, freedom of speech, and the right to have access to information.
- Study the risks with information dominance and information monopoly.
- Study the development of social information.
- Examine relevant legislation and ethical standards.

3. Noise
- Study the technical problems creating noise.
- Study the effect of information overload, a kind of "mental noise."

The sender

The production of a message commences with an idea occurring to someone or with the need to convey information to a given target group. When an outline is ready, then the generation of text, draft sketches, editing, graphical design, the production of originals, masters, and, ultimately, a given quantity will begin. The sender produces a representation of reality. Other tasks for the sender are stock-keeping, distribution, marketing, advertising, selling, billing, bookkeeping, etc.

A message/content with a given design/form is conveyed by the sender to the receiver with the aid of a medium. The various media today are undergoing comprehensive (technical) changes, changes in terms of production, duplication, stock-keeping, distribution, and presentation of contents. Some of these developments are proceeding in the same direction and working together. Others are on separate paths. Some are even counteracting one another.

Costs and revenue represent both limitations and opportunities. We know that interest in buying and paying for entertainment, education, news, and factual information varies. We also know that the development of systems for, e.g., DTP (desktop publishing) offers individuals an opportunity to produce graphical products at relatively low cost. At the same time, facilities are being developed for the production of "distributed databases" in the form of small, compact optical discs with a large storage capacity. This option makes it possible to create completely new types of informational materials in which text, pictures, sound, and numerical information interact in an extremely flexible way.

This part, "the sender," includes these areas of activities: framing a verbo-visual message, producing an original, master and edition, and "sending" a verbo-visual message. There are several different questions at issue within each of these areas.

1. Framing a verbo-visual message
- Analyze the problem and the need for information.
- Define the target group or the target groups.
- Frame the objectives in measurable terms.
- Select the method (the way the objectives can be achieved).
- Select the presentation method and the medium.
- Select the time for the presentation.
- Determine the contents of the verbo-visual message.
- Collect facts and reference materials.
- Write the different text components: headings, main text, and legends.
- Process and edit the texts.
- Visualize the pictures: describe and draft the sketches.
- Create the pictures: draw, animate, paint, photograph, and film.
- Process and edit the pictures: correct, crop, enlarge, reduce, and supplement.
- Integrate words, pictures, sound, and graphical design to informative units.
- Study the development of information ergonomics.
- Study the development of psychological information theory.
- Evaluate legibility and readability of the verbo-visual message.
- Consider the specific properties of different media.

2. Producing an original, master and edition
- Produce an original: words, pictures, sound, and graphical design.
- Select different production methods and produce the master.
- Produce the edition: printing, copying, etc.
- Consider the technical quality, choice of different materials, costs.

3. "Sending" a verbo-visual message
- Market verbo-visual messages: storage, advertising, sales, and invoicing.
- Distribute verbo-visual messages: lectures, newspapers, books, films, TV, video, exhibitions, and databases.
- Post-testing can lead to correction of information, correction of the choice of method or media, or detection of new information needs. In the latter instances, the procedures start all over again from the beginning.

The representation
This part, "the representation," includes three areas of activities: analyzing a verbo-visual message, studying the relationships of the message, and studying the development of new media. There are several different questions at issue within each of these areas.

1. Analyzing a verbo-visual message
- Study visuals as linguistic expressions; analyze the structure and properties of visual languages.
- Study the levels of meaning, sub-meanings, complete meanings, in visual languages.
- Create methods for analyzing verbo-visual messages and the interaction between text, visuals, and graphic design.

— Create methods for analyzing the quality of verbo-visual messages; aesthetic, informative, and also technical quality.
— Create methods for classifying verbo-visual messages, descriptions of types of representations, terminology, etc.
— Compare the receiver's perception with the sender's intentions.
— Note the problem of objectivity – subjectivity.

2. Studying the relationships of the message
— Compare how a message is presented in different media.
— Compare how a message is perceived in different media.
— Create methods for relating representations to the sender.
— Create methods for relating representations to the receiver.
— Create methods for relating representations to reality.
— Study the process of selection of contents. When and how are different messages designed?

3. Studying the development of new media
— Study the specific properties of typical presentations in different media.
— Study how we present messages with the aid of different media. How can presentations be improved?
— Study the development of information technology.
— Study the development of new technology for production of verbo-visual messages.

The receiver

The receiver's perception of a given message is not likely to coincide with the sender's perception of or intention for a given message/content. A number of studies have shown that there is a very considerable difference between intended and perceived message/content. In one instance, the differences amounted to 22 units when a scale ranging from 0 to 100 was used.

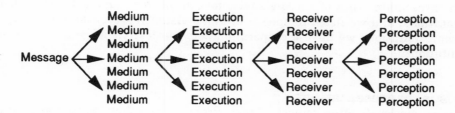

The sender's message and receiver's perception of that message do not always coincide.

We know that both texts and pictures can be interpreted in many different ways. As far as information is concerned, text and pictures should therefore convey the same message/content so as to reduce the number of potential interpretations and increase the learning effect. Captions are needed to "tie down" one of many possible interpretations of text.

How do we receive information about the outside world? We can smell, taste, feel, listen, see, and examine our surroundings. We can also ask questions. We ultimately learn to interpret and "read" different coded messages, such as those contained in, e.g., text.

This part, "the receiver," includes three areas of activity: receiving a verbo-visual message, understanding a verbo-visual message, and reacting to a verbo-visual message. There are several different questions at issue within each of these areas.

1. Receiving a verbo-visual message
– Study biological and cultural prerequisites for receiving of verbo-visual messages.
– Study individual and subjective perceptions of verbo-visual messages.
– Study perception of text and pictures: viewing, reading, studying, experiencing, understanding, and interpreting.
– Study the receiver's opportunities for reacting with the prevailing medium.

2. Understanding a verbo-visual message
– Study the development of the ability to understand verbo-visual messages.
– Study the importance of prior experience and knowledge.
– Study the understanding of facts presented in textbooks and reference books.
– Study the understanding of instructions presented in manuals and instructions.
– Study the understanding of contexts presented in maps and business graphics.

3. Reacting to a verbo-visual message
– Study how we learn from verbo-visual messages.
– Study how we remember verbo-visual messages.
– Study the impact of verbo-visual messages in advertising and propaganda.
– Study the receiver's actions.

Presentation

Based on how the *verbal information* is presented to the receivers, we can distinguish between three main types of verbo-visual information. We *read* text in lexi-visual representations, and we *listen to* speech in audio-visual representations. In multi-visual representations we have a cooperation between lexi-visual and audio-visual representations.

Lexi-visual representations

Information materials often consist of text. Probably no other instructional device leads to more consistently beneficial results than does adding pictures to a text. There can be no doubt that pictures combined with texts can produce strong facilitative effects on retention and learning. These effects prove to be valid for a broad range of texts, pictures, learner characteristics, and learning tasks (Levie & Lentz, 1982; Levin & Lesgold, 1978; Pettersson, 1989). Lexi-visual representations can be manually produced, "manual productions," or manufactured graphical media, "technical productions." In each group there are several ways of combining the verbal and the visual information.

1. Manual productions
Production of one or a few copies of lexi-visual representations, to some extent "historical infology."
– Interplay of written text, pictures, and graphic design (in manuscripts, textiles with verbo-visual messages, letters, drawings, etc).

2. Technical productions
Production of lexi-visual representations in graphical media such as books and newspapers, and also presentations on computer screens as well as computer print-outs.
– Interplay of printed text and graphic design, typography.
– Interplay of printed text and pictures.
– Interplay of printed text, pictures, and graphic design.
– Interplay of printed words and various cartographic symbols in maps.
– Interplay of printed text, pictures, symbols, and tables in infography.

Audio-visual representations
Audio-visual representations may consist of "oral presentations" and "recorded representations." In each group there are several ways of combining the verbal and the visual information.

1. Oral presentations
The use of speech and pictures in business presentations and lectures.
– Speech and body language.
– Speech and demonstrations.
– Speech and stills: "chalkboard pictures," overhead transparencies, slides, prints, flip charts, and maps.
– Speech and short sequences of moving pictures.

2. Recorded representations
All "traditional" information and training programs on film, video, and TV for linear use belong to this group.
– Interplay of words, sound, and pictures in film productions.
– Interplay of words, sound, and pictures in TV productions.

Multi-visual representations
In interactive systems and simulator systems it is possible to have an active cooperation between lexi-visual and audio-visual representations. In each group there are several ways of combining the verbal and the visual information. It is possible to create the "total information material" and the "total teaching aid" with completely new dimensions.

1. Interactive systems
In various optical media with databases it is possible to create the presentation of the information according to the specific needs and special preferences of the individual user.
– Cooperation between lexi-visual and audio-visual representations.

2. Simulator systems
In advanced simulator systems it is possible to generate real-time three-dimensional computer graphics in true colors.
– Cooperation between lexi-visual and audio-visual representations.

REFERENCES AND SUGGESTED READINGS

Aero, R., & Weiner, E. (1983). *The Brain Game.* New York: Quill.

Agrawal, B. C., Deshpanday, N., & Sinha, A. K. (1987). *Visual Symbols in Mass Media: Continuity of Collective Memories.* Paper presented at the Symposium on Verbo Visual Literacy: Research and Theory. Stockholm, June 10–13.

Akanbi, M. R., & Dwyer, F. M. (1989). The effect of inductive and deductive instructional strategies on students' ability to profit from visualized instruction. In R. A. Braden, D. G. Beauchamp, L. V. W. Miller, & D. M. Moore (Eds.). *About Visuals: Research, Teaching, and Applications.* Readings from the 20th Annual Conference of the International Visual Literacy Association. Blacksburg: Virginia Tech University.

Argyle, M., & Trower, P. (1979). *Person to Person.* Amsterdam: Multimedia Publications.

Arnheim, R. (1969). *Art and Visual Perception.* Berkeley: University of California Press.

Arnheim, R. (1986). *New Essays on the Psychology of Art.* Berkeley: University of California Press.

Aronsson, K. (1983). *Verklighetens mångtydighet och pekbokens begränsningar. Om bild och begrepp i språkläromedel.* I L. Gustavsson och H. Hult. (Red.). *Text och bild i läromedel,* SIC 4, 7–24. Linköping: Universitetet i Linköping. Tema Kommunikation.

Arvidsson, H., & Engman, R. (1989). *Skolledarperspektiv på bildspråket i skolan.* Stockholm: Skolöverstyrelsen, Sk 89:8 / Specialinformation till skolledare.

Ausburn, L. J., & Ausburn, F. G. (1978). Visual literacy: Background, theory, and practice. *Programmed Learning & Educational Technology, 15,* 292–297.

Backman, J., & Eklund, S. (1989). *Efter konferensen. Diskussioner och förslag.* J. Backman & S. Eklund (Red.). *Bilder, bildmedier, tänkande och kreativitet. Rapport från ett kulturpedagogiskt seminarium.* Umeå: Umeå universitet. Institutionen för bildlärarutbildning. Rapport nr 9, 22–27.

Backman, J., Berg, T., & Sigurdson, T. (1988). *Grundskoleelevers produktion och reception av bilder.* Umeå: Umeå universitet. Institutionen för bildlärarutbildning. Rapport nr 7.

Barnhurst, K. G., & Whitney, D. C. (1991). Visual literacy training: Changing how journalism students reason about layout. In D. G. Beauchamp, J. Clark-Baca, & R. A. Braden (Eds.). *Investigating Visual Literacy.* Selected Readings from the 22nd Annual Conference of the International Visual Literacy Association. Blacksburg: Virginia Tech University.

Baron, L. J. (1980). Interaction between television and child-related characteristics as demonstrated by eye movement research. *ECTJ, 28,* 4, 267–281.

Baron, N. S. (1981). *Speech, Writing, and Signs.* Bloomington: Indiana University Press.

Barry, A., & Leaver, A. (1989). Teaching visual literacy through newspeak: A unit model for integrating visual literacy principles and practices in the secondary English classroom. In R. A. Braden, D. G. Beauchamp, L. V. W. Miller, & D. M. Moore (Eds.). *About Visuals:*

Research, Teaching, and Applications. Readings from the 20th Annual Conference of the International Visual Literacy Association. Blacksburg: Virginia Tech University.

Batley, S. (1988). *Visual Information Retrieval: Browsing Strategies in Pictorial Databases.* In *Online Information 88.* 12th International Online Information Meeting. London 6–8 December. Proceedings Volume 1, 373–381. Oxford and New Jersey: Learned Information (Europe) Ltd.

Baudoiun, A., & Anker, P. (1984). *Kartperception of EDB-assistert kartografi.* Oslo: Norwegian Computing Center. Publication 744.

Beauchamp, D. G., & Braden, R. A. (1987). Catering to the visual audience: A reverse design process. In R. A. Braden, D. G. Beauchamp, & L. V. W. Miller (Eds.). *Visible & Viable: The Role of Images in Instruction and Communication.* Readings from the 18th Annual Conference of the International Visual Literacy Association. Commerce: East Texas State University.

Beauchamp, D. G., Clark-Baca, J., & Braden, R. A. (Eds.). (1990). *Investigating Visual Literacy.* Selected Readings from the 22nd Annual Conference of the International Visual Literacy Association. Blacksburg: Virginia Tech University.

Beauchamp, D. G. (1988). Developmental techniques to promote research and learning with visuals in the affective domain. In R. A. Braden, D. G. Beauchamp, & L. V. W. Miller (Eds.). *Visual Literacy in Life and Learning.* Readings from the 19th Annual Conference of the International Visual Literacy Association. Blacksburg: Virginia Tech University.

Becker, A. D. (1987). Tracing the codes of educational and instructional television. In R. A. Braden, D. G. Beauchamp, & L. V. W. Miller (Eds.). *Visible & Viable: The Role of Images in Instruction and Communication.* Commerce: East Texas State University.

Bennett, L. T. (1989). Visual literacy: A factor of text design and reading instruction. In R. A. Braden, D. G. Beauchamp, L. V. W. Miller, & D. M. Moore (Eds.). *About Visuals: Research, Teaching, and Applications.* Readings from the 20th Annual Conference on the International Visual Literacy Association. Blacksburg: Virginia Tech University.

Benson, P. J. (1985). Writing visually: Design considerations in technical publications. *Technical Communications Journal. Fourth Quarter,* 35–39.

Berefelt, G. (1976). *AB Se om Bildperception.* Liber Läromedel, Lund.

Bertin, J. (1967). *Sémiologie Graphique.* Paris and the Hague, Mouton and Gauthiers-Villars.

Besser, H. (1987). Computers for art analysis. In R. A. Braden, D. G. Beauchamp, & L. V. W. Miller (Eds.). *Visible & Viable: The Role of Images in Instruction and Communication.* Commerce: East Texas State University.

Blakeslee, T. R. (1980). *The Right Brain: A New Understanding of the Unconscious Mind and Its Creative Powers.* Anchor Press: Doubleday. I svensk översättning 1984. *Högra hjärnan. En ny syn på det omedvetna själslivet och dess skapande förmåga.* Värnamo: Hammarström & Åberg.

Braden, R. A., & Hortin, J. A. (1982). Identifying the theoretical foundations of visual literacy. *Journal of Visual Verbal Languaging,* 2(2), 37–51.

Braden, R. A. (1983). Visualizing the verbal and verbalizing the visual. In A. D. Walker, R. A. Braden, & L. H. Dunker (Eds.). *Seeing Ourselves: Visualization in a Social Context.* Blacksburg: Virginia Tech University.

Braden, R. A. (1987). *High Impact Technology and Visual Literacy: Reacting to Change.* Paper presented at the Symposium on Verbo-Visual Literacy: Research and Theory. Stockholm, June 10–13, 1987.

Braden, R. A., & Beauchamp, D. G. (1986). Catering to the visual audience: A reverse design process. Presentation at the 18th Annual Conference of the International Visual Literacy Association. Madison, Wisconsin, Oct. 30–Nov. 2. In R. A. Braden, D. G. Beauchamp, & L. W. Miller (Eds.). (1987). *Visible & Viable: The Role of Images in Instruction and Communication.* Readings from the 18th Annual Conference of the International Visual Literacy Association. Commerce: East Texas State University.

Braden, R. A., & Clark-Baca, J. (1991). Toward a conceptual map for visual literacy constructs. In D. G. Beauchamp, J. Clark-Baca, & R. A. Braden (Eds.). *Investigating Visual Literacy: Selected Readings from the 22nd Annual Conference of the International Visual Literacy Association.* Blacksburg: Virginia Tech University.

Braden, R. A., Beauchamp, D. G., & Clark-Baca, J. (Eds.) (1990). *Perceptions of Visual Literacy.* Selected Readings from the 21st Annual Conference of the International Visual Literacy Association. Conway: University of Central Arkansas.

Braden, R. A., Beauchamp, D. G., Miller, L. V. W., & Moore, D. M. (Eds.). (1989). *About Visuals: Research, Teaching, and Applications.* Readings from the 20th Annual Conference of the International Visual Literacy Association. Blacksburg: Virginia Tech University.

Brigthouse, G. (1939). A Study of Aesthetic Apperception. *Psychological Monographs, 51,* 1–22.

Brun, T. (1974). *The International Dictionary of Sign Language.* Halmstad: Spektra, Swedish translation.

Buswell, G. T. (1935). *How People Look at Pictures.* Chicago: University of Chicago Press.

Cassidy, M. F., & Knowlton, J. Q. (1983). Visual literacy: A failed metaphor? *ECTJ, 31 (2),* 67–90.

Cermak, L. S., & Craik, F. I. M. (Eds.). (1979). *Levels of Processing in Human Memory.* Hillsdale, NJ: Lawrence Erlbaum Associates.

Chomsky, N. (1959). Review of verbal behaviour. In B. F. Skinner (Ed.). *Language, 35,* 26–58.

Clark-Baca, J., & Braden, R. A. (1990). The delphi study: A proposed method for resolving visual literacy uncertainties. In R. A. Braden, D. G. Beauchamp, & J. Clark-Baca (Eds.). *Perceptions of Visual Literacy.* Selected Readings from the 21st Annual Conference of the International Visual Literacy Association. Conway: University of Central Arkansas.

Clark-Baca, J. (1990). *Identification by Consensus of the Critical Constructs of Visual Literacy: A Delphi Study* (Doctoral dissertation, East Texas State University, 1990).

Cochran, L. (1976). Defining Visual Literacy. *AECT Research and Theory Division Newsletter, 5,* 3–4.

Cochran, L. M. (1987). *Visual/Verbal Languaging as Metaphor.* Paper presented at the Symposium on Verbo-Visual Literacy: Research and Theory. Stockholm, June 10–13.

Considine, D. M. (1986). Visual literacy & children's books: An integrated approach. *School Library Journal,* September, 38–42.

Cossette, C. (1982). *How Pictures Speak: A Brief Introduction to Iconics.* Paper presented at the 32nd International Communication Association Conference, Boston May 1–5. Translated from French by Vincent Ross, Quebec.

Dahlstedt, K. H. (1979). *Språk och massmedier.* Presentation at the IVth Nordic Conference for Mass Communication, Umeå University.

Debes, J. L. (1969). The loom of visual literacy. *Audiovisual Instruction, 14,* 25–27.

Debes, J. L. (1970). The loom of visual literacy – an overview. In C. M. Williams & J. L. Debes (Eds.). *Proceedings: First National Conference on Visual Literacy.* New York: Pitman Publishing Corporation.

Debes, J. L., & Williams, C. (1978). *Visual Literacy, Languaging, and Learning: Provocative Paper Series 1.* Washington, DC: Gallaudet College.

Doblin, J. (1980). A structure for nontextual communications. In P. A. Kolers, M. E. Wrolstad, & H. Bouma (Eds.). *The Processing of Visible Language: Vol. 2.* New York: Plenum Press.

Dondis, D. A. (1973). *A Primer of Visual Literacy.* Cambridge, MA: Massachusetts Institute of Technology.

Duchastel, P. C. (1978). Illustrating instructional texts. *Educational Technology, 18,* 36–39.

Duchastel, P. C. (1983). Text llustrations. *Performance and Instruction, 22,* 3–5.

Duchastel, P. C., & Waller, R. (1979). Pictorial illustration in instructional texts. *Educational Technology, 19,* 20–25.

Duffy, B. (Ed.) (1983). *One of a Kind. A Practical Guide to Learning Styles 7–12.* Oklahoma State Department of Education.

Duncan, H. F., Gourlay, N. (1973). *A Study of Pictorial Perception Among Bantu and White Primary School Children in South Africa.* Johannesburg: Witwaterstand University.

Dwyer, F. M. (1972). *A Guide for Improving Visualized Instruction.* State College, PA: Learning Services.

Dwyer, F. M. (1978). *Strategies for Improving Visual Learning.* State College, PA: Learning Services.

Dwyer, F. M., & Dwyer, C. A. (1989). Enhancing visualized instruction: A research overview. In R. A. Braden, D. G. Beauchamp, L. V. W. Miller, & D. M. Moore (Eds.). *About Visuals: Research, Teaching, and Applications.* Readings from the 20th Annual Conference of the International Visual Literacy Association. Blacksburg: Virginia Tech University.

Eco, U. (1971). *Den frånvarande strukturen. Introduktion till den semiotiska forskningen.* Lund, Swedish translation.

Eco, U. (1976). *A Theory of Semiotics.* Bloomington: Indiana University Press.

Ekwall, E. (1977). *Diagnosis and Remediation of the Disabled Reader.* Boston: Allyn and Bacon.

Elkind, D. (1975). We Can Teach Reading Better. *Today's Education, 64,* 34–38.

Eriksson, R. (1986). Språkpedagogisk forskning. In F. Marton (Ed.). *Fackdidaktik. Volym II. Svenska och främmande språk. Samhällsorienterande ämnen.* Lund: Studentlitteratur, 47–74.

Esdale, B., & Robinson, R. (1982). *Viewing in Secondary Language Arts.* Edmonton, Alberta: Alberta Education.

Evans, M. A., Watson, C., & Willows, D. M. (1987). A naturalistic inquiry into illustrations in instructional textbooks. In H. A. Houghton & D. M. Willows (Eds.). *The Psychology of Illustrations: Vol. 2. Instructional Issues.* New York: Springer-Verlag.

Fast, J. (1971). *Body Language.* Stockholm, Swedish translation.

Ferm, R., Kindborg, M., & Kollerbaur, A. (1987). *A Flexible Negotiable Interactive Learning Environment.* Paper presented at HCI'87, Exeter, England.

Fleming, M. L. (1970). *Perceptual Principles for the Design of Instructional Materials.* Washington, DC: Office of Education Bureau of Research.

Fleming, M., & Levie, W. H. (1978). *Instructional Message Design.* Englewood Cliffs, NJ: Educational Technology Publications.

Fork, D. J., & Jonassen, D. H. (1976). Research in Visual Literacy: Where to Begin? *AECT Research and Theory Division Newsletter, 5,* 12–14. (ERIC Document Reproduction Service No. ED 136 822).

Fredriksson, I. (1979). *Konsten spränger ramarna. John Hartfield och det politiska fotomontaget.* Stockholm: Akademilitteratur.

Gardner, H. (1983). *Frames of Mind: The Theory of Multiple Intelligence.* New York: Basic Books.

Garoian, C. R. (1989). Teaching visual literacy through art history in high school. In R. A. Braden, D. G. Beauchamp, L. V. W. Miller, & D. M. Moore (Eds.). *About Visuals: Research, Teaching, and Applications.* Readings from the 20th Annual Conference of the International Visual Literacy Association. Blacksburg: Virginia Tech University.

Gazzaniga, M. (1967). The split brain in man. *Scientific American, 217,* 24–29.

Goldberg, A., & Kay, A. (1977). Personal dynamic media. *IEEE COMPUTER,* March.

Goldsmith, E. (1980). Comprehensibility of illustraion—an analytical model. *Information Design Journal, 1,* 204–213.

Goldsmith, E. (1984). *Research into Illustration: An Approach and a Review.* Cambridge, England: Cambridge University Press.

Goldsmith, E. (1986). Learning from illustrations: Factors in the design of illustrated educational books for middle school children. *Word and Image, 2,* 11–121. London: Taylor & Francis Ltd.

Goldsmith, E. (1987). The analysis of illustration in theory and practice. In H. A. Houghton & D. M. Willows. (Eds.). *The Psychology of Illustrations. Vol.2. Instructional Issues.* New York: Springer-Verlag.

Good, B. L. (1987). K–12 curriculum integrated library media skills: The impact of visual motivators. In R.A. Braden, D.G. Beauchamp, & L.W. Miller (Eds.). *Visible & Viable: The Role of Images in Instruction and Communication.* Commerce: East Texas State University.

Gregory, M., & Poulton, E. C. (1970). Even versus uneven right-hand margins and the rate of comprehension in reading. *Ergonomics, 13,* 427–434.

Griffin, R. E. (1989). A comprehensive study of the types of visuals used in business and engineering presentations. In R. A. Braden, D. G. Beauchamp, L. V. W. Miller, & D. M. Moore (Eds.). *About Visuals: Research, Teaching, and Applications.* Readings from the 20th Annual Conference of the International Visual Literacy Association. Blacksburg: Virginia Tech University.

Griffin, R. E. (1990). *Important Facts about Business Presentations.* State College: Penn State University.

Griffin, R. E., & Whiteside, J. A. (1984). Visual literacy: A model for understanding the discipline. In A. D. Walker, R. A. Braden, & L. H. Dunker (Eds.). *Visual Literacy: Enhancing Human Potential.* Blacksburg: Virginia Tech University.

Gunnemark, E., & Kenrick, D. (1985). *A Geolinguistic Handbook.* Kungälv: Goterna.

Gustafsson, C. (1980a). *Läromedlens funktion i undervisningen.* En rapport från utredningen om läromedelsmarknaden. DsU 1980:4.

Gustafsson, C. (1980b). *Läromedlens funktion i undervisningen. Bilagedel.* En rapport från utredningen om läromedelsmarknaden. DsU 1980:5.

Haber, R. N. (1979). How we remember what we see. *Scientific American, 222,* 104–115.

Haber, R. N., & Erdelyi, M. H. (1967). Emergence and recovery of initially unavailable perceptual material. *Journal of Verbal Learning and Verbal Behavior, 6,* 618–628.

Haber, R. N., & Myers, B. L. (1982). Memory for pictograms, pictures, and words separately and all mixed up. *Perception, 11,* 57–64.

Hanson, J. R. (1988). Learning styles, visual literacies, and a framework for reading instruction. *Reading Psychology: An International Quarterly, 9,* 409–430.

Hanson, J. R., Silver, H. F., & Strong, R. W. (1988). Learning styles and visual literacy: Connections and actions. In R. A. Braden, D. G. Beauchamp, & L. Miller (Eds.). *Visual Literacy in Life and Learning.* Blacksburg: Virginia Tech University.

Hardin, P. (1983). Investigating visual communication in diagrams. In A. D. Walker, R. A. Braden, & L. H. Dunker (Eds.). *Seeing Ourselves: Visualization in a Social Context.* Blacksburg: Virginia Tech University.

Hartley, J. (1987). Designing electronic text: The role of print-based research. *Educational Communications and Technology Journal, 35,* 3–17.

Heinich, R., Molenda, M., & Russell, J. D. (1993). *Instructional Media and the New Technologies of Instruction.* New York: Macmillan

Henney, M. (1981). The effect of all-capital print versus regular mixed print as displayed on a micro-computer screen on reading speed and accuracy. *Educational Communications and Technology Journal, 31,* 126.

Hobbs, R. (1989). Taft school media project, year one: Uniting video production and critical television viewing. In R. A. Braden, D. G. Beauchamp, L. V. W. Miller, & D. M. Moore (Eds.). *About Visuals: Research, Teaching, and Applications.* Readings from the 20th Annual Conference of the International Visual Literacy Association. Blacksburg: Virginia Tech University.

Hocking, F. O. (1978). A nationwide survey to determine visual literacy goals, constraints, and factors influencing their selection. (Doctoral dissertation, University of Colorado, 1978). *Dissertation Abstracts International,* 1978, *39,* 2699A. (University Microfilm No. 78-20520).

Holliday, W. (1980). Using visuals to teach concepts. *Science and Children, 17,* 9–10.

Hortin, J. A. (1980). *Sources for Developing a Theory of Visual Literacy.* (ERIC Document Reproduction Service No. ED 204 716).

Hortin, J. A. (1982). A Need for a Theory of Visual Literacy. *Reading Improvement, 19,* 257–267.

Hortin, J. A. (1983). Imagery in our daily lives. In A. D. Walker, R. A. Braden, & L. H. Dunker (Eds.). *Seeing Ourselves: Visualization in a Social Context.* Blacksburg: Virginia Tech University.

Hunter, B., Crismore, A., & Pearson, P. D. (1987). Visual displays in basal readers and social studies textbooks. In H. A. Houghton & D. M. Willows (Eds.). *The Psychology of Illustrations: Vol. 2. Instructional Issues.* New York: Springer-Verlag.

Isaacs, G. (1987). Text screen design for computer-assisted learning. *British Journal of Educational Technology, 18,* 41–51.

Jacobson, R. (1976). *Språket i relation till andra kommunikationssystem.* In K. Aspelin & B. A. Lundberg (Eds.). *Tecken och tydning. Till konsternas semiotik.* Stockholm.

Jay, A. (1970). *Effective Presentation, the Communication of Ideas by Words and Visual Aids.* London: British Institute of Management.

Johnson, L. (1988). Cable television—public schools—visual literacy. In R. A. Braden, D. G. Beauchamp, & L. Miller (Eds.). *Visual Literacy in Life and Learning.* Blacksburg: Virginia Tech University.

Jonassen, D. H. (1982). *The Technology of Text.* Englewood Cliffs, NJ: Educational Technology Publications.

Jonassen, D. H., & Fork, D. J. (1975). *Visual Literacy: A Bibliographic Survey.* Paper presented at The Pennsylvania Learning Resources Association Annual Conference. (ERIC Document Reproduction Service No. ED 131 837).

Karp, S. A. (Ed.). (1962). *Kit of Selected Distraction Tests.* Brooklyn, NY: Cognitive Tests.

Keller, J., & Burkman, E. (1993). Motivation principles. In M. Fleming & W. H. Levie (Eds.). *Instructional Message Design* (2nd ed.). Englewood Cliffs, NJ: Educational Technology Publications.

Kindborg, M., & Kollerbaur, A. (1987). *Visual Languages and Human Computer Interaction.* Paper presented at HCI'87, Exeter, England.

Kollerbaur, A. (1983). *Final Report from the PRINCESS-Project* (Swedish title: *Slutrapport från PRINCESS-Projektet*). Stockholm: University of Stockholm, Department of Computer Science.

Krauss, D. A. (1984). A phototherapy project. In A. D. Walker, R. A. Braden, & L. H. Dunker (Eds.). *Visual Literacy: Enhancing Human Potential.* Blacksburg, VA: Virginia Tech University.

Lacy, L. (1987). An interdisciplinary approach for students in K–12 using visuals of all kinds. In R. A. Braden, D. G. Beauchamp, & L. W. Miller (Eds.). *Visible & Viable: The Role of Images in Instruction and Communication.* Commerce: East Texas State University.

Lacy, L. (1988). Thinking skills and visual literacy. In R. A. Braden, D. G. Beauchamp, & L. Miller (Eds.). *Visual Literacy in Life and Learning.* Blacksburg: Virginia Tech University.

Larssen, A. K., & Skagert, P. (1982). *Hur fungerar annonser?* Aftonbladets Annonstest, Södertälje.

Lawson, L. (1968). Ophthalmological factors in learning disabilities. In H. Myklebust (Ed.). *Progress in Learning Disabilities, Volume 1.* New York: Grune and Stratton.

Leahy, S. B. (1991). Visual literacy: Investigation of visual literacy concepts as historically developed in writings of selected western philosophers from the pre-Socratics to Comenius. In D. G. Beauchamp, J. Clark-Baca, & R. A. Braden (Eds.). *Investigating Visual Literacy.* Selected Readings from the 22nd Annual Conference of the International Visual Literacy Association. Blacksburg: Virginia Tech University.

Lee, D. (1959). *Freedom and Culture.* Englewood Cliffs, NJ: Prentice-Hall.

Lenze, J. S. (1991). Serif vs. san serif type fonts: A comparison based on reader comprehension. In D. G. Beauchamp, J. Clark-Baca, & R. A. Braden (Eds.). *Investigating Visual Literacy.*

Selected Readings from the 22nd Annual Conference of the International Visual Literacy Association. Blacksburg: Virginia Tech University.

Levie, W. H. (1978). A prospectus for instructional research on visual literacy. *ECTJ, 26,* 25–36.

Levie, W. H., & Lentz, R. (1982). Effects of text illustrations: A review of research. *ECTJ, 30,* 4, 195–232.

Levin, J. R. (1981). On functions of pictures in prose. In F. J. Pirozzolo & M. C. Wittrock (Eds.). *Neuropsychological and Cognitive Processes in Reading.* New York: Academic Press.

Levin, J. R., & Lesgold, A. M. (1978). On pictures in prose. *ECTJ, 26,* 233–243.

Levin, J. R., Anglin, G. J., & Carney, R. N. (1987). On empirically validating functions of pictures in prose. In D. M. Willows & H. A. Houghton (Eds.). *The Psychology of Illustration: Vol. 1. Basic Research.* New York: Springer-Verlag.

Lidman, S. , & Lund, A. M. (1972). *Berätta med bilder.* Stockholm: Bonniers.

Limburg, V. E. (1987). *Visual "Intrusion": A Two-way Street in Visual Literacy.* Paper presented at the Symposium on Verbo-Visual Literacy: Research and Theory. Stockholm, June 10–13.

Limburg, V. E. (1988). Ethical considerations in visual literacy. In R. A. Braden, D. G. Beauchamp, & L. Miller (Eds.). *Visual Literacy in Life and Learning.* Blacksburg: Virginia Tech University.

Lindström, A. (1990). Bilder i läromedel, lärarsynpunkter. Stockholm: Stockholms Universitet. Konstfack, Institutionen för bildpedagogik.

Littlewood, W. (1984). *Foreign and Second Language Learning.* Cambridge: Cambridge University Press.

Lloyd-Kolkin, D., & Tyner, K. (1990). Media literacy education needs for elementary schools: A survey. In R. A. Braden, D. G. Beauchamp, & J. Clark-Baca (Eds.). *Perceptions of Visual Literacy.* Selected Readings from the 21st Annual Conference of the International Visual Literacy Association. Conway: University of Central Arkansas.

Lodding, K. (1983). Iconic Interfacing. *Computer Graphics and Applications, 3,* 2, 11–20.

Lotman, J. (1973). *Die Struktur des künstlerischen Textes.* Frankfurt am Main.

MacDonald-Ross, M. (1977). How numbers are shown: Review of research on the presentation of quantitative data in texts. *AV Communication Review, 25*(4), 359–409.

MacDonald-Ross, M. (1978). Graphics in text. *Review of Research in Education, 5,* 49–85.

Mangan, J. (1978). Cultural conventions of pictorial representation: Iconic literacy and education. *Educational Communications and Technology, 26,* 245–267

Marsh, P. O. (1983). *Messages That Work: A Guide to Communication Design.* Englewood Cliffs, NJ: Educational Technology Publications.

Martinello, M. L. (1985). Visual thinking in the elementary curriculum: Strategies and learning activities. In L. W. Miller (Ed.). *Creating Meaning.* Readings from the Visual Literacy Conference at California State Polytechnic University at Pomona.

Matsushita, K. (1988). *A Summary Version of the Comprehensive Report on Hi–OVIS PROJECT Jul. '78–Mar. '86.* Tokyo: New Media Development.

McKim, R. H. (1980a). *Thinking Visually: A Strategy Manual for Problem Solving.* Belmont, CA: Lifetime Learning Publications.

McKim, R. H. (1980b). *Experience in Visual Thinking,* 2nd edition. Monterey, CA: Brooks/Cole.

Melin, L. (1986a). *Text, bild, lexivision. En studie i text-bild-samverkan i en lärobok.* Stockholm: Stockholm University, Department of Nordic Languages.

Melin, L. (1986b). *Termer—Ett kompendium om terminologi och termbildning.* Stockholm: Stockholm University, Department of Nordic Languages.

Metallinos, N. (1991). High definition television: New perceptual, cognitive, and aesthetic challanges. In D. G. Beauchamp, J. Clark-Baca, & R. A. Braden (Eds.). *Investigating Visual Literacy.* Selected Readings from the 22nd Annual Conference of the International Visual Literacy Association. Blacksburg: Virginia Tech University.

Metallinos, N., Muffoletto, R., Pettersson, R., Shaw, J., & Takakuwa, Y. (1990). *The Use of Verbo-visual Information in Textbooks–A Crosscultural Experience.* Paper presented at the International Visual Literacy Association Symposium 1990. Verbo-Visual Literacy. Mapping the Field. July 10–13. University of London, Institute of Education.

Miller, L. W. (1987). Visual literacy across the curriculum. In R. A. Braden, D. G. Beauchamp, & L. W. Miller (Eds.). *Visible & Viable: The Role of Images in Instruction and Communication.* Commerce: East Texas State University.

Miller, L. W. (1989). Teaching visual literacy with films and video. In R. A. Braden, D. G. Beauchamp, L. V. W. Miller, & D. M. Moore (Eds.). *About Visuals: Research, Teaching, and Applications.* Readings from the 20th Annual Conference of the International Visual Literacy Association. Blacksburg: Virginia Tech University.

Moore, D. M. (1988). The effects of presentation order and contextual background on cognitive style. In R. A. Braden, D. G. Beauchamp, & L. Miller (Eds.). *Visual Literacy in Life and Learning.* Blacksburg: Virginia Tech University.

Morris, D. (1985). *Body Watching. A Field Guide to the Human Species.* London: Jonathan Cape Ltd.

Muffoletto, R. (1984). Visual literacy and teacher education; A pedagogical strategy. In A. D. Walker, R. A. Braden, & L. H. Dunker (Eds.). *Visual Literacy: Enhancing Human Potential.* Blacksburg, VA: Virginia Tech University.

Muffoletto, R. (1988). Teaching visual literacy to teachers. In R. A. Braden, D. G. Beauchamp, & L. Miller (Eds.). *Visual Literacy in Life and Learning.* Blacksburg: Virginia Tech University.

Mulcahy, P., & Jay Samuels, S. (1987). *Three Hundred Years of Illustrations in American Textbooks.* In H. A. Houghton & D. M. Willows (Eds.). *The Psychology of Illustrations: Vol. 2. Instructional Issues.* New York: Springer-Verlag.

Neurath, O. (1936). *International Picture Language.* London: Kegan Paul.

Oudejans, M. (1988). The photograph: An icon of violence or peace? In R. A. Braden, D. G. Beauchamp, & L. Miller (Eds.). *Visual Literacy in Life and Learning.* Blacksburg: Virginia Tech University.

Paivio, A. (1979). *Imagery and Verbal Processes.* Hillsdale, NJ: Lawrence Erlbaum Associates.

Paivio, A. (1983). The empirical case for dual coding. In J. C. Yuille (Ed.). *Imagery, Memory, and Cognition.* Hillsdale, NJ: Lawrence Erlbaum Associates.

Perfetti, C. (1977). Language comprehension and fast decoding: Some psycholinguistic prerequisites for skilled reading comprehension. In J. Guthrie (Ed.). *Cognition, Curriculum, and Comprehension.* Newark, DE: International Reading Association.

Peterson, L. (1984). *Seriealbum på myternas marknad.* Stockholm: Liber.

Pettersson, R. (1983a). *Visuals for Instruction.* (CLEA–Report No. 12). Stockholm: Stockholm University, Department of Computer Science.

Pettersson, R. (1983b). Factors in visual language: Image framing. *Visual Literacy Newsletter, 9 and 10.* Also (CLEA–Report No. 11). Stockholm: Stockholm University, Department of Computer Science.

Pettersson, R. (1984a). Picture legibility, readability, and reading value. In A. D. Walker, R. A. Braden, & L. H. Dunker (Eds.). *Enhancing Human Potential.* Readings from the 15th Annual Conference of the International Visual Literacy Association. Blacksburg: Virginia Tech University.

Pettersson, R. (1984b). Numeric data, presentation in different formats. Presentation at the 16th Annual Conference of the International Visual Literacy Association. Baltimore. Nov. 8–11. In N. H. Thayer & S. Clayton-Randolph (1985). *Visual Literacy: Cruising into the Future.* Readings from the 16th Annual Conference of the International Visual Literacy Association. Bloomington: Western Sun Printing Co.

Pettersson, R. (1985a). Intended and perceived image content. Presentation at the 17th Annual Conference of the International Visual Literacy Association. In L. W. Miller (Ed.). *Creating*

Meaning. Readings from the Visual Literacy Conference at California State Polytechnic University at Pomona.

Pettersson, R. (1985b) Interplay of Visuals and Legends. *Visual Literacy Newsletter,* 5.

Pettersson, R. (1986a). See, look, and read. *Journal of Visual Verbal Languaging, Spring,* 33–39.

Pettersson, R. (1986b). Image–word–image. Presentation at the 18th Annual Conference of the International Visual Literacy Association. Madison, Wisconsin, Oct. 30–Nov. 2. In R. A. Braden, D. G. Beauchamp, & L. W. Miller (Eds.). (1987). *Visible & Viable: The Role of Images in Instruction and Communication.* Readings from the 18th Annual Conference of the International Visual Literacy Association. Commerce: East Texas State University.

Pettersson, R. (1986c). Picture Archives. *EP Journal.* June, 2–3.

Pettersson, R. (1987a). *Interpretation of Image Content.* Paper presented at the 19th Annual Conference of the International Visual Literacy Association. Tulsa, Oklahoma, Oct. 28–Nov. 1. 1987.

Pettersson, R. (1987b). Picture processing. *EP Journal,* June.

Pettersson, R. (1989). *Visuals for Information: Research and Practice.* Englewood Cliffs, NJ: Educational Technology Publications.

Pettersson, R. (1990a). Teachers, students, and visuals. *Journal of Visual Literacy, 10,* 1, 45–62.

Pettersson, R. (1990b). *What Is Infology?* Paper presented at the International Visual Literacy Association Symposium 1990. Verbo-Visual Literacy. Mapping the Field. July 10–13. University of London, Institute of Education.

Pettersson, R. (1991). *Bilder i läromedel.* Tullinge: Institutet för Infologi.

Pettersson, R., Carlsson, J., Isacsson, A., Kollerbauer, A., & Randerz, K. (1984). *Color Information Displays and Reading Efforts.* (CLEA–Report No. 18a). Stockholm: Stockholm University, Department of Computer Science.

Pettersson, R., Metallinos, N., Muffoletto, R., Shaw, J., & Takakuwa, Y. (1991). The use of verbo-visual information in teaching of geography—views from teachers. Presentation at the 23rd Annual Conference of the International Visual Literacy Association. In J. Clark-Baca, D. G. Beauchamp, & R. A. Braden (Eds.) (1992). *Visual Communication: Bridging Across Cultures.* Selected Readings from the 23rd Annual Conference of the International Visual Literacy Association. Blacksburg: Virginia Tech University.

Piaget, J. (1963). *The Origin of Intelligence in Children.* New York: Norton.

Postman, N. (1979). *Teaching as a Conserving Activity.* New York: Delacorte Press.

Poulton, E. C., & Brown, C. H. (1968). Rate of comprehension of an existing teleprinter output and of possible alternatives. *Applied Psychology, 52,* 16–21.

Quirk, R., Greenbaum, S., Leech, G., & Svartvik, J. (1985). *A Comprehensive Grammar of the English Language.* London: Longman.

Ragan, T. J. (1988). Foundations for a visual perceptual development curriculum. In R. A. Braden, D. G. Beauchamp, & L. Miller (Eds.). *Visual Literacy in Life and Learning.* Blacksburg: Virginia Tech University.

Reynolds Myers, P. (1985). Visual literacy, higher order reasoning, and high technology. In N. H. Thayer & S. Clayton-Randolph (Eds.). *Visual Literacy: Cruising into the Future.* Readings from the 16th Annual Conference of the International Visual Literacy Association. Bloomington: Western Sun Printing Co.

Rezabek, L. (1990). Teaching visual literacy using a computer-based audiographic telecommunication system. In R. A. Braden, D. G. Beauchamp, & J. Clark-Baca (Eds.). *Perceptions of Visual Literacy.* Selected Readings from the 21st Annual Conference of the International Visual Literacy Association. Conway: University of Central Arkansas.

Ringom, B. (1988). *Tänk positivt.* Falun: Larson.

Robinson R. S. (1988). An investigation of narrative television comprehension: Factors of visual literacy. In R. A. Braden, D. G. Beauchamp, & L. Miller (Eds.). *Visual Literacy in Life and Learning.* Blacksburg: Virginia Tech University.

Robinson, R. S. (1991). Investigating visual literacy: Developing skills across the curriculum. In D. G. Beauchamp, J. Clark-Baca, & R. A. Braden (Eds.). *Investigating Visual Literacy.* Selected Readings from the 22nd Annual Conference of the International Visual Literacy Association. Blacksburg: Virginia Tech University.

Romare, E. (1989). Bildens betydelse i läroboken. En text-och bildanalys av religionsböcker från 1940-tal och 1980-tal. *Spov, 7,* 45–64.

Rudisill, M. (1951–1952). Children's preferences for colour versus other qualities in illustrations. *Elementary School Journal, 52,* 444–457.

Schallert, D. L. (1980). The role of illustrations in reading comprehension. In R. J. Spiro, B. C. Bruce, & W. F. Brewer (Eds.). *Theoretical Issues in Reading Comprehension: Perspectives from Cognitive Psychology, Linguistics, Artificial Intelligence, and Education.* Hillsdale, NJ: Lawrence Erlbaum Associates.

Schiller, H. A. (1987). Visual literacy in ancient and modern man (part one). In R. A. Braden, D. G. Beauchamp, & L. W. Miller (Eds.). *Visible & Viable: The Role of Images in Instruction and Communication.* Commerce: East Texas State University.

Scüsseleder, N., & Troedsson, A. (1988). *Användning av ikoner i datorprogram.* Undergraduate thesis. Stockholm: University of Stockholm, Department of Computer and Systems Science.

Selander, S. (1988). *Lärobokskunskap. Pedagogisk textanalys med exempel från läroböcker i historia 1841–1985.* Lund: Studentlitteratur.

Sinatra, R. (1986). *Visual Literacy Connections to Thinking, Reading, and Writing.* Springfield, IL: Charles C. Thomas.

Skinner, B. (1957). *Verbal Behavior.* New York: Appleton-Century-Crofts.

Skolöverstyrelsen (1979). *Bilder i gymnasieskoleundervisningen.* Stockholm: Rapport 1979–05–28.

Skolöverstyrelsen (1980). *Lgr 80. Läroplan för grundskolan. Allmän del. Mål och riktlinjer. Kursplaner. Timplaner.* Stockholm: Liber Utbildningsförlaget.

Slobin, D. (1973). Cognitive prerequisites for the development of grammar. In C. Ferguson & D. Slobin (Eds.). *Studies of Child Language Development.* New York: Holt, Rinehart, & Winston.

Smith, M. R., & Blinn, L. M. (1985). Visual information for the consumer: An undergraduate course with a multi-disciplinarey focus. In N. H. Thayer & S. Clayton-Randolph (Eds.). *Visual Literacy: Cruising into the Future.* Readings from the 16th Annual Conference of the International Visual Literacy Association. Bloomington: Western Sun Printing Co.

Sperry, R. (1973). Lateral specialization of cerebral functions in the surgically separated hemispheres. In F. J. McGuigan & R. A. Schoonever (Eds.). *The Psychophysiology of Thinking: Studies of Covert Processes.* New York: Academic Press.

Sperry, R. (1982). Some effects of disconnecting the hemisphere. *Science, 217,* 1223–1226.

Suhor, C., & Little, D. (1988). Visual literacy and print literacy—theoretical considerations and points of contact. *Reading Psychology, 9* (4), 469–482.

Sutherland, N. S. (1973). Object recognition. In E. C. Carterette & M. P. Friedman (Eds.). *Handbook of Perception, III.* New York, London: Academic Press.

Sutton, R. E. (1992). *Information Literacy Meets Media Literacy and Visual Literacy.* Presentation at the 29th Annual Conference of the International Visual Literacy Association, Pittsburgh, Sept. 30–Oct. 4.

Thurstone, L. L. (1937). *Psychological Tests for a Study of Mental Abilities.* Chicago, IL: University of Chicago Press.

Tinker, M. A. (1963). *The Legibility of Print.* Ames: Iowa State University Press.

Trice, R. W. (1986). *Development of a Videodisc Database.* Presentation at the AECT Conference, Las Vegas.

Twyman, M. (1982). The graphic presentation of language. *Information Design Journal, 3,* 1, 2–22.

Vogel, D. R., Dickson, G. W., & Lehman, J. A. (1986). Driving the audience action response. *Computer Graphics World,* August.

Walker, A. D. (1990). Examining visual literacy, 1983–1989: A seven-year bibliography. In R. A. Braden, D. G. Beauchamp, & J. Clark-Baca (Eds.). *Perceptions of Visual Literacy.* Selected Readings from the 21st Annual Conference of the International Visual Literacy Association. Conway: University of Central Arkansas.

Waller, R. (1987). *The Typographic Contribution to Language: Towards a Model of Typographic Genres and Their Underlying Structures.* Reading: University of Reading, Department of Typography & Graphic Communication.

Weidenman, B. (1988). Der flüchtige Blick beim stehenden Bild: Zur oberflächlichen Verarbeitung von pädagogishen Illustrationen. (The Careless View in the Case of Standing Picture.) *Zeitschrift für Lernforschung, 16,* 3, 43–57.

Weiser, J. (1984). Phototherapy—becoming visually literate about oneself. In A. D. Walker, R. A. Braden, & L. H. Dunker (Eds.). *Visual Literacy: Enhancing Human Potential.* Blacksburg, VA: Virginia Tech University.

Whiteside, C. (1985). Visual literacy awareness in college-level educational media courses. In L. W. Miller (Ed.). *Creating Meaning.* Readings from the Visual Literacy Conference at California State Polytechnic University at Pomona.

Wileman, R. (1993). *Visual Communicating.* Englewood Cliffs, NJ: Educational Technology Publications.

Williams, E. E. (1988). How I teach video literacy in my basic educational media class. In R. A. Braden, D. G. Beauchamp, & L. Miller (Eds.). *Visual Literacy in Life and Learning.* Blacksburg: Virginia Tech University.

Winn, W. (1993). Perception principles. In M. Fleming & W. H. Levie (Eds.). *Instructional Message Design: Principles from the Behavioral and Cognitive Sciences.* Englewood Cliffs, NJ: Educational Technology Publications.

Wisely, F., Kennett, D., & Bradford, J. (1989). Development of visual communication courses. In R. A. Braden, D. G. Beauchamp, L. V. W. Miller, & D. M. Moore (Eds.). *About Visuals: Research, Teaching, and Applications.* Readings from the 20th Annual Conference of the International Visual Literacy Association. Blacksburg: Virginia Tech University.

Witkin, H. A. (1985). *Personality Through Perception.* New York: Harper and Brothers.

Zachrisson, B. (1965). *Studies in the Legibility of Printed Text.* Stockholm: Almqvist and Wiksell.

Zakia, R. D. (1985). Advertising and sexual ethic. *International Journal of Visual Sociology, 3,* 1, 42–58.

Zimmer, A., & Zimmer, F. (1978). *Visual Literacy in Communication: Designing for Development.* Hulton Educational Publications Ltd., in cooperation with the International Institute for Adult Literacy Methods, Teheran.

Chapter 4

CLASSIFICATION OF VISUALS

A visual always has a sender and a receiver, as can be seen in the communications models. A visual also has a content seen in the image. The visual is executed, e.g., as a drawing. It is structured or executed, e.g., according to size, shape, etc. The visual has a physical form, a format, e.g., as a 35mm slide. The visual is used in a context, e.g., as an illustration in a textbook.

Visuals can be classified according to various criteria, such as sender, receiver, content, execution, format, and context, and even according to criteria such as function, use, and the means of production, etc. With reference to the distance to and size of the motif, photographers may classify pictures as long shots, full-length portraits, half-length portraits, and close-ups. In picture archives, pictures may be stored, e.g., according to content categories.

Doblin (1980) classifies iconographic (visual) information into several categories: *ideogrammatic* (symbols that attempt to convey a single meaning, such as a road sign), *diagrammatic* (charts, graphs, or diagrams), and *isogrammatic* (photography, drawing, and drafting). Hunter, Crismore, & Pearson (1987) present a classification as points along a continuum from realistic to abstract: photography, artwork, diagrams and maps, graphics and formulae, tables and charts, and orthography (icons). In their study on "Visual Displays in Basal Readers and Social Studies Textbooks," they used the following categories: sequential graphs, quantitative graphs, maps, diagrams, tables and charts, and verbal-visual displays.

For Wileman (1993) all kinds of representations of an object are symbols. He argues that there are three major ways to represent objects—as pictorial symbols, as graphic symbols, and as verbal symbols—ranging from concrete to abstract representations.

The first group, pictorial symbols, includes photographs and illustrations or drawings. Viewers should easily be able to translate a pictorial symbol to a real-world example.

The second group, graphic symbols, has image-related graphics, concept-related graphics, and arbitrary graphics. Image-related graphics can be characterized as silhouettes or profiles of the object. Concept-related graphics look like the object but have less detail than image-related graphics. Arbitrary graphics are abstract symbols for objects, constructed out of the designer's imagination.

The third group, verbal symbols, is divided into two sub-groups, verbal descriptions and nouns or labels. Verbal symbols can be understood only by people who comprehend the language used to describe the objects.

There seem to be no major difference in "abstractness" between abstract arbitrary graphic symbols and verbal symbols. Thus, I prefer to talk about two categories of representations: figurative and non-figurative. Figurative representations include two groups; *visuals* and *graphic symbols*. Visuals include three-dimensional images, photographs, realistic drawings, and schematic drawings. Graphic symbols include pictorial symbols, abstract symbols, and arbitrary symbols. Non-figurative representations or verbal symbols include verbal descriptions, nouns or labels, and letters and characters.

Thus, there are many possibilities for classification. However, one and the same visual can and will be classified in different ways at the same time depending on the criteria applied. Often the borders between different groups partially overlap each other.

THE PICTURE CIRCLE

The "picture circle" is an attempt to exemplify one model of classification. Many visuals are made to affect us in one way or another. Pictures which affect us in an unambiguous way can be referred to as *symbols*. Signposts, traffic signs, labels, etc., belong to this category. They are unambiguous by convention. We agree and decide on their meaning. All other pictures are representations of reality. As is the case for other kinds of representations, pictures are always open to different interpretations by different people at different times. Some pictures are open to many interpretations, others to only a few.

In many situations we need to use *schematic pictures* such as maps, charts, graphs, engineering drawings, etc. Schematic pictures are representations of reality, but they are often non-iconic and may lack any resemblance with reality.

Objective documentation of a product, situation, or course of events by means of photographs, documentary drawings, X-rays, satellite photographs, thermographic pictures, and ultrasonograms is often necessary. These pictures are frequently *realistic* and simulate reality in ways unique to each documentation process. However, apparently objective documentation can occasionally be extremely subjective and suggestive when the choice of images, the cropping, layout, and caption contents are overtly selective. The expression "the camera never lies" can often be very wrong indeed!

As far as ambiguous pictures are concerned, there is often a major difference between their denotation, i.e., their literal meaning, and their various connotations, i.e., their associative meanings. By exaggerating perspective, deforming shapes, making symbolic use of colors, etc., a picture creator can easily create works which evoke extra associations in viewers. This is in fact the very idea behind an artistic picture. However, the informative picture should not be open to different interpretations. The picture's message should then be the message intended by the person/agency commissioning the picture.

Ambiguous pictures, which often express moods and emotions, are usually referred to as *suggestive pictures*. Even here the creators of the pictures are out to influence the viewer in some way. Paintings often belong to this category. It is often difficult and sometimes impossible to make clear distinctions between different kinds of pictures. Advertising pictures, propaganda pictures, pictures for information or instruction, or educational pictures can be both ambiguous and unambiguous.

Visuals that are used in materials for information or instruction are very often schematic and/or realistic. The role of such a picture is to convey a given piece of factual information in the simplest and most effective manner possible. But the picture may also have the task of conveying moods or of arousing the viewer's interest and involvement by disseminating certain information.

A hand-crafted visual such as a painting, drawing, diorama, or sculpture takes a long time to make, is highly personal, exists only in individual, unique copies, and only reaches a narrow public. Pictures made by children, for example, often display considerable spontaneity and reveal a great deal about their personality, degree of development, and maturity. In all hand-crafted pictures the relationship of information presented to reality is totally controlled by the artist. Photographic pictures, though, are records of an event or object which actually existed.

Technically crafted visuals can be made in a relatively brief period of time and easily reach a wide public. A TV camera can take live pictures viewed simultaneously by millions of people in different countries. In this way, we can "attend" various happenings, such as sporting events, no matter where they occur. The ease with which news pictures can be produced and distributed may influence the selection of pictures. Sensational events, such as a disaster, may be assigned a relatively large amount of space in the mass-media because pictures such as these attract widespread interest. Here, the mass-media bear an enormous responsibility in their editing and selection of pictures.

Hand-crafted pictures are now easy to reproduce in newspapers, books, television, etc., but the technical reproduction processes do rob them of some of their original character. The halftone dots of the printing process or the special characteristics of electronic images are incapable of doing justice to, e.g., a painting made with vivid colors and applied paint. This is even more true for sculptures, dioramas, and other three-dimensional pictures. In the future, holograms, stereo, and laser techniques may hopefully solve some of these problems and re-create the third dimension. Current methods for making three-dimensional pictures require considerable development.

The manner in which we perceive a picture and the efficiency with which the image communicates the image creator's intentions depend not only on the technical reproduction method chosen but also on the manner and presentation to a large degree. We often need help and guidance in order to interpret a picture's message. Different captions or sound effects enable us to respond to one and the same picture in widely differing ways. This is especially true of moving pictures. The relative size of the picture, cropping, lighting, and the location on the cover of a book or newspaper page are also important to the way in which the picture is perceived by people with differing values, feelings, attitudes, experience, background knowledge, and philosophy. Pictures often serve as amplifiers, i.e., the viewer often readily accepts information verifying his or her own opinion on a given issue.

Pictures are always related in some way to reality. But they must never be confused with reality and are incapable of replacing reality. The "picture circle" is an attempt to provide a simple graphic description of the relationship between different types of pictures. The spot in the center, the "bull's eye," represents scribble, which is the same all over the world and our first attempt to make pictures.

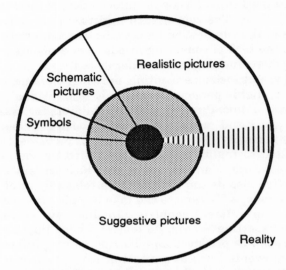

This is the picture circle. We have symbols, schematic pictures, realistic pictures, and suggestive pictures. The borderline between realistic and suggestive pictures is indistinct. Scribble (the dark spot) is followed by hand-crafted visuals (grey) and technically crafted visuals. Visuals that are used in materials for information or instruction are very often schematic and/or realistic pictures.

Every ring in the circle encompasses *symbols,* such as signs, signposts; *schematic pictures,* such as blueprints and maps; *realistic pictures* for objective documentation; and *suggestive pictures* with mythological representations, artistic pictures, advertising, propaganda pictures, news pictures, etc. The borderline between realistic and suggestive pictures is indistinct. Some visuals may be considered as suggestive pictures in one context but as realistic pictures in another context.

Symbols

Symbols are signs representing objects or ideas. Functional, instructive graphic symbols are actually older than words. They are found in every culture however primitive. In specific areas symbols are a supplement to all languages to help create better and faster understanding. Symbols have evolved to the point of universal acceptance in such areas as music, mathematics, and many branches of science.

Some figurative graphic symbols are *pictorial* or *representational.* They are "image related" and simplified pictures. Pictorial symbols resemble the objects they represent. They can be characterized as silhouettes or profiles with no surface detail. A traffic sign with a silhouette of a locomotive, to denote a railroad crossing, is an example of a pictorial symbol.

In the design process, some pictorial symbols may be successively simplified into figurative and *abstract* graphic symbols. They still look like the objects they represent but have less detail than pictorial symbols.

Some figurative symbols are *arbitrary* graphic symbols. They are invented and constructed out of the designer's imagination. Usually arbitrary graphic symbols have no resemblance at all to the objects or ideas that they represent. Many are based on geometric shapes. Signposts are often good examples of arbitrary symbols. They are unambiguous by convention. We agree and decide on their meaning.

Many non-figurative verbal symbols, written characters, and letters of various alphabets have evolved from simplified pictures. Verbal symbols are used in written languages and in many branches of science.

Taking up only a very small amount of space, symbols can convey a message containing a large amount of varying information, equivalent to one or more sentences of text. Image perception is very rapid, virtually "instantaneous." Reading and comprehending the equivalent message in words takes much more time. So symbols permit *rapid reading*. This is important in numerous situations, e.g., in traffic, industry, and aviation.

Design of symbols

Quirk, Greenbaum, Leech, & Svartvik (1985) note that pictograms most reliably can substitute for words in "block language"—single-word captions, headings, and labels—as distinct from sentenced language. Eco (1976) suggests that the verbal equivalent of an iconic sign is not a word but a phrase or indeed a whole story. This is, of course, also the case with the large number of Chinese kanji-characters, designating different words or sometimes phrases. The modern symbols typically found in airports and travel guides are intended to convey generalities of the same order of abstractness as words. Their characteristic graphic neutrality is perhaps the most significant aspect of their invention by the Isotype Institute (Neurath, 1936). Keates (1982) notes that discriminatory responses to map symbols depend on contrast in form, dimension, and color. The problem of discrimination is generally more critical in monochrome maps, in which only contrasts in form and dimensions are possible for lines and small symbols.

Symbols are often composed of simple graphical elements, i.e., lines, circles, ovals, squares, rectangles, triangles, or combinations thereof. Distinctively shaped letters are often utilized. Regular, simple, geometrical figures are identified more quickly than complex ones.

Symbols often employ bright colors, such a pure yellow, red, blue or green, white and black, or combinations of the same. According to Keates (1982), the use of color on maps introduces a large number of variables which can enhance contrast, and therefore extend the number of perceptual differences that can be employed in discrimination. The effect is to aid legibility, and therefore to increase the total range of information which the map can present.

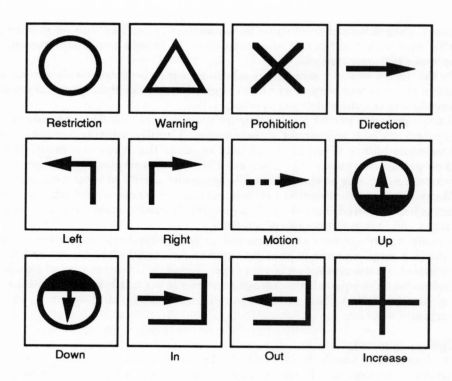

Here are some basic symbols that appear and reappear in many different situations in various countries throughout the world.

Shape and color components are often used for designating a link or relationship between groups of messages. In traffic, for example, a triangle is used for warning signs, a circle for restriction signs, and a rectangle for informative signs. The recognition of geographical features is much enhanced when areas are differentiated by hue. At the same time, complex color arrangements may raise problems in discrimination, so that although multi-color maps enlarge the graphic possibilities, they also increase the probability of errors in the judgment of discrimination. According to Keates (1982), the most common case of quantitative judgment on maps occurs in the use of proportional symbols, that is, point or line symbols constructed to represent specific quantities.

A good symbol is designed so it can be used in many different situations. For example, the McDonald's M or "arch" is designed to work in every conceivable size from a few millimeters high in a brochure to more than six feet high in outdoor signs.

Use of symbols

Many pictograms are culturally biased (Mangan, 1978) and thus arbitrary to those from other cultures. For example, when using a guidebook with numerous pictographic symbols, we often have to look them up in a key in much the same way as we look up unfamiliar words in a dictionary. Their iconic origins may only become apparent after we are aware of their intended meaning (Waller, 1987). Baron (1981) reports that iconicity is a surprisingly unimportant factor in the learning of sign-languages for the deaf, autistic, or mentally retarded.

Symbols can be used for *creating an overview* and providing a holistic perspective. This property is utilized in maps and informative signs as well as in, e.g., catalogues and project reports.

Symbols can be used for *supplying instructions and information* about appropriate behavior in different situations. Numerous examples can be found in catalogues and timetables. Various traffic signs also belong to this category.

Symbols can be used for *illustrating* the spatial and geographic *position* of different objects or services. One example is the floor plan of an exhibition hall with symbols designating the location of telephones, lavatories, information booths, and refreshment sites. Other examples are maps with numerous cartographic symbols for objects and conditions.

Symbols can be used for illustrating size relationships and to supply numerical/statistical information.

Symbols can be used to *represent* an organization, service, or product. Trademarks and logos are utilized in marketing, advertising, public relations, etc. As a rule, promotion of the representation begins with text (e.g., a company or product name), followed by text + a symbol. Ultimately the symbol alone suffices. Examples: McDonald's yellow M and Shell's scallop shell.

Symbols are employed in different media. They are static and immutable in graphical media. They may be more changeable in computer media. When you select, e.g., a brush in the menu for a Macintosh drawing program, the brush icon switches from positive to reverse video. This "acknowledgment" shows the user that the command has been understood. This makes communications more "reliable."

It can be concluded that every situation/context demands *consistent utilization of symbols*, an explanation of the symbols used, and learning the meaning of those symbols. Well-designed symbols can be used and will work in different cultures in different parts of the world.

Schematic pictures

There are several ways to classify schematic pictures. We can study how schematic pictures are executed, how and when they are used, and of what the content consists.

The following is an attempt to classify schematic pictures with respect to type of illustration and purpose. The purpose can be to show the relationship between variables or to explain and show abstract contents. A pictorial representation displays at a glance much of the quantitative behavior of the variables involved.

1. Word visuals have words and/or figures and digits.
    1.1.   Words, verbal summaries, headlines, lists, quick facts, quotations
    1.2.   Tables
    1.3.   Word visuals with pictograms
    1.4.   Word visuals with pictures

2. Graphs are pictorial representations of numerical data or a geometric relationship between quantities. The graph of an equation shows pictorially the relation of independent variables to dependent variables. When a variable y is a mathematical *function* of another variable x, then the pictorial graph of that function will represent the *locus* of all points (x, y) that satisfy the specific relationship. The line representing the relationship between or among variables on a graph is called a curve, even when it is straight.

    2.1.   Single scale
    2.2.   Coordinate grid
    2.3.   Nomogram
         2.3.1.   Abac
         2.3.2.   Alignment chart
    2.4.   Straight line graph
    2.5.   Normal curve
    2.6.   Exponential curve
    2.7.   Cumulative curve
    2.8.   Multiple line graph
    2.9.   Segmented graph, stacked curves, or stacked area graph
    2.10. Scattergram, scatter plot, scatter graph, or scatter plot graph
    2.11. Frequency polygon
    2.12. Multiple frequency polygons
    2.13. Histogram
    2.14. Multiple histograms

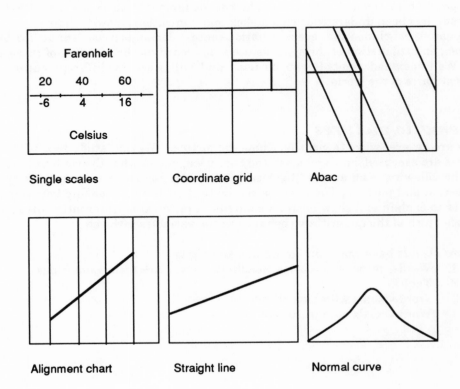

Single scales   Coordinate grid   Abac

Alignment chart   Straight line   Normal curve

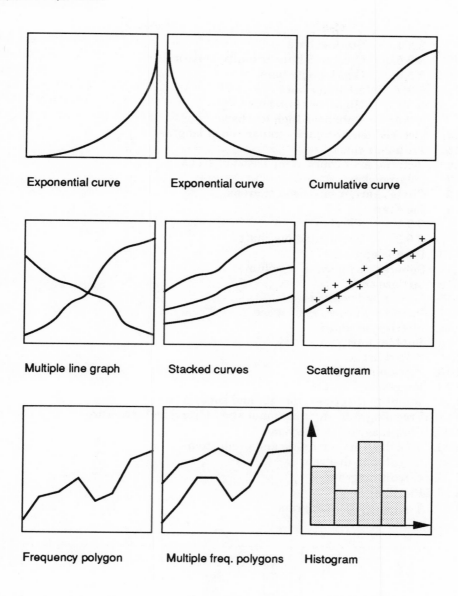

Exponential curve   Exponential curve   Cumulative curve

Multiple line graph   Stacked curves   Scattergram

Frequency polygon   Multiple freq. polygons   Histogram

3. Diagrams are illustrations that systematically show the relationship between various factors. There are many kinds of diagrams. It is far too easy to make diagrams confusing, difficult to understand, and/or misleading. Diagrams need to be correct and simple.

    3.1.   Pictograph or isotype system chart, each icon represents a given quantity
    3.2.   Line diagram, e.g., a "time line"
    3.3.   Bar chart
        3.3.1.   Vertical bar chart or column chart
        3.3.2.   Horizontal bar chart
        3.3.3.   Segmented bars

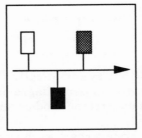
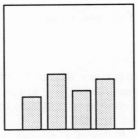

Pictograph   Line diagram   Vertical bar chart

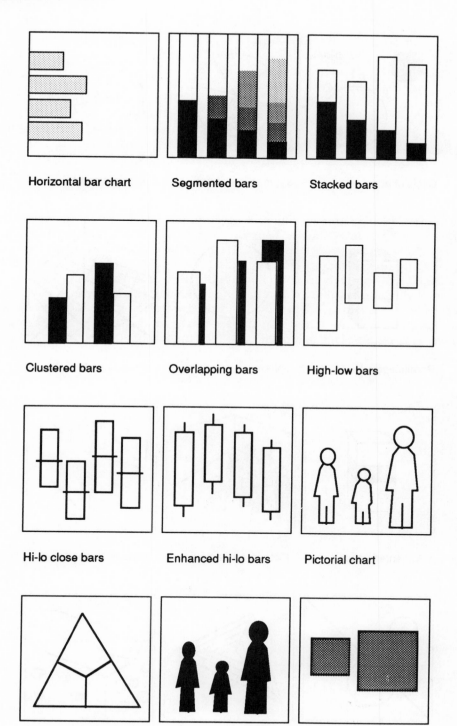

Horizontal bar chart

Segmented bars

Stacked bars

Clustered bars

Overlapping bars

High-low bars

Hi-lo close bars

Enhanced hi-lo bars

Pictorial chart

Tri-linear chart

Pictorial chart

Polygon chart

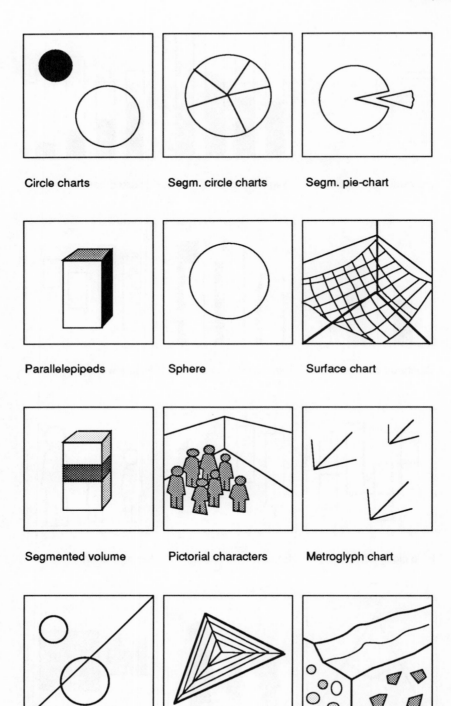

Circle charts   Segm. circle charts   Segm. pie-chart

Parallelepipeds   Sphere   Surface chart

Segmented volume   Pictorial characters   Metroglyph chart

Bubble chart   Kite chart   Block diagram

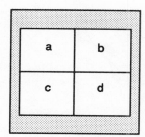

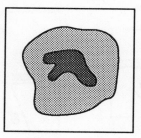

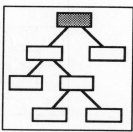

Field diagram   Quantity diagram   Tree diagram

4. Matrices are mathematical quantities consisting of rectangular arrays of numbers.
    4.1.   Four-field matrices
    4.2.   Multiple field matrices
    4.3.   Complex matrices

5. Plans show plans for various constructions and systems
    5.1.   Construction drawings
    5.2.   Floor plans and layouts

6. Maps are heavily reduced flat images of the surface of the earth. A map enables the user to see a generally complete representation of the world at one time. Mapmaking, or cartography, attempts to reproduce portions of the earth with a minimum of distortion. The information contained in a map should be as accurate as possible. The scale of a map is the relationship between a distance on the map and the corresponding real distance.

Theoretically, an infinite variety of map types exists. Most of the commonly used map types are either cultural or physical in nature. Common types of maps are distributional maps, geologic maps, soil maps, land-use maps, economic maps, zoological and botanical maps, statistical maps, political maps, topographic maps, meteorological maps, transportation maps, and historical maps.

Map projections can be placed in one of three general groups, based on the method in which the information on the round earth is transferred to the flat map—azimuthal, conic, or cylindrical.

The following examples are based on the contents in maps.
    6.1.   Overview or location maps
    6.2.   Detail maps
    6.3.   Map with figures
    6.4.   Cloropleths
    6.5.   Dot maps
    6.6.   Isopleths
    6.7.   Circle chart maps
    6.8.   Pie chart maps
    6.9.   Bar chart maps
    6.10. Flow maps

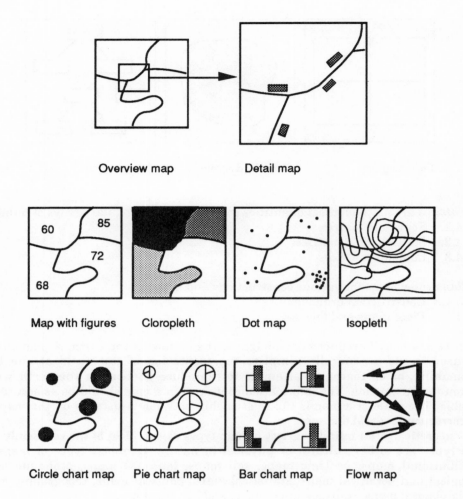

Overview map   Detail map

Map with figures   Cloropleth   Dot map   Isopleth

Circle chart map   Pie chart map   Bar chart map   Flow map

7. *Metaphorical pictures* are used for something that has a similarity with the actual image contents. Some examples are mentioned here.

    7.1.   Staircase leading to a target
    7.2.   Pieces in a jigsaw puzzle
    7.3.   Concentric circles around a center
    7.4.   Circulations
    7.5.   Spirals showing circular continuity

8. *Drawings* may be created in many artistic styles. The purpose of schematic drawings is basically to inform, not to decorate. Schematic drawings must not be excessively imaginative nor unnecessarily abstract. Clarity is the most important factor.

    8.1.   Stylized drawings
    8.2.   Informative drawings, figures and objects
    8.3.   Analytical drawings working in concert with photographs

8.4. Cross sections
8.5. Exploded drawings
8.6. Cut-away drawings
8.7. Panaromas
8.8. Silhouettes
8.9. Cartoons
8.10. Comic strip sequences

9. Integrating text and pictures with the use of legends, headings, explanatory texts, and labels.

10. Integrating drawings and photographs makes it possible to combine the advantages from both categories. Photographs are documentary and drawings can be analytical.

PICTURE ARCHIVES

Pictures are now being created more rapidly than at any time in history. Millions of pictures are produced every day. Sweden alone (with a population of under 10 million) accounts for more than 200 million amateur photographs each year. And each of the country's 2,000 professional photographers produces a half million photographs before retiring. Many pictures are put to active use in various ways. But a large portion ends up in collections. Some collections evolve into archives. There are four main types of archives:
• Personal, private collections
• Commercial photo agencies
• (Personal) research archives in different fields
• Collections in museums and other public institutions

Many photo collections are small enough to be accessed without any special index. The owner knows which pictures she/he has and where they are stored. This ease of access is no longer possible in large photo archives holding hundreds of thousand or even millions of photographs. So a large number of different indexing systems have been devised. Pictures may be indexed according to category, motif, or subject. Era, geographic area, and persons may be other classification concepts. Accession and negative indices and information on the dates photographs were taken, copyright, etc., may also be provided. Commercial photo agencies usually permit direct, manual, and visual perusal of originals or copies in each category. The feeling here is that the indexing or cataloguing of individual photographs takes too long, costs too much, and conveys no decisive advantages. Institutional photo archives, as used in research and education, are usually unable to manage without some kind of cataloguing. Many indexing systems are based on hierarchic classification of picture subjects according to some pre-determined code or on systematic catalogues in which every index word has a corresponding alphabetical or alpha-numerical designation.

PICTURE DATABASES

The ability to store photographs in a database for simultaneous display of pictures and texts would be an attractive option to most people with a picture archive and facilities for database searches of indices or texts. A picture stored in digital form requires a vast amount of storage space compared to text. So some systems employ analog storage of pictures. An optical video disc is capable of storing up to 100,000 PAL-TV-quality images, i.e., 250,000 pixels per picture. Pictures are individually numbered and can be sought and displayed within seconds. Spectrum, a Dutch publisher, has stored its pictures on a single analog, optical videodisc. The disc is used as a kind of "catalogue" in marketing the picture archives. A customer can obtain all the facts about a sought photograph on a computer screen at the same time as the photograph is displayed on a TV monitor. A similar system has been developed by Image Bank, in collaboration with Brignoli Inc. in New York. Video discs holding picture archives provide people in different parts of the world with access to pictures previously unavailable to them. Art treasures from the world's leading museums can be displayed to the public, scientists, and educators using this medium.

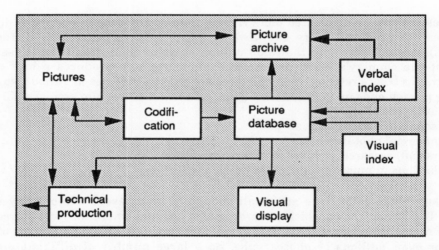

In a picture archive pictures are stored as objects, that is, as originals or as copies. This is a *primary storage*. For storage in a picture database a transformation of the image content to analogous or digital signals is needed. This is a *secondary storage*. Individual images can be found with the use of a verbal and/or verbal-numerical index. For technical production and mass communication, pictures are taken from picture archives, and image signals are collected from picture databases.

A large number of indexing systems have been devised to guide access to individual images (Pettersson, 1986a). However, real-life experience, as mentioned above, shows that it is often very hard to find the intended image. It is known from several experiments that images are perceived in many different ways by various subjects (Pettersson, 1985, 1986b). Even simple line drawings evoke many associations. Vogel *et al.* (1986) showed that image enhancement intended to improve interpretation of image content sometimes got in the way of the message. They concluded that image enhancement graphics should be used selectively and carefully. When in doubt, they recommended, plain text should be used. Limburg (1987) pointed out that receivers have even more ambiguity or semantic diversity with visual images than with most expressions of written language with its manifold meanings. Lodding (1983) reported on the problems with misinterpretations of icons used in computer systems. However, he concluded that people find naturalness in dealing with images either as an aid to or, in some circumstances, as the sole means of communicating.

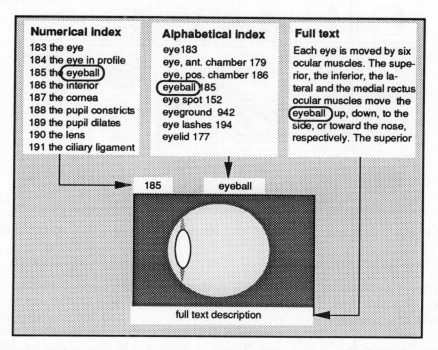

A verbal search for a picture. Examples are taken from a numerical index, an alphabetical index, and a free-text database.

A picture in a database can be sought with the aid of verbal and visual indices. Each picture has a picture number as a heading and a verbal description. The pictures can be listed systematically in numerical order in a numerical index. Or they can be listed in alphabetical order (according to their headings) in an alphabetical index. Picture descriptions are stored in a free-text (or full-text) database, making it possible for users to access a picture via a number of different descriptive terms.

A verbal description of a picture should be rather comprehensive. It may sometimes apply to an entire picture series. A database search based on certain descriptive terms could produce several different pictures with the same description. All such pictures would then be displayed in separate "windows" on the terminal screen. Entry of a command causes full-screen display of any of the windowed pictures. For children it might be easy to point with a finger at the window on the screen. Pictures can be stored in files stored in other files, etc., in a kind of a tree structure. When a file containing pictures is opened, the file contents are displayed in "windows" which can be as small as 1.5 x 1.5 cm. Thus, verbal searches are used on higher levels and visual, iconic searches on lower levels in the storage structure. Users who know in which file a desired picture is resident can go straight to that file. Index searches are employed when the whereabouts of a given picture is unknown.

A visual search for a picture. Examples of "windows" with small images that may be shown on the screen.

Batley (1988) experimented with retrieval of pictorial information from a database on a videodisc. The videodisc was created specifically for the experiment. It contained 950 photographs selected from a collection of 40,000 photographs by a Victorian photographer. The photographs were arranged into broad subject groupings such as: Cathedrals, Castles, and Rivers. A program in the authoring language Microtext provides access to the database. The program allows users to scan through images in the database using a joystick ("serendipitous browsing"); step through groups of related photographs ("specific browsing"); or type in key-word descriptors ("key-word search"). Summary files keep a record of each user's interaction with the database. Users may request text information about the photograph currently displayed on the screen and store a record of photographs they retrieve. The findings indicate that the search strategies adopted by users are dependent upon two factors: the nature of the information need and the individual user characteristics. Batley offers three proposals for the design of visual information systems:

1. Emphasis should be on providing a range of search options for the user—to accommodate both narrowly defined and exploratory searching and to accommodate individual user preferences.
2. Care must be taken in the design of the user interface—the emphasis should be on ease of use—so that the system is accessible to both naive and expert users.
3. Some attempt should be made to individualize searching—by allowing users the option of selecting their own range of scanning speeds, choosing between menu

selection and typing commands, choosing which input devices to use, designing a screen layout, etc.

Research is being conducted on the possibility of using a computer to search picture files for image structures or patterns. So far, these systems have very limited capabilities and are only being employed in, e.g., industrial robots programmed for taking certain components from a conveyer belt and creating assemblies with other components. Developments are most advanced in the military sector, e.g., in target-seeking missiles capable of reading terrain and comparing readings to a pre-programmed map and a predetermined route to the target (e.g., the Tomahawk cruise missiles used in the Persian Gulf War).

But there is yet another major, unsolved problem, since one and the same structure may occur in different pictures. Empirical studies (Pettersson 1987a) have shown that subjects given a number of image elements combine them to form many different picture contents.

PICTURE STYLE

An illustration is a picture complementing words in a verbo-visual presentation. Illustrations are printed in lexi-visual presentations. In audio-visual and multi-visual presentations illustrations may have many other formats. Illustrations are a "subset" of all visuals.

Sloan (1971) discussed four pictorial artistic styles: (1) photographic, (2) representational, (3) expressionistic, and (4) cartoon. *Photographic style* was defined as a colored photograph of the subject. *Representational style* was defined as an artist's rendition of the subject which conforms to the subject in its true form. *Expressionistic style* was defined as an artist's rendition of the subject which leans heavily towards abstraction. *Cartoon style* was defined as an animated caricature of the subject. These four artistic styles form a realistic to an abstract continuum.

Dondis (1973) discussed the anatomy of a visual message. We express and receive visual messages on three *levels*: (1) representationally, (2) symbolically, and (3) abstractly. Representational forms of illustrations are actual photographs of things. In symbolical forms pictures show one thing and connote another. In abstract forms illustrations provide minimal visual information on the phenomenon illustrated.

In addition to size, shape, color, etc., the way pictures are shot is important. The aesthetic value of a long shot is different from that of a medium shot or close-up. According to Zettl (1990) a scene can be presented (1) objectively (usually a long shot), (2) subjectively (usually a close-up), or (3) creatively (created by the medium itself, for example, superimposition, picture montage, etc.). Metallinos (1990) has developed a schema which explains these three forms of picture presentations in accordance with their functional aesthetic value. We can (1) remain totally objective and *look at* an event, (2) become subjectively involved and *look into* an event, and (3) where the event is totally dependent on the medium for its existence, we can *create* an event.

Depending on the *execution* illustrations can be divided in three main categories: (1) art work, (2) photographs, and (3) technically crafted visuals.

1. Art work
Art work consists of cartoons, line art, realistic drawings, schematic drawings, stylized drawings, drawings of animate objects, drawing of inanimate objects, exploded views, X-ray drawing, blueprints, panorama drawings, paintings, and others.

2. Photographic pictures
Photographic pictures are realistic records of an event or object which actually existed like product photos, portraits, situation photos, landscapes, etc.

3. Technically crafted visuals
Technically crafted visuals may be computer generated maps (plotting maps, detailed maps, figurative maps, cartograms), diagrams (bar diagrams, linear diagrams, pie charts, block diagrams, pictograms), scales (time scales, distance scales, size scales), or charts (flow charts, organizational charts). Technically crafted visuals are also produced with TV cameras, thermographs, radiographs, and ultrasonograms.

COMPUTER PICTURES

Computers are currently capable of displaying many kinds of pictures on their monitors. Rapid technological innovations constantly increase the range of images displayable by computer. Computer-displayable pictures are always converted to digital form at some stage, i.e., a series of zeros and ones. The computer can process picture information as *vector* or *pixel* images. A vector image is based on mathematical functions and is composed of lines and closed polygons. A pixel image is composed of a large number of individual picture elements, i.e., pixels whose grey scale and color scale are variable. The following classification, based on picture function and intended use, is proposed to facilitate discussions of various issues in the field of "computer pictures." Computer pictures may be classified in four groups: (1) computer processed pictures, (2) pictures analyzed by computer, (3) computer generated pictures, and (4) computer distributed pictures.

1. Computer processed pictures
Computer systems are being used to an increasing degree for editing, correcting, processing, retouching, and supplementing the contents of pictures for books, magazines, or other printed matter, or for slides or overhead transparencies. The basic picture, such as a drawing or photograph, must be digitized with the aid of a scanner or special video camera. The computer can then feed the digitized images to some peripheral such as a laser printer, dot matrix printer, plotter, film, or printing plate.

2. Pictures analyzed by computer
Pictures analyzed by computer may be divided into the following two groups: (1) measurement pictures, and (2) photographic pictures.

2.1. Measurement pictures
Measurement pictures are representations of various measurements in, e.g., medicine. Ultrasonograms and CAT scans are examples of pictures employed for identifying differences in the density of body tissues. The brain's activity can be visualized and measured with a positron camera. Measurement of thermal radiation is another example.

2.2. Photographic pictures
Photographic pictures are of several origins. Satellites with multispectral scanners continuously record and transmit digital TV images of the Earth. These images are analyzed and used for many different purposes in meteorology, geology, agriculture, and forestry. The interpretation of satellite pictures is a widespread activity. Photographic pictures are also used for a wide range of military applications.

3. Computer-generated pictures
The concept of computer-generated pictures, i.e., computer graphics, is employed in many different ways. However, image generation by computer is the common denominator. Computer generated pictures may be divided into the following four groups: (1) computer art, (2) information graphics, (3) design pictures, and (4) entertainment graphics.

3.1. Computer art
Computer art is a young art form comprising visual presentations whose aesthetic aspect predominates. Computer art consists of images created on an interactive basis and of images and patterns generated at random. Computer art often contains animated sequences and is displayed at, e.g., exhibitions, art galleries, etc. Computer art can also be displayed on paper. Image information is often stored pixel by pixel, and not as mathematical functions.

3.2. Information graphics
Information graphics may be divided into several subgroups. Business and news graphics are often generated by computer. Sales, stock, or production statistics are often illustrated with graphics. If the values of individual variables are stored separately, the user is often able to illustrate the information in different ways. Histograms, bar charts, pie charts, or curves are examples of the options available. The graphics are usually reproduced on film (as a slide or overhead transparency) or paper. Graphics are being used to an increasing degree for presenting information in research and development.

3.3. Design pictures
Design pictures comprise the subgroups of drawings, maps, and patterns.

Drawings, two-dimensional representations of mathematical descriptions of objects, can be generated by various CAD (computer-aided design) systems. The systems are often able to "twist and turn" a depicted object to show it from different angles before the object ever leaves the drawing board stage. Car parts, ships, aircraft, machinery, buildings, etc., are examples of objects being designed with the aid of CAD. CAD systems are often used in conjunction with CAM (computer-aided manufacturing) systems.

Maps are successfully produced in CAD systems, combined with vector systems. The systems make it easy to change both the scales and contents of maps.

Patterns, e.g., for textiles are also produced in CAD systems. But these CAD systems can also be used for producing patterns for, e.g., wallpaper, wrapping paper, and book covers.

3.4. Entertainment graphics

Entertainment graphics such as electronic games and animations are also produced in computer systems. Many kinds of interactive *electronic games* are on the market. Players manipulate space-ships, robots, heroes, and bandits in fantasy worlds. The electronic games often feature dramatic colors, symbols, changes in perspective, and sound effects. Developments move at a furious pace. Only a few years ago, graphics were very primitive, but their sophistication and resolution have been vastly improved. Animation is becoming increasingly commonplace. Computers are being used to create advanced animation effects in *movies, TV,* and *video.*

4. Computer distributed pictures

Computer distributed pictures may be divided into image databases and fax.

4.1. Image databases

Various forms of videotex belong to this category. They all entail transmission of information via ordinary telephone networks. Several online systems have very high transmission capacities. These systems usually store their information on magnetic media.

Optical storage media have a much greater text and picture storage capacity (hundreds of thousands of documents on each disc) than magnetic media. Each of the stored documents can be quickly retrieved and displayed on a screen or printed as hard copy if desired. *Filing* is a main application for optical storage media.

4.2. Fax

Fax is a collective designation for electronic copying and transmission of text and/or pictures to a receiver in which a facsimile of the transmitted information is reproduced.

REFERENCES AND SUGGESTED READINGS

Baron, N. S. (1981). *Speech, Writing, and Signs.* Bloomington: Indiana University Press.

Batley, S. (1988). Visual information retrieval: Browsing strategies in pictorial databases. In *Online Information 88,* 12th International Online Information Meeting. London 6–8 December. Proceedings Volume 1, 373–381. Oxford: Learned Information (Europe) Ltd.

Doblin, J. (1980). A structure for nontextual communications. In P. A. Kolers, M. E. Wrolstad, & H. Bouma (Eds.). *The Processing of Visible Language: Vol. 2.* New York: Plenum Press.

Dondis, D. (1973). *A Primer of Visual Literacy.* Cambridge, MA: MIT Press.

Eco, U. (1976). *A Theory of Semiotics.* Bloomington: Indiana University Press.

Griffin, R. E. (1989). A comprehensive study of the types of visuals used in business and engineering presentations. In R. A. Braden, D. G. Beauchamp, L. V. W. Miller, & D. M. Moore (Eds.). *About Visuals: Research, Teaching, and Applications.* Readings from the 20th

Annual Conference of the International Visual Literacy Association. Blacksburg: Virginia Tech University.

Hunter, B., Crismore, A., & Pearson, P. D. (1987). Visual displays in basal readers and social studies textbooks. In H. A. Houghton & D. M. Willows (Eds.). *The Psychology of Illustrations: Vol. 2. Instructional Issues.* New York: Springer-Verlag.

Keates, J. S. (1982). *Understanding Maps.* London and New York: Longman.

Limburg, V. E. (1987). *Visual "Intrusion": A Two-Way Street in Visual Literacy.* Paper presented at the Symposium on Verbo-Visual Literacy: Research and Theory. Stockholm, June 10–13.

Lodding, K. (1983). Iconic interfacing. *Computer Graphics and Applications, 3,* 2, 11–20.

Mangan, J. (1978). Cultural conventions of pictorial representation: Iconic literacy and education. *Educational Communications and Technology, 26,* 245–267.

Metallinos, N. (1990). Three dimensional video: Perceptual and aesthetic drawbacks. In R. A. Braden, D. G. Beauchamp, & J. Clark-Baca (Eds.). *Perceptions of Visual Literacy.* Selected Readings from the 21st Annual Conference of the International Visual Literacy Association. Conway: University of Central Arkansas.

Neurath, O. (1936). *International Picture Language.* London: Kegan Paul.

Pettersson, R. (1984). Numeric data, presentation in different formats. Presentation at the 16th Annual Conference of the International Visual Literacy Association. Baltimore, Nov. 8–11. In N. H. Thayer & S. Clayton-Randolph (Eds.). (1985). *Visual Literacy: Cruising into the Future.* Readings from the 16th Annual Conference of the International Visual Literacy Association. Bloomington: Western Sun Printing Co.

Pettersson, R. (1985). Intended and perceived image content. Presentation at the 17th Annual Conference of the International Visual Literacy Association. In L. W. Miller (Eds.). *Creating Meaning.* Readings from the Visual Literacy Conference at California State Polytechnic University at Pomona.

Pettersson, R. (1986a). Image–word–image. Presentation at the 18th Annual Conference of the International Visual Literacy Association. Madison, Wisconsin, Oct. 30–Nov. 2. In R. A. Braden, D. G. Beauchamp, & L. W. Miller (Eds.). (1987). *Visible & Viable: The Role of Images in Instruction and Communication.* Readings from the 18th Annual Conference of the International Visual Literacy Association. Commerce: East Texas State University.

Pettersson, R. (1986b). Picture Archives. *EP Journal,* June, 2–3.

Pettersson, R. (1987a). Interpretation of image content. Paper presented at the 19th Annual Conference of the International Visual Literacy Association. Tulsa, Oklahoma, Oct. 28–Nov. 1. In R. A. Braden, D. G. Beauchamp, & L. V. Miller (Eds.). (1988). *Visual Literacy in Life and Learning.* Readings from the 19th Annual Conference of the International Visual Literacy Association. Blacksburg: Virginia Tech University.

Pettersson, R. (1987b). Picture Processing. *EP Journal.*

Quirk, R., Greenbaum, S., Leech, G., & Svartvik, J. (1985). *A Comprehensive Grammar of the English Language.* London: Longman.

Sloan, M. (1971). *Picture Preferences of Elementary School Children and Teachers.* Ann Arbor, MI: University Microfilms.

Sutherland, N. S. (1973). Object recognition. In E. C. Carterette & M. P. Friedman (Eds.). *Handbook of Perception, III.* New York, London: Academic Press.

Trice, R. W. (1986). *Development of a Videodisc Database.* Presentation at the AECT Conference, Las Vegas.

Vogel, D. R., Dickson, G. W., & Lehman, J. A. (1986). Driving the audience action response. *Computer Graphics World,* August.

Waller, R. (1987). *The Typographic Contribution to Language: Towards a Model of Typographic Genres and Their Underlying Structures.* Reading: University of Reading. Department of Typography & Graphic Communication.

Wileman, R. E. (1993). *Visual Communicating.* Englewood Cliffs, NJ: Educational Technology Publications.

Zettl, H. (1990). *Sight, Sound, Motion: Applied Media Aesthetics* (2nd ed.). Belmont, CA: Wadsworth Publishing Co.

Chapter 5

VISUAL CONTENT

In the design and production of visual information, we have to consider the characteristics of visual languages. We need to know how the illustrations will be used. We should consider image variables related to content, graphic execution, context, and format.

Motifs, facts, "action," drama, violence, time shifts, parallel events, metaphorical (symbolic) descriptions, the degree of realism, the degree of detail, the credibility of contents, comparisons and statistics, movement, time, space, sounds in the form of speech, music, sound effects, and emotions are examples of variables related to picture contents.

Before starting to design visual information, it is very important to define how the illustrations can be used. The most important factors seem to be informational or educational objectives and user characteristics. Visuals may not always be really necessary but are useful in many situations. However, in some situations, pictures may be distracting. In these cases illustrations should not be used.

In the design and production of visuals for instruction or for education, pictures must contain the information they are intended to convey. The visuals must be relevant to the situation. Without clear content, the visual will not be able to function well.

We should carefully define the objective of each visual. What information or knowledge is the visual intended to convey? Who is the sender? Who are the receivers? And in which medium or media is the visual to be distributed? Cues for understanding the message in a visual are different in various cultures as well as in different socioeconomic groups. It is very important to consider these factors in each specific situation. Messages including visuals are preferred by most subjects and attract attention. Generally speaking, humans, especially their faces, are the kind of content that will get maximum attention in images. It is also known that objects and pictures of objects are remembered better than their names. Adding illustration to textual material, however, may fail to enhance attitude change. Results depend on how pictures are executed and how they are used. Association is facilitated when items are shown together.

STRUCTURE

A well-defined structure of content facilitates learning. There is a need for structure in complete material as well as within parts of that material. Normally the structure of the instructional message is built to be continuous, to form a connected whole that presents the message clearly to learners. The instruction progresses logically, step by step. After an initial orientation or instruction, instructional materials should develop at a pace that is suitable for the intended audience. A major factor in instructional effectiveness is repetition. Also, summaries will help learners to remember the most important points of the specific subject matter. Background colors, shades, frames, and special use of fonts and type size can be used to achieve unity.

When the learner doesn't see, read, or hear what s/he *expects* to see, or can't find agreement between verbal and visual content, the message is likely to be misunderstood. Since the competition for our attention is very fierce in commercial arts and in advertising, discontinuity is often used intentiona' y to attract and even to hold attention. The intended message may be hidden within verbal or visual puns, metaphors, satires, parodies, or humor. In these cases, designers break the traditional rules of instructional design. It might also be possible to use the unexpected to attract attention to instructional material as well.

Realism

A visual should usually possess a moderate and selected degree of realism and be true-to-life. Rather often this means culturally accurate detailed drawings in natural color. Recognition of familiar objects is remarkably high. But some objects, for example, a fire or a river, are not readily described in line drawings.

Informative pictures should be "unambiguous," i.e., not too "artistic" and therefore ambiguous. Cartoons, line drawings, and photographs represent a continuum of realism in visuals.

Cartoons, line drawings, and photographs represent a continuum of realism in visuals.

The more realistic a visual, the closer it is to reality. Too little or too much realism in a visual can interfere with the communication and learning processes. Learning is always related to the needs of the learners and to the level of objectives in each specific situation. Low-level objectives, such as naming of objects, need only a limited amount of information. High-level objectives, such as synthesis and analysis,

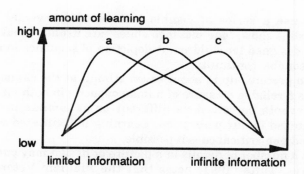

Low (a), medium (b), and high (c) level objectives demand various degrees of realism for a high amount of learning.

need a lot of information. Learners being exposed to "new" information may profit optimally from line drawings, whereas learners who are familiar with the content area may profit from more realistic types of illustrations.

Degree of detail

A visual should contain the details that are essential in communicating the intended message. Too many details and too much complexity give rise to distracting "interference" and reduce the interest for the content and the impact of the important part of the content in the visual. Thus, we should avoid unnecessary elements in the picture. Too few details or too little complexity makes it impossible to understand the picture. For each picture there is an optimal degree of detail. (This depends, e.g., on the content, the format, the intended audience, and the objectives.)

The amount of information and the degree of detail should be tailored to the medium and the visual format. Slides and overhead transparencies often include far too much information, making them impossible for the listeners to read and comprehend in a short time. It is usually not possible to directly transfer printed images to slides or overhead transparencies. Pictures should be re-designed to best fit the medium.

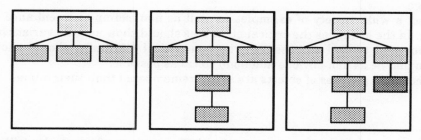

In AV-productions, it is usually a good idea to deliver the message step by step. A sequence of pictures can aid communication.

If necessary, use a series of visuals instead of one visual overloaded with information. In a slide show, "one-message slides" are usually ideal. This is also true for print material designed for children. A depiction of sequence in a series of frames should have a reasonable continuity.

We are able to perceive up to about seven stimuli at the same time. It has been found that 7+/–2 is a reliable measure of human capacity in both vision and audition.

Objects and events perceived as different or as similar in any way will be grouped and organized in our perception. Learning is facilitated when critical cues are apparent. Avoid non-critical cues if possible.

In some cases a number of details in a picture or design may cumulate into larger coherent structures. Tufte (1991) notes that the Vietnam Veterans Memorial in Washington, D.C. achieves its visual and emotional strength by means of micro/macro design. From a distance the entire collection of names of 58,000 dead soldiers arrayed on the black granite yields a visual measure of what 58,000 means, as the letters of each name blur into a grey shape, cumulating to the final toll. When a viewer approaches, these shapes resolve into individual names.

FACTUAL CONTENT

In instructional message design, the content is very often factual. "Realistic" pictures can provide reasonably objective documentation of an object or a product.

Objects

The type of subject should be commonplace, easy to recognize, and neither uncommon nor abstract. The visuals should not contain any strange or unknown codes. The more familiar a message is to its audience, the more readily it is perceived. Familiarity with the depicted objects themselves is basic to understanding. Also, the purpose of the visual should be obvious to the readers for whom the message is intended. In developing countries, pictures of people are most easily understood. Parts of the body like arms, hands, legs, and feet are more difficult to recognize. Even more difficult to recognize are tools and objects in the environment. People should, however, be dressed appropriately. Facial resemblance to members of the community is often an advantage.

Select a wide variety of examples as well as non-examples to enhance concept learning. In the examples the critical attributes should show as little variation and be as obvious and typical as possible. The non-critical attributes should show much variation and be as non-obvious and non-typical as possible.

Objects and pictures of objects are better remembered than their names.

Time

A still picture is a "frozen moment in time." The passage of time is best illustrated with a series of illustrations which show details in the course of an event. However, illiterate people in developing countries may have difficulties in understanding that adjacent frames show the same people in a time sequence.

Picture context and picture composition can illustrate an age, year, season, time of day, etc. Enhance comprehension with the aid of caption. Sometimes a time-scale may be useful.

For AV productions it should be remembered that the perception of time durations and time intervals is relatively inaccurate without a standard or frame of reference. Time that is filled with activity appears to pass more rapidly than time that is not filled with activity. Time is an essential factor in television and film. We can distinguish between objective time (clock time) and subjective time (psychological time).

People seem to prefer programs with fast pace and action. Such programs also result in greater learning efficiency.

Place

The location of objects may be shown in various kinds of scales, graphs, and maps. (There is a large literature in cartography and the design of maps. However, these topics are not discussed in this volume.)

Statistics

Numeric data are often used to illustrate situations such as relationships between variables and parts of a whole. Data can be presented in many formats. Graphical formats include comparisons of numbers, lengths, areas, volumes, positions, and also comparisons of different combinations of these. Discriminations are most readily learned when the differences between stimuli are maximal. If you wish to be clear, choose clear examples. Tufte (1983) wrote (p. 51): "Graphical excellence is that which gives the viewer the greatest number of ideas in the shortest time with the least ink in the smallest space."

Quantitative information should be made to stand out from the supporting information by ensuring that the different items on a graph can be easily distinguished visually. People cannot compare sizes of areas or volumes readily or exactly. It is far easier to distinguish between lines than between areas or volumes. In most contexts, the difference in the sizes of circles, squares, triangles, ellipses, and several other two-dimensional symbols are underestimated.

Distorting graphs by adding an artificial perspective or adding shadows will make it harder for readers to understand the information.

It is easier to assess "parts of a whole" than "relationships between variables." When relationships between variables are to be presented, comparisons of lengths give the best results. When parts of a whole are to be presented, pie charts may be used. However, don't use too many segments!

The bars in a bar chart should be equidistant from one another, and the bars should be wider than the empty spaces between them. Design of individual graphic elements is important. Patterns of bars should be discrete and not disturbing. Usually it is better to avoid mixtures of patterns and keep it as plain as possible. If

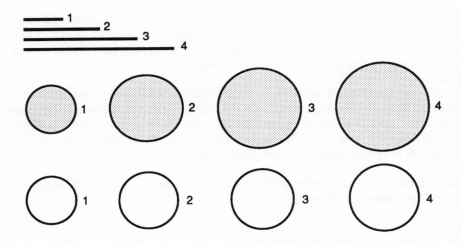

Comparisons of lengths, areas, and volumes. In this example, using the units 1, 2, 3, and 4, it is easier to distinguish between lines than between areas (grey) or between volumes (white).

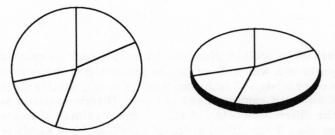

Adding perspective to a pie chart makes comparisons between segments very difficult. Avoid artificial perspectives.

stacked bar charts must be used, it is best to have dark tones at the bottom and lighter tones on top.

It is far too easy to convey misleading information about statistical relationships by using misleading illustrations or scales that are difficult to understand. Use a scale break only when it is necessary. If a break cannot be avoided, the break must be very distinct and easy to understand.

Tufte (1983) provides guidelines for the "friendliness" of graphs. In *friendly graphs*, words are spelled out, they run from left to right (in western societies), data are explained, and elaborately encoded shadings, cross-hatching, and colors are avoided; graphics attract viewers, colors are easy to distinguish, type is clear and precise, and is done in upper and lower case with serifs. In *unfriendly graphs,* abbreviations abound, words run vertically and in several other directions, the graphic is repellant and cryptic with obscure coding, the design is insensitive to color-deficient viewers, red and green are used for essential contrasts, and type is clotted and in all capitals, sans serif.

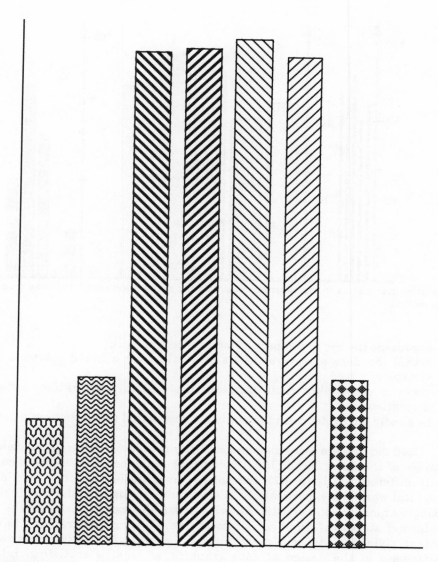

This is a **horrible example** of the misuse of patterns in a bar chart. Avoid disturbing, ugly, and misleading mixtures of patterns. They may influence our perception of the actual content.

According to Tufte (1983), excellence in statistical graphics consists of complex ideas communicated with clarity, precision, and efficiency. Graphical displays should (p. 13):

- show the data;
- induce the viewer to think about the substance rather than about methodology, graphic design, the technology of graphic production, or something else;
- present few numbers in a small space;
- make large data sets coherent;

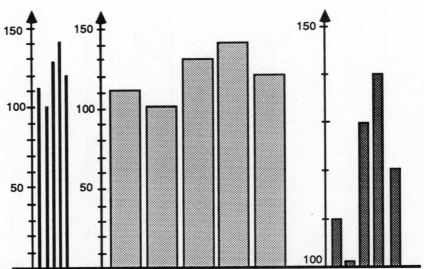

The three bar graphs in this illustration contain the same information, but they give us different impressions.

- encourage the eye to compare different pieces of data;
- reveal the data at several levels of detail, from a broad overview to the fine structure;
- serve a reasonably clear purpose: description, exploration, tabulation, or decoration; and
- be closely integrated with the statistical and verbal descriptions of a data set.

Good designs are intriguing and curiosity-provoking, drawing the viewer into the wonder of the data. Tufte (1983) noted that graphical competence demands three quite different skills (p. 87): the substantive, statistical, and artistic. Yet most graphical work today, particularly in news publications, is under the direction of but a single expertise—the artistic. Allowing artist-illustrators to control the design and content of statistical graphics is almost like allowing typographers to control the content, style, and editing of prose. Substantive and quantitative expertise must also participate in the design of data graphics, at least if statistical integrity and graphical sophistication are to be achieved.

EVENTS

Several kinds of image contents are related to events. "Action," humor, drama, violence, time displacement, parallel action, metaphoric descriptions (symbolic actions), and change are all examples of events that may be the content in visuals.

It is known that pictures showing events usually are more interesting and more effective instructional materials than static pictures. Activity is best shown in film or TV-sequences.

Motion

Obviously, several types of content benefit from being shown in moving media such as film and TV.

The best way to illustrate motion in a still picture is to depict a natural movement in contrast to a static situation. The impression of motion can be enhanced with graphical motion symbols such as speed lines. The meaning of these symbols has to be learned and in fact is easily learned by young children.

Motion in a visual attracts attention. The relation of figure to ground is particularly determinative of motion perception, which is highly related to depth perception. Perception of motion is influenced by contextual variables.

Rhythm consists of regular changes between different levels of a variable. This can be illustrated by arraying image elements into distinct groups.

Sound

The impression of sound in a still picture is most readily conveyed with onomatopoetic combinations of letters combined with graphical symbols and legends.

Examples of some onomatopoetic combinations of letters

Comic strips enclose the text in different kinds of bubbles.

In AV productions, words and sound effects can enhance perception of the visual stimuli. However, there should be a redundant relationship between these different stimuli.

Humor and satire

Humor and satire are often used in cartoons to point out a special situation, occurrence, or event. In instructional material humor may sometimes be used as a visual pun to attract attention or dramatize certain portions of a visual. However, humor should be used with great care in instructional material. Misuse of humor and "funny people" may ruin the intended message. This is sometimes referred to as the "vampire-effect."

Relationships

Visuals may express relationships between people. For example, in various cultures the distance between people tells the viewer a lot about their relationship.

EMOTIONS

A picture is able to express emotions in at least three different ways. It may suggest an image of some emotional concept, i.e., a picture may look the way an emotion feels, e.g., "happy" or "sad." A picture may arouse emotional response in a viewer, i.e., the viewer may feel pleasure, excitement, or fright. A picture may also express and reflect the picture creator's feelings about a given subject, such as politics or religion.

Examples of onomatopoetic combinations of graphical symbols in comic strips.

Visuals with an emotional content support and extend the attitudes we already have.

Pictures will usually not change our attitudes, but they make us more convinced that we already hold the "right" views.

If people like the content in a visual, they like it even more when the visual is presented in color and vice versa.

In the western cultural sphere, people tend to associate colors with emotions or moods in the following way. The red and yellow part of the spectrum is often said to be warm and is felt to be active, exciting, happy, and clear. Green to blue is described as cold and are perceived as being passive, comfortable, controlled, and peaceful.

Emotions and moods are readily conveyed with onomatopoetic combinations of graphical symbols. However, we have to remember that the meaning of the symbols must be learned by the readers.

CREDIBILITY

A visual should depict reality in a manner appropriate to the content and be as relevant and credible as possible. If possible use familiar pictures.

High-credibility sources (for most people today), like television, film, and radio, exert a more persuasive influence than low-credibility sources, like newspapers and magazines. However, if attention is assured, the degree of credibility does not affect the amount learned.

The most important components of credibility are expertise and trustworthiness. The endorsements of real people are memorable and persuasive. In the production of educational materials it is very important to note the issues of multiethnicity and gender equality. These have often been overlooked.

The use of misleading illustrations in comparisons and statistics reduces the credibility of the message itself.

According to Tufte (1983), misleading or lying graphics cheapen the graphical art everywhere. Since the lies often show up in news reports, millions of images are printed. When a chart on television lies, it lies tens of millions of times over; when a major newspaper chart lies, it lies hundreds of thousands of times over to a great many important and influential readers. Tufte offers six principles which will result in graphical integrity (p. 77):

- The representation of numbers, as physically measured on the surface of the graphic itself, should be directly proportional to the numerical quantities represented.
- Clear, detailed, and thorough labeling should be used to defeat graphical distortion and ambiguity. Write out explanations of the data on the graphic itself. Label important events in the data.
- Show data variation, not design variation.
- The number of information-carrying (variable) dimensions depicted should not exceed the number of dimensions in the data.
- Graphics must not quote data out of context.

SYMBOLISM

As mentioned earlier, there is often a major difference between the *denotation*, the literal meaning, and the various *connotations*, associative meanings, and *private associations*. Many visuals have a *symbolic content* and meaning. Look at images used in most religions, in folklore, in mythology, in propaganda, in advertising, and in political campaigns.

Some contemporary photographs and paintings are well known by people all over the world. A photograph with a national flag is much more than an ordinary photograph. To every person the flag of her or his nation is a symbol that means "my country." A lion is the symbol for courage, a lamb suggests gentleness, and the dove with an olive branch symbolizes peace.

Sometimes symbolic pictures are simplified to symbols. Visual details are reduced to a minimum. A symbol cannot have detailed information.

VIEWER COMPLETION

Experienced artists usually leave out most details. They only draw the lines that are necessary to understand the content. Our minds constantly fills in missing details and complete images, most of the time without our realizing that it has happened. The most probable interpretation of the message is created as a meaningful whole. However, the human imagination may be triggered by the design to provide details that will increase viewers' attention and possibly also facilitate learning.

In drawings the lines that are missing may be as important as those that actually are there. This is often seen in cartoons.

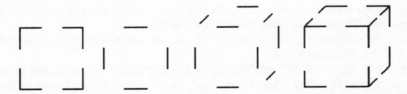

Some lines are more important than others at giving key information. This is clearly shown in these examples of squares and cubes.

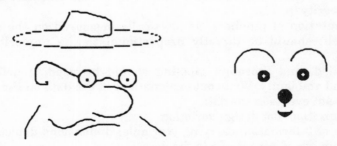

Our minds fill in missing details and make the best possible interpretation of a given stimulus. To the left we may see a person with a hat, not just a few lines. To the right we may see an animal face.

REFERENCES AND SUGGESTED READINGS

Ackmann, D. (1984). *Advanced Business Graphics Forms.* CAMP/ 84. Computer Graphics Applications for Management and Productivity. Berlin Sept 25–28. Proceedings: AMK Berlin.

Allander, B. (1974). TV-rutans verklighet. In B. Allander, S. S. Bergström, & C. Frey. *Se men också höra.* Stockholm.

Anderson, R. C., & Faust, G. W. (1973). *Educational Psychology: The Science of Instruction and Learning.* New York: Dodd, Mead & Co.

Belson, W. A. (1978). *Television Violence and the Adolescent Boy.* London: Saxon House.

Berefelt, G. (1976). *AB Se om Bildperception.* Lund: Liber läromedel.

Chaprakani, T. K., & Ehrenberg, A. S. C. (1976). *Numerical Information Processing.* London: London Business School.

Colwell, C., Mangano, N., & Hortin, J. A. (1984). Humour and visual literacy: Keys to effective learning. In A. D. Walker, R. A. Braden, & L. H. Dunker (Eds.). *Visual Literacy: Enhancing Human Potential.* Readings from the 15th Annual Conference of the International Visual Association. Blacksburg: Virginia Tech University.

Cook, B. L. (1981). *Understanding Pictures in Papua New Guinea.* Elgin, IL: David C. Cook Foundation.

Cox, D. R. (1978). Some remarks on the role in statistics of graphical methods. *Applied Statistics, 27,* 4–9. Cited by E. R. Misanchuk. (1992). *Preparing Instructional Text: Document Design Using Desktop Publishing.* Englewood Cliffs, NJ: Educational Technology Publications.

Dondis, D. A. (1973). *A Primer of Visual Literacy.* Cambridge, MA: Massachusetts Institute of Technology.

Duck, S. W., & Baggaley, J. (1975). Audience reaction and its effect on perceived expertise. *Communication Research, 2,* 79–85.

Dwyer, F. M. (1972). *A Guide for Improving Visualized Instruction.* State College, PA: Learning Services.

Dwyer, F. M. (1978). *Strategies for Improving Visual Learning.* State College, PA: Learning Services.

Dwyer, F. M., & Dwyer, C. A. (1989). Enhancing visualized instruction: A research overview. In R. A. Braden, D. G. Beauchamp, L. V. W. Miller, & D. M. Moore (Eds.). *About Visuals: Research, Teaching, and Applications.* Readings from the 20th Annual Conference of the International Visual Literacy Association. Blacksburg: Virginia Tech University.

Filipson, L. , & Schyller, I. (1980). *Barnens tittande, 3–8-åringars TV tittande 2. 18 May 1979.* Stockholm: SR/PUB 2.

Fleming, M., & Levie, W. H. (1978). *Instructional Message Design.* Englewood Cliffs, NJ: Educational Technology Publications.

Fleming, M., & Levie, W. H. (Eds.) (1993). *Instructional Message Design* (2nd ed.). Englewood Cliffs, NJ: Educational Technology Publications.

Griffin, R. E. (1991). The visual business presentation: An international comparison. In D. G. Beauchamp, J. Clark-Baca, & R. A. Braden (Eds.). *Investigating Visual Literacy.* Selected Readings from the 22rd Annual Conference of the International Visual Literacy Association. Blacksburg: Virginia Tech University.

Heinich, R., Molenda, M., & Russell, J. D. (1993). *Instructional Media and the New Technologies of Instruction.* New York: Macmillan.

Kince, E. (1982). *Visual Puns in Design.* New York: Watson-Guptill Publication.

Kowalski, K. (1977). *Barn och bildskapande. Hur man stimulerar barns föreställningsförmåga, fantasi och idéer.* Stockholm: W&W.

Legatt, A. L. S. (1983). *Financial Information on Teletext.* London: The City University, Centre for Information Science, M. Sc. Thesis.

Lindsten, C. (1975). *Hembygdskunskap i årskurs 3. Att inhämta, bearbeta och redovisa kunskaper.* Lund: Liber Läromedel.

MacDonald-Ross, M. (1977). How numbers are shown. A review of research on the presentation of quantitative data in texts. *AV Communication Review, 25* (4), 359–409.

McLachlan, J., & LaBarbara, P. (1978). Time- compressed TV commercials. *Journal of Advertising Research, 18*, 11–15.

Murch, G. M. (1973). *Visual and Auditory Perception.* Indianapolis: The Bobbs-Merrill Co.

Myatt, B., & Carter, J. M. (1979). Picture preferences of children and young adults. *ECTJ, 27* (1), 45–53.

Pettersson, R. (1982). Cultural differences in the perception of image and color in pictures. *ECTJ, 30* (1), 43–53.

Pettersson, R. (1984a). Factors in visual language: Emotional content. *Visual Literacy Newsletter, 13*, 3 and *13*, 4.

Pettersson, R. (1984b). *Factors in Visual Languages: Motion.* CLEA–Report, No. 17. Stockholm: Stockholm University, Department of Computer Science.

Prawitz, M. (1977). Varför förstår du inte vad jag säger, när jag hoppar, skuttar och målar? In G. Berefelt. *Barn och bild.* Stockholm: AWE/Gebers..

Reidhaar, J. W. (1984). An overview of nontabular methods for statistical presentation of data before this century. *Information Design Journal, 4* (1), 25–35.

Rickards, J. P. (1976). Stimulating high-level comprehension by interspersing questions in text passages. *Educational Technology, 16* (11), 13–17.

Rock, I. (1975). *An Introduction to Perception.* New York: Macmillan Publishing Co.

Ryan, M. (1975). The impact of television news film on perceived media credibility. *Journal of Applied Communications Research, 3*, 69–75.

Rydin, I. (1979). *Hur barn förstår TV II, Från frö till telefonstolpe. Med rörlig bild eller stillbild?* Stockholm: SR/PUB, Projekt Nr. 747073.

Thayer, N. (1984). *Verbal-Visual Mis-literacy: Creative Discontinuity.* Presentation at the 16th Annual Conference of the International Visual Literacy Association, Baltimore, Nov. 8–11.

Tufte, E. R. (1983). *The Visual Display of Quantitative Information.* Cheshire, CT: Graphics Press.

Vinberg, A. (1981). *Designing a Good Graph.* San Diego: Integrated Software Systems.

Wainer, H. (1984). How to display data badly. *The American Statistician, 38*, 137–147.

Wileman, R. (1993). *Visual Communicating.* Englewood Cliffs, NJ: Educational Technology Publications.

Winn, W., & Everett, R. J. (1978). *Differences in the Affective Meaning of Color and Black and White Pictures.* Paper presented at the annual meeting of the Association for Educational Communications and Technology. Kansas City, Missouri, April, 23 pp. Document ED 160 067.

Zimmer, A., & Zimmer, F. (1978). *Visual Literacy in Communication: Designing for Development.* Hulton Educational Publications, Ltd., in cooperation with the International Institute for Adult Methods, Teheran.

Chapter 6

EXECUTION OF EFFECTIVE VISUALS

Picture type (i.e., drawings, painting, photos, computer-generated images, etc.), shape (external shape, external contour), size (picture, motif, depth), color (hue, nuance, grey scale, contrast, location), perspective (depth, angle of view, level), technical quality, characters, and intra-image "passwords," pace, speed changes (slow, fast), editing, zooming in, zooming out, panning, visual complexity, and visual effects are examples of pictorial factors and components. Informative pictures should always be designed so they are easy to read. The goal should be *clarity of communication*. Several authors have pointed out that "form follows function." Industrial products are often shaped by what they do. To make life easier we want to have products with as good a function as possible. However, in message design the subjective tastes of the individual designers are often allowed to dominate, sometimes with serious malfunctions occurring in effective communication.

PRODUCTION

Perception is always organized. We perceptually construct relationships, groupings, objects, events, words, and people. We see dots, lines, areas, light, dark, etc., in an organized way. One of the most simple perceptual organizations is that of "figure and background." Some elements in a visual are selected as the figure. The remaining elements constitute the background. Our ability to distinguish the boundaries of an image is usually very high.

"Good figures," i.e., in the sense of simplicity, regularity, and stability, are closed and exhibit a continuous contour. A given contour can belong to only one of the two areas it encloses and shapes. Whichever side, the contour shapes will be perceived as a figure. Reversible figures lack sufficient cues as to which side of a contour is figure and which is the background. This is often used to create illusions. We have all seen a reversible figure that is perceived as a vase or as two heads facing each other.

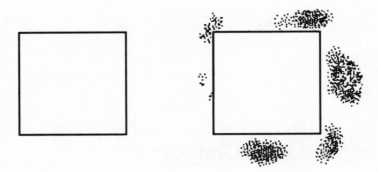

In these two illustrations, we easily recognize two squares as "figures" against the white (left) and also against the dotted background (right).

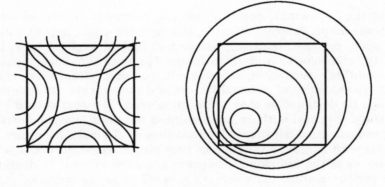

In these two illustrations, the properties of "figure and background" cannot be sharply distinguished. Despite our perceptions, the squares are of the same size with straight sides.

Highly developed perceptual abilities are needed to detect the bounds of a single image within a complex structure. Small children may find it difficult to switch attention from parts to the whole and back again.

In camouflage the intention is to make a figure as much like the background as possible.

When lines overlap or compete, emerging figures have good continuation. The most symmetrical and simplest figures constructed will be perceived.

The simplest image components should be arrayed so that the picture's message is brought out as clearly as possible. This can be combined with high demands on aesthetic quality, but it is difficult to make any general recommendations on how, e.g., various drawing styles should be used. Fine details in the texture of a drawing disappear in the dot screen structure of the printed image. Even more detail is lost in a TV image. To save money, pictures could be tailored to the technical limitations of the systems that are used to make originals, masters, and print runs in the respective medium/distribution channel.

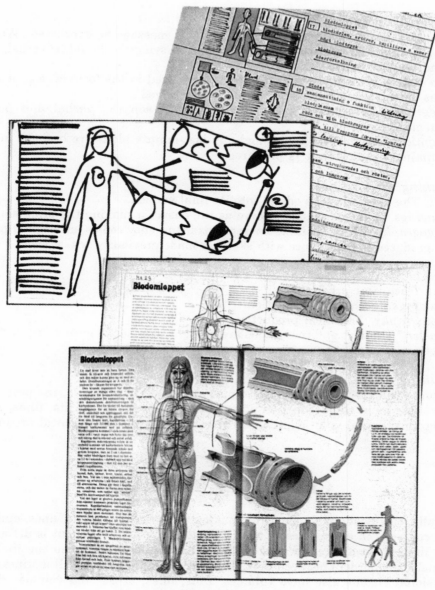

From visualization to the final print.

When visuals are produced for informative purposes, it is always a good idea to start by trying to "visualize" the information to be conveyed. "Visualizing" a message means that you attempt to materialize it in an effective synthesis of words and pictures. So visualization is always a composite task, never a single act on its own, and requires the collaboration of several different parties. The stages in the production of instructional material from visualization to the finished product are listed below:

A. *Visualization*
- *Synopsis*. Define the message! How can this message be expressed? What are the required characteristics and conditions? A synopsis should be verbal, take a broad view, be concise, and to the point.
- *Idea conception*. The idea should be materialized in the form of, e.g., a sketch. Ideas for the text, sound, and visuals are conceived.
- *Integration*. An interplay is organized between the verbal and pictorial information.
- *Graphical design*. The layout and any last-minute ideas are brought in and a preliminary manuscript is prepared.

B. *Making the original*
- *Text*. The manuscript is edited into its final version.
- *Drawings*. Previous sketches serve as the basis for making the originals.
- *Photography*. Prints suitable for repro, transparency copies, or original pictures are produced in accordance with sketches made previously or test shots.

C. *Making the "master"*
- *Text*. Technical production.
- *Drawings*. Technical production.
- *Photography*. Technical production.
- *"Master."* The text and the visuals are brought together to form a "master" which can be used to print a run.

D. *Run*
- *Copies*. The specified number of copies are made. In principle, the procedure is the same as in the production of graphical products, AV media, films, and TV programs. Sound is an additional representation in non-graphical products.

GRAPHICAL ELEMENTS

Generally, the most simple elements making up a visual are dots, lines, and areas, which can vary in a great many ways. Whether a graphic element is defined as a dot, a line, or an area is related to the size and the scale of the specific visual. Obviously, the borders between dots, lines, and areas are not at all distinct. Three-dimensional visuals also have volumes. Dots, lines, areas, and volumes all have various properties, and together they build up the visuals.

A dot (left) may vary in size. A line (middle) may be defined as a dot that is extended, at least to the length of two dots, and usually more dots. An area (right) may be defined as a line that is broadened. Thus, the smallest area has the size of four dots.

Basic properties of graphic elements

Dots	Lines	Areas	Volume
size	point of origin	size	size
shape	length	"emptiness"	shape
color	direction	shape	color
value	curvature	color	surface
grain	shape	value	structure
position	thickness	grain	contour
context	evenness	texture	direction
	points of	shaded	weight
	change	non-shaded	position
	printing	grey scale	material
	color	combination of	light
	value	colors	architecture
	grain	brightness	stability
	brightness	context	balance
	orientation		proportions
	terminus		gravity
	context		context

Dots

With respect to the technique and the different types of visuals, dots can vary in size, shape, color, value, grain, context, and position. The ability of a series of dots to direct our attention is greater the closer the individual dots are to one another. When the dots are really close to one another, they cannot be individually recognized any more. The series of dots form a line. A line could also be defined as the "track of a dot in motion."

When dots are close they form a line.

Lines

A line may be varied with respect to its starting point, length, direction, curvature, shape, thickness, evenness, points of change, printing, color, value, grain, brightness, orientation, terminus, and context. A line has one of two functions. It can lead from one place to another, or it can be a border between two areas. Since we always perceive graphical elements with respect to the context, the meaning of a simple and single line will vary.

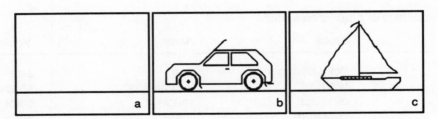

A horizontal line can serve, e.g., as a horizon (a), a street (b), or a sea (c).

Vertical and horizontal lines, parallel to the borders of the picture give the impression of calm and stability. Horizontal lines give the impression of depth. Vertical lines often stop eye movement. Diagonal lines give the impression of movement. There is a tendency for curved lines and smooth shapes to stand out more than straight lines and shapes made out of straight lines. Lines that reach out from one point in different directions may be perceived as aggressive or violent.

There are several good reasons for using lines in drawing.

- Line is the natural way to draw. Infants begin with line and adults continue throughout life.
- Line is restless and never static.
- Line is a quick way to visualize ideas.
- Line needs a minimum use of time and material.
- Line drawing materials are least expensive.
- Line emphasizes the basic structure and composition of a drawing.
- Other drawing techniques may be added.
- Line drawings are the most readily recognizable form of depiction in general.
- Line drawings are effective stimuli for learning.
- Line can take many different moods.
- Line is a tool for notation systems.
- Line describes shape.

There are many different kinds of lines and arrows. Here are a few versions.

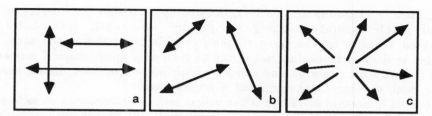

Vertical and horizontal lines (a) are harmonious and flat. Diagonal lines disrupt harmony and add depth to the visual (b); reaching out from one point they may be perceived as violent (c).

Lines should usually be solid (left) and not filled with a pattern (middle and right), which will be hard to recognize.

Areas

An area can be varied with respect to size, "emptiness," shape, color, value, grain, texture, shaded, non-shaded, grey scale, color combinations, brightness, and context. Roundness is the most common form in nature. When ink, water, or any other liquid material is dropped on a surface, it assumes a rounded form.

Squares and rectangles are rare in nature. An area may be described by a line. It may also be described by a shade or by a color. An area may have a geometric, an abstract, or a representational shape. The size of an individual area is always relative. It depends on our knowledge of its surroundings.

The size of a rectangle (a) means little to us. A person sitting behind the rectangle gives it the size of a desk (b). A car in front of it makes it the size of a building (c).

A square is an example of a static area. A rectangle is perceived as more active. A volume has a three-dimensional form. The form may be actual or simulated. In two-dimensional representations of three-dimensional objects, shadows are key cues for simulated volumes. We structure the three-dimensional field into various depth planes, or grounds, a foreground, a middleground, and a background.

In printing technology, graphic elements may be defined as type for letters and lines, and screen points for visuals. In work with digital images in computerized image processing, graphic elements can be defined in one of two systems: either mathematically as points and vectors, defined by cartesian coordinates, or in the form of pixels (minute rectangular picture elements), defined by raster coordinates. A vector can be assigned basic graphic properties in the same way as attributes in display fountains, but it has as such only mathematical properties. A pixel is in fact a minute area and can vary with respect to color. Lines, areas, and symbols, such as letters, are composed of several pixels.

The most important elements of the visual may be emphasized so as to enhance attention and perception. Design all visual material taking into account dots, lines, and areas, so that the important content will stand out and be easy to perceive.

Volumes

Like lines and areas, volumes also have several basic properties, such as size, shape, color, surface, structure, contour, direction, weight, position, material, light, architecture, stability, balance, proportions, gravity, and context. A volume has a three-dimensional form. The form may be actual or simulated.

Study the works of good artists, painters, and sculptors. Most artists use many of the possibilities in the visual language. However, some artists have made paintings, drawings, etc., using mainly one or two different elements with limited basic properties. Here are just a few examples.

Vincent van Gogh only used dots and lines in some paintings. In numerous paintings, Roy Lichtenstein used the screen of dots and lines from comics in newspapers. Paul Cezanne used hues in different areas.

Pablo Picasso is most well-known for his paintings, in which he often used areas in different shapes. Picasso was, however, very active also in other fields. He introduced "construction" in sculpture. He assembled pieces of wood, cardboard, paper, string, and other materials. Thus, Picasso gave sculpture a potential freedom which is not yet fully explored. Marcel Duchamp used everyday objects like the famous "Bottle Rack" directly as sculpture.

Auguste Rodin was the master of modeling clay, with special articulation of the surface of the sculpture. Replicas of his sculptures can now be found in many countries. Constantin Brancusi exploited Rodin's discovery of material as the fundamental determinant of form. He explored materials like timber and stone, and used forms inherent in these materials. He also used polished bronze.

Henry Moore was a master of lines and volumes in his sculptures. In his sculptures there is an intense interaction of space, light, shadows, contours, balance, composition, proportions, relations, and stability.

TYPE OF VISUAL

Look around! In your home, at work, and in other places you will see that there are many different types of visuals. You may see drawings, paintings, collages, montages, mosaics, maps, pictures or textiles, lithographs, photographs, and pictures in books, magazines, newspapers, and television. The visual register is very large and we see a good deal of it every day. Visuals showing the same subject can be executed in many different ways.

Preference for a particular visual format does not necessarily result in increased learning. Yet, in the absence of more substantial data, information based on student preference has a meaningful role to play in affecting learning from instructional texts. All other things being equal, we should provide formats which are preferred by the viewer, thus making the text more attractive, and hopefully more motivating.

Visuals for instruction should be attractive but "unambiguous," i.e., not too "artistic" and therefore ambiguous. Visuals that are attractive and that people like also have greater impact. It might be a good idea to use a blend of several kinds of visual types, such as diagrams, drawings, photos, etc.

Generally speaking, it is not possible to rank the different types of visuals. Often the type of visual which should be used must be determined in each individual case with a view to various demands on the picture and the prevailing budget framework. It is often easier to control the production of a drawing than the production of a photograph. It is usually easier to reduce multiple visual factors and only show the essential in a drawing than in a photograph. For these reasons a drawing may be the only realistic alternative in many instances.

SUBJECT

A subject may be presented in several different ways. The part of the subject that is important must be large and clear, take up a large proportion of the image area, and be perceivable as an entirety. Symbolic illustrations are easier to do but they may be more difficult to recognize.

From the age of about seven years most children will understand images with figures truncated by the picture frame. However, for children up to the age of about seven years, the entire subject must be clearly visible. No important part of the subject may be hidden in or missing from the visual. Absent items do not really exist, in the minds of many children. To a large extent this is also true for illiterate adults in developing countries. The "personal space" between people in a visual is important, with different meaning to readers belonging to different cultures.

LIGHT

Light is essential to the appreciation of three-dimensional images like sculptures. Whether the light is coming from the left or from the right, the top or the bottom, makes a crucial difference in the appearance of the forms. Soft light helps us appreciate subtle undulations. Strong light accentuates details on the surface.

The word photography has its origin in Greek and means "writing with light." Drawers as well as painters and photograpers make use of various lighting conditions, light, shadows, and darkness to create perceptions of volume in two-dimensional pictures. A person or an object depicted in hard or soft light will be perceived differently.

The physicist defines light as visible radiant energy. Actually, light is invisible. We can see it only at its source and when reflected. Light has outer as well as inner orientation functions.

Outer orientation functions

Light will articulate our outer orientation with respect to space, texture, and time. Without any shadows we can make out the basic contour of an object. Shadows define space. The *attached shadow* is on the actual object. It helps to reveal the basic form and dimensions of that object.

The *cast shadow* is frequently observed as being independent of the object that caused it. Depending on the angle of the light source, the cast shadow may reveal the basic shape and location of the object that caused it. The surface appears to be curved when the light falls off gradually. A highly directional (hard) light produces fast fall-off. Thus, a curved surface is emphazised. A highly diffused and nondirectional (soft) light produces slow fall-out. Prominent cast shadows caused by hard light from a low angle emphasize texture. Soft light, on the other hand, de-emphasizes texture. Thus, both hard and soft light may be used successfully for spatial and tactile orientation, for example, in portrait photography. In daylight the background is usually bright. The cast shadows are very pronounced and the fall-off is fast. In a night time scene the background is dark. The lighting from various light sources is highly selective. Shadows are prominent.

Inner orientation functions

As well as light can articulate space, texture, and time, it can also articulate inner orientation functions. In motion picture and TV production, light, especially combined with music and sound effects, can evoke a great variety of specific feelings and emotions within us. Minor position changes of principal light sources may have drastic effects on our perception of mood and atmosphere. For example, a face lighted from below may appear unusual, ghostly, and brutal.

TEXTURE

In a picture the optical texture serves as a stand-in for the qualities of actually touching and sensing the real thing. In a photograph we may recognize and "sense" the hard bronze surface in a sculpture and the soft and warm yarn in a textile. We can experience the surface of paper, plastics, stone, wood, and many other materials. To be able to do this the lighting and the shadows are very important. Actually most of our textural experience is optical, and not tactile, in the real world. We see and we believe.

SHAPE

There are three basic and fundamental shapes: the circle, the equilateral triangle, and the square. The basic shapes express visual directions. Circles suggest curved directions, triangles suggest diagonal directions, and squares suggest horizontal and vertical directions. Basic and regular shapes are dominated by irregular and unpredictable shapes. These shapes attract more attention.

For small children (three to six years), color stimuli have greater impact than shape stimuli. However, the reverse is true of older children, i.e., shape becomes more important than color.

Shape constancy is our tendency to judge shapes as the same despite changes in distance, viewing angle, and illumination.

The picture area in drawing, painting, and still photography can have any shape and orientation. Most pictures, though, are cropped and published in square or rectangular formats. However, the visual's external shape should be "free-form," round, or oval, and not delineated by straight lines. Perception of shape is influenced by contextual variables.

Classical formats are based on the proportions of the golden section or golden rectangle, 3:5, 5:8, 8:13, 13:21, 21:34, etc. The proportions of the golden section are 1:1.618. Television as well as film screens are horizontally oriented, since we basically experience the world on a horizontal, rather than a vertical, plane. When HDTV was developed it was found that people preferred the aspect ratio of 3 x 5 or 9 x 16 (1:1.778) over the 3 x 4 (1:1.333) ratio of the current television system.

The visual's external contour should be blurred and unclear so the visual fades in/out of the background and never clear enough to stand out against the background. A printed image should fade in/out from the (white) page and a projected image should fade in/out from the (dark) screen. It is possible that very distinct framing diverts interest from the actual content in the visuals.

Illustrations in early European books frequently had gently rounded contours. Many artists still frequently draw free-form visuals which are not delineated by straight lines and which fade in/out of the background. In one study typical primary school textbooks from Ghana, Japan, and Sweden were compared. Irregularly shaped, oval, or round image shapes were predominant in the Ghanian and Japanese books. In the Swedish book fewer than one-fourth of the illustrations were "free" or rounded images.

SIZE

It is easier for us to distinguish between lines than between areas or volumes. When we judge the size of objects, e.g., areas, we are apparently most influenced by the length of horizontal lines or horizontal distances. In most contexts the differences in the sizes of circles, squares, triangles, ellipses and other two-dimensional symbols are underestimated.

Size constancy is our tendency to judge the size of an object as the same despite changes in distance, viewing angle, and illumination.

Size of visual

In materials for information, the size of a visual should never be decided with
respect to "available space" or "prettiness." The size of a visual should be decided
with respect to the possibility to communicate the intended message. For example,
illustrations in textbooks for early grades are both large and frequent. In later
grades the visuals are smaller and less frequent.

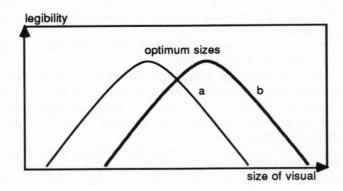

The size of a visual should be large enough for the image to be legible. There is an optimum size for
each visual.

Quite often readers will interpret the size of a visual as a measure of
importance. By tradition the bigger a picture is on a page the more important it is
considered to be. However, a visual should neither be too small nor too large. There
is an optimum size for each visual. The size must be large enough for the image to
be legible. A visual with a "large content" and many details must be larger than a
visual containing a more limited amount of information.

If one picture is larger than the others in an array, this picture will attract the
most attention. "Noise" in the visual results in a need for a larger size.

A picture 4–5 cm (1 1/2 to 2 inches) wide in a book corresponds to the eye's
perception of the width of a TV screen at a normal viewing distance and is adequate
in some cases. In TV the spectacle of things is de-emphasized, but human actions
gain prominence. A large Cinemascope image is more overpowering than the
small TV image. In film, people as well as objects attain spectacular dimensions.

Size of subjects

The most important part of the subject must be large and clear, take up a large
proportion of the image area, and be perceivable as an entirety. Large visual
elements attract the attention of the reader.

The perception of size is influenced by color and grey scale. Open and light
forms are perceived as being larger than closed and darker forms of the same
shape.

These circle areas all have the same size but we may easily perceive them as different in sizes because of the variation in the grey levels.

The perception of size is very much influenced by contextual variables. There can be no large without small. We need to show the scale and the contrast. It is usually a good idea to include some familiar object to supply the scale for judging the size of an unfamiliar object.

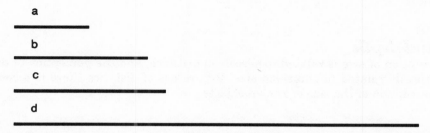

In this illustration line b can be considered long compared with line a. At the same time b is shorter than c which is short compared with d.

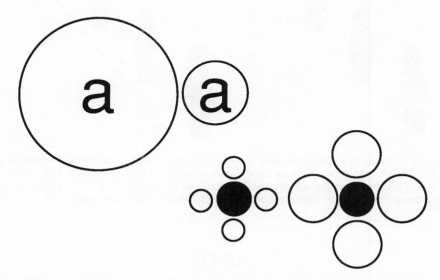

Cover the right part of this illustration with a piece of paper or with your hand. Compare the size of the two "a's." Move the cover to the the left part of the picture. Compare the size of the two dark circles. The perceived size of an object is relative to the size of nearby objects. Above, the letter 'a' is equal in both contexts; so is the dark circle in the other pair.

People vary greatly in their ability to perceive proportional relationships. The perceived size of an object is relative to the size of other objects. The size of unfamiliar objects is perceived as relative to the size of familiar objects. Sometimes it is possible to include a scale in the visual. Any simple and distinct part of an image can be visually superimposed to measure proportional relationships of the whole. In caricatures, however, proportions are deliberately wrong. Deliberate distortions create aesthetic tension between the caricature and the normal image of the subject. This induces emotional responses in viewers. Feelings are readily aroused by a departure from what is considered visually correct or normal. Photographers can also produce "caricatures" by using unusual angles and/or distorting lenses. When we need visuals for instruction, caricatures are usually not the best choice.

When the size of an object changes in a story from one page to another or even on the same page, children up to seven years of age often believe that the objects are different.

Size and depth

The perception of size is related to perceived distance, and the perception of distance is reciprocally related to perceived size. Regardless of distance there is a constancy in the perception of the size of known objects.

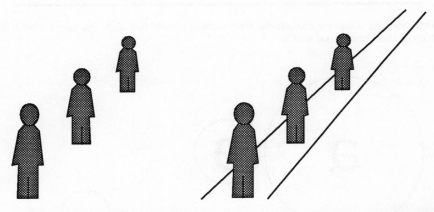

Cover the right part of this illustration with a piece of paper or with your hand. The group of three persons (to the left) can now easily be considered as different in size. Move the cover to the left part of the picture. Now the addition of the two lines (in the right part of the picture) makes it easy to perceive that group of three persons as people seen on different distances.

COLOR

A visual should usually be in color but not in unrealistic colors. It is possible for us to see the difference between several million colors. However, we can only distinguish about 10,000 different colors. Color can be described in technical, physiological, psychological, and aesthetic terms. Color is capable of enhancing communication, adding clarity and impact to a message.

Yellow-green lies in the region of the eye's greatest sensitivity. Sensitivity decreases markedly toward the red and blue ends of the spectrum. Perception of color is strongly influenced by and dependent on contextual variables such as lighting conditions and other surrounding colors.

Color constancy is our tendency to judge surface colors as the same despite changes in distance, viewing angle, and illumination.

People in different cultures and in different socio-economic groups use colors in different ways and with different meanings. In cultures in Africa, Central and South America, and Indonesia bright colors and high contrast are common in illustrations.

Color preferences

People prefer surface colors according to this ranking: (1) blue, (2) red, (3) green, (4) violet, (5) orange, and (6) yellow.

Children prefer colors that are light, distinct, and shining better than colors that are dark and gloomy. Color intensity should be strong and color contrast should be clear.

Color visibility

Color intensity influences our perception of shapes and objects. When colors of equal intensity are compared, the most visible colors are white, yellow, and green, in that order. The least visible colors are red, blue, and violet.

In information graphics and statistical presentations, the most important elements should have the brightest colors, with the best contrasts to the background.

In multi-color map design, the contrast effect of different hues provides the most dominating visual clue in differentiating different symbols.

The most legible combinations of print colors is black or dark brown text on a light yellow background. Other combinations may attract more attention but are less legible and, thus, require bigger letters.

Attentional use of color

Colors are good aids in drawing attention to circumstances that need highlighting. It is hard to recognize an image when it has many colors. It has been found that even if color is not adding any information it is still contributing to better learning because the interest for the picture increases. There are many ways to use colors to get attention to certain information.

Affective use of color

Color enhances the perception of a visual message. If people like the content in a picture they like it even more when the visual is presented in color. From many experiments, it is quite clear that people prefer color in visuals. Advertising is known to be much more effective when visuals are in color than in black and white.

Tests have indicated that viewers feel they have a better understanding when TV images are displayed in color, although the use of black and white sometimes would be sufficient. However, an improper use of color can produce negative results. It can be distracting, fatiguing, and upsetting.

Cognitive use of color

Color is important in a visual when it carries information that is vital for the content in the visual. It is, for example, easier to learn to distinguish between various species of birds or butterflies when color illustrations are used instead of black and white. It is known that highlighted information tends to be better remembered. Colors can easily be used for highlighting, separating, defining, and associating information. In line drawings or in black and white photos, for example, the addition of one color may be very efficient. To avoid confusion and misunderstanding, it is very important that color be used consistently.

Color coding

Colors are often used for color coding, for example, of objects. This is used also in different signs and symbols. The number of color codes should be very limited. As the number of color coded items increases, the value of color as a cue for selecting important information decreases. In videotex, for example, subjects tend to dislike the use of more than four or five colors at the same time.

A color-coding process may enable learners to retain critical information and disregard redundant and/or irrelevant information. An effective, systematic color code in a learning material assists the learner in organizing and categorizing stimuli into meaningful patterns.

Decorative use of color

There are many situations where colors can be used for decoration. However, a decorative use of color should never be mixed with other uses of color. It must always be easy to understand when color is used for decoration and when the use is cognitive.

Color psychology

In spite of the large quantity of research, color perception still only seems to be partially understood. It could be concluded that:
- Colors can be associated with temperature and emotions.
- The human reactions to color stimuli cannot be standardized. Depending on sex, age, and culture, the subjective reactions to color are different. People might see colors in the same way. However, no two persons experience color in *precisely* the same way.

- There are likes and dislikes of color, based on general and personal associations.

CONTRAST

In nature, as well as in art, contrast is of major importance for perception. The contrast, i.e., the difference between the brightest and the dimmest parts of a visual, should be clear. This is regardless of the color chosen and color-contrast effects. It is known that high contrast between objects attracts attention. Children prefer "light" visuals as compared to dark visuals in relation to whiteness-blackness, i.e., the grey scale. In the comparison of the darkness of tones on a graphic display, differences in tones will be overestimated.

It is far too common that illustrations, e.g., in textbooks do not have good contrast. Instead, it is often a more or less even shade of grey.

It is not easy to distinguish between more than ten shades of grey. In printed materials grey is a combination of black ink and white paper, measured as a percentage of full black.

A grey scale can usually serve the same function as a color scale, e.g., in a map. A color scale, however, may be nicer and more attractive. Tone is more important to contrast than color. According to Dondis (1973) the broadest range of distinctly different grey tones in pigment is about thirty-five. Without light upon it, the whitest of whites will not be seen.

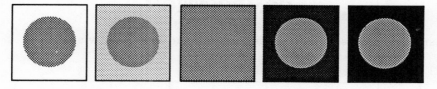

Our perception of one tone of grey can change when it is placed on a tonal scale.

EMPHASIS

Emphasis is used to attract or direct attention or dramatize certain points of a visual. A dark dot in a light field or a jog in a line are examples of emphasis. The contrast of the dark area against the light background draws attention to the dot. The more dots, the lower the degree of contrast and the less effective the emphasis. Many dots form a pattern of light and dark areas that compete with each other. Neither shade dominates nor demands more attention. The more competition for attention, the less effective is the emphasis.

Many different elements in a visual can cause emphasis. Light against dark, color against no color, detail against no detail, change in size, arrows, implied motion, circles or ovals around objects, stars, shaded areas, tonal contrast, isolation, complexity, directionality, line drawings in photos, words, position or placement of elements, line intersections, or any other unexpected change or variation out of context will create emphasis. Furthermore, emphasis on the message is achieved by reducing the number of details in the picture to those that are really essential.

Inappropriate use of graphical elements may direct learner attention away from essential learning cues and depress subsequent achievement. To avoid disinterest and boredom, we should use varied methods for emphasis.

Explanatory words, numbers, or other symbols should be incorporated into the picture as reading aids when this facilitates comprehension and learning. These aids must not then be distracting, large, or ugly. Simple styles and fonts are more easily read than complex ones. Symbols are of special value and importance in maps.

Relationships, moods, sound, and movements can be conveyed in a picture with the aid of signs and symbols. However, symbols have to be learned by the readers. Usually they are not naturally understood. Especially in developing countries, symbols must be introduced slowly and patiently.

In audio-visual materials, such as slides, filmstrips, and screen presentations, lettering must be considered carefully. Fifteen to twenty words on a slide are maximum for effective communication. Letters should be medium to medium-bold. Lettering height should be no less than one twenty-fifth the height of the artwork to be transferred. Generally speaking, lower-case letters are more legible than capitals.

COMPOSITION

Composition is discussed here mainly within the individual visual.

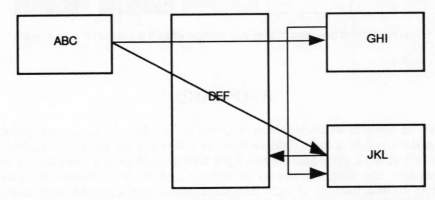

The schematic picture above is not very well-organized. Crossing arrows make it hard to see the relationships between the four items ABC, DEF, GHI, and JKL. The following schematic is much better organized.

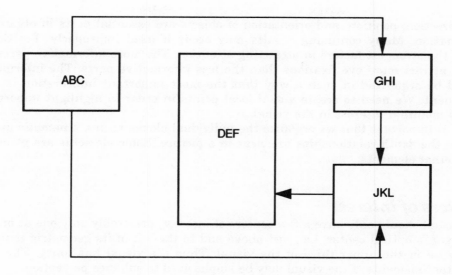

This schematic picture is much better organized than the previous one.

Organization

The elements in a visual may be arranged in a pattern that is easy for the reader to comprehend. Organization provides a pattern that facilitates learning. By organizing the graphic elements it is possible to direct the eye movements within the picture.

Perceptually, we group things on the basis of similarity and distinguish between things on the basis of disparity. Certain stimuli, such as contour lines, unusual colors, or graphical symbols, are accentuated in perception while others, such as uniform areas, are not.

Horizontal and vertical lines are more intense than other lines, i.e., they evoke more mental activity and they are more easily compared. Organizing a message can make perception much easier and learning more efficient. The visual should have a moderate degree of complexity. Complexity without order produces confusion, and order without complexity produces boredom. Differences in texture and grain may help organizing information.

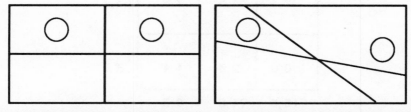

In this example, two rectangles are divided into four fields, in each case by two lines. The rectangle to the left has balance and harmony. The rectangle to the right has imbalance and contrasting composition.

Direction, position, and orientation of objects are essential parts in organizing information. Many confusing results may occur if used improperly. Position is one of the strongest factors in attracting attention. The more informative parts of a visual attract more eye fixations than the less informative parts. The information should be organized in such a way that the most important information is most prominent. We need to create visual focal points in order to highlight importance and to maintain interest in the visual.

It is important that we organize the individual elements in a schematic picture so that the depth relationships are clear in a picture. Some elements are placed on top of other elements.

Centers of interest

The visual should only have a few centers of interest, preferably only one at or near the visual's optical center, i.e., just above and to the left of its geometric center or otherwise in the upper third of the visual. Thus the visual has unity. The most important elements of the visual may be emphasized to enhance perception.

41	20
25	14

In the U.S., viewers tend to begin looking at a visual from the left side, particularly the upper left portion (41%). The optical center is above and to the left of the geometrical center.

Young children may chose to pay attention either to the whole picture or to specific parts of it. For children until about nine years of age it might be difficult to switch attention between a part and the whole.

13,5	19,0	0,0	32,5
2,3	53,5	7,9	63,7
0,0	2,3	1,4	3,7
15,8	74,8	9,3	

In one experiment, adult subjects looked at a drawing of two flying house martins. The distribution of fixations (%) within different parts of the image area is shown in this figure. More than half of the 215 fixations made by the seventeen subjects were in the central field.

According to the "rule of thirds" the center of interest may be selected at any one of the four points where equidistant vertical and horizontal lines divide a picture in three parts.

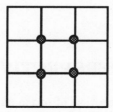

Centers of interest according to "the rule of thirds."

Balance

In nature balance is normal. A visual should usually display the best possible balance. Elements of the visual should fit together in a harmonious relationship in a manner which is interesting but not distracting.

Man has an intuitive sense of balance. Imbalance creates an uncomfortable feeling in the reader and should be avoided. Imbalance, however, can be used to attract attention within a picture or within a material. Unexpected, irregular, and unstable design will attract attention. As soon as instability is introduced in a picture the result is a provocative visual expression. The eye will struggle to analyze the relationships and the balance within the picture.

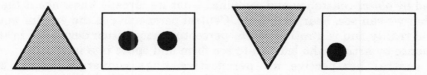

Here are two examples of balance (left) and two examples of imbalance (right).

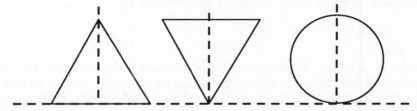

An upright vertical visual "axis," a "felt axis," and a stable horizontal base, express the unseen fields of balance. When we look at a circle we supply it with stability.

Balance could be formal with total symmetry or informal. Formal balance is felt to be static. Informal balance contributes to a feeling of dynamism.

However, the mind needs stimulation and surprise. Contrast and imbalance in a picture can dramatize an image and attract attention. Several artists use a visual strategy, such as combinations of dark and bright, large and small, round and square, to sharpen meaning.

PERSPECTIVE

Spatial perception is not the perception of space as such but of the learned meaning of the relationship between different objects seen in space.

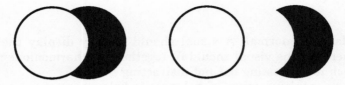

We see this pattern (left) as a black disc partially occluded by a white disc (the natural way of things). However, the figure may actually represent an incomplete black disc nestled against the white disc, as demonstrated to the right (the discs now separated).

We have to distinguish between an optical and a perceptual reality. Optical reality is governed by geometry and is only visual. However, perceptual reality is governed by *object constancy* and combines what we already know about the subject with what we can see, hear, smell, etc. Central perspective is the graphic equivalent of optical reality and is a rather recent perceptual acquisition developed in the early Renaissance by artists who learned to see form and space in a new way.

In central perspective all perspective lines converge toward common vanishing points. The accurate proportion is established by our intuitive experience. People in some cultures do not see our central perspectives. An orthographic projection is the graphic equivalent of our perceptual reality. A mechanical orthographic drawing shows proportions exactly.

Depth

The perception of depth is related to the relative size of known objects, to illumination and shadows, judicious croppings, linear perspective, change of line weight, texture gradients, upward angular location of grounded objects, overlap inter-position, and filled space. Image elements conveying a sense of depth should be clear and easy to comprehend. Depth perception is also based on different colors' varying wavelengths. Warmer colors emphasize foreground. Cooler colors emphasize background.

A visual must not incorporate any built-in optical illusions or geometric patterns making it possible to interpret the image in different ways.

In the new visual communication media, like video games and computerized pictures, the use of depth composition is common. The combination of rapid inward-outward movement, distorted depth of field, and forceful direction of visual elements placed on the Z-axis disturbs viewer comprehension and diminishes the aesthetic appreciation of such images.

Depth of field

Photographs often have well defined foregrounds and backgrounds and parts in between. During photography the depth of field is influenced by the distance to the object and the camera aperture. The depth of field can vary from several meters to a few decimeters.

By making the foreground sharp and background blurred, interest is directed to the foreground and vice versa. Obviously, it is also possible for an artist to choose depth of field in her or his drawing.

Uneasy backgrounds should be avoided in visuals for instruction. Instead balance and harmony should be present in any picture. Very often it could be recommended to move in closer on the object and thus avoid uneasy components in the background.

Picture angle

A picture angle corresponding to the angle of normal vision is preferable to bottom views, top views, wide-angle views, or telescopic views. However, regardless of the angle there is a constancy in the perception of known objects.

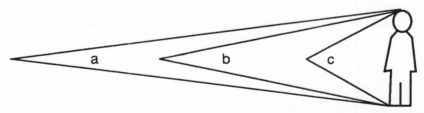

Regardless of the angle (in this example a, b, and c) there is a constancy in the perception of known objects.

Picture height

A frontal projection in which the subject is rendered from normal eye level is easier to comprehend than other projections and angles.

An unusual view of a person.

TECHNICAL QUALITY

Obviously, the technical quality of a visual should be "good" and tailored to the medium. A printed picture should be matte and distinct, not blurred, overly glossy, or dazzling. Resolution should be sufficient for the reproduction of the desired details. Remember that fine details in the texture of a visual disappear in the dot screen structure of the printed image. Even more detail is lost in a TV image.

Poor technical quality is far too common in instructional message design. The result of most of the previous work on visualization and making originals can easily be destroyed by a single error in the making of the master or in the actual production of the copies.

PICTURE EDITING

When we find "good" pictures we cannot take for granted that we can use them as they are. There is usually a need for cropping and/or changing the scale of selected pictures. Sometimes it is also possible to manipulate the picture by changing the projection, expanding or compressing the image, changing, adding, deleting, moving, or turning specific picture elements in various ways.

Selection

Every published visual has been selected, not only once but usually several times. First the picture creator, the photographer, and/or the artist makes a selection of the subject matter. In any given situation a lot of different pictures may be produced. Then the editor, art director, and/or the designer makes a selection among various pictures in a collection or in an picture archive. In instructional materials a picture should never be used just because it is pretty. Every picture should have some information to convey—if it doesn't, it should be left out.

Usually several sketches or outlines make a basis for decisions necessary in the production of the final drawings. A selected photo often needs cropping. By cropping, distracting and/or uninteresting parts of the image will be eliminated.

Cropping

An original picture can often be improved by removal of irrelevant or distracting elements. Usually pictures can be cropped a little bit from all sides. In practice the photographer always performs some "initial cropping" while taking the actual photograph. When composing or taking a photograph, the photographer sets the boundaries or "frame" of the picture. The same is also true for the artist who makes a "mental cropping" before s/he starts the actual drawing process.

The following simple pictures (below and on pages 264–265) will illustrate how cropping can be done. It may be a good idea to take some pictures, for example, from a magazine, and two set-squares cut out of white cardboard and practice cropping.

A complicated picture can be cropped and divided into two or more parts, each supplied with their individual legends. Sometimes images can be cropped to non-rectangular shapes like ovals or soft round shapes. Cropping and changing of scale are the most common methods used in picture editing.

Changing scale

Pictures should always be adjusted to fit into their final context. An image may be scaled up or down. There is an optimum size for each visual. The content remains the same but the chosen scale can influence our perception of it. The size of the visual should be large enough for the image to be legible. If the plane of projection is changed the relations between various parts in the picture will be influenced.

Usually drawings are produced in a larger size than the intended size in the finished product. When scaling down, lines get thinner, tighter, sharper, and more distinct. Drawings look better because lines appear to be more confident. However, small details may disappear. Scaling up has the opposite effect. Lines tend to dissolve and small mistakes become more obvious.

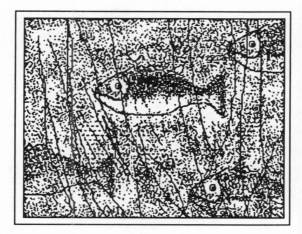

This simple illustration will serve as an example of a picture that may be cropped. In this case we want to show only the whole fish in the center of the picture, and not the environment with small parts of other fish.

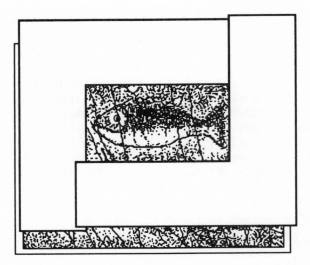

To find the most interesting part of the visual we can use two set-squares cut out of white cardboard. Move them around until you find the best cropping possible. Mark the desired cropping on an overlay or on a plain copy of the picture. Be very careful with the original print. The actual cropping is usually done in a scanner at the print shop.

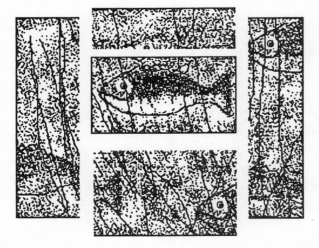

In some rare situations you will actually have to cut the picture to the desired size (center) and then manually paste it on the page. This might be the case with originals for offset printing or copying in an office copying machine.

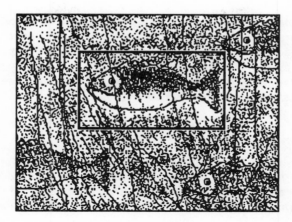

In desktop publishing systems you sometimes can make the cropping of an image electronically. You will then have to define the area that you want to keep (center) and remove the other parts or make a copy of the defined area.

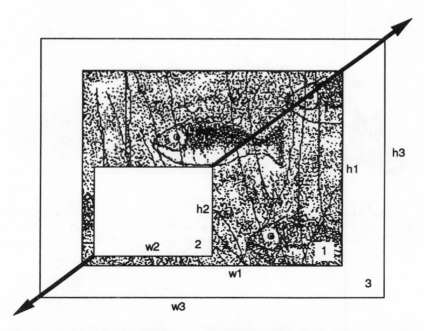

An image (1) can be reduced (2) or it can be enlarged (3). (When scaling w1/h1 = w2/h2 = w3/h3.) Draw a diagonal on an overlay on top of the image. Decide on the desired width of the scaled version, and then measure the height. Or do it the other way around.

A bit-mapped image, created and stored in a computer, may be scaled. However, no new information is added when the image is enlarged and important information is lost when the image is reduced. Thus, it is normally best to create bit-mapped images in the correct sizes.

Another possibility is to create a bit-mapped image in a large size, scale it down with a repro-camera or with a copying machine and then paste it as an original. Object oriented objects may, however, be scaled without loss of quality.

Sometimes it might be a good idea to enlarge interesting parts of a picture. Several consecutive enlargements of a specific part will help the reader to understand the detailed structure of an object.

Image manipulation

Modern computer-based graphical systems have great built-in possibilities for manipulating the image. The image can usually be modified and changed in several ways. We can change projection, expand, compress, reduce, delete, modify, move, turn, supplement, isolate, or combine various image elements.

A bit-mapped image (2), created and stored in a computer may be scaled. However, no new information is added when the image is enlarged (3) and important information is lost when the image is reduced (1). Thus, it is normally best to create bit-mapped images in the correct sizes from the beginning. The small cat will be almost black, and a very large cat will be very light grey.

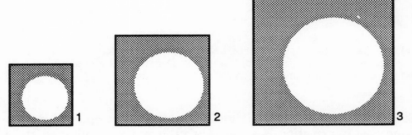

An object oriented image (2) may be scaled down (1) or scaled up (3) without loss of quality.

Changing projection

The projection plane can be altered through image modification or shrinkage. This distorts size relationships within the picture and affects our perception of image contents. It can be used in a creative and positive way to enhance or restore the content of an image.

Changing the projection plane will distort size relationships within a picture (middle and right). This is easy to experience when using OH-transparencies or slides without a proper set-up of projector and screen.

Expansion and compression

An image can be vertically and/or horizontally stretched out. This will of course change the size relationships within the image, but may sometimes be necessary.

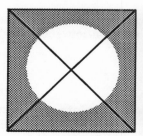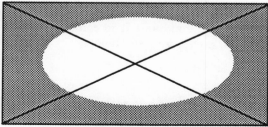

In this example the picture to the left has been expanded horizontally (right). Turn the book 90 degrees and you will see a vertical expansion. The circle and the square were choosen to clearly demonstrate the effects of expansion. See also compression below.

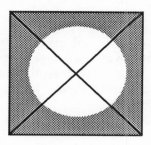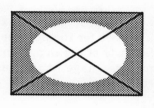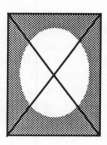

In this example the illustration to the left has been compressed in two different versions. The circle and the square were choosen to clearly demonstrate the effects of compression. See also expansion above.

A picture can also be "compressed," i.e., squashed from the sides or from the top and bottom. Expansion and compression will always result in a distortion of the original image. Sometimes this can create useful effects.

Changes and deletions

To focus the reader's attention on the main content in a picture, individual picture elements can be changed so as to improve contrast, acuity, sharpness, grey scale, or color scale.

Surrounding parts can be made paler, darker, or out of focus. The visual's external contour can be blurred and unclear so the picture fades in/out of the background. Good photographers select focusing and depth of field to achieve the same goal—better clarity and better communication.

The grey scale can sometimes be transformed into optional colors.

Distracting or undesirable details in a picture can be removed by painting with an appropriate retouching color or shade. This is also a way to isolate parts of a picture.

Deletion can be used for partial silhouetting of a picture so that an important part of the picture pokes beyond the frame. Deletion can also be used for full silhouetting to get rid of all background disturbance. The outline of an image can be softened.

Addition

The relation between width and height of the image can be changed by the addition of space. To achieve emphasis it is common to add information such as shadows, contrasts, colors, signs, and symbols.

Move and turn

Individual picture elements or rather groups of picture elements can be moved or turned around within an image for the sake of better balance and harmony. Groups of picture elements can also be copied from one place in an image and moved to one or more other positions within the image. It is also possible to move parts of an image to other pictures.

Supplement

Letters of the alphabet, numerals, lines, arrows, circles, and other symbols or markings can be added to a picture for the purpose of enhancing image content and focusing attention to specific parts of the image and links to the legend. The superimposition of text onto a picture image usually impairs our ability to absorb the contents of both text and picture.

Isolation

An attractive, interesting, or amusing detail in a picture can be isolated by, say, peeling and cropping. The detail can then be used independently or as a part of other pictures.

Combination
A few thousand "stock" pictures with standard backgrounds and foregrounds, such as landscapes, scenic views, people, vegetation, animals, etc., can be combined to form an infinite number of compositions. For example, clip art programs are available for several personal computers.

Tilting
A picture can be tilted on the page. Tilting of a picture may draw special attention to it.

Framing
Image framing makes a clear distinction between image and background. An image may be framed in a frame appropriate to the subject. The frame may be a window, a keyhole, or the like.

Shadow
A cast shadow, or drop shadow, behind two edges of a picture may create feelings of three dimensions and depth. If this is done correctly, the picture seems to be floating above the page. However, cast shadows may create a lot of confusion and they may actually impair communication. Usually it is better not to use shadows.

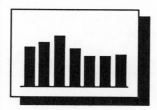

A cast shadow behind a visual may create a feeling of depth.

The picture in context
Pictures should always be adjusted to fit into their final context. Image framing makes a clear distinction between image and background. Fading is used to make the image gradually appear on the page. Layout is the integration of text and images, i.e., on an opening in a book. Legends give the reader necessary guidance in understanding the image content.

REFERENCES AND SUGGESTED READINGS

Annis, R. C., & Frost, B. (1973). Human visual ecology and orientation anistropics in acuity. *Science, 182 (4113)*, 729–731.

Arnheim, R. (1954). *Art and Visual Perception.* Berkeley: University of California Press.

Berlin, B., & Kay, P. (1969). *Basic Color Terms.* Berkeley: University of California Press.

Bertin, J. (1967). *Sémiologie Graphique.* Paris and the Hague: Mouton and Gauthiers-Villars.

Cook, B. L. (1981). *Understanding Pictures in Papua New Guinea.* Elgin, IL: David C. Cook Foundation.

Cosette, C. (1982). *How Pictures Speak: A Brief Introduction to Iconics.* Paper presented at the 32nd International Communication Association. Conference, Boston, May 1–5. Translated from French by Vincent Ross, Quebec.

Dodwell, P. C. (1975). Pattern and object perception. In E. C. Carterette & M. P. Friedman (Eds.). *Handbook of Perception (Vol. 5).* New York: Academic Press.

Dondis, D. A. (1973). *A Primer of Visual Literacy.* Cambridge, MA: Massachusetts Institute of Technology.

Dwyer, F. M., & Dwyer, C. A. (1989). Enhancing visualized instruction: A research overview. In R. A. Braden, D. G. Beauchamp, L. V. W. Miller, & D. M. Moore (Eds.). *About Visuals: Research, Teaching, and Applications.* Readings from the 20th Annual Conference of the International Visual Literacy Association. Blacksburg: Virginia Tech University.

Dwyer, F. M., & Lamberski, R. J. (1983). A Review of the Research on the Effects of the Use of Color in the Teaching-learning Process. *International Journal of Instructional Media, 10*(4), 303-327.

Ehlers, H-J. (1982). *How Color Can Help Visualize Information.* Online Review 6th International, 'Online Information' Meeting held 7–9 Dec. in London. Oxon: Learned Information (Europe) Ltd.

Evans, R. M. (1974). *The Perception of Color.* New York: John Wiley.

Eysenck, H. J. (1941). A critical and experimental study of color preferences. *American Journal of Psychology, 54,* 385– 394.

Falk-Björkman, S. (1978). LMN – är det något för mig? In K. Wearn. *Mot en ekologisk världsbild – En ny väg för naturvetenskaplig undervisning.* Malmö: Liber Läromede.

Feilitzen, C., Filipson, L., & Schyller, I. (1978). *Blunda inte för barnens tittande. Om barn, tv och radio nu och i framtiden.* Stockholm: Sveriges Radios Förlag.

Fleming, M., & Levie, W. H. (1978). *Instructional Message Design.* Englewood Cliffs, NJ: Educational Technology Publications.

Fleming, M., & Levie, W. H. (Eds.). (1993). *Instructional Message Design* (2nd ed.). Englewood Cliffs, NJ: Educational Technology Publications.

Fuglesang, A. (1973). *Applied Communications in Developing Countries: Ideas and Observations.* Uppsala: Dag Hammarskjöld Foundation.

Gregory, R. L. (1978). *Eye and Brain* (3rd ed). New York: McGraw-Hill.

Hayashi, K. (1982). Research and development on high definition television. *SMPTE Journal, 3,* 178–186.

Heider, E. R. (1972). Universals in color naming and memory. *Journal of Experimental Psychology, 93,* 10–12.

Herbener, G. F., Van Tubergen, G. N., & Whitlow, S. S. (1979). Dynamics of the frame in visual composition. *ECTJ, 27* (2), 83–88.

Higgins, L. C. (1980). Literalism in the Young Child's Interpretation of Pictures. *ECTJ, 28* (2), 99–119.

Kaar, H. (1976). The color preferences of a young girl in pre-puberty, puberty, and adolescence: Observations over an eight-year period with Luscher color test. *British Journal of Projective Psychology and Personality Study, 21,* 21–30.

Kanner, J., & Rosenstein, A. (1960). Television in army training: Color vs Black and White. *AV Communication Review, 8,* 243–252.

Katzmann, N., & Nyenhuis, J. (1972). Color vs black and white effects on learning, opinion, and attention. *AV Communication Review, 20,* 16–28.

Kossllyn, S. M. (1975). Information representation in visual images. *Cognitive Psychology, 7,* 341–370.

Krishna, K. P. (1972). Color preference as a function of age and sex. *Journal of the Indian Academy of Applied Psychology, 9,* 10–13.

Lamberski, J. R., & Dwyer, F. M. (1983). The instructional effect of coding (color and black and white) on information acquisition and retrieval. *ECTJ, 31* (1), 9–12.

Legatt, A. L. S. (1983). *Financial Information on Teletext.* London: The City University, Centre for Information Science, M. Sc. Thesis.

Lenze, S. J. (1992). Lexi-visual design of instructional materials. In J. Clark-Baca, D. G. Beauchamp, & R. A. Braden (Eds.). *Visual Communication: Bridging Across Cultures.* Selected Readings from the 23rd Annual Conference of the International Visual Literacy Association. Blacksburg: Virginia Tech University.

Lynch, M. P. (1980). Designing effective visual images. *Visual Literacy Newsletter, 4.*

MacDonald-Ross, M. (1977). How numbers are shown: A review of research on the presentation of quantitative data in texts. *AV Communication Review, 25* (4), 359–409.

Mangan, J. (1978). Cultural conversations of pictorial representation: Iconic Literacy and Education. *ECTJ, 26* (3), 245–267.

Moore, D. M., & Sasse. E. B. (1971). Effect of size and type of still projected pictures on inmediate recall of content. *AV Communication Review, 19,* 437–450.

Morris, L. L. (1974). The effects of ball color and background color upon the catching performance of second, fourth, and sixth grade youngsters. *Dissertation Abstracts International, 35,* 6-a 3556.

Murch, G. M. (1973). *Visual and Auditory Perception.* Indianapolis: The Bobbs-Merrill Co.

Murch, G. M. (1983). Perceptual considerations of color. *Computer Graphics World, 6* (7), 32–40.

Myatt, B., & Carter, J. M. (1979). Picture preferences of children and young adults. *ECTJ, 27* (1), 45–53.

Noble, G. (1975). *Children in Front of the Small Screen.* Beverly Hills: Sage.

Otto, W., & Askov, E. (1968). The role of color in learning and instruction. *Journal of Special Education, 2,* 155–165.

Pett, D. P., & Burbank, L. (1991). Research on color: A summary. In D. G. Beauchamp, J. Clark-Baca, & R. A. Braden (Eds.). *Investigating Visual Literacy.* Selected Readings from the 22rd Annual Conference of the International Visual Literacy Association. Blacksburg: Virginia Tech University.

Pettersson, R. (1981). *Bilder Barn och Massmedia.* Stockholm: Akademilitteratur.

Pettersson, R. (1982a). Cultural Differences in the Perception of Image and Color in Pictures. *ECTJ, 30* (1), 43–53.

Pettersson, R. (1982b). Factors in visual languages: Shape. *Visual Literacy Newsletter, 10,* and *11.*

Pettersson, R. (1983). *Factors in Visual Language: Size.* (CLEA–Report No. 13). Stockholm: Stockholm University, Department of Computer Science.

Posekaney Pruisner, P. A. (1992). The effects of color code in graphic presentation and assessment on remembering verbal material. In J. Clark-Baca, D. G. Beauchamp, & R. A. Braden (Eds.). *Visual Communication: Bridging Across Cultures.* Selected Readings from the 23rd Annual Conference of the International Visual Literacy Association. Blacksburg: Virginia Tech University.

Prawitz, M. (1977). Varför förstår du inte vad jag säger, när jag hoppar, skuttar och målar? In G. Berefelt. *Barn och bild.* Stockholm: AWE/Gebers.

Rock, I. (1975). *An Introduction to Perception.* New York: Macmillan Publishing Co.

Samit, M. L. (1983). The Color Interface, making the most of color. *Computer Graphics World*, 7, 42–50.

Sivik, L., 1970 (1979): *Om färgers betydelse*. Skandinaviska Färginstitutet, Stockholm.

Sporrstedt, B. (1980). Kring en bildvärld. *Synpunkt, populär tidskrift för konst*, 5, 6–7.

Weismann, D. L. (1974). *The Visual Arts as a Human Experience*. Englewood Cliffs, NJ: Prentice-Hall.

Wileman, R. (1993). *Visual Communicating*. Englewood Cliffs, NJ: Educational Technology Publications.

Winn, W. (1976). The structure of multiple free associations to words, black and white pictures, and color pictures. *AV Communication Review*, 24 (3), 273–293.

Winn, W. & Everett, R. J. (1978). *Differences in the Affective Meaning of Color and Black and White Pictures*. Paper presented at the Annual Meeting of the Association for Educational Communications and Technology, Kansas City, Missouri, April, 23 pp., Document ED 160 067.

Zimmer, A., & Zimmer, F. (1978). *Visual Literacy in Communication: Designing for Development*. Hulton Educational Publications Ltd., in cooperation with the International Institute for Adult Methods, Teheran.

Chapter 7

CONTEXT IN GRAPHIC DESIGN

A picture has both an *internal* and an *external context*. I regard factors inside the medium as "internal context." I regard the entire communications situation, i.e., senders and their intentions for the picture and receivers and their circumstances (e.g., time available), as "external context."

Graphic design is a tool with which we can manipulate the raw materials—words in different typefaces, sizes, styles, empty space, illustrations, color, paper and ink, and the final number of pages—to achieve the best possible communications between people. Most people read instructional materials selectively. Readers rarely, if ever, begin at the beginning and read straight through to the end. Usually we use a combination of browsing, reading headings, looking at illustrations and legends, reading certain parts carefully, skimming others, and avoiding some parts completely. Keller & Burkman (1993) noted that it is important to create a positive impression and give courseware a comfortable image to gain and maintain learner attention and to build confidence.

The goal for graphic design should be *clarity of communication*. Typography for information, or typography for instruction, aids communication and is also aesthetically pleasing.

In this chapter different aspects of typography, page design, and layout will be discussed. Some guidelines for "good" typography will also be presented. Many of these guidelines are based on practical experience rather than on formal, empirical research.

DIFFERENT CONTEXTS

In books internal context is the interplay between text and illustrations, between illustrations and layout. Movies and TV programs have sound with speech, music, and sound effects plus visual and audio metaphors. Some computer programs contain advanced animation with interaction between text, images, and even sound.

The context in which a visual message is presented has a major impact on the way the message is perceived. For example, the context may consist of text, speech, music, sound effects, or other visuals. Our attention is on either the sound or the image when we view a film or a TV program. This is even more obvious when we look at a multi-image slide and film presentation. As soon as the film starts, our attention is directed towards the movement in the film from the surrounding stills. It is just impossible for viewers not to be influenced by the film.

Our perception of a stimulus is thus not only determined by the characteristics of the main stimulus but also by those of the context. This is, however, not the case with young children. A background which might give extra information to an adult reader cannot be assumed to fulfill the same function for a child. It may actually hinder the child from perceiving the picture at all.

a, **A B C**   b, **12 13 14**

The same pattern is identified as "B" in the first sequence (a) and as "13" in the second sequence (b). Context is important.

Perception of brightness, color, size, shape, pattern, and motion have all been shown to be influenced by contextual variables. One and the same visual can be perceived in different ways in different contexts. A single picture taken from a series of pictures may be hard to decipher, but the visual's content becomes easier to comprehend when that picture is returned to its proper sequential context. Thus, we should be very careful in selecting contexts for our messages.

Several factors can be regarded as external context variables. In an oral presentation the audience is influenced not only by the presenter and her/his projected images but also by other things like the temperature, the furniture, the room itself, outside noise, noise from the projector, and noise from other persons. The lighting conditions may be the most important variable for our perception of all kinds of images.

A projected image is perceived as having high image quality in a dark room. When the light increases, the perceived quality decreases. A printed image is perceived as having high image quality in a light room. When the light decreases, the perceived quality decreases.

A "poor" slide will always give a poor projected image, which will be perceived as having low quality. A "good" slide with high quality contents and execution may be perceived as having anything between low and high quality. When a "medium good" slide is projected under optimal conditions, that image may be perceived as better than a "good" picture which is projected under poor conditions.

The listeners usually have very small or no possibilities to influence the lighting conditions or other contextual variables in oral presentations. When there is too much light in the room the images will be poor. However, when we watch television or read a book, a magazine, or a newspaper, we can usually adjust the context lighting.

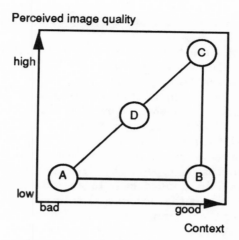

A "poor" slide will always give a poor projected image which will be perceived as having low quality (A). A "good" slide with high quality contents and execution may be perceived as having anything between low (B) and high (C) quality. When a "medium good" slide is projected under optimal conditions, that image (D) may be perceived as better than a "good" picture (B) which is projected under poor conditions.

The external context may have its focus on the receiver or on the sender. Thus, we can talk about a "receiver context" as well as about a "sender context." It is also possible to discuss an "inner context," a context within the picture itself, with respect to the use of various graphic elements.

In graphical media the reader usually can spend as much time as she/he feels is needed to read the text as well as the pictures. This is also true for video. The viewer is usually free to stop the tape and look at a specific sequence several times. However, in oral presentations, in films, and in television, the viewer has to follow the pace set by the sender or the producer. It may sometimes be very hard to follow a presentation and be able to accurately read the image content. Also, in oral presentations it is important to find the optimal pace. A slide should not be on too long nor too short. Quite often it is the length of the text that decides for how long a specific image is used.

TYPE

Lenze (1991) noted that private documents may invite the use of ornate and stylish looking fonts. Professional documents, however, require maximum legibility (Tinker, 1963; Benson, 1985; Pettersson, 1989). Type can be created in a variety of styles. A change in type style can signal a change of purpose, a new section, or degree of importance. Typographical techniques can alert learners to such things as main ideas, important concepts, rules, sections, subsections, and more. However, multiple type styles on a page tend to be confusing rather than facilitating. The decision of which font to use should rest largely on the purpose and audience of the document (Benson, 1985).

Systems for desktop publishing are now common. Easy to handle software gives the layman the opportunity to combine verbal and visual messages. This technological revolution enables us to do anything we have in mind to do on a page. We are no longer restricted by the mechanical processes of typesetting and makeup. Unfortunately, most desktop publishers know little about typography, graphic design, and visual information. With the new systems it is almost too easy to manipulate a text and make use of all the possibilities to change the appearance of a page. It is far too easy to create confusion or even a complete mess-up. As White (1987) put it: "The distinguished art and craft of typography developed over centuries by sensitive craftsmen/artists cannot be handed over to an indifferent typist keyboarding a machine (however marvelous the technology) with results of equal excellence and stature. The reader feels the difference in terms of the piece's ease of reading, charm, and comfort." It is wrong economy to cut back on investment in quality, believing the readers won't know the difference. Winn (1993) noted that in text, attention is drawn to words or passages that stand in contrast to the rest of the body of the text. To encourage readers to pay attention to relevant information, text designers should help the reader to control his or her cognitive processes during learning (Mayer, 1993).

In the following subsections some typefaces, sizes of type, and stylistic variations of type will be presented.

Typefaces

To achieve optimum legibility it is known that:
— Common typefaces are easier to read than uncommon typefaces.
— Serif typefaces are often considered to be easier to read than sans serif typefaces, except for small letter sizes.
— Running text should be in lower case letters. All-capital printing has been shown to markedly reduce the speed of reading.
— Proportionally spaced type is usually easier to read than monospaced type.

Individual characters can be designed in many different ways. The differences between many typefaces are subtle. It is not always possible to see the differences without special training. They can be identified by looking for classic traits, such as the shape of lower-case letters.

During the little more than 500 years of western printing history, probably more than 10,000 typefaces have been designed. A complete assortment of characters of the same style and size is called a *font of type*. Thus, each typeface appears in many different fonts. In theory it is possible to choose from far more than 100,000 fonts. However, in computer manuals the word font is sometimes used to mean typeface.

Many have tried to develop classification schemes of typefaces. Classification systems may be based, e.g., on chronology, on evolution, and on various elements of letter shapes. Most systems are incomplete and more or less confusing. The system that has enjoyed the largest general favor divides typefaces into four main classes: Roman, Sans Serif, Script, and Black letter. Within these classes groups of type designs with important similarities form "type families."

Roman type includes most of the typefaces used in modern printing. Roman type has *serifs*. Serifs are the finishing strokes at the ends of the letterforms. Serifs are not just for decoration. They help us distinguish between characters. Serifs makes it easier to follow horizontal text lines. Thus, serifs increase legibility and aid reading (Tinker, 1963).

An example of a letter with serifs (left) and an example of a letter without serifs (right).

Typefaces are often named after the designers who created them or after the printers who first used them. Baskerville, Bodoni, Bookman, Caslon, Century, Palatino, and Times are all popular Roman typefaces.

Sans serif type has no serifs on the characters. Avant Garde, Futura, Gill, Helvetica, Univers, and Venus are examples of popular sans serif typefaces.

Script type looks somewhat like modern handwriting which is carefully executed with a brush dipped in India ink. The individual characters are joined together. It is not possible to use script type for whole words in upper case. Examples are Constance, Palace Script, and Zaph Chancery.

Black letter type resembles old German manuscript handwriting. Black letter type is difficult to read and rarely used in the US. Examples are Fraktur, Rotunda, Schwabacher, and Textura.

A more modern classification scheme is the serif-evolution system. This system provides eight main classes: Venetian, Old Style (Dutch-English and French), Transitional, Modern, Contemporary (sans serif and square serifs), Black letter, Scripts, and Decorative letters.

Most typefaces are *proportionally spaced*. Different letters are assigned different spacing in accordance with their individual sizes and shapes. However, on most typewriters and some printers the typefaces are *monospaced*. In such typefaces all the letters have the same amount of space. The letter "i" takes the same space as the letter "m." Proportionally spaced type is usually easier to read than monospaced type.

As mentioned earlier, thousands of fonts are available. In the practical work with *graphic design for information*, we need only a few typefaces in different versions. Here are six examples of the same text rendered with different typefaces; *serif typefaces:* Times, Palatino, Bookman, New Century Schoolbook, and *sans serif typefaces:* Helvetica and Avant Garde. These typefaces are all available from Adobe for desktop publishing. In the following examples all six typefaces are set in 12 point.

Times
abcdefghijklmnopqrstuvwxyzABCDEFGHIJKLMNOPQRSTUVWXYZ,.;:!?"()/
&%+-=><*1234567890

Infology is the science of verbo-visual presentation of information. On the basis of Man's prerequisites, infology encompasses studies of the way a verbo-visual representation should be designed in order to achieve optimum communications between sender and receiver. Some studies concentrate on the sender, others on the receiver, representation, or communications process as such.

Palatino
abcdefghijklmnopqrstuvwxyzABCDEFGHIJKLMNOPQRSTUVWXYZ,.;:!?
"()/&%+-=><*1234567890

Infology is the science of verbo-visual presentation of information. On the basis of Man's prerequisites, infology encompasses studies of the way a verbo-visual representation should be designed in order to achieve optimum communications between sender and receiver. Some studies concentrate on the sender, others on the receiver, representation, or communications process as such.

Bookman
abcdefghijklmnopqrstuvwxyzABCDEFGHIJKLMNOPQRSTUVWXYZ,
.;:!?"()/&%+-= ><*1234567890

Infology is the science of verbo-visual presentation of information. On the basis of Man's prerequisites, infology encompasses studies of the way a verbo-visual representation should be designed in order to achieve optimum communications between sender and receiver. Some studies concentrate on the sender, others on the receiver, representation, or communications process as such.

New Century Schoolbook
abcdefghijklmnopqrstuvwxyzABCDEFGHIJKLMNOPQRSTUVWXYZ,.
;:!?"()/&%+-=><*1234567890

Infology is the science of verbo-visual presentation of information. On the basis of Man's prerequisites, infology encompasses studies of the way a verbo-visual representation should be designed in order to achieve optimum communications between sender and receiver. Some studies concentrate on the sender, others on the receiver, representation, or communications process as such.

Helvetica

abcdefghijklmnopqrstuvwxyzABCDEFGHIJKLMNOPQRSTUVWXYZ,.;:!?"()/&%+-=><*12 34567890

Infology is the science of verbo-visual presentation of information. On the basis of Man's prerequisites, infology encompasses studies of the way a verbo-visual representation should be designed in order to achieve optimum communications between sender and receiver. Some studies concentrate on the sender, others on the receiver, representation, or communications process as such.

Avant Garde

abcdefghijklmnopqrstuvwxyzABCDEFGHIJKLMNOPQRSTUVWXYZ,.;:!?"()/&%+-=><*1234567890

Infology is the science of verbo-visual presentation of information. On the basis of Man's prerequisites, infology encompasses studies of the way a verbo-visual representation should be designed in order to achieve optimum communications between sender and receiver. Some studies concentrate on the sender, others on the receiver, representation, or communications process as such.

As we can see from the examples above, the different typefaces have their individual characteristics. Typefaces vary in their visual appeal. Some are more legible and some are less legible. In the US children usually learn to read using textbooks with serif typeface like New Century Schoolbook. In European countries it is not unusual that sans serif typefaces are used in textbooks. Children in China learn to read the complicated Chinese characters. And we can find equally good readers in all these countries. *As a matter of fact, the reader should never become too conscious of the typeface.* A "good" typeface might actually be one that is more or less "invisible" to us as readers. We shouldn't be too concerned with the design of the typeface. The typefaces in common use are all more or less equally legible (Tinker, 1963, 1965; Paterson & Tinker, 1932). However, readers are likely to have strong preferences about the aesthetics of typefaces. One important aspect of the design of a typeface is the perceived size of the individual characters. Some type looks big and some type looks small. This depends on the design of the characters and their x-height.

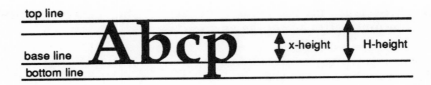

Letters are positioned on a base line.

A typeface *can influence* our appraisal of a printed message. Thus, it might be important to make a choice so that typography reinforces the message.

The original *"Times New Roman"* was created in 1932 by the graphic designer Stanley Morrison for the London newspaper "The Times." The mission was to create a typeface with very good legibility even in small sizes. Several versions of Times have been developed. Typefaces and fonts belonging to "the Times family" are all easy to read. They are compact and are also often considered attractive. Times typefaces are used in newspapers and magazines as well as in books. They are probably the most widely used serif typefaces in the world.

Palatino was created by Hermann Zapf in 1950. He was inspired by the handwritings in manuscripts from the 14th century. Palatino is considered to be a "formal" typeface. Thus, it is often used in various business proposals and business reports.

Bookman was created by C.H. Griffith in 1936. It is a classic typeface with open and round letter shapes. Bookman is often used in books as well as in printed matter and in many other kinds of graphical media. Misanchuk (1989) asked learners to compare samples of text made up of all possible combinations of the fonts Bookman, Courier, Helvetica, New Century Schoolbook, and Times, all in 10-point size. They were asked to make their judgments based on the question, "Which of these two pages of text do you think it would be most easy to read and study from?" The order of preference was Bookman, New Century Schoolbook, Courier, Helvetica, and Times.

New Century Schoolbook was originally developed by Morris Fuller Benton in 1926 for use in school textbooks. It is a rather wide typeface which is easy to read. New Century Schoolbook is often used in textbooks and also in many other books. In this book, New Century Schoolbook is used for the running text as well as for the headings.

Helvetica was created by Max Miedinger in 1957. Helvetica is designed with simple, striking lines in a compact way. Like Times, Helvetica has been developed in many typefaces and font versions. Helvetica typefaces are very useful for titles, headings, legends, and tables of various kinds but they might be hard to read in running text. Running text will need extra space between the lines. Helvetica is often used for reader slides, overhead transparencies and in business graphics. Today Helvetica typefaces may be the most widely used sans serif typefaces in the world (Collier & Cotton, 1989). In this book Helvetica has been used for the figure legends.

Avant Garde was created in 1970 by the well known American graphic designer Herb Lubalin. Avant Garde has a geometric and symmetrical appearance. It is often used for titles and headings in different kinds of printed matter. Avant Garde is also used on signs and in visual communications but it is not good for running text.

Size of type

Our perception of size is relative. According to White (1987), some 10-point type looks gigantic and some minuscule. It all depends on the design of the face and its x-height. Letters can be varied in size and even by type to differentiate different types of data (Hartley, 1987). To achieve optimum legibility it is known that letter size must be adjusted to the visual format and the reading distance. According to Tinker (1963) text smaller than nine points is too small to be considered legible. Text which should be read in a continuous manner should be set between nine and twelve points (Tinker, 1963; Haber & Haber 1981; Benson, 1985; Braden, 1983, 1985; Pettersson, 1989). According to Lenze (1991) font size above twelve points slows the reading process because the reader must examine each letter individually to recognize it. Thus, we can conclude that *type should be "large enough."* A larger type size in a single column is preferable to a smaller type size in a double column layout.

Letter size is designated in typographical points -p. In the US one point is .346 mm (nearly 1/72 of an inch). However, in many European countries one point is .376 mm.

Hot metal type is cast in sizes ranging from 4 point to 144 point. Photo-typesetting machines can produce even larger characters. The sizes of type which are in most common use are 6, 7, 8, 9, 10, 11, 12, 13, 14, 18, 24, 30, 36, 42, 48, 60, and 72 point. Characters should obviously neither be too small, nor too large. In the first case we cannot read them at all. In the latter case we can only have a few words on each line. Too small or too large lettering impairs reading. As an example, a text on a poster should be at least five times larger than a corresponding text in a book. Newspaper print is usually 8 or 9 point. In books 10 to 12 point is common; this book uses 10 point type.

Here are seven examples of the same text in different size versions: Times 8, 9, 10, 11, 12, 13, and 14 points.

Times 8 p
abcdefghijklmnopqrstuvwxyzABCDEFGHIJKLMNOPQRSTUVWXYZ,.;:!?"()/&%+=><*1234567890.

Information ergonomics comprises research and development of the ergonomic design of Man-machine systems. The design of an information system must be based on studies of the information user's aims, knowledge, experience, and way of working.

Times 9 p
abcdefghijklmnopqrstuvwxyzABCDEFGHIJKLMNOPQRSTUVWXYZ,.;:!?"()/&%+-=><*1234567890.

Information ergonomics comprises research and development of the ergonomic design of Man-machine systems. The design of an information system must be based on studies of the information user's aims, knowledge, experience, and way of working.

Times 10 p
abcdefghijklmnopqrstuvwxyzABCDEFGHIJKLMNOPQRSTUVWXYZ,.;:!?"()/&%+-=><*12345
67890.

Information ergonomics comprises research and development of the ergonomic design of
Man-machine systems. The design of an information system must be based on studies of the
information user's aims, knowledge, experience, and way of working.

Times 11 p
abcdefghijklmnopqrstuvwxyzABCDEFGHIJKLMNOPQRSTUVWXYZ,.;:!?"()/&%+-=
><*1234567890.

Information ergonomics comprises research and development of the ergonomic
design of Man-machine systems. The design of an information system must be based on
studies of the information user's aims, knowledge, experience, and way of working.

Times 12 p
abcdefghijklmnopqrstuvwxyzABCDEFGHIJKLMNOPQRSTUVWXYZ,.;:!?"()/
&%+-=><*1234567890.

Information ergonomics comprises research and development of the ergonomic design of Man-machine systems. The design of an information system
must be based on studies of the information user's aims, knowledge, experience,
and way of working.

Times 13 p
abcdefghijklmnopqrstuvwxyzABCDEFGHIJKLMNOPQRSTUVWXYZ,.;:
!?"()/&%+-=><*1234567890.

Information ergonomics comprises research and development of the ergonomic design of Man-machine systems. The design of an information
system must be based on studies of the information user's aims, knowledge,
experience, and way of working.

Times 14 p
abcdefghijklmnopqrstuvwxyzABCDEFGHIJKLMNOPQRSTUVWX
YZ,.;:!?"()/&%+-=><*1234567890.

Information ergonomics comprises research and development of
the ergonomic design of Man-machine systems. The design of an
information system must be based on studies of the information user's
aims, knowledge, experience, and way of working.

As we can see from these examples different size versions give very different impressions. It is important to find a balance between our need for and possibility of a general view and a good legibility of individual words.

In books, magazines, and newspapers larger type is used for headlines. Below are some examples of the same information in larger size versions: Times 18, 24, 30, 36, 42, 48, and 60 point.

Times 18 p

Times 24 p

Times 30 p

Times 36 p

Times 42 p

Times 48 p

Times 60 p

Stylistic variation of type

With respect to width and line thickness a character can be designed in different versions. A typeface may be available as light condensed, light, light expanded, bold condensed, bold, bold expanded, regular condensed, regular, regular expanded, extra bold condensed, extra bold, and extra bold expanded. With respect to inclination a typeface may be designed in italic letter style versions. A typeface may also be available as outlined, inlined, and shadowed.

To achieve optimum legibility it is known that regular type is easier to read than uncommon type. Boldface or italics should normally not be used for continuous text. Italic print is read more slowly than regular type and is also disliked by many readers (Tinker, 1965). However, boldface and italics may be used for *emphasis*.

Italics may be used for small parts in a running text, for headings, and for legends. Bold type may be used for headings. Different style manuals have different recommendations for when italic and bold type versions should and shouldn't be used.

The use of underlining and all capital letters should be restricted to headings and titles, if they are used at all. Usually bold and italics are quite sufficient. Underlining in the middle of a sentence makes the lower line more difficult to read (Isaacs, 1987). Shadow and outline letters should be avoided.

Here are four examples of the same text in different type versions of the same typeface; Times 12p regular, italic, bold, and bold italic.

Times 12p regular
abcdefghijklmnopqrstuvwxyzABCDEFGHIJKLMNOPQRSTUVWXYZ,.;:!?"()/
&%+-=><*1234567890.

Information technology (IT) is a science dealing with the technical systems used for making production, distribution, storage, and other information handling more efficient. This includes, e.g., computer technology and electronics.

Times 12p italic
abcdefghijklmnopqrstuvwxyzABCDEFGHIJKLMNOPQRSTUVWXYZ,.;:!?" ()/&
*%+-=><*1234567890.*

Information technology (IT) is a science dealing with the technical systems used for making production, distribution, storage, and other information handling more efficient. This includes, e.g., computer technology and electronics.

Times 12p bold
abcdefghijklmnopqrstuvwxyzABCDEFGHIJKLMNOPQRSTUVWXYZ,.;:!?
"()/&%+-=><*1234567890.

Information technology (IT) is a science dealing with the technical systems used for making production, distribution, storage, and other information handling more efficient. This includes, e.g., computer technology and electronics.

Times 12p bold italic
abcdefghijklmnopqrstuvwxyzABCDEFGHIJKLMNOPQRSTUVWXYZ,.;:!?"()/
&%+-=> < * 1 2 3 4 5 6 7 8 9 0.

Information technology(IT) is a science dealing with the technical systems used for making production, distribution, storage, and other information handling more efficient. This includes, e.g., computer technology and electronics.

As we can see from these examples, different type versions have their individual characteristics. The most common type versions are easier to read than uncommon type versions. We should avoid odd type versions like outline, shadow, and reverse type like white type on black background. Boldface and/or italics should not be used for running text but rather for emphasis of important parts of the text. Typography can be used to modulate a message. We should remember, though, that content is more important than form. A text will retain its content even when type design is changed. Graphic design can be and should be used to build consistency and aid communication.

Glynn, Britton, & Tillman (1985) reviewed studies on the effect of "typographic cueing" on learning. Typographic cueing generally refers to the use of bold or italic type or underlining to signal the important ideas in a text. There is little doubt that cueing does work in drawing attention to the cued material. The consensus is that readers are more likely to remember cued ideas than uncued ideas.

PAGE COMPOSITION

An "empty" page can be considered as an available area or space. This area may be and should be used in many ways. However, the appearance of a book page is governed by the fact that Western readers begin at the top left of a page and read right a line at a time until they get to the bottom of the text column. Often the main part of the page is the text-face. Depending on the page size the page may be used for one or more columns.

Hartley & Burnhill (1977a) have done extensive research on psychological research on typography based on basic principles of typographic decision-making. The three main principles are: the consistent use of space to convey information structure, the use of standard page sizes, and the use of grids for pre-planning of pages.

Use of space

In all printed matter, space can be used to convey the structure of the information. The information can be grouped in various ways. Margins, headings, and "empty" white space can be used to aid communication.

According to Waller (1987), the observations on which the Gestalt theory is based form a basic part of the graphic designer's craft knowledge. These principles might be seen as relatively inflexible perceptual rules that act as a fundamental constraint for the typographer alongside such conventional rules as the left-to-right direction of the writing system. By *grouping* headings, paragraphs, illustrations, and legends the designer aids communication. An "empty" line might separate paragraphs, two lines a subsection, and three or four lines a new section. In this process the principles from the Gestalt theory can be utilized. When we use *space* to group graphic components, we employ the "proximity principle" or the "proximity law." When we use a consistent type to signal a particular kind of graphic component, we employ the "similarity principle." When we use grid systems these are based on the "closure principle," together with the "continuity principle."

Often the main part of the page is the text-face. The white space is important for the structure of the page. There are four *margins*; a header (or top margin) and footer (or bottom margin), an inner, and an outer or outside margin. Usually the margins differ in size. According to Hartley (1985) and Lichty (1989), margins should occupy about 50% of the space on the page. Some guidelines call for even larger margins (Burns, Venit, & Hansen, 1988). Misanchuk (1992) concludes that readers expect margins to occupy 40–50% of the page, although this amount can be reduced in professional or scholarly text, such as this book.

Margins have three main functions. They provide space for headings, page numbers, comments, and illustrations. They provide space for fingers to hold the book. They make it possible to make notes.

With very thick books, the part of the page that is bound will have a section that we cannot see. Thus, thick books need to have wide inner margins. This part of the page is called the gutter. On a two-page spread the right side of the left page is the gutter, and the left side of the right page is the gutter.

Page size

In traditional as well as in desktop publishing the available paper defines the possible page sizes. The use of standard page sizes can aid communication.

Hartley & Burnhill (1977b) are strong advocates of international standard paper sizes. Their own experimental materials are printed on A4 paper.

We may choose from different kinds of page formats.

A *quadratic format* is static. It is often considered uninteresting and it is seldom used.

Wide formats correspond with our vision. In printed materials wide formats may be used to present pictures in large sizes.

Tall formats are very suitable for presentation of printed text and are the most common format for books.

Classical formats are based on the proportions of the golden section, 3:5, 5:8, 8:13, 13:21, 21:34, etc. Each new number in the scale is the sum of the previous two numbers.

Many experiments have shown that there is an optical center on a page.

Grid systems

Look at different books, reports, magazines, and papers and study the variety of page sizes and page designs. In many books the page has only one column, which is very good for undisturbed and *easy reading*. However, a wide page has to be divided. Too wide lines impair reading. Book pages with two columns are quite common. Even three columns can be used, e.g., in dictionaries and reference books. Pages with four or more columns are very rare. One-column layouts are the most used layouts in instructional materials. It is easy to work with, especially when materials may have to be revised frequently. Davies, Barry, & Wiesenberg (1986) suggest that one, two, or three columns per 8 1/2" x 11" page are reasonable for reports, papers, and other similar documents.

In magazines it is common that different sections have their individual page designs. One section may have three columns, another section four columns, and a third five columns. Pages with six or more columns are very rare. In newspapers it is common that a page has six, seven, or eight columns. Newspaper pages with four or five as well as with nine or ten columns may also be used. Pages with eleven or more columns are very rare.

It is very easy to create complicated typography and page layout. However, simplicity and consistency are very important. Complexity usually interferes with communication. Readers should not be forced to search on the page for headings and page numbers. Typographic grids may be used to ensure that space and print are used consistently. It is important that the printed page provide a reliable frame of reference from which the learner can return without confusion.

By dividing a page into smaller sections, a specific topic may be presented in a variety of combinations of grid sections. A grid establishes a structure to build upon. There are different kinds of grid systems. We can distinguish between *one-column grids, multi-column grids, modular grids*, and *irregular grids*.

Many books and other documents use a standard page with a fixed text-face, a live area. The text-face is occupied by the type and other graphic elements. The grid establishes the exact location of the text-face, the inner and outer margins, the header, and the footer on each page.

Traditionally graphic designers work with grid sheets printed in light blue ink. The "non-repro" blue ink will not show up on films, printing plates, or on the final print. The grid is used to ensure that type and graphic elements are pasted on correct locations. In electronic page layout systems the software can create electronic grids. They are called *master pages*. A master page is shown on the screen but does not print.

In *columnar grids* the text flows from one column to another. Dictionaries and telephone directories are examples of simple columnar grids.

In *parallel columnar grids* the text flows in columns that are related horizontally. This system is sometimes found in multilingual manuals with the same text in different languages.

The *modular grid* is the classical Swiss grid. It is based on regular rows as well as columns. Often a modular grid system is used for "blocked grids." For example, it is possible to use columns with different widths to present texts and illustrations. Usually "topic frames" are rectangular. The purpose is to create clear visual gestalts.

Many tabloid newspapers use *irregular grids*. The topic frames are often not rectangular. Editorial stories are mixed with advertising items. The purpose of irregular grids is actually to prevent clear visual gestalts. The reader can never get an understanding of the page at only one glance.

Oppositions

By tradition page layout is based on symmetrical page design. Centered as well as justified texts are examples of *symmetrical layout*. Symmetry is axial balance. It is logical and simple to design. Symmetrical page design is static and may be perceived as boring. An *asymmetrical layout* can be based on contrasts of size, strength, shape, area, or color. Unjustified text flushed left or right are examples of asymmetrical layout. Symmetrical as well as asymmetrical layouts can have a good balance.

The favoring of uniformity in the use of design elements is *regularity*. The opposite, called *irregularity*, emphasizes the unusual and unexpected. A layout may be built on simplicity using few and simple elements and simple forms. The opposite strategy is based on complexity. Dondis (1973) discusses the use of several pairs of oppositions as techniques for visual communication. These are:

Balance	–	Instability
Symmetry	–	Asymmetry
Regularity	–	Irregularity
Simplicity	–	Complexity
Unity	–	Fragmentation
Economy	–	Intricacy
Understatement	–	Exaggeration
Predictability	–	Spontaneity
Activeness	–	Stasis
Subtlety	–	Boldness
Neutrality	–	Accent
Transparency	–	Opacity
Consistency	–	Variation
Accuracy	–	Distortion
Flatness	–	Depth
Singularity	–	Juxtaposition
Sequentiality	–	Randomness
Sharpness	–	Diffusion
Repetition	–	Episodicity

These different visual design techniques overlap and reinforce meaning. They present the graphic designer with effective means of making expressive visual communication.

TEXT LAYOUT

A layout is the result of graphic design. The purpose of this work is to find a suitable presentation for the content with respect to the receiver, the subject matter, and the financial situation. Reference material, such as telephone books, dictionaries, etc., are examples of highly structured information. Here, a carefully thought-out, functional layout can facilitate the reader's ability to find the desired information quickly, easily, effectively, and reliably.

The text-face is surrounded by margins. White or "empty" space on a page can contribute to the creation of a harmonious and functional product. Text must have a typography which facilitates its legibility. Headings, sub-headings, main text, legends, boxes, summaries, etc., must be clearly distinguished from one another. Here are a few examples illustrating the vast possibilities of text design.

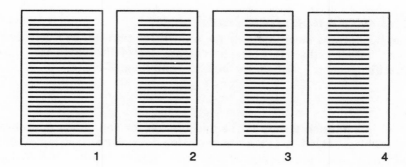

In the first example, the whole page is used with a compact column of text. In 2 the left margin is quite wide. This is good for printing on only one side of the page. In 3 the left margin is even wider. This column is probably very easy to read fast. In 4 the text is centered.

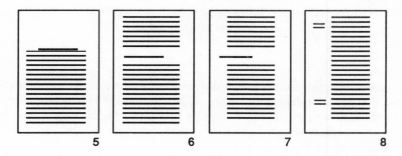

In 5 the text starts down the page. This is usual in new chapters. In 6 a sub-heading is located within the text column. In 7 the sub-heading is poking out. In 8 there are notes in the margin.

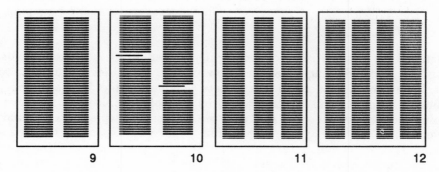

In 9 the text is divided into two columns. In 10 sub-headings are located within the text columns. In 11 the text is divided into three, and in 12 into four columns.

Justified or unjustified text?

The text can be justified or unjustified. An unjustified text can be flushed left, center justified, or flushed right. Here are four examples of the same text in different versions; justified, center justified, flushed left, and flushed right:

Justified text:

Psychological information theory is the designation for one of the main branches of cognitive psychology. It refers to the study of Man's mental processing of information, i.e., mental information processing. A major principle in cognitive psychology is that Man organizes impressions and knowledge into meaningful units. This process starts at the perception stage.

Center justified text:

Psychological information theory is the designation for one of the main branches of cognitive psychology. It refers to the study of Man's mental processing of information, i.e., mental information processing. A major principle in cognitive psychology is that Man organizes impressions and knowledge into meaningful units. This process starts at the perception stage.

Flushed left text:

Psychological information theory is the designation for one of the main branches of cognitive psychology. It refers to the study of Man's mental processing of information, i.e., mental information processing. A major principle in cognitive psychology is that Man organizes impressions and knowledge into meaningful units. This process starts at the perception stage.

Flushed right text:

Psychological information theory is the designation for one of the main branches of cognitive psychology. It refers to the study of Man's mental processing of information, i.e., mental information processing. A major principle in cognitive psychology is that Man organizes impressions and knowledge into meaningful units. This process starts at the perception stage.

Justified text (sometimes called right-justified text) is commonly used for running text in books, magazines, and newspapers. To achieve a justified text the technical system inserts extra space between words and between characters. According to Kleper (1987), the practice of having text justified is a tradition in the publishing industry which originated with the scribes who copied text by hand before the invention of movable type. At that time paper was expensive and the scribes attempted to put as much text as possible onto every page, filling each line completely. Burns, Venit, & Hansen (1988) pointed out that the use of metal type required that the right edges of type align in the page form so that the type could be locked into place. Until recently anything other than justified text had been regarded as unprofessional by most publishers. Lang (1987) argues that justified text is aesthetic, it serves to define the right margin, and it is familiar to the readers. Like Lang, Lichty (1989) also argues that it is easier to read lines of the same length than lines with markedly varying righthand ends.

Today flushed left text with a "ragged–right–hand" edge is commonly used for running text in books, magazines, and some newspapers. A century ago flushed left text was restricted to poetry. At that time it was considered very odd and peculiar. Hartley (1985) and Hartley & Burnhill (1977a) argue that justified text is not a good idea for instructional materials. The variable spacing between words as well as the use of hyphenation makes reading less smooth and more difficult. The advantage with flushed left and ragged right text is that it retains the optimal spacing between letters and between words and so keeps the visual rhythm constant. This aids reading, especially for young and inexperienced readers. Poor readers have difficulty reading justified text (Zachrisson, 1965; Gregory & Poulton, 1970). However, whether the text is justified or unjustified causes no significant difference in search time and comprehension of the information for advanced readers (Hartley, 1987). Justification should especially be avoided with narrow columns in multi-columnar layouts (Davies, Barry, & Wiesenberg, 1986). Misanchuk (1992) claims that there are no good arguments at all for using justified text. However, many readers find justified text much more aesthetically pleasing than flushed left text. They may even feel that the ragged right is ugly and repulsive.

Center justified texts are often used for menus and sometimes for poetry and also for tables of contents. Flushed right texts can be used for legends positioned to the left of the pictures or for tables of contents. This is only possible when the line length is short.

Line length

According to Tinker, readers tend to dislike both very short and very long line lengths. West (1987) suggests that the line length should be 35–40 characters. Quite often the optimum line length seems to be about 1 1/2 alphabets—42 characters (Pettersson, 1989; Walker, 1990). This is nine to eleven centimeters with optimum character size, ten to twelve point, at a normal reading distance. Parker (1988) suggests 50 characters. Burns, Venit, & Hansen (1988) suggest up to 60 characters. Miles (1987) suggest 60–65 characters. It is quite clear that too wide lines impair reading. In my opinion the maximum line length should not be much more than 60-70 characters, except for books intended for highly skilled readers. Costs often force people to use more characters on each line, so that the total number of pages can be reduced. The longer the lines the wider the space between them needs to be (Waller, 1987).

The length of a line will affect reading speed (Duchnicky & Kolers, 1983). Different kinds of publications should use different line lengths. The optimum line length should be found for each individual purpose and audience.

The width of a line of type is traditionally measured in *picas*. A pica equals 12 points. There are six picas to an inch. As systems for desktop publishing become more common, line lengths will be measured in inches or centimeters instead of picas.

The line length may vary considerably. The longer the line is, the larger the type size should be. The shorter the line is, the smaller the type size can be. If justified text is set in lines too short, you get rivers of space between words, or characters spaced out to fill. Following are examples (two each) of different line length with the same type size; too short lines, short lines, optimum line length, and long lines. All examples are given with unjustified as well as with justified lines:

Too short lines 1:
In philosophy,
semantic in-
formation the-
ory refers to
the information
supplied by a
proposition in
terms of the
proposition's
probability,
and specifies
the principles
for measuring
information.

Too short lines 2:
In philosophy,
semantic in-
formation the-
ory refers to
the information
supplied by a
proposition in
terms of the
proposition's
probability,
and specifies
the principles
for measuring
information.

Short lines 1:
In philosophy, semantic
information theory refers to
the information supplied by a
proposition in terms of the
proposition's probability, and
specifies the principles for
measuring information.

Short lines 2:
In philosophy, semantic information theory refers to the information supplied by a proposition in terms of the proposition's probability, and specifies the principles for measuring information.

Optimum line length 1:
In philosophy, semantic information theory
refers to the information supplied by a proposition in terms of the proposition's probability,
and specifies the principles for measuring
information.

Optimum line length 2:
In philosophy, semantic information theory
refers to the information supplied by a proposition in terms of the proposition's probability,
and specifies the principles for measuring
information.

Long lines 1:
In philosophy, semantic information theory refers to the information supplied by a proposition in terms of the proposition's probability, and specifies the principles for measuring
information.

Long lines 2:
In philosophy, semantic information theory refers to the information supplied by a proposition in terms of the proposition's probability, and specifies the principles for measuring
information.

As we can see from these examples, short lines cannot handle justified setting
very well. The distance between the words is too long. We get white "rivers" of space
in the text column.

Interline distance

The "interline distance," "interline spacing," or "vertical spacing" is the distance
between the base lines in the text. A 12-point text may be set on a 13-point line. This
is written as 11/13, and read as "eleven on thirteen." The term "leading" may refer to

the extra space between lines. In this case the interline distance is 13 points, and thus leading is 2 points. (This volume's text is set ten on twelve.)

The leading may vary considerably. The longer the lines, the wider it should be. The reader needs to be able to find the next line without any trouble. In general, the opinion is that as the line length is increased, the need for more leading and larger type increases (Misanchuk, 1992). For maximum legibility Tinker (1963) and Pettersson (1989) recommend a leading of 1 to 2 points in a continuous text when text size is optimal, Hartley (1987) recommends 1.5 points, and Benson (1985) recommends 2 points. Kleper (1987) recommends a leading of about 20% and Lichty (1989) recommends 25%. Children need more leading than adult readers.

Here are six examples of different interline spacings; Times 12/12, 12/13, 12/14, 12/15, 12/16, and 12/17:

Times 12/12
Social information, i.e., the result of all information measures whose aim is to make it easier for citizens to know what their rights, privileges, and obligations are, is studied in social science subjects. Good social information should be readily accessible, tailored to local requirements, readily grasped, adapted to individual needs, and capable of creating a state of preparedness in the receiver.

Times 12/13
Social information, i.e., the result of all information measures whose aim is to make it easier for citizens to know what their rights, privileges, and obligations are, is studied in social science subjects. Good social information should be readily accessible, tailored to local requirements, readily grasped, adapted to individual needs, and capable of creating a state of preparedness in the receiver.

Times 12/14
Social information, i.e., the result of all information measures whose aim is to make it easier for citizens to know what their rights, privileges, and obligations are, is studied in social science subjects. Good social information should be readily accessible, tailored to local requirements, readily grasped, adapted to individual needs, and capable of creating a state of preparedness in the receiver.

Times 12/15
Social information, i.e., the result of all information measures whose aim is to make it easier for citizens to know what their rights, privileges, and obligations are, is studied in social science subjects. Good social information should be readily accessible, tailored to local requirements, readily grasped, adapted to individual needs, and capable of creating a state of preparedness in the receiver.

Times 12/16

Social information, i.e., the result of all information measures whose aim is to make it easier for citizens to know what their rights, privileges, and obligations are, is studied in social science subjects. Good social information should be readily accessible, tailored to local requirements, readily grasped, adapted to individual needs, and capable of creating a state of preparedness in the receiver.

Times 12/17

Social information, i.e., the result of all information measures whose aim is to make it easier for citizens to know what their rights, privileges, and obligations are, is studied in social science subjects. Good social information should be readily accessible, tailored to local requirements, readily grasped, adapted to individual needs, and capable of creating a state of preparedness in the receiver.

Spacing

Wendt (1979) inserted additional space between the constituents of the sentences to better convey the phrase structure of the text but found no difference in learning efficiency when compared with traditional text in one or in two columns. Text with a generous amount of space within it is rated as "easier" and "more interesting" than text which has a more solid appearance. For comfortable reading it must be easy to distinguish between words. The distance between words should be relatively small. When the text has optimal spacing we can keep the reading rhythm constant. The distance between characters is sometimes too long. This is especially true for headlines in capitals. In hand typesetting spacing of type is done by using thin strips of metal from .5 point upwards. In electronic systems "empty space" is added automatically between the words and between letters when the text is set with justified lines.

The amount of space between words and between letters varies in each line depending on the actual words and the actual line length. First the system adds word-spacing and then, if the space between words becomes too excessive, the system will add letter-spacing.

Here are five examples of the same text (Times 18 points) with different spacings between the words: (1) condensed, (2) normal, (3) expanded with one space, (4) expanded with two spaces, (5) expanded with three spaces, and (6) expanded with four spaces:

1 Visual information.
2 Visual information.
3 Visual   information.

4 Visual   information.
5 Visual   information.
6 Visual   information.

In photo-typesetting *kerning* is used to individually correct the distance between characters to achieve a better type. For example, when a capital A and a capital T, V, or Y are set without kerning, there is too much space between the letters. The A, V, and Y have slanted shapes, and the T has empty space on the bottom. Thus, the space between these letters is exaggerated. With kerning, selected pairs of letters can be pushed together and overlap to create the correct visual spacing between the letters. Hewson (1988) notes that it isn't worthwhile kerning any type under 18 points. It is worthwhile to use kerning for headings and also for texts on OH transparencies.

In photo-typesetting it is also possible to automatically and systematically reduce the distance between characters, or to *condense* the text. It is also possible to automatically and systematically increase the distance between characters, or to *expand* the text. This is also possible in some systems for desktop publishing.

Here are six examples of the same text (Times 18 points) in different spacing versions: (1) condensed with one point, (2) normal spacing, (3) expanded with one point, (4) expanded with two points, (5) expanded with three points, and (6) expanded with four points.

1 Visual information
2 Visual information
3 Visual information
4 Visual information
5 Visual information
6 Visual information

Headings

The structure of the text is very important for readability, and a structured text is much easier to read and comprehend than a text without any distinct structure. The structure should be as clear as possible. The structure of a text can be divided into *internal* and *external* textual structure. Internal structure is built into the text itself. External textual structure relates to the embedded strategies which focus a learner's attention on particular parts of the text (Jonassen & Kirschener, 1982).

Headings, or headlines, should always be relevant and identify the subject matter. The purposes of headings are to attract the attention of the readers, make the subject matter readily apparent, and indicate the relative importance of items. To avoid too large masses of text, it is a good idea to divide the text into sections and subsections. Headings on different hierarchic levels will provide the readers with reference points and help them organize information cognitively for better retention and recall. Headings set in different type versions aid comprehension of the text content (Jonassen, 1982).

To achieve a clear structure we can use a combined numbering and lettering system (Jonassen, 1982). Main points in a text are traditionally labeled with Roman numerals (I, II, III, etc.). Subpoints of the first degree are traditionally labeled with capital letters (A, B, C, etc.). Second degree subpoints are traditionally labeled with Arabic numerals (1, 2, 3, etc.). The labeling hierarchy is I., A., 1., a., (1), (a). In Europe it is common to use a numbering system only (e.g., 1, 1.1, 1.2, 1.3, 2, 2.1, 2.2, 2.3, 3, 3.1, 3.2, 3.3, etc.).

Numbering and lettering systems can be combined with typographic cueing of headings. Headings set in different type versions aid comprehension of the material. We can use a special typeface for headings. We can vary the type size and/or use different type versions. According to a rule of thumb called the "Rule of X's," the height of the upper-case X of a smaller typeface should be the same as the height of the lower-case x of a larger typeface in a hierarchy. Also, the use of space and the actual placement of a heading can be used to enhance the hierarchic structure.

Paragraphs

Readers prefer small text paragraphs to big ones. Often it is quite easy to divide the text in hierarchic and natural parts, portions, or sections. Natural breaks emphasized by typography are helpful. Providing "white space" between portions of the text provides cues to the learners that a new section or a new type of activity follows. The end of a sentence should be determined by syntax rather than by a set width of a line (Hartley, 1980; Bork, 1982). Paragraph indents or spaces between paragraphs can be used for emphasis.

There are usually no problems with continuation of text in books. The text fills up page after page. However, in magazines and other periodical publications, it is sometimes necessary to use continuation marks like arrows or triangles and a reference to page numbers. In these situations it might also be a good idea to use "terminal-marks" after the last paragraph in the article. Such a mark is often a circle or a square, filled or unfilled. Sometimes the terminal mark is the initials or the signature of the writer.

It is considered to be bad typography to allow an indent on the bottom line of a page. It is also considered bad to end a paragraph on the first line of a page. To avoid this it might be possible to edit the text until it fits.

The extra space between paragraphs may vary, depending on the material.

Tables

Numeric data can be used to illustrate several different situations, such as chronological changes in single quantities or sets of quantities, parts of a whole, and relationships between two or more variables. There are different ways to present numeric data. In print media numeric data can be presented in text, as figures and digits, in tables, or in various graphical formats. No more than one or two items of numeric data should be presented in prose form. Often one or more tables is a good solution. Many people find tables confusing and difficult to understand (Wright, 1968). Tables should be structured and compact for easy accessibility. Tables can be produced with or without markings for rows and/or columns. Columns should not be too far away from each other.

Readers prefer vertically oriented tables where it is easy to see the target entries, and then find the data (Wright, 1968; Wright & Fox, 1972). Horizontally oriented tables are harder to use and understand. According to Tinker (1963) type in tables should be no smaller than 8-point, no larger than 12-point. Like pictures, all tables should be integrated with the text. In a text, tables should be put between paragraphs, and not forced to break paragraphs.

The following two examples show the different looks of a vertically and a horizontally oriented table with some made-up data:

Table 1. This is a vertically oriented table, with some made-up data indicating sales of five different products during two years:

	Sales	
Products	*1992*	*1993*
abc	1000	1200
def	2000	1800
ghi	2000	2200
jkl	3000	3200
mno	3200	3300

Table 2. This is a horizontally oriented table, with some made-up data indicating sales of five different products during two years:

			Products		
Sales	*abc*	*def*	*ghi*	*jkl*	*mno*
1992	1000	2000	2000	3000	3200
1993	1200	1800	2200	3200	3300

Wright & Fox (1970) offer the following guidelines for the construction of tables for the general public and non-professional audiences (p. 241):
- All the information the learner will need should be presented in the table. That is, the learner should not be required to interpolate, combine entries, draw inferences, or otherwise manipulate the contents of the table in order to determine the correct answer. Rather, the learner should only be required to scan the list to find the correct target entry.
- Type size used in the table should be between 8 and 12 point.
- Items should be arranged vertically in the table rather than horizontally (i.e., the list of target entries should be vertical).
- Items within columns should be grouped and separated from other groups by either white space or rules (lines) in order to facilitate reading without accidentally moving to another row. Groups should contain no more than five items.

- Redundant abbreviations of units should not be included within the table entries [although they should be included in the column or row headings].
- 'Landmarks' or sub-headings—certain target entries in the table highlighted by using bold type or a larger font (e.g., every tenth entry, starting with 10, 20, 30, etc.) as an intended aid to locating entries—should not be used, since they appear to be ineffective and possibly confusing.
- It is useful to have adjacent columns printed in different fonts or styles to distinguish between them. That is, there is less chance of erroneous reading of the table if the column of target entries is in normal text (for example) and the column of associated answers is in boldface text.
- Related pairs of items in adjacent columns should be spaced closely together (i.e., the eyes should not have to traverse a great distance between the target entry and the associated answer).
- Whenever possible, columns should be arranged so that the target entries are to the left of the answers.

Ehrenberg (1977) gives some more general guidelines for the construction of tables for the general public and non-professional audiences:
- Numbers should be rounded off to no more than two significant figures to facilitate learners' making comparisons.
- Averages of rows and columns (as appropriate) should be given to facilitate learners' making comparisons of individual cell entries to them.
- Put the most important comparisons into columns (rather than rows), as columns make for the easiest comparisons.
- Numbers in rows or columns should be arranged in some meaningful order whenever possible (e.g., increasing or decreasing).

Legends

We may find legends with several apparently different functions. Sometimes legends (or captions) are used just as labels. They may convey factual content, or information about events. They may also evoke emotions. Books legends may instruct and direct the reader what to study in the picture. Every visual should always be supplied with a legend.

Legends are very important in all kinds of instructional materials. We need to explain the pictures. We need to tell the reader or viewer what we want her/him to see and learn from the illustration. Thus, every visual should always be supplied with a legend, which should be brief and easy to understand. The legends may also be "bridges" between the main text and the illustrations. The function of the legend is to help the reader select the intended content in the picture. Winn (1993) notes that students often need specific instructions as to how to look at and interpret a picture. Legends can effectively direct attention where the designer wishes it to be directed.

Content of legend

The legend and the visual should interact as parts of a whole. A legend should describe image contents and govern the way a picture is read: a picture producer's intentions about what the reader is supposed to see and learn from each illustration should be as clear as possible. The legend should be redundant in relation to the visual, i.e., the legend should supply approximately the same information as the visual.

Form of legend

A legend should be edited to fit different reader categories, such as general readers (children, teenagers, adults...), technical readers, and specialist readers. The legend should be brief and easy to understand.

A general reader knows little, if anything, about the subject matter. The legends and the pictures are kept simple, attractive, and informative. They should not be too complicated and, thus, distracting to the reader.

A technical reader will understand technical concepts but may not be familiar with special terminology.

A specialist reader has a good understanding of the subject matter. Both the text and illustrations, which may consist of detailed drawings, graphs, technical photographs, ultra-sonograms, or other realistic pictures or symbols, may be detailed.

The legend should be brief and cogent. An excessively long legend diverts the reader's attention from the main thread in the overall text. Just as it is natural for the main text to refer to the legend, it is equally important for the reader to be able to make her/his way with ease from the legend to the main text—not merely the readers who shift back and forth between the main text and the legend! This also applies to an equal degree to the many readers who begin with the pictures and legends without any intention of reading the entire main text and who are only interested in obtaining detailed information on a particular illustrated section.

Placement of legend

A legend may be placed in many ways. The legend should always be located close to the picture. Readers usually expect to find the legends beneath the pictures. However, legends can also be placed above, to the left, or to the right, of the picture, but never inside the picture frame.

Different ways to place legends. Readers usually expect, though, to find legends beneath the picture.

Use flushed right text if you want to put the legend to the left of the picture. Use flushed left text if you want to put the legend to the right of the picture. When the legend is put above or beneath the picture, we can use justified text or flushed left text and sometimes even centered text. Sometimes triangles or arrows pointing from the legend towards the picture are used, especially when pictures are gathered together many on a page, e.g., in a magazine.

Placing the legend inside the picture makes it harder for people to read both the picture and the text. Nor should the legend be located on some other page, as happens far too often in reference books and school books. A legend can have a heading as an additional link between the visual and the legend.

Title of legend
The legend and the visual should interact as parts of a whole. A legend may have a heading or a title which summarizes the contents. The title of a legend should be short and distinct. It could give answers to questions like these: Who? What? When? Where? Why? and How?

Typography of legend
The legend should have a different typographic size or even a different typeface so it can be easily distinguished from the main text. The legends should not be in negative form in a color picture since the slightest misalignment in printing makes the legends extremely difficult to read. Never make the legend type larger than the main text. The title of the legend could be printed in boldface.

Miscellaneous
This section contains short notes on items like color, credits, footnotes, indexes, introductions, line numbers, lines and patterns, page numbers, paper and ink, references, special designs, tables of content, and tables.

Boxes.

> Specially important messages like summaries can be boxed-in to gain special attention. If the lines are shorter the effect is even more obvious. Boxes usually have thin lines. Boxes may sometimes be filled with a background color.

Bullets. Bullets (•) are commonly used in lists of items in "point form" without numbers. Bullets are more powerful than hyphens (-) or asterisks (*).

Capitals. It is known that all capital letters are harder to read than a "normal" combination of upper and lower case letters (Poulton & Brown, 1968; Henney, 1981). Without sufficient white space around words in all capitals, the words will become too difficult to read (Kinney & Showman, 1967). Thus, all-capital printing has been shown to markedly reduce the speed of reading (Tinker, 1965).

Check box. Check boxes (❑) can be used in instructional materials when learners may make check marks when they have finished assignments.

Credits. In books it is quite common to give credits to artists and photographers in a special "List of illustrations." In magazines and in newspapers credits are usually put next to the actual illustration, often in a vertical position. Credits to the author are usually in the form of a byline.

Color is regularly used in printed materials, not only in illustrations, but also in the text itself. Color can be used to clarify the structure of the text and to make learning easier. Certain parts of the text may be printed with colors or printed on top of backgrounds in different colors.

Dash. With typewriters we had to create a dash (—) with two hyphens (--). With desktop publishing and typography this is not necessary. In desktop publishing we can create the em dash (—), the en dash (–), as well as the hyphen (-). The em dash is used to indicate a break in thought. There should be no space before or after the em dash. The en dash is used between numerals (e.g., pp. 33–45 and as a minus sign (e.g., –12).

Diagrams. If a diagram is to be understood by the ordinary reader it has to be very simple. Diagrams should not become confusing, over-imaginative, or illogical.

Dingbats. See Ornaments.

Drop caps. See Initial letters.

Ellipsis. An ellipsis (...) is normally used to indicate that text is missing in a quotation.

Fill-in blanks. Fill-in blanks (_) can be used in assignments, and in lists of various kinds.

Footers. When present, footers appear at the bottom of every page. Like headers, footers may carry page numbers. Footers should provide information that will help the reader navigate in a document.

Footnotes are placed at the bottom of the page or at the end of the chapter or the article. Usually a smaller type size or a different typeface is used. A horizontal line can be used to separate the footnotes from the running text.

Graphical markers. Arrows, boldface type, headings, and white space are all examples of external textual structure (Hartley, 1987; Jonassen & Kirschner, 1982). Arrows can be used for cueing when information is located in places other than in the normal directional flow (Winn, 1989).

Grouping. By grouping headings, paragraphs, illustrations, and legends, the designer aids communication.

Headers. When present, headers, or running heads, appear at the top of every page. In this book every left-hand page has the title of the book, and every right-hand page has the name of the chapter. Headings may also carry page numbers. Headers should provide information that will help the reader navigate in a document.

Hyphenation. Lines can be broken according to different principles. According to one principle, lines can be broken only between words. According to another principle, lines can be broken also within words. This can be done phonetically or according to etymology. In mechanical word breaks, lines are broken at the most convenient point, regardless of meaning. It is known that poor readers have difficulty reading hyphenated text (Gregory & Poulton, 1970; White, 1983; Lichty, 1989). Misanchuk (1992) provides guidelines for hyphenation.

Indexes. Like the reference list, the index might be bulky. To aid overview and easy access, an index is often arranged in two or three columns. The index text is set in type on shorter lines than the running text. As with the reference list, an indented text may be used.

Initial letters. Sometimes initial letters are larger than the running text. Initial letters may be lowered as "drop caps" or raised as "raised initial letters." Because of the possibility to create fancy initial letters in desktop systems, this medieval practice is becoming common again. Misanchuk (1992) argues that fancy initial letters are not likely to help readers.

Introductions. Introductions to chapters in a book or to articles in a magazine or newspaper are very often set in different type than the following running text. Sometimes the introduction is set with larger type size, sometimes in italic or bold typefaces.

Ligatures. Ligatures are letters combined to new characters. Examples are Æ (A+E) and Œ (O+E).

Line numbers. Non-arbitrary numbering systems include the numbering of lines where line endings are meaningful. This might be the case in computer programs, in dictionaries, and in texts used for linguistic analysis. Non-arbitrary numbering systems also include the numbering of paragraphs and the numbering of headed sections.

Lines. Various lines are often used for decoration to make a more aesthetically pleasing or artistic product. However, lines can also be used to aid communication.

Horizontal lines can separate sections or paragraphs or hold them together. Horizontal black lines are usually one to four points. When printed in other colors horizontal lines may be wider.

When two or more columns are used on a page, vertical lines can be used to clearly separate the text blocks. By tradition vertical lines are thin, usually half a point or one point.

Lists. Putting information into list form can facilitate comprehension (Hartley, 1987; Frase & Schwartz, 1970).

Marks. In magazines and other periodical publications, it is sometimes necessary to use continuation marks like arrows or triangles and a reference to page number, and "terminal marks" after the last paragraph. A terminal mark is often a circle or a square, filled or unfilled. Sometimes the terminal mark is the initials or the signature of the writer.

Ornaments. Various ornaments and patterns can be used to separate different sections in a text. In instructional materials they are often used to mark specific activities. They can also be used for decoration, to make a more aesthetically pleasing or artistic product. Dingbats is a special PostScript font in desktop publishing systems. Here are some examples of such characters (from the Zapf Dingbats series):

Orphans. In typography an "orphan" is defined as the last line of a paragraph when it is alone at the top of a column. See widows.

Outdention. Outdention or hanging indent is the reverse of indentation. In this book it is used in lists with bullets, and in the reference lists, for the lines following the initial line in a reference.

Page numbers. In all kinds of reference materials, it is important to have page numbers, *folios*. The reader can find information in the material by using the table of contents and/or the index. Page numbers should be *clear and easy to find*. There are many possibilities for placement of the page numbers. They can be put to the left, in the middle, or to the right in the header or in the footer. Page numbers are sometimes also put in the margin. In products with large page sizes, it is usual to put page numbers in the header. In products with small page sizes, it is quite common to put page numbers in the footer. However, this should not to be considered a rule. The important thing is consistency.

Page numbers indicate arbitrary divisions of the text. For technical reasons many books contain more than one series of page numbers. For example, technical manuals and instructional materials often use a separate numbering series for each chapter. Then a single chapter can be updated without reprinting the whole manual.

The running head includes the name of the publication, the issue date, or other header or footer style material.

Paper and ink. In all graphical media the quality of the paper and ink is of vital importance for the final result. The paper has its specific grain, texture, finish, bulk, and weight. It may be stiff or floppy. It may be glossy and shining or matte and maybe dull. It may be thick or thin. Thin lines, in serifs on small type sizes, may require a harder paper than normal lines and larger type. The printing technique used will affect the type of paper needed. The quality of ink is also an important factor in graphical communication.

All these factors affect legibility and our reading comfort and also our perceived value of the product. The degree of contrast between the color of the ink and the color of the paper should be optimum. For text printed in black all paper surfaces are equally legible if they have a reflectance of at least 70%. (The paper used in this book is at that level.) The most legible combination is a black text on a light yellow background. In a normal reading situation, black print on white paper is over 10% more efficient than white on black.

Raised initial letters. See Initial letters.

References. References to cited works are usually put in a reference list at the end of a chapter or at the end of a book. A reference list may be bulky and set in smaller type than the running text. To aid the reader's possibilities to find a desired reference, it might be a good idea to use outdented text, e.g., the opposite to the indents used in running text at the beginning of a paragraph.

Rules. Vertical and horizontal lines that are used in typography and layout are called rules. Horizontal lines can be used to separate sections in a text and rows in a table. Vertical lines can be used to separate columns of text on a page or columns in a table. It is, however, often better to use white space as a separating device.

Runarounds. When text is "wrapped" around an irregularly shaped illustration this is known as a "runaround." Runarounds almost never represent any improvements and should be avoided.

Separation. Use of separation devices such as bullets, numbers, and letters facilitate recall of information in list form.

Special designs. Chemical, mathematical, astronomical, and medical signs are important for use in these subject matters.

Summaries. Specially important messages like summaries can be boxed-in to gain special attention. If the lines are shorter, the effect is even more obvious. Boxes usually have thin lines. Boxes may sometimes be filled with a background color.

Symbols. Various symbols can be used to aid communication in a book or magazine. Examples are marks for continuation (>) or for termination (□).

Table of contents. There are many ways to make a table of contents. Justified or unjustified text may be used. The important thing is that the structure of the content is visible. The references to page numbers must be clear.

Widows. In typography a "widow" is defined as the first line of a paragraph alone at the bottom of a column. Sometimes a widow refers to the last line of any paragraph with only a few words. See Orphans.

LAYOUT OF TEXT AND PICTURES

A layout is the result of graphic design. The purpose of this work is to find a suitable presentation for the content with respect to the receiver, the subject matter, and the financial situation.

Image placement

A picture may be placed on a page in many different ways. It is usually, but not necessarily, adjusted to the width of the text column. A page with more than one column has more possibilities for placement of pictures.

A few examples of pages with text and pictures. Each picture has its legend.

A picture may expand beyond the width of the column and cover the margins and sometimes the whole page. "Bleed" (covering the entire page, with no margins) may be used constructively and creative to expand the impact of important attention-getting images.

In materials for information a picture should be located as close to the relevant text passage as possible (Lidman & Lund, 1972; MacDonald-Ross, 1977; Hartley & Burnhill, 1977a; Haber & Hershenson, 1980; Wright, 1982; Braden, 1983; Benson, 1985; Pettersson, 1989). It is usually a good idea to put pictures between paragraphs. Pictures within a paragraph will disturb the reading of the text.

Pictures on odd-numbered pages attract more attention than pictures on even pages. In newspapers and magazines it is quite often a correlation between placement of pictures and perceived importance. The higher up on a page a picture is placed, the more important it is considered to be.

Many visuals have a built in "direction," e.g., a person on a photograph may be looking to the left. Such a picture should usually be placed on the right page for the person to look into the gutter and not out of the book or the magazine.

Image framing

A frame or box around an image, or sometimes around an illustration and text, may have different functions. Image framing can be functional and/or attentional. A frame will separate the image from the surrounding context and draw special attention to information within the frame. In a newspaper, framing is a way of helping the readers to combine the corresponding text and pictures on the page.

Interplay of visuals

In many situations it is a good idea to use more than one visual to be able to convey information. We can use image pairs or sequences of images.

Image pairs

In many situations it is a good idea to use pairs of visuals in which one is true-to-life, such as a photograph, and the other represents an analytical representation, such as a simple line drawing. The analytical visual makes it easier for us to understand the content, and the realistic visual enables us to believe in the content. So the two visuals should be closely linked in a carefully thought-out relationship.

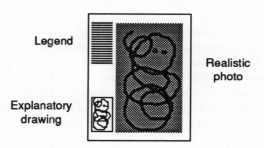

An example of a page with interplay of a realistic photo (right), an explanatory drawing (bottom left), and a legend.

To enhance communication it is very good if there is a logical *relationship* between pictures placed next to each other. This relationship may be based on consistency or on continuity.

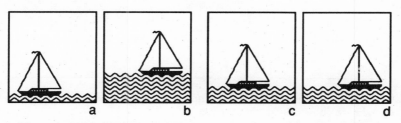

The c-d combination is usually better to use than the a-b combination.

The actual size of two pictures may reflect a natural relationship of scale but it may also reflect a relationship of importance.

Image sequences

Sometimes it is necessary to divide a message content into a series of visuals. The amount of details can be great or the content can include a certain period of time. Time scales and charts provide a reference in time and space.

A sequence of pictures can be used to explain a development over time. It can be used in instructions. A sequence of pictures telling parts of the same story can be used to hold a chapter together to enhance the depth dimension in a printed material. A series of pictures can approximate the impression of a motion picture sequence.

Several consecutive enlargements of a specific part will help the reader to understand the detailed structure of an object.

Understanding of a series of pictures is dependent upon the ability to recognize that the object or person in each frame is the same.

For an exhibition pictures and prints can be put on a wall or on a board in many different ways. It may be a good idea to create balance in the layout of the exhibition. Balance can be achieved by putting all pictures on a joint base line or bottom edge. Balance can also be achieved by putting all pictures centered on a "central" line. A third possibility is to put all the pictures on the wall with a joint upper edge.

When we want to have two rows of pictures on the wall we can achieve balance with reference to a central line or cross or with reference to joint bottom and upper edges and joint side edges.

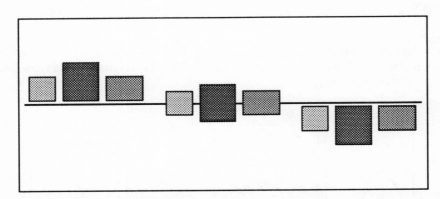

This example shows three ways of arranging a group of three pictures with reference to a "line of balance." (Legends are not visible in this example.)

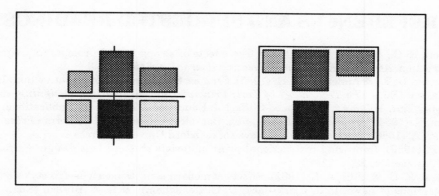

This example show two ways of arranging two rows of each three pictures for a balanced layout. (Legends are not visible in this example.)

Layouts

In *newspaper layout* many different messages have to be communicated. The problem is to communicate a series of disconnected messages of infinitely varying significance within a limited space, time, and economy with a recognizably consistent style for each section of the paper. Many readers will only spend time on a limited amount of information in a newspaper. It is known that elements like headlines, photos, drawings, and information graphics attract attention and often are entry points into a page. Size and placement of such elements influence how the reader will read a page. It is possible that many readers may jump over too large pictures and never look at them at all.

In *magazine layout* visuals are often very large. The visuals have no or a very limited contact with the text. Here White (1987) asks for less typographic amusement and more character building. *Fiction layout* certainly does not work very well in instructional message design. Even in traditional non-fiction publishing, it is often very hard to access the information.

Picture placement has very often been based on aesthetic rather than instructional characteristics. The appearance of elements on the page can provide powerful cues to the reader. Thus, visuals should be located in close proximity to the parts of the text in which pictured motifs are discussed. Visuals plus their captions should preferably be inserted into the text between two paragraphs, not in the middle of a paragraph, so they do not disrupt reading rhythm. Legends and visuals are often piled up in different areas and sometimes even on different pages. Here, an effort should really be made to achieve the best possible interplay of words and visuals. Visuals interact with the legends, other visuals, headings, running text, tables, maps, etc., on a page and on a spread in a book, magazine, or newspaper. The layout of the whole spread should be attractive. However, the mere use of a lot of pictures is not enough. In an *artistic layout*, the message may be effectively hidden. The message is more effectively conveyed by an *informative layout*.

REFERENCES AND SUGGESTED READINGS

Anderson, R. C., & Faust, G. W. (1967). The effects of strong formal prompts in programmed instruction. *American Educational Research Journal, 4*, 345–352.

Armbruster, B. B., & Anderson, T. H. (1985). Frames: Structures for informative text. In D. H. Jonassen (Ed.). *The Technology of Text: Principles for Structuring, Designing, and Displaying Text. Volume 2.* Englewood Cliffs, NJ: Educational Technology Publications.

Arnheim, R. (1954). *Art and Visual Perception.* Berkeley: University of California Press.

Baddaley, A. (1986). *Working Memory.* New York: Oxford University Press.

Balan, P. (1989). Improving instructional print materials through text design. *Performance and Instruction, 28,* 7, 13–18.

Barnhurst, K. G., & Ellis, A. L. (1992). Effects of modern & postmodern design styles on reader perceptions of news. In J. Clark-Baca, D. G. Beauchamp, & R. A. Braden (Eds.). *Visual Communication: Bridging Across Cultures.* Selected Readings from the 23rd Annual Conference of the International Visual Literacy Association. Blacksburg: Virginia Tech University.

Bausell, R. B., & Jenkins, J. R. (1987). Effects on prose learning of frequency of adjunct cues and the difficulty of the material cued. *Journal of Reading Behaviour, 9,* 227–232.

Benson, P. J. (1985). Writing visually: Design considerations in technical publications. *Technical Communications Journal. Fourth Quarter,* 35–39.

Bernard, R. M. (1990). Effects of processing instructions on the usefulness of a graphic organizer and structural cueing in text. *Instructional Science, 19,* 207–217.

Bild och Ordakademin. (1988). News Graphics. Effective news presentation using text and pictures. Exhibition and documentation.

Booth-Clibborn, E., & Baroni, O. (1980). *The Language of Graphics.* London: Thames & Hudson.

Bork, A. (1982). *Information Display and Screen Design.* Paper presented at the American Educational Research Association Conference. New York.

Braden, R. (1983). Visualizing the verbal and verbalizing the visual. In R. Braden & A. Walker (Eds.). *Seeing Ourselves: Visualization in a Social Context.* Readings from the 14th Annual Conference of the International Visual Literacy Association. Blacksburg: Virginia Tech University.

Braden, R. (1985). The stylish look: A format for visual literacy writers. In N. H. Thayer & S. Clayton-Randolph (Eds.). *Visual Literacy: Cruising into the Future.* Readings from the 16th Annual Conference of the International Visual Literacy Association. Bloomington, IN: Western Sun Printing Co.

Brody, P. J. (1982). Affecting instructional textbooks through pictures. In D. H. Jonasson (Ed.). *The Technology of Text.* Englewood Cliffs, NJ: Educational Technology Publications.

Burg, K. F., Boyle, J. M., Evey, J. R., & Neal, A. S. (1982). Windowing versus scrolling on a visual display terminal. *Human Factors, 24,* 385–394.

Burns, D., Venit, S., & Hansen, R. (1988). *The Electronic Publisher.* New York: Brady

Chomsky, N. (1959). Review of verbal behaviour. In B. F. Skinner (Ed.). *Language, 35,* 26–58.

Christ, R. E. (1975). Review and analysis of color coding research for visual displays. *Human Factors, 17,* 542–578.

Collier, D., & Cotton, B. (1989). *Basic Desktop Design and Layout.* Cincinnati, OH: North Light Books.

Cox, D. R. (1978). Some remarks on the role in statistics of graphical methods. *Applied Statistics, 27,* 4–9. Cited by E. R. Misanchuk (1992). *Preparing Instructional Text: Document Design Using Desktop Publishing.* Englewood Cliffs, NJ: Educational Technology Publications.

Crouse, J. H., & Idstein, P. (1972). Effects of encoding cues on prose learning. *Journal of Educational Psychology, 63,* 309–313.

Dahlbak, H., & Öystein, K. (1982). *Bildet i Journalistikken*. Fredrikstad: Institutt for Journalistikk.

Davies, F. E., Barry, J., & Wiesenberg, M. (1986). *Desktop Publishing*. Homewood, IL: Dow Jones-Irwin.

Dillon, A., & McKnight, C. (1990). Towards a classification of text types: A repertory grid approach. *International Journal of Man-Machine Studies, 33*, 623–636.

Dodge, R. W. (1962). What to report. *Westinghouse Engineer, 22*, 108–111.

Dondis, D. A. (1973). *A Primer of Visual Literacy*. Cambridge, MA: Massachusetts Institute of Technology Press.

Duchnicky, R. L., & Kolers, P.A. (1983). Readability of text scrolled on visual display terminals as a function of window size. *Human Factors, 25*, 683–692.

Dwyer, F. M. (1978). *Strategies for Improving Visual Learning*. State College, PA: Learning Services

Eco, U. (1971). *Den frånvarande strukturen. Introduktion till den semiotiska forskningen*. Lund, Swedish translation.

Egidius, H. (1969). *Praktisk Psykologi*. Stockholm: Läromedelsförlagen.

Ehrenberg, A. S. C. (1977). Rudiments of numeracy. *Journal of the Royal Statistical Society, 140*, 277–297. Cited by E. R. Misanchuk (1992). *Preparing Instructional Text: Document Design Using Desktop Publishing*. Englewood Cliffs, NJ: Educational Technology Publications.

Ekwall, E. (1977). *Diagnosis and Remediation of the Disabled Reader*. Boston: Allyn and Bacon.

Elkind, D. (1975). We can teach reading better. *Today's Education, 64*, 34–38.

Evans, H. (1973). *Editing and Design. Newspaper Design*. London: Heinemann.

Evans, H. (1978). *Editing and Design. Pictures on a Page*. London: Heinemann.

Fleming, M., & Levie, W. H. (1978). *Instructional Message Design*. Englewood Cliffs, NJ: Educational Technology Publications.

Forgus, R. H. (1966). *Perception*. New York: McGraw-Hill Book Company.

Foster, J. J. (1979). The use of visual cues in text. In P. Kolers, M.E. Wrolstad, & H. Bouma (Eds.). *Processing of Visible Language*. New York: Plenum.

Frase, L. T., & Schwartz, B. J. (1970). Typographical cues that facilitate comprehension. *Journal of Educational Psychology, 71*, 197–206.

Gagné, R. M., Briggs, L. J., & Wager, W. W. (1988). *Principles of Instructional Design* (Third Edition). New York: Holt, Rinehart, & Winston.

Gazzaniga, M. (1967). The split brain in man. *Scientific American, 217*, 24–29.

Glynn, S. M., Britton, B. K., & Tillman, M. H. (1985). Typographic cues in text: Management of the reader's attention. In D. H. Jonassen (Ed.). *The Technology of Text: Principles for Structuring, Designing, and Displaying Text. Volume 2*. Englewood Cliffs, NJ: Educational Technology Publications.

Gombrich, E. H. (1972). The visual image. *Scientific American, 227*, 82–96.

Gould, J. D., & Grischkowsky, N. (1984). Doing the same work with hard copy and the cathode-ray tube (CRT) computer terminals. *Human Factors, 26*, 323–337.

Grabinger, R. S. (1989). Screen layout design: Research into the overall appearance of the screen. *Computers in Human Behavior, 5*, 175–183.

Grabinger, R. S., & Albers, S. (1988). *The Effect of CRT Screen Design on Learning*. Paper presented at the AECT conference, New Orleans, LA.

Grabinger, R. S., & Amedeo, D. (1988). CRT text layout: Perceptions of viewers. *Computers in Human Behavior, 4*, 189–205.

Gregory, M., & Poulton, E. C. (1970). Even versus uneven right-hand margins and the rate of comprehension in reading. *Ergonomics, 13*, 427–434.

Haber, R. N., & Haber, L. R. (1981). Visual components of the reading process. *Visual Language, 15*, 149.

Haber, R. N., & Hershenson, M. (1980). *The Psychology of Visual Perception.* New York: Holt, Rinehart, & Winston.

Haber, R. N., & Myers, B. L. (1982). Memory for pictograms, pictures, and words separately and all mixed up. *Perception, 11,* 57–64.

Hartley, J. (1980). Spatial cues in text: Some comments on the paper by Frase and Schwartz (1979). *Visible Language, XIV,* 62–79.

Hartley, J. (1985). *Designing Instructional Text* (second edition). London: Kogan Page.

Hartley, J. (1986). Planning the typographical structure of instructional text. *Educational Psychologist, 21,* 315–332.

Hartley, J. (1987). Designing electronic text: The role of print-based research. *Educational Communications and Technology Journal, 35,* 3–17.

Hartley, J., Bartlett, S., & Branthwaite, A. (1980). Underlining can make a difference—sometimes. *Journal of Educational Research, 73,* 218–223.

Hartley, J., & Burnhill, P. (1977a). Fifty guidelines for improving instructional text. *Programmed Learning and Educational Technology, 14,* 65–73.

Hartley, J., & Burnhill, P. (1977b). Understanding instructional text: Typography, layout, and design. In M. J. A. Howe (Ed.). *Adult Learning.* London: John Wiley.

Helson, H. (1974). Current trends and issues in adaption-level theory. In P. A. Fried (Ed.). *Readings in Perception: Principle and Practice.* Lexington, MA: D. C. Heath and Co..

Henney, M. (1981). The effect of all-capital print versus regular mixed print as displayed on a micro-computer screen on reading speed and accuracy. *Educational Communications and Technology Journal, 31,* 126.

Hewson, D. (1988). *Introduction to Desktop Publishing.* San Francisco, CA: Chronicle Books.

Holliday, W. G., Brunner, L. L., & Donais, E. L. (1977). Differential cognitive and affective responses to flow diagrams in science. *Journal of Reasearch in Science Teaching, 14,* 2, 129–138.

Horn, R. E. (1982). Structured writing and text design. In D. H. Jonassen (Ed.). *The Technology of Text: Principles for Structuring, Designing, and Displaying Text. Volume 1.* Englewood Cliffs, NJ: Educational Technology Publications.

Horn, R. E. (1985). Results with structured writing using Information Mapping™ writing service standards. In T. M. Duffy & R. H. W. Waller (Eds.). *Designing Usable Texts.* Orlando, FL: Academic Press.

Ibison, R. A. (1952). *Differential Effect on the Recall of Textual Materials Associated with the Inclusion of Colored and Uncolored Illustrations.* Unpublished Doctoral Dissertation, Indiana University, Bloomington.

Isaacs, G. (1987). Text screen design for computer-assisted learning. *British Journal of Educational Technology, 18,* 41–51.

Jahoda, G., Cheyne, W. M., Deregowski, J. B., Sinha, D., & Collingbourne, R. (1976). Utilization of pictorial information in classroom learning: A cross cultural study. *AVCR, 24,* 3, 295– 315.

Jarvella, R. J. (1971). Syntactic processing of connected speech. *Journal of Verbal Learning and Verbal Behavior, 10,* 409–416.

Jonassen, D. H. (1982). *The Technology of Text: Principles for Structuring, Designing, and Displaying Text. Volume 1.* Englewood Cliffs, NJ: Educational Technology Publications.

Jonassen, D. H. (1985). *The Technology of Text: Principles for Structuring, Designing, and Displaying Text. Volume 2.* Englewood Cliffs, NJ: Educational Technology Publications.

Jonassen, D. H., & Kirschener, P. A. (1982). Introduction to section 2: Explicit techniques for structuring text. In D. H. Jonassen (Ed.). *The Technology of Text: Principles for Structuring, Designing, and Displaying Text. Volume 1.* Englewood Cliffs, NJ: Educational Technology Publications.

Kallison, J. M. (1986). Effects of lesson organization on achievement. *American Educational Research Journal, 23,* 2, 337–347.

Katzman, N., & Nyenhuis, J. (1972). Color vs. black-and-white: Effects on learning, opinion, and attention. *AV Communication Review, Spring,* 16–28.

Keller, J., & Burkman, E. (1993). Motivation principles. In M. Fleming & W. H. Levie (Eds.). *Instructinal Message Design* (2nd ed.). Englewood Cliffs, NJ: Educational Technology Publications.

Kinney, G. C., & Showman, D. J. (1967). The relative legibility of upper-case and lower-case typewritten words. *Information Display, 4,* 34–39.

Kintsch, W., & van, Dijk, T. A. (1978). Towards a model of text comprehension and production. *Psychological Review, 85,* 363–394.

Kleper, M. L. (1987). *The Illustrated Handbook of Desktop Publishing and Typesetting.* Blue Ridge Summit, PA: Tab Books.

Kolers, P. A., Duchnicky, R. L., & Ferguson, D. C. (1981). Eye movement measurement of readability of CRT displays. *Human Factors, 23,* 517–524.

Lamberski, R. J. (1972). *An Exploratory Investigation of the Instructional Effect of Color and Black and White Cueing on Immediate and Delayed Retention.* Masters Thesis, The Pennsylvania State University.

Lang, K. (1987). *The Writer's Guide to Desktop Publishing.* London: Academic Press.

Lawson, L. (1968). Ophthalmological factors in learning disabilities. In H. Myklebust (Ed.). *Progress in Learning Disabilities, Volume 1.* New York: Grune and Stratton.

Lenze, J. S. (1991). Serif vs. san serif type fonts: A comparison based on reader comprehension. In D. G. Beauchamp, J. Clark-Baca, & R. A. Braden (Eds.). *Investigating Visual Literacy.* Selected Readings from the 22nd Annual Conference of the International Visual Literacy Association. Blacksburg: Virginia Tech University.

Levie, W. H., & Lentz, R. (1982). Effects of text illustrations: A review of research. *ECTJ, 30,* 195–232.

Levin, J. R., & Lesgold, A. M. (1978). On pictures in prose. *ECTJ, 26,* 233–243.

Lichty, T. (1989). *Design Principles for Desktop Publishers.* Glenview, IL: Scott Foresman and Co.

Lidman, S., & Lund, A. M. (1972). *Berätta med bilder.* Stockholm: Bonniers.

Lindsten, C. (1975). *Hembygdskunskap i årskurs 3. Att inhämta, bearbeta och redovisa kunskaper.* Lund: Liber Läromedel.

Lorch, R. F., & Chen, A. H. (1986). Effects of number signals on reading and recall. *Journal of Educational Psychology, 76,* 263–270.

MacDonald-Ross, M. (1977). How numbers are shown: A review of research on the presentation of quantitative data in texts. *AV Communication Review, Winter,* 359–409.

MacDonald-Ross, M. (1978). Graphics in text. *Review of Research in Education, 5,* 49–85.

Magne, D., & Parknäs, L. (1962). The learning effects of pictures. *British Journal of Educational Psychology, 33,* 265–275.

Marsh, P. O. (1983). *Messages That Work: A Guide to Communication Design.* Englewood Cliffs, NJ: Educational Technology Publications.

Martin, J. (1973). *The Design of Man-Computer Dialogues.* Englewood Cliffs, NJ: Prentice-Hall.

Mayer, R. E. (1993). Problem-solving principles. In M. Fleming & W. H. Levie (Eds.). *Instructional Message Design* (2nd ed.). Englewood Cliffs, NJ: Educational Technology Publications.

Melin, L. (1986a). *Text, bild, lexivision. En studie i text-bild-samverkan i en lärobok.* Stockholm: Stockholm University, Department of Nordic Languages.

Melin, L. (1986b). *Termer—Ett kompendium om terminologi och termbildning.* Stockholm: Stockholm University, Department of Nordic Languages.

Meyer, B. J. F. (1985). Signaling the structure of text. In D. H. Jonassen (Ed.). *The Technology of Text: Principles for Structuring, Designing, and Displaying Text. Volume 2.* Englewood Cliffs, NJ: Educational Technology Publications.

Miles, J. (1987). *Design for Desktop Publishing.* San Francisco: Chronicle Books.

Misanchuk, E. R. (1989). *Learner Preferences for Typeface (font) and Leading in Print Materials.* Saskatoon, SK: Division of Extension and Community Relations, The University of Saskatchewan. (ERIC Document Reproduction Service No. ED 307 854). Cited by E. R. Misanchuk (1992). *Preparing Instructional Text: Document Design Using Desktop Publishing.* Englewood Cliffs, NJ: Educational Technology Publications.

Misanchuk, E. R. (1992). *Preparing Instructional Text: Document Design Using Desktop Publishing.* Englewood Cliffs, NJ: Educational Technology Publications.

Murch, G. M. (1973). *Visual and Auditory Perception.* Indianapolis: The Bobbs-Merrill Co.

Paivio, A. (1979). *Imagery and Verbal Processes.* Hillsdale, NJ: Lawrence Erlbaum Associates.

Paivio, A. (1983). The empirical case for dual coding. In J.C. Yuille (Ed.). *Imagery, Memory, and Cognition.* Hillsdale, NJ: Lawrence Erlbaum Associates.

Parker, R. C. (1988). *The Aldus Guide to Basic Design* (2nd ed.). Seattle, WA: Aldus Corporation.

Paterson, D. G., & Tinker, M. A. (1932). Studies of typographical factors influencing speed of reading: X. Styles of type face. *Journal of Applied Psychology, 16,* 605–613.

Paterson, D. G., & Tinker, M. A. (1940). *How to Make Type Readable.* New York: Harper

Perfetti, C. (1977). Language comprehension and fast decoding: Some psycholinguistic prerequisites for skilled reading comprehension. In J. Guthrie (Ed.). *Cognition, Curriculum, and Comprehension.* Newark, DE: International Reading Association.

Pettersson, R. (1983a). Factors in visual language: Image framing. *Visual Literacy Newsletter, 12,* 9 and *12,* 10.

Pettersson, R. (1983b).*Visuals for Instruction.* (CLEA–Report No. 12). Stockholm: Stockholm University, Department of Computer Science.

Pettersson, R. (1984). *Interplay of Visuals and Legends.* Presentation at the Information Design Conference. Dec. 17–19.

Pettersson, R. (1985). *Intended and Perceived Image Content.* Presentation at the 17th Annual Conference of the International Visual Literacy Association. Claremont, CA. Nov. 1–2.

Pettersson, R. (1986a). See, look, and read. *Journal of Visual Verbal Languaginge,* Spring, 33–39.

Pettersson, R. (1986b). *Image-Word-Image.* Presentation at the 18th Annual Conference of the International Visual Literacy Association. Madison, Wisconsin, Oct. 30 – Nov. 2.

Pettersson, R. (1989). *Visuals for Information: Research and Practice.* Englewood Cliffs, NJ: Educational Technology Publications.

Pettersson, R. (1990). *What Is Infology?* Paper presented at the International Visual Literacy Association Symposium 1990. Verbo-Visual Literacy. Mapping the Field. July 10–13. University of London, Institute of Education.

Postman, N. (1979). *Teaching as a Conserving Activity.* New York: Delacorte Press.

Poulton, E. C., & Brown, C. H. (1968). Rate of comprehension of an existing teleprinter output and of possible alternatives. *Applied Psaychology, 52,* 16–21.

Rambally, G. K., & Rambally, R. S. (1987). Human factors in CAI design. *Computing Education, 11(2),* 149–153.

Reynolds Myers, P. (1985). Visual literacy, higher order reasoning, and high technology. In N. H. Thayer & S. Clayton-Randolph (Eds.). *Visual Literacy: Cruising into the Future.* Readings from the 16th Annual Conference of the International Visual Literacy Association. Bloomington: Western Sun Printing Co.

Romiszowski, A. J. (1986). *Developing Auto-Instructional Materials: From Programmed Texts to CAL and Interactive Video.* New York: Nichols Publishing.

Rothkopf, E. Z. (1970). The concept of mathemagenic activities. *Review of Educational Research, 40(3),* 325–336.

Rubens, P.M. (1986). A reader's view of text and graphics—implications for transactional text. *Journal of Technical Writing and Communication, 16,* 73–86.

Samuels, S. J. (1970). Effects of pictures on learning to read, comprehension, and attitudes. *Review of Educational Research, 40,* 397–407.

Samuels, S. J., Biesbrock, E., & Terry, P. R. (1974). The effects of pictures on children's attitudes towards presented stories. *Journal of Educational Research, 67*, 243–246.

Schwarz, E., Beldie, I. P., & Pastoor, S. (1983). A comparison of paging and scrolling for changing screen contents by inexperienced users. *Human Factors, 25(3)*, 279–282.

Sinatra, R. (1986). *Visual Literacy Connections to Thinking, Reading, and Writing*. Springfield, IL: Charles C. Thomas.

Sperry, R. (1973). Lateral specialization of cerebral functions in the surgically separated hemispheres. In F. J. McGuigan & R. A. Schoonever (Eds.). *The Psychophysiology of Thinking: Studies of Covert Processes*. New York: Academic Press.

Sperry, R. (1982). Some effects of disconnecting the hemisphere. *Science, 217*, 1223–1226.

Sporrstedt, B. (1980). Kring en bildvärld. *Synpunkt, populär tidskrift för konst, 5*, 6–7.

Stine, E. A. L. (1990). The way reading and listening work: A tutorial review of discourse processing and aging. In E. A. Lovelace (Ed.). *Aging and Cognition: Mental Processes, Self Awareness, and Interventions.* North Holland: Elsevier Science Publishers.

Taylor, J. F. A. (1964). *Design and Expression in Visual Arts*. New York: Dover.

Thompson, P., & Davenport, P. (1980). *The Dictionary of Visual Language*. London: Bergstrom & Boyle.

Tinker, M. A. (1963). *The Legibility of Print*. Ames: Iowa State University Press.

Tinker, M. A. (1965). *Bases for Effective Reading*. Minneapolis: University of Minnesota Press.

Tobias, S. (1984). *Macroprocesses, Individual Differences, and Instructional Methods*. EDRS. ED 259 019.

Tufte, E. R. (1983). *The Visual Display of Quantitative Information*. Cheshire, CT: Graphics Press.

Walker, P. (1990). A lesson in leading. *Aldus Magazine*, March/April, 45–47.

Waller, R. (1987). *The Typographic Contribution to Language: Towards a Model of Typographic Genres and Their Underlying Structures*. University of Reading, Department of Typograhy & Graphic Communication.

Weidenman, B. (1988). Der flüchtige Blick beim stehenden Bild: Zur oberflächlichen Verarbeitung von pädagogishen Illustrationen. (The Careless View in the Case of Standing Picture.) *Zeitschrift für Lernforschung, 16*, 3, 43–57.

Weismann, D. L. (1974). *The Visual Arts as a Human Experience*. Englewood Cliffs, NJ: Prentice-Hall.

Weitzman, K. (1970). *Illustrations in Role and Context*. Princeton: Princeton University Press.

Wendt, D. (1979). An experimental approach to the improvement of the typographic design of textbooks. *Visible Language, 13*, 2, 108–133.

West, S. (1987). Design for desktop publishing. In the Waite Group (J. Stockford, Ed.). *Desktop Publishing Bible*. Indianapolis, IN: Howard W. Sams.

Whalley, P., & Fleming, R. (1975). An experiment with a simple recorder of reading behavior. *Programmed Learning and Educational Technology, 12*, 120–124.

White, J. (1983). *Mastering Graphics*. New York: Bowker.

White, J. (1987). *New Strategies for Editing and Design*. Presentations at Trialog 87, Stockholm.

Whiteside, C., & Blohm, P. (1985). The effects of CRT text color and decision making tasks on learners' recall. In N. H. Thayer & S. Clayton-Randolph (Eds.). *Visual Literacy: Cruising into the Future*. Readings from the 16th Annual Conference of the International Visual Literacy Association. Bloomington, IN: Western Sun Printing Co.

Whiteside, J. A., Whiteside, F. M., & Griffin, R. E. (1989). *The Structured Writing Technique of Visually Organizing Content: Its Roots and Fruits*. Paper presented at the 21th Annual Conference of the International Visual Literacy Association. Scottsdale, Oct. 25–29.

Winn, W. (1989). The design and use of instructional graphics. In H. Mandl & J. R. Levin (Eds.). *Knowledge Acquisition from Text and Pictures*. North-Holland: Elsevier Science Publishers.

Winn, W. (1993). Perception principles. In M. Fleming & W. H. Levie (Eds.). *Instructional Message Design* (2nd ed.). Englewood Cliffs, NJ: Educational Technology Publications.

Wright, P. (1968). Using tabulated information. *Ergonomics, 11(4)*, 331-343.

Wright, P. (1980). The comprehension of tabulated information: Some similarities between reading tables. *NSPI Journal, 19(8)*, 25–29.

Wright, P. (1982). A user-oriented approach to the design of tables and flowcharts. In D.H. Jonassen (Ed.). *The Technology of Text: Principles for Structuring, Designing, and Displaying Text.* Englewood Cliffs, NJ: Educational Technology Publications.

Wright, P., & Fox, K. (1970). Presenting information in tables. *Applied Ergonomics, 1(4)*,234–242.

Wright, P., & Lickorish, A. (1983). Proof-reading texts on screen and paper. *Behavior and Information Technology, 2(3)*, 227–235.

Zachrisson, B. (1965). *Studies in the Legibility of Printed Text.* Stockholm: Almqvist and Wiksell.

Zettl, H. (1973). *Sight. Sound. Motion.* Belmont, CA: Wadsworth.

Zimmer, A., & Zimmer, F. (1978). *Visual Literacy in Communication: Designing for Development.* Hulton Educational Publications Ltd., in cooperation with the International Institute for Adult Methods, Teheran.

Chapter 8

MEDIA FORMATS

Our perception of a visual is affected by its medium, e.g., as a photograph, a printed image, a slide projected on a white screen, a view-finder image, a computer-generated image, etc. A movie evokes completely different perceptions when a viewer watches it alone on TV (possibly via a VCR) or in a crowded movie theater with a wide-screen and high-quality sound and images.

An image is a multidimensional representation of an inner or external reality, depicting the physical structure of the objects or events it represents. An image can also be described as a more or less complicated sense of vision, i.e., awareness of the stimulation of the eye's vision perception cells, with a specific message/content. An inner image, a visual experience, can originate in thoughts and in dreams. It may be caused by words, e.g., a picture description, without any help of pictures. Every possible visual, every format has different possibilities of supplying specific message/content. This depends on the choice of material and type of production.

IMAGE MORPHOLOGY

Mirror images and other virtual images, created by mirrors, lenses, and other optical systems, can be seen but not "captured" and shown on a screen of any sort. A virtual image is located in a point from which divergent light beams seem to start before they have passed the optical system. Like our inner images, e.g., memories, virtual images lack an obvious physical format. All other kinds of images have a physical format.

An artist or a painter producing a picture may use lead, crayons, India ink, various kinds of paint, paper, canvas, and several other kinds of material in a variety of different combinations. The image is gradually produced by combinations of dots, lines, and areas. The actual picture is built up from materials and pigments which, according to intentions, can be completely separated or gradually mixed.

In technical systems the whole motif may be captured at once with a traditional camera, or it may be scanned line by line with a TV-camera. Except for the printing of line drawings, all other pictures have to be *divided into small elements*, picture elements, or *pixels*, in the technical process of duplication, e.g., in the printing of books or in the broadcasting of television. The image has vertical (y) and horizontal (x) resolution and it has also "depth resolution" (z). An individual pixel may vary with respect to shape, size, position, value, grain, color, and grey scale.

Normally these pixels are very small. At normal reading distance they can hardly be seen. In fact *an image with "good quality" must have a resolution that is better than that of our own vision.*

The necessary number and size of individual pixels will be defined by:
* the size of the object depicted,
* the size of the image,
* the viewing distance,
* the image content, and
* the actual material carrying the image (paper, film, glass, etc.).

Close viewing distances require the images to be divided into many small pixels. For long viewing distances it is enough with fewer and larger pixels.

Perception of pixels

Pixels are always small in relation to the screen on which they are displayed. The greater the number of pixels used by a system for image formation in a given area, the greater the system's sharpness and resolution. When resolution is good, a black or white pixel cannot be distinguished from other adjacent black or white pixels. This applies both to monitor screens and copies on paper, plastic, or film. However, an individual white (black) pixel is highly visible when surrounded by black (white) pixels. When black and white pixels are evenly distributed in an image, individual pixels become indistinguishable. The image then assumes a grey appearance. Thus, our perception of an individual pixel is always heavily influenced by the context in which the pixel appears. The relative distribution of black and white pixels, or the "sum" of each pixel's context, is decisive to our perception of image content. Purely random distribution of pixels produces a grey, uninteresting pattern. A controlled, *intentional* distribution of pixels can result in different patterns or depictions. Moving or changing the pixels in a picture enables us to create thousands of new images. Computers process each variation as a different picture. But a human viewer may regard these images as functionally identical or equivalent. Analogously, a text can be presented in many different ways, with different typefaces and pitches, etc., with no major effect on perception of the text's content.

Normally speaking, an individual pixel is insignificant from a visual language point of view. A surprisingly large number of pixels can be deleted from an image. When performing image analysis, a computer is usually incapable of deciding whether or not an individual pixel is significant to the image. A pixel may be an important feature of a basic graphic image element (a dot, a line, or an area) or of a simple shape, thereby contributing to a visual sub-meaning or syntagm. So we can delete, add, or shift information in an image without drastically affecting perception of image contents. The pixels which form borders/edges between different shapes are more important to picture perception than other pixels. Since the brain fills in missing information and always strives to make the best possible interpretation of a given stimulus, the deletion of even some meaningful parts of a picture is also possible. In cartoons, absent lines can be as important as the lines actually present. The ability to utilize the "right" amount of graphic image elements and to find the "right" balance in a picture are characteristics of experienced and skilled artists, photographers, and graphic designers. Too little information results in an inadequate picture. Too much information results in a picture which is hard to decipher and comprehend. There is an ideal trade-off for every type of picture content and for every application.

Analog and digital coding

Whether information is stored in analog or digital codes is of major importance. Analog coding takes up much less space than digital coding. Video data stored in analog form is suitable, for example, for entertainment when sequential viewing of a program from beginning to end is desired.

The following example illustrates the difference between analog and digital storage of information. A single page of a book can hold about 2,500 characters (i.e., 50 lines containing 50 characters, including spaces). Storing the same page information in digital form would require 20,000 bits of information (binary ones and/or zeros).

This may seem like a great deal but is still almost negligible compared to the storage and transmission of information in other media. Here are some equivalents: a line drawing is equivalent to five pages of text, one second of FM radio to ten pages of text, one second of digital sound on a compact disc to 35 pages of text, one second of TV to 250 pages of text, one second of HDTV to 1,500 pages of text, and one frame (a scene) from the SPOT-satellite is equivalent to no less than 50,000 pages of text.

Thus, digitally stored information always takes up much more space than information stored in analog form. Provided that the number of pixels is large enough, digitally stored information offers numerous opportunities for easy and convenient "manipulation" and editing of text, sound, or image in different ways. This may be highly important in different kinds of interactive applications, such as multimedia systems for education and training.

The editing of a written text can result in the production of a "message" with fewer words. In speech synthesis, i.e., computer-generated speech, the amount of transmitted information can sometimes be reduced by 99% with no loss of message comprehension, even if the aesthetic quality of the speech may decline. In a similar manner, the number of pixels in an image can be reduced without any major impact on the image's message. Thus, it is possible to more effectively make use of computer memory capacity.

COMPUTER IMAGES

Computer images are *digital*. In some image systems the square or rectangular pixel is either white (light) or black (dark). In other systems the pixels can be varied in a grey-scale and/or in a color range.

The number of colors that can be reproduced depends on which computer, which operating system, which program, and which computer screen is used. Quite often eight bits of information is used for red, green, and blue colors, respectively, and eight bits for text and graphical effects. Each color can be stored in 256 levels. In total it is possible to create 16 millions of nuances in the image.

Pixels are always small compared to the screen. The more pixels within a given area the better the sharpness and the more details in the system. Pixels in large systems can actually be much larger than whole screens in smaller systems.

Creation of computer images

For too long the creation of illustrations was time-consuming, expensive, and usually required the use of an outside artist or design service. As a result of this many publications were created without illustrations or with only a few. Now several very easy-to-use drawing programs, charting programs, and even digital clip-art files make it possible for anyone to create simple but good-looking graphics and other line drawings. Pictures can be handled in bit-mapped form, as object oriented descriptions or as a combination of the same.

A *bit-mapped picture* consists of a large number of small pixels or picture elements, e.g., small squares. These pixels have either a color (usually black, but they may also be, e.g., green or blue, depending on the design of the screen) or no color at all. All pixels have the same size. In "paint-programs" like MacPaint for the Macintosh you have a lot of different painting tools. You can draw all kinds of figures in free hand and you can easily change any individual pixel. Bit-mapped graphics can be modified, stretched, condensed, inverted, rotated, and outlined. Programs like MacPaint are effective multi-purpose drawing tools.

When a bit-mapped picture is printed the black pixels get the color of the print medium (usually black), and the white pixels get the color of the paper (usually white). The relative distribution of printed and non-printed pixels builds the image. The more pixels, the better the resolution. Normally the resolution is not at all "good enough" to create a suitable picture. This is especially true if we need to change the scale of a picture. Apart from lines in vertical and horizontal positions, all other lines get a rugged appearance. The image quality is the same when printed with a laser printer or with an advanced photo-typesetter.

An *object oriented picture* is defined by a number of mathematical algorithms. A coordinate system holds all the information on where lines, circles, squares, rectangles, and other shapes start and stop. Shapes can be filled with various patterns and delineated with different lines. This means that an image can be scaled up and scaled down without loss of quality. The image is re-drawn according to the specifications set by the new size. For object oriented pictures the quality is defined by the quality of the printer. The better the printer, the better the technical quality of the picture. MacDraw is an example of an object oriented program. Object oriented programs are especially suited for more advanced uses such as drafting and charting. Some programs can handle really large drawings.

The production of charts and graphs may be very time-consuming. Several computer programs can convert traditional tabular data to various kinds of graphics. These programs allow you to enter all the values needed, into a spreadsheet-style grid. They take the information, do all the calculations and present the results as line charts, bar charts, pie charts, scatter charts, and combinations of those styles. Once data is entered you can usually choose from several different presentations.

A *hybrid picture* is created by using programs combining the bit-map and the object oriented programs.

A number of "clip art" packages containing ready-to-use drawings of people, buildings, cars, boats, tools, animals, plants, etc., are available. Clip art programs are usually created in bit-map technique. The drawings may easily be changed and modified to fit a special style. Like all other computer pictures they can be integrated with text.

Computer screens

Computer screens can be constructed and manufactured in many different ways and have very different characteristics. Picture tubes, liquid crystals, plasma screens, magnetic field boards, light emitting diodes, projection systems, and head up displays will be mentioned here.

Picture tubes

A picture tube or a *cathode ray tube* is the unit that produces and shows the picture on a TV-receiver, computer, or terminal screen. The picture tube consists of an airless glass-tube. Its rear end contains a device which emits electronic rays, while the front part forms the screen. The back of the screen is illuminated when hit by the electrons; and, by steering the ray over the screen, a picture is built up. For color synthesis in a cathode ray tube a range of colors can be produced by the additive combinations of a very limited amount of radiation. The *additive color combination* starts in dark adding light to produce color.

Liquid crystals

Liquid crystals can be used for instrument displays or screens:

LCD

An LCD, Liquid Crystal Display, contains a liquid whose molecules lie parallel when an electronic current passes. Between polarizing filters the crystals then look dark. The technique is common in, for example, wrist watches. Here every element in the digits is connected so that it can be turned on and off. In larger screens there is a net of crossing semi-conductors behind the crystal layer. A dark dot appears in every crossing when the current is turned on. A picture is built up quite slowly.

FLCD

An FLCD, Ferro-electric Liquid Crystal Display, is a flat screen with liquid crystals. The ferro-electric crystals work tens of thousands times faster than the normal LCD. They give better contrast and use less energy.

Plasma screens

Plasma screens are flat screens with a network of anodes and cathodes. When the points are made live, a neon-like gas starts glowing. Plasma screens are sharper but require more energy than LCD-screens.

Magnetic field board

At the Electronic Publishing Exhibition in Tokyo in 1989 an electronic magnetic field board was presented. The board consists of small hexagons containing a black magnetic material, like iron filings. Close-up the board looks like a honeycomb. By using a magnetic head, a "page" with text or images can be built up. The information is put in by a computer. The board is "erased" by changing the magnetic field. It is also possible to write directly on the board with either a magnetic pen or with markers of different colors.

Light-emitting diodes

Comview and ComFuture are modular designed image systems, *LED-displays*, for indoor and outdoor use. The picture area may vary between one square meter and 48 m^2. The system is directed by a computer which can adapt a signal from a videotape recorder or a computer. The resolution is 6,400 pixels per m^2. The pixels consist of red and green light-emitting diodes with high efficiency, i.e., low power consumption and long life. So far no blue diodes have been developed.

Screens with light-emitting diodes are used for advertising. By turning the diodes on and off it is possible to create simple animations, for example, text and simple graphics moving across the screen.

Projection systems

There are several possibilities of projecting computer images. A transparent or semitransparent flat screen with liquid crystals can be placed on an overhead projector, which transfers the image to a projection screen.

Head up displays

A Head Up Display, a HUD, is a special type of helmet used in advanced flight simulators and recently in Virtual Reality systems. Computer generated images are projected by fiber-optics onto the curved visor in front of the pilot's face. In the simulator the pilot gets a flying experience very true to life.

In simpler simulator systems computer-graphics are projected onto several screens, replacing the windows, or located just outside the cockpit of the boat, car, or aircraft.

GRAPHICAL PICTURES

Single copies of graphical visuals can be hand-crafted using a number of different techniques like drawing with a pencil, charcoal, crayons, and pens; painting in water colors, acrylics, oils, etc. Multiple copies of graphical visuals can be produced using technical equipment for printing, print out, or copying.

There are many kinds of visuals and we can use several different criteria for classification. As far as *production technology* is concerned it is practical to distinguish between line-art or "full-tone pictures" and "half-tone pictures" like photographs.

Full-tone pictures

All line-art or "full-tone pictures" are built up by dots, lines, and areas of solid paint. Line drawings, schematic illustrations, maps, and business graphics all belong to this category. Full-tone pictures can be in black-and-white as well as in color. When color pictures are printed we need one printing plate for each color. To be able to achieve this we have to produce one original for each color. Thus, the picture is "manually" divided into its various color components.

Half-tone pictures

To be able to reproduce the fine nuances of a photograph or some fine art the original picture must be divided into small picture elements. A *reproduction camera* is used for photographical separation (analog technology). Here raster-screens are used to transfer the original image into a raster-image. It is also possible to use a scanner (digital technology) to create the raster-image. In the scanner a light beam scans the complete picture area. The beam "reads" all the nuances in the picture. This information is converted to the raster-dots that are employed in the printing of the picture. In both cases the number of raster-dots within an area will define the quality of the final printed image.

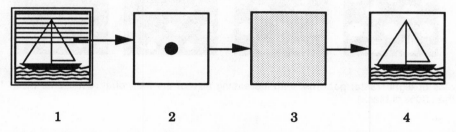

1   2   3   4

A photograph is read in a scanner (1) e.g., with 100 lines per inch. Then each registered pixel (2) gets a value between 0 and 100% of, e.g., black. In the photo-typesetter this "grey level" is transformed to a raster-dot within the "pixel-area" (3). The raster-dots can be created with a resolution of, e.g., 1,200 lines per inch. In the printed picture (4) the individual printed dots may be seen with the aid of a magnifying glass.

Black and white

The photos we see in books and newspapers are really collections of small dots. These printed dots vary in size within the fixed "pixel-area" from nothing or a very small dot to gradually increasing dot-sizes, until the dot covers the complete "pixel-area." Smaller dots give the *impression* of light grey areas, and larger dots give the *impression* of darker tones. Thus, it is possible to reproduce photos, drawings, and other originals with (perceived) scales of grey. (Note that half-tone rasters will only *simulate grey*, due to the imperfection of our vision. The only way to really achieve the color grey is to print with grey printing ink.)

In newspaper production, rasters with a density of 50 to 65 lines per inch may be used in the pre-press process. For book production, rasters with a density of 100 to 133 lines, or more, per inch may be used. Higher-quality printing allows half-tone rasters of up to 300 lines per inch, resulting in images with dots so small that you can hardly see them at all.

The films that are used to make printing plates may be produced using photo-typesetting machines, working with resolutions of 600 lines per inch for the newspaper plates and 1,200 lines per inch for the book plates. An image, say a two by two inch portrait, may be printed with 10,000 dots in a newspaper and 40,000 dots in a book.

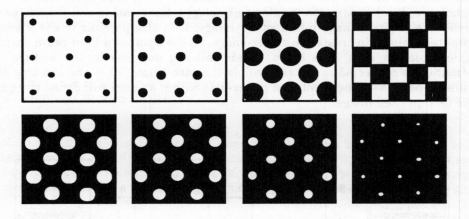

Examples of eight "raster patterns" with increasing size of the individual raster dots (from 10% to more than 90% of black).

A large outdoor placard printed with low resolution may be at least one thousand times larger than the same advertisement printed with high resolution in a magazine. Both images may have an equal number of pixels.

Color

Images in color have to be separated using different color filters. This can be done photographically with a reproduction camera (analog technology) or electronically with a scanner (digital technology). Images in color are separated into four different half-tone films: blue, yellow, red, and black. A printing plate is generated from each film. The picture is then printed in each color, resulting in a "four-color-process" visual.

Looking at a picture printed in color we experience a *subtractive color combination*. The inks, dyes, and pigments function like filters for the white light. The light is absorbed in different ways. When printing on white paper, yellow and red ink produce orange. Blue and yellow create green. Red and blue give purple. Yellow, red, and blue will become black. However, since black ink is used for printing of the text, it is also used for the printing of pictures. The black ink gives the picture a distinct sharpness and more solid dark parts. To achieve the best possible print quality the red color that is used (magenta) is somewhat violet, and the blue color used (cyan) is somewhat light. For the printing of black and white pictures, only one film and one plate are needed.

The easiest way to understand printed dots is to examine a printed picture. In a newspaper, the printed dots can be seen with the aid of a magnifying glass. On outdoor advertisements, and posters you can often see the individual printed dots even without a magnifying glass if you look at it from a normal reading distance.

Scanners

There are several types of scanners, from equipment designed for amateurs to equipment for professional use. Desktop digitizers and drum scanners will be mentioned here.

Desktop digitizers

Since photography includes a full spectrum of greys it is not possible for a computer, working in a bit-mapped mode, to represent the shades of grey. It can only show black and white.

There are different kinds of digitizers. A *scanner* allows the user to digitize all kinds of illustrations on a paper. Desktop scanners work with CCD-technology (Charge Coupled Device). A CCD-cell consists of a number of light sensitive crystals that can transform light into digital codes. Most desktop scanners work with 300 or 400 dots per inch. The scanner can digitize an image either as a full-tone picture or as a half-tone picture. In full-tone pictures each pixel is black or white.

However, desktop systems are more or less only at a halfway point in the reproduction of photographs and fine arts. The low resolution of computer screens, scanners, and laser printers, and the vast amount of storage that it takes to store a high-resolution image electronically make digitized images possible only as low-quality simulations of photographs.

So far good half-tones can only be produced by professional printers. A positive half-tone on paper can be pasted on the printout from the laser printer. The other alternative is to leave an empty space for the picture so that the printer can add a half-tone film negative in the pre-press process.

Drum-scanners

Large systems for integrated image and text processing often contain a drum-scanner. The original, a slide, or a print is fixed on a rotating drum. A laser beam reads the picture with a resolution of up to 300 lines per inch creating up to 75 dots per inch for yellow, cyan, magenta, and black, respectively.

The digital image information can then be processed in different ways. It is possible to change the scale, crop the picture, and manipulate the contents. It is, for example, possible to move picture elements, make copies, put in text or symbols, etc.

Printers

Digital computer pictures can be printed by several types of printers. Laser printers, photo-typesetters, plotters, thermal printers, ink-jet printers, color bubble-jet printers, telefax, telephoto, and dot matrix printers will be mentioned here.

Laser printers

A laser printer is an electrostatic device in which a laser beam is scanned across the surface of an electrically charged selenium coated drum. This is done with a rotating polygonal mirror. The charge of the drum surface is modulated according to the dot matrix character patterns. A whole page with text and images is built up by a page description language (for example, PostScript) and then transferred to a paper as in a conventional Xerographic printer.

Laser printers often have had a resolution of 300 or 400 dots per inch. For these printers it is hard to reproduce more than a few grey levels. When printing many grey levels the dots get far too large and the resolution too poor as they are built up by available "dots." However, some laser printers manage 1,200 dots per inch horizontally and 600 dots per inch vertically. This is enough for good reproduction of half-tone pictures. Laser printers with 600 DPI appeared commonly worldwide toward the end of 1992 and soon will be the world standard for desktop users, rendering 300 dot printers obsolescent.

Usually laser printers have one toner that mainly consists of coal powder. There are, however, also toners in blue, brown, green, yellow, magenta, cyan, and red.

Photo-typesetters

A photo-typesetter usually works with high quality such as 1,250–2,600 dots per inch. This is good enough to create very small and close raster dots and to reproduce a great number of grey levels. Print-outs are made on photographic materials, paper, or film, which are then used to produce printing plates. In order to get really good half-tone pictures, the quality of a photo-typesetter is required.

Plotters

A plotter works with one or more exchangeable pens which draw lines, graphs, diagrams, drawings, or pictures in ink in several colors directly on paper or film in different formats.

The resolution is normally 50-100 dots per inch. The highest known resolution produced by a plotter is 300 dots per inch. In a flat bed plotter the paper is placed on a plane surface. The prints can often be carried out in large formats.

Thermal printers

Thermal printers print dot matrix characters. A font is equipped with small needles. These point to an especially prepared, heat-sensitive paper. The needles are heated in a pattern which corresponds to the character to be printed, and the heat-sensitive paper is affected. Thermal printers usually have a resolution of 200 dots per inch.

To create color pictures, foils with yellow, magenta, and cyan color are used. By combining these foils a great number of colors can be produced. In desktop systems the number of colors is 256. In this system the color is heated over to the image paper point by point. There are also thermal printers which heat up small ampoules inside a special paper so that the color spreads inside the paper.

Ink-jet printers

An ink-jet printer is an impact printer where the characters are formed by an ink jet on normal office paper. The ink-jet printer does not work with raster-dots but varies the number of ink drops within a given area. Few drops give light colors. Many drops give darker colors. The system is thus creating the same kind of effect as the systems working with half-tone pictures. Many ink-jet printers work with pictures printed out with a resolution of 200-250 dots per inch.

Color Bubble-Jet Printers

In this printer each of four high-density bubble-jet print heads has 128 vertically arranged nozzles. With this printer digitally stored images can be printed in full color with a vertical and horizontal resolution of 400 dots per inch. The maximum image width is 472 mm. Plain paper, in 50 meter rolls, is used. It is possible to use four out of seven colors (black, red, green, blue, yellow, magenta, and cyan).

In this system all ink dots have the same size. However, the number of dots within an area can be altered. Many dots create dark tones and few dots create light tones. Each nozzle has a heater. When the heater operates the heat produces small bubbles. Ink evaporates abruptly and the bubbles inflate. After cooling, each bubble contracts. The ink splashes out of the nozzle and the bubbles disappear.

Telefax

The telefax is used to send text and image information via the telephone network. The area of the paper is usually divided into approximately 2 million pixels: 50 dots per inch horizontally and 90-385 dots per inch vertically. The very best resolution divides an A4-paper into 6 million pixels.

It is common that telefax machines work thermally with heat sensitive paper in rolls of approximately 100 meters. There are, however, also fax machines built on laser printers. Many telefax machines can be connected to personal computers and then can be used both as scanners and printers.

Telephoto

Telephoto or *photofax* is a special kind of telefax equipment used for sending and receiving pictures in a full grey scale. There is also a system for color pictures that transmits the pictures color-separated. The transmission is done over the radio or the telephone network. Telephoto pictures are mostly used by newspapers and by some TV stations.

Dot matrix printers

A dot matrix printer is an impact printer. It produces dot matrix characters by pressing thin needle points, "needles" arranged in a matrix pattern, 5 x 7, 7 x 7, or 7 x 9, to a carbon paper or a ribbon lying close to a paper. The needles form different characters, letter, digits, or parts of a picture.

Dot matrix printers work with a resolution of 50-100 dots per inch. This is the same resolution as that of many computer screens but considerably inferior to the print-out quality of laser printers.

Photographic copies
Photographic copies have the highest hard copy quality. The chemical constitution of film and paper gives the limits for resolution.

Printing
Printing is the process of producing multiple copies of an original using a printing press. A printing press consists of some means for feeding the paper (or some other material) in contact with an inked image carrier and a system for delivering of the copies. There are four major categories of printing processes: relief, intaglio, the planographic process, and screen printing. In all systems text and pictures are reversed in the printing forms that transfer the printing ink onto the paper, where it appears in the correct position.

Relief printing
In relief printing the printing areas are raised above the nonprinting areas, and the impression is made directly from the inked raised surface to the paper. There are several relief printing technologies: woodcut, wood engraving, letterpress, and flexography.

Woodcut
The image is cut in a plate of wood, a wood block, which transfers the printing ink to the paper. It is very hard to produce text in small fonts on a plate of wood. The lines in the picture are usually rough.

The woodcut is the oldest form of printmaking. It can be traced back to ancient Egypt, Babylonia, and China, where wooden stamps were used to make decorative patterns or symbols in wax or clay. Blocks may have been used to print textiles in India as early as 400 B.C.

Wood engraving
In wood engraving, also called *xylography*, the artist engraves the image in the cross-end of hard timber. This method was invented in England 1775 and became very important for the production of illustrated newspapers during the 19th century. To be able to prolong the life of the wood engravings, casts in metal, *stereotypes*, were produced during the middle of the 19th century. Today this method is mainly used as a fine arts technique by graphic artists.

Letterpress
In the letterpress process the image carriers can be cast-metal type, etched-metal plates, or photopolymer plates on which the image or printing areas are raised and the non-image areas are below the surface of the printing areas.

In the production of books photoengravings used to be very common for the printing of illustrations. Photoengraving was first done in 1824. The screen principle was introduced in 1852. The first successful process-color engraving was done in 1893.

There are two kinds of photoengravings: *autotypi* or half-tone block and *fototypi* or line cut. A half-tone picture is photographed in a reproduction camera using a raster to create a raster-image. The raster-image is copied to a photo-sensitive plate of zinc. The plate is etched resulting in a relief. Prior to printing the plate is mounted in the printing form.

There are several kinds of letterpress printing machines, both sheet-fed and web-fed presses. Presses include the platen press, the flatbed cylinder press, and the rotary press.

Flexography

In flexography rubber or plastic plates on cylinders are used. Low costs and solvent inks to speed ink drying are making inroads into book printing, magazines, and even newspapers. Flexography is being used extensively in heat-transfer printing for textiles. It is also a method for production of packaging materials, labels, and wallpaper.

Intaglio

In intaglio, or *gravure*, the image areas are below the surface in "ditches," and ink is removed from the non-printing areas by the scraping action of a metal blade. There are several gravure printing technologies: copperplate engraving, steel-die, dry-point engraving, mezzotint, etching, aquatint engraving, gravure, and rotogravure printing.

Copperplate engraving

In engravings the image or design to be printed is cut directly into a metal surface by the engraver. In copperplate engraving the image is engraved in a plate of copper, which transfers the printing ink to the paper. The line is very distinct and ends in a fine point.

The oldest copy of a copperplate engraving was printed 1446, but it is supposed that the technology existed already a hundred years earlier. Copperplate engravings were first used for book production in 1476. During the 17th century copperplate engraving became the most important method for production of pictures in books. Today this method is mainly used as a fine arts technique by graphic artists.

Mezzotint

In mezzotint the entire surface of the copperplate is first covered with hundreds of small pricks. These are burnished and scraped to create light areas. Mezzotint was invented in the 17th century and was used extensively until the early 19th century. It was the only method by which the many nuances in oil paintings could be reproduced.

Etching

The image is scratched in a flat print plate covered with a layer of an acid-resistant coating, like wax. When the plate is placed in an acid solution the lines are cut, or etched, into the metal. By varying the time for the etching process, it is possible to decide the thickness and blackness of the lines. An etched line has blunt endings. The method of etching has been known since 1523.

Drypoint etching

In drypoint etching the artist works the copper plate with a fine point tool. The line in drypoint engraving is soft and fluffy.

Aquatint
Aquatint engraving is a type of etching specially used for areas with many shades and nuances. In tonal quality aquatint is similar to the wash effect of a watercolor drawing. Aquatint is often combined with other printing techniques, such as line etching. The method has been known since the 17th century.

Gravure
Gravure was first developed in 1875. The printing surface is divided, by means of a screen, into a series of cells etched below the plate surface. The surface may be treated in various ways to produce cells of varying size and depth. Sheet-fed and web-fed presses may be used in gravure. Gravure printing gives good picture quality, but text is fluffy and ragged.

Web-fed presses have the plate wrapped around a cylinder and they can operate at high speeds. They are called cylindrical, or rotary, presses. Such a printing process is called *rotogravure* and is extensively used for printing of weekly publications, catalogues, and brochures in large runs.

Planographic processes
In a planographic process, or *lithography*, the image and non-image areas are on the same plane and are distinguished by making use of the principle that grease and water do not mix. There are two different planographic printing processes: lithography and offset lithography.

Lithography
Originally all lithographs were printed from a flat, lithographic limestone on a flatbed press. The image is drawn on the flat surface of the stone with a greasy crayon, an oily wash, or with India ink. After a chemical treatment the parts of the stone without the image elements are susceptible to water. The printing ink is transferred to the paper from the surface with the image. Lithography was invented in 1798 and has been used for printing of lithographic art, but also posters, placards, cards, advertisements, etc. By 1834 specially treated zinc plates began to replace the heavy stones. The use of photomechanical metal plates in the early 1900s made the technique of hand-transferring from stones obsolete. In the 1930s the deep-etch process was introduced.

Offset lithography
In offset printing, text and images are copied to a photo-sensitive plate of zinc, plastic, or paper. In platemaking the image area is covered with an ink that is grease-receptive, and the non-printing areas are made water-receptive. The plate is mounted on a rotary press. During the printing water and printing ink are supplied by special rollers. The paper or other substrate picks up the impression of the image as the paper travels between the rubber-covered blanket cylinder and an impression cylinder. There are many kinds of offset printing machines, from small office printing machines to very large industrial printing machines. Sheet-fed and web-fed presses may be used. In large offset printing machines it is possible to print four colors directly in one combined process. Today offset printing is very common for printing of newspapers, books, and most kinds of graphical products, including this book.

Screen-printing

In screen-printing, or *silk-screen-printing*, the image is on a screen stencil on silk, plastic, or metal through which ink is forced to the paper. Screen printing originated during the Middle Ages in the art of stencil printing of China and Japan. It was practiced with great delicacy and intricacy. Until the 20th century, screen printing was a decorative and commercial medium, used to enhance fabrics, wallpaper, furnishings, and advertising. Screen printing was introduced in the US about 1910.

In screen-printing the printing form is a fine-meshed screen, mounted over a frame. It was a hand process for many years, used for making signs, banners, posters, and personal greeting cards. In the 1950s techniques for making screen stencils photomechanically were developed. The pores of the mesh are blocked by the stencil in the background or non-image areas, and left open in the areas to be printed. Ink is spread over the screen and pushed through the open mesh areas with a rubber- or plastic-bladed squeegee to produce a print. Screen-printing can lay down the thickest ink film of any of the printing processes. Screen-printing is used for printing on paper, plastic, wood, metal, glass, foil, and textile fabrics. The method is used for printing of posters, placards, and advertisements of various kinds. Silk-screen-printing is also used for many other industrial applications, e.g., for printing of electronic circuit cards. Special equipment can be used for printing of labels on bottles.

In *serigraphy* the stencils are hand-cut by artists for the production of screen prints as a fine art, *serigraphs*.

In *transfer-printing* or *decal-printing* the image is printed with silk-screen-printing on a paper which is then used to transfer the image to T-shirts and other textiles.

Electro-press

Electro-press is a new method for printing, developed by Harris Graphics Corp. in the US in 1990. The system functions like a copying machine but it has "magnetic ink" instead of a coal-based powder. This gives a better print quality. A computer gives impulses to a number of diodes charging the drum. The charged ink is attracted to parts of the drum and it is possible to print single pages or sheets.

Copying

The development of copying machines in recent years has been remarkable. Modern zoom optics in combination with micro-electronics have given birth to small and handy copying machines that automatically reduce and enlarge, retaining good quality. Concurrent with simpler handling and better quality, the consumption of copies increases. The Swedish public administration produces about three billion copies each year. In average that means 5,000 copies per public employee, which means approximately 25 copies per working day. The figure for the whole world must be enormous.

Xerography

Xerography is a dry copying process. The text or image to be copied is projected onto a drum so that an electrostatic discharge is conveyed where the drum is illuminated and stays where the image is black. After that the charged (unilluminated) surface attracts an ink (color) powder. This is transferred to the paper or to the material onto which the image is to be transmitted. The ink powder is fixed on and inside the paper by heat and pressure.

Color laser copier

In Canon's Color Laser Copier a scanner "reads" the original picture and converts it into digital signals. The scanning resolution is 400 dots per inch. The scanner reads the image four times, for magenta, yellow, cyan, and black. Then the digital information about the image can be processed and transmitted to the laser printer for production of color copies.

The picture elements form 8 x 8 pixel raster-dots. Each pixel may be printed with magenta, yellow, cyan, or black, or with combinations of those. Thus, the printed copies can have 64 gradations per color. A pixel can also be non-printed and thus have the color of the paper. The print resolution is 400 dots per inch.

Since the image is handled in digital form, it can be edited in many ways. For example, the image may be reduced, enlarged, stretched, or slanted. Individual colors can be changed. A projector can be used for making full-color copies from 35mm slides—even negative film can be used.

PHOTOGRAPHY

When the film is exposed to light in a camera, the chemical composition of the film is changed. Polygon crystals of silver halogens are reduced to silver. The film is developed and fixed. The grains of the film, i.e., the "pixels of photography," are a few thousandths of a millimeter in size and different in shape. Different films have different light sensitivity and different granularity. Today there are film materials for many different purposes: from "normal daylight films" to films sensitive to infrared light, X-rays or other invisible radiations. Such special films are mostly used for research. The film resolution may vary from 500,000 to several millions for each square inch. The theoretical upper limit is usually put to 800 million grains for a square inch of film.

By changing lenses or by using a lens with changeable focal distance the image area is changed. A camera can be aimed at a subject from different angles. At a low angle the subject is seen from below. At high angle the subject is seen from above. At normal angle the subject is on the same level as the camera. A telephoto lens includes a small section of the subject. A wide-angle lens includes a large section of the subject.

There have been many different formats for still photography with miniature formats, film discs, film cassettes, standard 35mm film, and several larger formats. The individual grains, pixels, are irregular and run into and partly cover each other. This is particularly true for color film where the light-sensitive grains are formed in layers. The film's light-sensitive grains cannot really be compared to a computer's regular pixels.

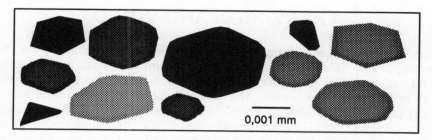

Examples of some of the grains in a film, here very much enlarged.

Apart from ordinary cameras there are several systems and different equipment for producing slides. Both Polaroid and Kodak have developed a series of hoods to be put in front of video and computer screens to take photos with direct films. After a minute or so the slide is ready to use.

Many other systems work essentially as reversed scanners. A laser beam exposes the film dot by dot. The film is handled in a traditional camera body.

Several camera manufacturers, for example Canon, Konica, Minolta, and Sony, have still video cameras which store up to 50 photographs on a small magnetic disc. Electronics, CCD, replaces the film. Via a TV-adapter the image information is transmitted to a color TV-receiver or to a TV-monitor, where the photograph is reproduced. The information can also be printed out by a video printer.

FILM

By showing a sequence of pictures describing a course of events so quickly that the eye cannot discern the individual pictures, the brain experiences movement. As early as the beginning of the 20th century, different toys with animated cartoons were experienced as "live" by the amazed audience.

Usually film is recorded and shown with 24 frames per second. Faster recording and projection gives a more stable picture. Film can also be projected with a different image frequency than that with which it was recorded. Recording with high frequency and projection with normal frequency results in slow motion. This is used for studies of fast or very fast and complicated courses of events, for example, a bullet leaving a rifle. Recording with low frequency and projection with normal frequency results in the opposite; fast motion. This is used for studies of slow or very slow courses of events, for example, a bud developing into a flower.

There are and have been many different kinds of film formats. Examples are standard 8mm film, S-8mm film, 16mm film, 35mm film, and 70mm film.

Usually "standard film" refers to 35mm film for movie production. The height-width relationship of this 35mm film is 1:1.33. At the middle of the screen the resolution is some 450 dots per square inch. There are several types of wide-film formats: VistaVision, CinemaScope, Cinerama, UltraVision, IMAX, and OMAX are examples.

TELEVISION AND VIDEO

The word "television" comes from the Greek word *téle*, distant, and from the Latin word *vidére*, to see. Television, or TV, is a tele-technical system for transmission of sound and images, stills, as well as motion pictures in both black and white and color.

In an analog television camera, the rays of light are projected from an image to an optical picture on a "picture plate" into the camera tube. By optic-electrical conversion the light variations are transformed into a low-frequency image signal, a so-called *video signal*. The image on the picture plate is scanned by a focused electron beam moving across the picture according to a set pattern, different brands working in different ways. Usually the picture is divided into picture elements by the electron beam moving in slightly inclined lines building up a so called TV-raster. At transmission, the light information is transmitted from one picture element at a time. These are projected reversed on the TV-receiver's picture tubes. The TV-image is of course built up, or "put together," in the same way as it was divided into picture elements earlier. The inertia of the eye makes us perceive the different picture elements as individual whole images or as motion pictures.

Most Western European countries have agreed on a color TV-system called PAL, Phase Alteration Line. PAL is also used in Australia and in several countries in Africa and in the Middle East. The TV-image is built up by 625 lines. Every line consists of a large amount of pixels. A color TV-receiver has a "shadow mask" with some 400,000 small holes for red, green, and blue, respectively. Our 50-periodical alternating current is used to produce 50 half images or 25 whole images per second. A black and white TV uses 450 effective lines with each 560 pixels. Thus, a black and white TV-image consists of 235,200 pixels.

Most video systems have considerably worse resolution than broadcast-TV. VHS has, for example, usually 248 lines. Super VHS has an improved resolution of 400 lines.

In the US, Canada, and Japan a system called NTSC is used. NTSC, National Television Standard Committee, is both the name of the authority which developed the American color TV-system and of the system itself. NTSC uses 525 lines.

France, Eastern Europe, the former Soviet Union, and Saudi Arabia use SECAM, Sequential Couleur à Mémoire. SECAM is so similar to PAL that it is possible to receive a SECAM-program in a PAL TV-receiver, but the color signals are produced in a different way.

In a digital TV or video camera there is a CCD-plate with normally more than 400,000 pixels.

TV-receivers

There are TV-receivers in a number of types and sizes. The image size is measured diagonally in inches. The most common sizes are 18–27 inches for domestic use and 28-38 inches for public use. Here are a few examples of less common TV-receivers:

Wrist-TV. In Japan a wrist-TV manufactured by Seiko has been sold since 1985. The system consists of three parts: the actual wrist-watch with a TV-screen, a receiver to be carried in one's inner pocket, and a headset with an antenna. The image is created by liquid crystals containing 32,000 pixels. The size of the screen is only 17 x 25 mm.

Pocket-TV. The Japanese electronics company Matsushita in 1983 developed a very compact "pocket TV" without a picture tube. The image is 2.4 inches diagonally and built up by liquid crystals. In August 1984 Seiko introduced a pocket color-TV. The image's diagonal is 2 inches. The set weighs 450 g. The screen consists of a thin film with a transistor in 52,800 individual pixels. The TV-image has 32,000 pixels. During 1989 Philips introduced a battery operated 3" color-TV. The screen is built on LCD-technology and has 264 x 384, that is, 101,376 pixels.

Jumbotron. At Tsukuba Expo '85 in Japan, Sony had built the world's largest video screen, 25x40 m, i.e., 1,000 m². The image was very bright and it could be seen by more than 50,000 people at the same time. The jumbotron image is built up by 150,000 pixels called Trini-lite, which are 80 x 45 mm. Every pixel consists of one blue, one red, and one green part. The jumbotron image is more than two million times larger than, for example, a wrist-TV.

Multivision or Video Wall is a display system where many TV-receivers (for example 16, 24, or 30) are put close together forming a check pattern. All screens can show the same image, differents parts of the same image, or different images in varying configurations. Multivision is used at, for example, shows, exhibitions, and sometimes in department stores.

Third generation-TV. In a few years there will be TV-sets with new functions. VLSI (Very Large Scale Integration) chips control the image quality in every individual TV-set. The TV-station's analog signal is transformed to digital signals, and they can then be processed in different ways. The image is cleared of shadows and noise, and its definition is improved. The picture can be zoomed in and "frozen." It is possible to produce prints of any still, simply by pressing the "print" button. A video printer produces the picture.

Third generation TV-systems might have a large, flat screen mounted on the wall with a possibility to open up several "windows" with different programs. It is not necessary to have an extra home computer for access to, for example, electronic shopping, home banking, and information retrieval in databases.

Video printers

There are several systems for printing TV and video images on paper. Some video printers use thermal copying, others use plotters, and some employ ink-jet printers or laser printers.

The German company Soro Electro-Optics GmbH has developed a laser printer which can produce print-outs of TV in formats up to 216 x 297 mm with high resolution. The photographic paper is stored in a cassette containing paper. The equipment is expected to be used for print-out/copying of satellite pictures in meteorology, biomedicine, etc.

Sony's thermal video printer *Mavigraf* produces color paper prints. The quality is not in the same class as paper color photographs. Color prints are printed out in 155 x 117 mm format with 116 pixels per inch on both paper and film. Panasonic's thermal printer gives pictures with 229,376 pixels in 2,100,000 colors on a format of 100 x 75 mm. The resolution is 448 x 512 pixels, 150 pixels per inch. Hitachi's thermal Color Video Printer also give pictures with 2,100,000 colors on a format of 105 x 147 mm.

The Japanese printing company Dai Nippon Printing has developed a method for catching the signals from high definition TV systems and transforming them to half-tone raster-dots printed out as color prints of high quality. The quality of this "video-to-print" method is superior to other methods.

Compact video

Video 8 is a video system using a cassette with an 8mm video tape. Many systems have the cassette player built into the portable and battery-powered TV-camera (CCD).

No fewer than 127 electronics companies have agreed on a standard for "compact video." The cassettes are only slightly larger than a normal sound cassette. They are of surprisingly good quality and have a playing time of up to two hours. When recording, the cassette is inserted directly into the small camera. When playing back, the camera is also used, connected to a TV-set. Video 8 has all possibilities of finally ending the life of S-8 filming.

High definition TV

High definition TV's are TV-systems with a higher definition than today's PAL, NTSC, and SECAM. In, for example, Hi-Vision the TV-image is built up by 1,125 lines compared to the 525 lines in the NTSC system (and 625 in PAL). Each line in Hi-Vision has 1,000 pixels. To manage the high definition TV-image's closer line construction, the band-width for each channel on the transmission side has to be increased to about 30 MHz. For conventional TV a band-width of 6 MHz is sufficient. A capacity of 30 MB per second is needed to handle moving high definition TV-images in a computer system.

To do full justice to a high definition TV, TV-screens larger than normal, preferably one meter wide, are required. To be accepted by the normal consumer the TV-picture tube must then be made flat so that it can be hung on the wall like a painting. Great research efforts have been made in recent years to solve the problem of flat picture tubes. New techniques like liquid crystals and plasma picture tubes are being evaluated as well as new types of picture tubes and TV-projection systems using new technology.

Experiments with high definition TV have been going on for a long time, with the latest research (mainly in Japan) aimed at digital systems, rather than the traditional analog images.

THREE-DIMENSIONAL PICTURES

Three-dimensional pictures can be produced with various kinds of technology. Mirror images and other virtual images are not discussed here.

Stereoscopic images

Our vision is binocular. This allows us to see the three dimensionality of the world. The *stereoscope* was created in 1833. This allowed each eye to see a different picture after exact placement of three mirrors. The *pseutoscope* used prisms to exchange the eyes' visual fields. At the turn of the century, primitive hand-held stereoscopes were widely used. A printed legend often conveyed information about the image content for each stereoscopic image pair. With the advent of motion pictures, systems for stereo-films were developed. Today advanced stereoscopic systems are widely used in science.

Anaglyphic images

The anaglyphic method for stereo images was developed at the end of the 19th century. This method is based on the perceptual principles of our binocular vision and the use of image pairs in complementary colors. The stereoscopic image pairs were colored red and blue (or green) and superimposed, for example, projected on a screen or printed on paper. Anaglyphic images are viewed with glasses with red and blue lenses acting as filters. Each eye sees only one of the superimposed images.

During the 1950s books were printed with anaglyphic pictures. Each book also carried glasses made of cardboard and celluloid filters in red and blue (or green). Experiments during the fifties and the sixties involved television and movies as well.

In 1983 the Swedish TV2 initiated three-dimensional TV-transmissions. The program was recorded at Philips research laboratories in Eindhoven, Holland.

Autostereo images

The raster method has several names. It is called "lenticular 3-D," "autostereoscopic 3-D system," or just "autostereo images." An autostereo image consists of a large number of very thin vertical strips of two or more pictures that have been sliced. The strips from different pictures are interlaced side-by-side and covered with a plastic foil with thin, long, narrow, embossed, vertical, and parallel lenses. When the head is held straight, the left eye only sees the strips forming the picture for the left eye. At the same time the right eye only sees the strips forming the picture for the right eye. The sum of these images is a three-dimensional experience. This system is used for the production of post cards, covers of books, and magazines and also for inserts.

Polarized light

Filters for polarized light were developed at the end of the 19th century. Glasses with polarizing filters can make the left eye see one picture and the right eye see another picture. Contrary to the anaglyphic method, true colors can be used. Throughout the fifties and sixties many movie films and TV-programs were made using this method.

Alternating view systems

A technique for 3-D TV has been developed by Stereographic Corp., San Rafael, California. Instead of the red-green glasses, they have developed glasses connected to the TV-receiver (a wireless model is also being developed). A *shutter* is alternately opened and closed in front of each eye synchronically with the film on TV and thus producing an optical illusion of 3-D movies.

The Japanese company Toshiba has developed a home video camera giving three-dimensional images. Glasses with *liquid crystals* are used darkening the right and the left eye alternatively, in time with the doubling NTSC-image frequency played back from a special video recorder and displayed in a special TV-set.

Alternating display systems

A system developed at the University of Jyväskylä, Finland, and supported by the Finnish TV-manufacturer Salora, uses rapid *image alteration* with images from two TV-cameras. The eye cannot discern the individual images and the viewer experiences only one three-dimensional TV-image.

By using CAD-technology it is possible to create three-dimensional experiences by having the computer generate one left and one right image alternatively.

Holograms

Today it is possible to create authentic 3-D-pictures with laser light, in which one can see "behind" objects, so-called holograms. This is a technique which today is where photography was at the turn of the last century. Integral white light holograms are used in art and advertising and can be produced on a commercial/industrial basis.

OmniView

In 1990 Texas Instruments presented *OmniView*, the first 3-D system for television which does not require glasses. A double helical translucent disc rotates at the end of a drive shaft. A laser beam scans the disc and an image is formed. As the disc rotates at ten times a second, the distance between the viewer and the disc varies. The laser modulates 10,000 times a second, which produces a 750 x 750 pixel picture. The use of red, green, and blue lasers results in color pictures.

REFERENCES AND SUGGESTED READINGS

Belland, J., & Best, T. (1992). Pixels instead of pens and paste. In J. Clark-Baca, D. G. Beauchamp, & R. A. Braden (Eds.). *Visual Communication: Bridging Across Cultures* Selected Readings from the 23rd Annual Conference of the International Visual Literacy Association. Blacksburg: Virginia Tech University.

Braden, R. A., & Hannemann, R. F. (1982). The evolution of publishing technology: Five eras of change. In J. Clark-Baca, D. G. Beauchamp, & R. A. Braden (Eds.). *Visual Communication: Bridging Across Cultures.* Selected Readings from the 23rd Annual Conference of the International Visual Literacy Association. Blacksburg: Virginia Tech University.

Deken, J. (1983). *Computer Images.* London: Thames and Hudson.

Dyring, E. (1984). *Nolla etta bild, den nya bildrevolutionen.* Stockholm: Prisma.

Finn, D. (1989). *How to Look at Sculpture.* New York: Harry N. Abrams.

Germundson, L., & Olsson, B. (1990). Bilden i tryck. *Reprokunskap för grafiker, trycksaksbeställare, fotografer och andra bildanvändare.* Halmstad: Bokförlaget Spektra.

Hallberg, Å. (1989). *Klart för tryck.* Halmstad: Bokförlaget Spektra.

Hayashi, K. (1983). Research and development on high definition television. *SMPTE Journal, 3,* 178–186.

Heinich, R., Molenda, M., & Russell, J. D. (1993). *Instructional Media and the New Technologies of Instruction.* New York: Macmillan.

Konomos, P., & Ragsdale, D. (1991). Investigating still video photography. In D. G. Beauchamp, J. Clark-Baca, & R. A. Braden (Eds.). *Investigating Visual Literacy.* Selected Readings from the 22rd Annual Conference of the International Visual Literacy Association. Blacksburg: Virginia Tech University.

Lax, L., & Olsson, M. (1983). NAPLPS standard graphics and the microcomputer. *Byte 8* (7), 82–92.

Lidman, S., & Lund, A.-M. (1972). *Berätta med bilder.* Stockholm: Bonniers.

Longley, D., & Shain, M. (1986). *Macmillan Dictionary of Information Technology.* London: Macmillan Press.

Mastroddi, F. (Ed.) (1986). *Commission of the European Communities. Electronic Publishing: The New Way to Communicate.* London: Kogan Page.

McLellan, H. (1990). From cubism to holography. In R. A. Braden, D. G. Beauchamp, & J. Clark-Baca (Eds.). *Perceptions of Visual Literacy.* Selected Readings from the 21st Annual Conference of the International Visual Literacy Association. Conway: University of Central Arkansas.

Metallinos, N. (1990). Three dimensional video: Perceptual and aesthetic drawbacks. In R. A. Braden, D. G. Beauchamp, & J. Clark-Baca (Eds.). *Perceptions of Visual Literacy.* Selected Readings from the 21st Annual Conference of the International Visual Literacy Association. Conway: University of Central Arkansas.

Metallinos, N., Muffoletto, R., Pettersson, R., Shaw, J., & Takakuwa, Y. (1990). *The Use of Verbo-visual Information in Textbooks: A Cross-Cultural Experience.* Paper presented at the International Visual Literacy Association Symposium 1990. Verbo-Visual Literacy. Mapping the Field. July 10–13. University of London, Institute of Education.

Pettersson, R. (1989). *Visuals for Information: Research and Practice.* Englewood Cliffs, NJ: Educational Technology Publications.

Pettersson, R. (1991a). *Medier, termer och begrepp.* Tullinge: Institutet för Infologi.

Pettersson, R. (1991b). *Bilder i läromedel.* Tullinge: Institutet för Infologi.

Pettersson, R. (1992). *Image Data Bases in Art and Science.* Presentation at the 24th Annual Conference of the International Visual Literacy Association. Pittsburgh, Sept. 30 –Oct. 4.

Pettersson, R., Metallinos, N., Muffoletto, R., Shaw, J. and Takakuwa, Y. (1992). The use of verbo-visual information in teaching of geography—views from teachers. In J. Clark-Baca, D. G. Beauchamp, & R. A. Braden (Eds.). *Visual Communication: Bridging Across Cultures.* Selected Readings from the 23rd Annual Conference of the International Visual Literacy Association. Blacksburg: Virginia Tech University.

Preston, J. M. (1988). *Compact Disc-Interactive: A Designer's Overview.* Deventer-Antwerpen: Kluwer Technical Books.

Roberts, R. S. (1981). *Dictionary of Audio, Radio, and Video.* London: Butterworths.

Sigel, E., Roizen, J., McIntyre, C., & Wilkinson, M. (1980). *Videotext: The Coming Revolution in Home/Office Information Retrieval.* White Plain, NY: Knowledge Industry Publications.

Tucker, W. (1974). *The Language of Sculpture.* London: Thames and Hudson.

Törneklev, L. (1987). *Grafisk tryckteknik. Metoder, material, mätteknik.* Halmstad: Bokförlaget Spektra.

Zelle, A., & Sutton, R. (1991). Image manipulation: Or the Zelig phenomenon. In D. G. Beauchamp, J. Clark-Baca, & R. A. Braden (Eds.). *Investigating Visual Literacy.* Selected Readings from the 22rd Annual Conference of the International Visual Literacy Association. Blacksburg: Virginia Tech University.

AUTHOR INDEX

SUBJECT INDEX